Schubert Studies
Problems of style and chronology

Schubert's death mask, front view (photograph of a bronze cast in the possession of the Curtis Institute, Philadelphia)

Schubert Studies
Problems of style and chronology

Edited by

Eva Badura-Skoda

and

Peter Branscombe

Cambridge University Press

Cambridge
London New York New Rochelle
Melbourne Sydney

Published by the Press Syndicate of the University of Cambridge
The Pitt Building, Trumpington Street, Cambridge CB2 1RP
32 East 57th Street, New York, NY 10022, USA
296 Beaconsfield Parade, Middle Park, Melbourne 3206, Australia

First published 1982

Printed in Great Britain
at the University Press, Cambridge

Library of Congress catalogue card number: 81-38528

British Library Cataloguing in Publication Data
Schubert studies.
1. Schubert, Franz
I. Badura-Skoda, Eva II. Branscombe, Peter
780′.92′4 ML410.S3
ISBN 0 521 22606 6

To the memory of

CHRISTA LANDON

Contents

List of illustrations *page* ix

Preface xi

WALTHER DÜRR
Schubert's songs and their poetry: reflections on poetic aspects of song composition 1

RUFUS HALLMARK
Schubert's 'Auf dem Strom' 25

ELAINE BRODY
Schubert and Sulzer revisited: a recapitulation of the events leading to Schubert's setting in Hebrew of Psalm XCII, D 953 47

MARIUS FLOTHUIS
Schubert revises Schubert 61

ELIZABETH NORMAN McKAY
Schubert as a composer of operas 85

PETER BRANSCOMBE
Schubert and the melodrama 105

CHRISTOPH WOLFF
Schubert's 'Der Tod und das Mädchen': analytical and explanatory notes on the song D 531 and the quartet D 810 143

PETER GÜLKE
In what respect a quintet? On the disposition of instruments in the String Quintet D 956 173

PAUL BADURA-SKODA
Possibilities and limitations of stylistic criticism in the dating of Schubert's 'Great' C major Symphony 187

ROBERT WINTER
Paper studies and the future of Schubert research 209

EVA BADURA-SKODA
The chronology of Schubert's piano trios 277

REINHARD VAN HOORICKX
The chronology of Schubert's fragments and sketches 297

ARNOLD FEIL
Rhythm in Schubert: some practical problems. Critical analysis, critical edition, critical performance 327

ALEXANDER WEINMANN
'Father Leopold Puschl of Seitenstetten' and 'Schubert's sojourn at Zseliz': the late Ignaz Weinmann's last contributions to Schubert research 347

Index 357

Illustrations

Schubert's death mask, front view (photograph of a bronze cast in the possession of the Curtis Institute, Philadelphia) *frontispiece*

A number of plaster casts and another bronze cast of this death mask are in the possession of the Historisches Museum der Stadt Wien, one cast is owned by the Wiener Schubert-Bund, and other copies are in private possession. For further information see *Österreichische Musikzeitschrift*, XXXIII (1978), pp. 578-95.

Hausmusik (Schubert making music with Josephine Fröhlich and Johann Michael Vogl), pencil drawing by Ferdinand Georg Waldmüller, 1827 (Albertina, Vienna) *page* 142

Portrait bust of Schubert, unsigned (most probably by Anton Dietrich), *c*. 1830 (private collection, Vienna) 186

Colour drawing of Schubert, by Moritz von Schwind, undated (collection of Wilhelm Kempff) 346

'Auf dem Strom' (Rufus Hallmark)

1 'Auf dem Strom', p. 1 of the autograph 31

2 'Auf dem Strom', p. 3 of the autograph (detail) 34

3 'Auf dem Strom', part of pp. 6 and 7 of the autograph 35

4 'Auf dem Strom', p. 11 of the autograph (detail) 38

(Reproduced by permission of the Houghton Library, Harvard University)

'Der Tod und das Mädchen' (Christoph Wolff)

1 *Freund Hain*, engraving: frontispiece to M. Claudius, *Asmus omnia sua secum portans* . . . (Hamburg, 1775) *page* 146

2-4 Drawings by Moritz von Schwind, from the series *Gräber oder Todesgedanken*, 1823 170

The 'Great' C major Symphony (Paul Badura-Skoda)

1 'Great' C major Symphony, first page of the autograph 207

(Reproduced by permission of the Gesellschaft der Musikfreunde, Vienna)

Paper studies and Schubert research (Robert Winter)

1-6 Sketches of watermarks: paper types Ia and Ib, IIa and IIb, III, IV, Va and Vb, VIb, VIIa-d, VIIIa and VIIIb 270-5

Schubert's piano trios (Eva Badura-Skoda)

1 Voll's *Chronologisches Verzeichniss* . . . for 1827-8, title-page 285

2 Voll's *Chronologisches Verzeichniss* . . . for 1827-8, extracts showing the Schuppanzigh Quartet's concert on 26 December 1827 and Schubert's 'Privat-Concert' on 26 March 1828 286

Preface

Extensive as is the literature on Mozart and Beethoven, the number of scholarly studies devoted to the other two great masters of Viennese classicism, Haydn and Schubert, is still comparatively limited. True, in recent years a spate of publications on Haydn and Schubert has reduced the gap; but in Schubert's case in particular large areas of the oeuvre have as yet received little attention. The operas, for instance, are still largely unknown territory, despite the welcome growth in the number of live performances and at least some attempt on the part of the record companies to place Schubert's stage works before the public. Yet in view of the fact that Schubert wrote a dozen operas and left several others sketched or unfinished, there is still much to be done, and several entrenched prejudices remain to be challenged, even if some of the criticisms directed against inept librettos are justified. The coming decades should see a better-informed and more positive revaluation of Schubert's dramatic works. Church music is another field where Schubert's works have been neglected to such an extent that it is only in recent decades that such masterworks as the 'Salve Regina' in A (D 676) or the A flat major Mass (D 678) have become at all widely known outside Austria. Even performances of the E flat major Mass (D 950) were still rare until the anniversary year of 1978. Here, too, it is to be hoped that interest in a neglected part of Schubert's oeuvre will result in the regular availability of good recordings.

Though there are still gaps in our knowledge of Schubert's life which further detailed study and more comprehensive publication of documents and other biographical material may be able to fill, the more urgent need is for analytical studies of his works. Therefore, as the subtitle of this book indicates, our authors have above all been concerned to bring a fresh clarity to our perception of the essentially individual aspects of Schubert's compositions. With the exception of the presentation of some relatively unfamiliar iconographical material, such as Schubert's death mask (frontispiece), biographical details with no special relevance to questions of the chronology of Schubert's music have found less attention here.

It should not be necessary to point to an anniversary in order to justify close attention being paid to Schubert, but naturally the celebrations in honour of the 150th anniversary of his death have given a valuable impetus to Schubert studies. The present collection of articles could not appear in time for the 1978 festivities for various reasons; but the later date of publication has had the benefit of permitting the greater completeness of some of the contributions, particularly those that deal with primary sources, and we trust that this will prove beneficial to the cause of Schubert research.

The majority of the contributions are concerned with compositions from Schubert's late years. A number of the contributors set out with the intention of demonstrating the limitations of narrowly applied stylistic criteria as the basis for the dating of individual works. Schubert was so inexplicable a genius that it has always been dangerous to attempt to maintain the thesis of steady and continuous improvement in the quality of his works. Especially in his Lieder he achieved brilliantly successful masterpieces in his early youth; but these were often followed by less inspired settings or re-settings. Nevertheless, at least in general terms a development of purely technical skills can be traced, though time and again we are surprised to realize on the basis of Schubert's own datings that a song was composed markedly earlier or later than intuition might have suggested. The problem is complicated by the fact that Schubert, whose melodic richness is his most obvious characteristic, occasionally re-used some of his finest tunes. For that reason there is an abiding fascination to the theme 'Schubert quotes Schubert'. Sometimes years separate the appearances of thematic material, as in such familiar examples as the song 'Die Forelle' and the 'Trout' Quintet; 'Der Wanderer' as song and as keyboard fantasy; the *Rosamunde* music and the theme of the B flat major Impromptu D 935 (op. 142); 'Der Tod und das Mädchen' and the String Quartet in D minor; or the less well-known connection between 'Der Zwerg' (D 771) and the Piano Sonata in A minor D 784 (op. 143). Also less familiar, but quite as interesting, is the way in which Schubert re-uses themes almost as leitmotifs in the operas or – whether openly or semi-concealed – in the various movements of a sonata. Such issues are touched on quite often, but the contributors have been alert to the danger of applying a stylistic yardstick when attempting to establish a chronology for works which Schubert left undated, or for which his dates are ambiguous. The method of O. E. Deutsch, who always strove to date works on the basis of documentary evidence and biographical data rather than on stylistic features, is and will remain exemplary. The numerous re-datings which Robert Winter has established on the basis of careful examination of paper types and watermarks take that process a stage further. Yet they also demonstrate Deutsch's remarkable powers of discernment in those cases where the autographs were undated. Deutsch was seldom far wrong; but he would have been the first to concede the need for certain corrections to his own findings, and to extol the virtues of more recent methods of scholarly investigation.

The essays in this volume have been ordered according to the thematic area with which they are most closely connected. Aspects of Schubert's vocal music have been chosen for study by several contributors – Walther Dürr examines the relationship between some of the songs and the poems on which they are based; Rufus Hallmark discovers interesting Beethoven reminiscences in Schubert's 'Auf dem Strom', one of only two Schubert songs with obbligato wind instrument as well as pianoforte; Schubert's church music is the field chosen by Elaine Brody, who focuses attention not on Schubert's music for the Roman Catholic Church but on his Hebrew setting of Psalm XCII; and Marius Flothuis, on the basis of examples from the Lieder, throws light on Schubert's creative processes as reviser of his own works. There follow an examination of Schubert's operatic style by Elizabeth Norman McKay and an outline study of Schubert's relationship to the tradition of melodrama by Peter Branscombe. The contiguous area of vocal and instrumental music has been chosen by Christoph Wolff for his study of 'Der Tod und das Mädchen', which also sheds light on one eighteenth-century attitude towards death, as a friend of mankind – a thought which must have appealed to Schubert. Instrumental music is represented by Peter Gülke's analysis of the String Quintet in C major, and orchestral music by Paul Badura-Skoda, who considers the possibilities and limitations of stylistic criteria in the dating of the 'Great' C major Symphony. The following three essays are concerned with chronology: besides Robert Winter's detailed analysis of paper types and watermarks in Schubert's manuscripts, mentioned above, Eva Badura-Skoda re-examines the chronology of Schubert's piano trios, and Reinhard Van Hoorickx studies the chronology of Schubert's fragmentary and sketched compositions. There follows an analytical essay in the field of performance practice by Arnold Feil, who studies Schubert's rhythmic characteristics; and finally Alexander Weinmann adds to our knowledge both of an important contemporary collection of Schubert's music and of Schubert's months in Zseliz by drawing attention to and filling out two studies by his late brother, Ignaz Weinmann.

It was a source of grief to us that of the fifteen authors who agreed to contribute to this symposium only fourteen were able to submit their essays. Christa Landon, one of the editors of the new complete edition of Schubert's works, had undertaken to write an article on the genesis and style of the F minor Fantasy for piano duet (D 940). In November 1977 she took all her material with her to Madeira, intending to work on her article during a holiday there. On the outward flight she was a victim of the airline disaster. We wish to pay tribute to her selfless service to the cause of Schubert's music by dedicating this volume to her memory. For years she gave herself wholeheartedly to the task of investigating textual problems, diligently checked the texts of the Neue Schubert-Ausgabe, and gladly helped her colleagues far and wide in every way she could.

Just a few words here about the frontispiece to the volume. Recent research has revealed the significance of a death mask of Schubert which had remained practically unknown to scholars as well as to the wider public, though casts of it have long been preserved in Viennese collections. The authenticity of the mask has been established with the help of an anthropological survey taking as model the plaster copy of Schubert's cranium (see *Österreichische Musikzeitschrift*, XXXIII (1978), pp. 578-95). The mask was reproduced in R. H. Schauffler's 1959 biography of Schubert (Schauffler owned a plaster cast of it); but its importance was not then realized, and only recently has it begun to arouse the interest of experts. Similarly little known are the Waldmüller and Schwind drawings, and the portrait bust which is almost certainly the lost bust by Anton Dietrich.

Finally, it is our duty and our pleasure to thank all those individuals and institutions who have made the appearance of this volume possible. The English versions of the articles by Dürr, Feil, Gülke, Paul Badura-Skoda and Weinmann were made by Mr L. W. Vyse, to whom we wish to express our gratitude. Our thanks go also to the private owners who allowed us to make use of their Schubert treasures, and to the directors and staffs of the libraries and archives in which we and our colleagues were granted access to autographs, manuscript copies and printed editions. In this context we would like to single out Dr Hedwig Mitringer and Dr Otto Biba of the Archiv der Gesellschaft der Musikfreunde in Vienna, and Dr Ernst Hilmar of the Vienna Stadt- und Landesbibliothek. Our warm thanks go also to Dr Walther Dürr, who kindly commented on the proofs of the whole book, and to the Cambridge University Press and its music editors.

E B-S
P J B

Schubert's songs and their poetry: reflections on poetic aspects of song composition*

WALTHER DÜRR

I

August Wilhelm Schlegel, at the beginning of his twenty-third lecture 'On Literature and the Fine Arts', treats of the difficulty of defining poetry:[1]

> The other arts have each a sphere of their own, as defined by the limitations of the medium or means of presentation, and this to some extent can be determined. Yet poetry employs that medium by means of which the human mind attains any kind of awareness, and brings its concepts under control, that it may order them and express them as it will – namely, language. Hence poetry is not bound by its subject-matter, but creates its own; it is the most comprehensive of the arts, being nearly that universal spirit which everywhere informs them. In works created in other art-forms, whatever raises us above the commonplace of daily life into a world of fantasy we call their poetic element . . . Every outward material representation is preceded by an inner representation in the mind of the artist, for which language always acts as the agent of consciousness . . . Language is not a product of Nature, but bears the impress of the human spirit, which commits to it the origin of its concepts and their affinities, with all the machinery of its operations. Thus in poetry what is already fashioned becomes fashioned anew; and the flexibility of its voice is as infinite as the faculty of the mind to examine itself by means of ever more intensified reflections.[2]

Language is here seen to be separate from poetry; it is its medium and the 'agent of consciousness'. This medium is of course 'already fashioned', is not 'a product of Nature', for the human mind thereby 'brings its concepts

* The principal sources cited in this article are referred to as follows: *Franz Schubert. Neue Ausgabe sämtlicher Werke* (Kassel, etc., 1964-), cited as '*NGA*'; O. E. Deutsch, *Schubert. Die Erinnerungen seiner Freunde*, 2nd edn (Leipzig, 1966), cited as '*Erinnerungen*'; English edn *Schubert. Memoirs by His Friends*, transl. R. Ley and J. Nowell (London, 1958), cited as '*Memoirs*'; O. E. Deutsch, *Schubert. Die Dokumente seines Lebens* (= *NGA*, Series VIII, vol. 5) (Kassel, etc., 1964), cited as '*Dokumente*'; English edn *Schubert. A Documentary Biography*, transl. E. Blom (London, 1946), cited as '*Documents*'.

1 A. W. Schlegel, *Vorlesungen über schöne Litteratur und Kunst*, Deutsche Litteraturdenkmale des 18. und 19. Jahrhunderts, 17, vol. 1 (Heilbronn, 1884), pp. 261f.

2 The German phrase, 'durch immer höhere potenzirte Reflexionen', also conveys a mathematical sense, 'raised to a higher power'.

under control, that it may order them and express them as it will'; but in poetry language 'becomes fashioned anew'. Schlegel is interpreting in a new way the old doctrine of imitation;[3] no longer does poetry imitate Nature directly, but rather man, by means of language; and ultimately, by virtue of 'ever more intensified reflections', it imitates itself. Schlegel describes this as 'the poetry of poetry'.

In saying this he also calls into question the role of music, which has always had the traditional task of imitating poetry in the word, and thereby of imitating Nature. This assumes that what precedes the music – namely, language – is also poetry, in the broader sense the real text. If however in the poetic work of art the identical nature of poetry and language is called in question, then music too can no longer unquestioningly be looked upon as its imitation.

It is true that, according to Schlegel, poetry is 'the most comprehensive of the arts', yet music plays a significant part in the poetics of Romanticism. It is frequently regarded not as imitation, but as a model for the poetic art. 'Poetry', says Friedrich Schlegel, is 'spiritual music'. Music, on the other hand, is 'the most universal of the arts', for 'every art obeys musical principles, and on the highest level itself becomes music'.[4] This estimation of music as 'the most universal of the arts' is of course connected with the altered role of instrumental music. The Romantics draw attention to this, and its subject-matter cannot by any means be either poetry, or Nature herself through poetry. 'The subject of music', as Friedrich Schlegel observes, 'is life itself'; if 'life' is also to be the subject of poetry, it is only natural that the latter should employ the techniques of music.

In the case of vocal music, such a reversal of the traditional relationship between poetry and music cannot be maintained; its subject-matter must always be the text to which it is set. Yet the work of poetic art and the text are not identical – only artistic and contextual implications make them so. The text is raw material for the musician, even as for the poet it is a medium for thoughts which transcend it. While the musician reshapes the text, i.e. the language, which thus becomes 'fashioned anew', he is also, working on parallel lines to the poet, creating new structures. These therefore do not merely repeat the poetic structures, thereby rendering them dispensable, but take their place beside them. The co-existence of musical and poetic structures – whether merely formal or determined by the content – and their partial incongruity or congruity, lead to a new perspective, to a stratification in depth, and at the same time to an openness of form which is certainly a characteristic feature of the Romantic art-song.[5]

3 See Wolfgang Preisendanz, 'Zur Poetik der deutschen Romantik, I: Die Abkehr vom Grundsatz der Naturnachahmung' in *Die deutsche Romantik. Poetik, Formen und Motive*, ed. Hans Steffen (Göttingen, 1967), pp. 54ff, esp. pp. 73f.

4 Ibid., p. 67.

5 See Arnold Feil, *Franz Schubert. Die schöne Müllerin. Winterreise* (Stuttgart,

Furthermore, in the words of E. T. A. Hoffmann, 'the composer is now not merely moved by the deep significance of the song . . . to seize upon every inflection of feeling, as though to make it a focal point, from which the melody shines forth':[6] the image refers especially to songs such as those written by Reichardt and Zelter – strophic songs, where the melody must embody the feeling of the whole, in order to do justice to every stanza. In the Romantic art-song, however, the process which led to the 'fashioning' of the poem is carried out once again in the music; the composition does not bring the whole text into the same focus, thereby to some extent becoming static, but is conceived as parallel to the poem, as having a goal – assuming that 'language', the antecedent of both music and poetry, implies such a goal.

The parallel 'fashioning' of the poem and its music, and the mutual conflict arising from the forms thus created, produces the effect which we call Romantic irony. Incongruities reveal the actual 'limitations', the imperfections of poetic and musical pronouncements in relation to their fundamental idea; they arouse musical as well as 'poetic reflection' (Friedrich Schlegel).[7] To be sure, if the listener is to become aware of such actual 'limitations' not only as a result of their inevitable and almost incidental incongruity, but also because Romantic irony gives them the status of an artistic principle, then this presupposes the conscious and 'reflective' application of Romantic poetic theory to the musical work. The composer then no longer follows the poem directly in every case, but rather the literary theory – the song may then be said to have been 'rendered literary'.

To regard the corpus of Schubert's songs with such questions in mind involves an inquiry into his connections with the literature of his time; it further requires consideration of the extent to which his songs are 'Romantic', i.e. composed with reflective irony, and to what extent music and poetry stand in a reciprocal relationship in which each throws light upon the other.

Yet in order to avoid misunderstanding, the term 'Romantic art-song' demands clarification. Here the word 'Romantic' has nothing to do with the often-stated contrast between 'classical' and 'romantic'. It is not by chance that the poetics of Romanticism when applied in a musical context are chiefly concerned with the 'classical' composers, in particular with Mozart and Beethoven but also with Haydn, and with Goethe and Schiller in the narrower sphere of poetry. In this case, 'classical' probably refers to certain compositional techniques of Haydn, Mozart and Beethoven, whereas 'romantic' implies that the artist preserves a sense of detachment from his own

1975), p. 51: 'Schubert's music cannot have originated "after" the text; text and music must rather have grown together in the same soil, which must have preceded the shaping of the text.'

6 Ernst Theodor Amadeus Hoffmann, *Schriften zur Musik*, ed. F. Schnapp (Munich, 1963), p. 238 (September 1814, from a review of W. F. Riem's *Zwölf Lieder*, op. 27).

7 See Ingrid Strohschneider-Kohrs, 'Zur Poetik der deutschen Romantik, II: Die romantische Ironie', in *Die deutsche Romantik*, ed. Steffen, pp. 83f.

creations, which are expressed in the ironic structures already described. The two concepts are in no way incompatible.

II

On 15 November 1831, Johann Michael Vogl wrote to Schubert's school-friend Albert Stadler:

> . . . But when you speak of manufacturing, producing, creating, I must beg to be excused, especially since I learnt from Schubert that there are two kinds of composition, one which, as in Schubert's case, comes into existence during a state of clairvoyance or somnambulism, without any conscious action on the part of the composer, but inevitably, by act of providence and inspiration. A work coming into existence in such a way can certainly be wondered at and delighted in, but it cannot be criticized . . . [8]

Later Stadler himself wrote to Ferdinand Luib, who had asked him for material for his projected biography of Schubert:

> If Schubert was with us, we shut him up in the *'Kamerate'* [the living-room *cum* study] during this interval, gave him a few scraps of manuscript paper, and any volume of poems which happened to be at hand, so that he could while away the time. When we returned from church there was usually something finished and this he gladly let me have. (*Erinnerungen*, p. 172; *Memoirs*, p. 147)

Both quotations exemplify a widespread preconception, which has developed from these and similar remarks, namely that Schubert seized avidly on every text which fell into his hands, and set it 'during a state of clairvoyance or somnambulism', so that later he sometimes did not even recognize his own work.[9] If such judgements are correct, there can clearly be no question of reflective irony in the process of creation.

The scope of Stadler's testimony must first be narrowed down. It applies of course exclusively to Schubert's early years – or, to be more precise, to 1815-16 – and principally to the composition of trios and quartets, the only works for which Stadler gives examples. These, as Anselm Hüttenbrenner confirms,[10] were above all incidental pieces, which Schubert composed for social occasions and 'gladly let [Stadler] have'.

8 Letter in the Vienna Stadt- und Landesbibliothek: see *Erinnerungen*, p. 172; *Memoirs*, p. 146.

9 See the account given by Johann Michael Vogl's wife Kunigunde to her daughter Henriette: *Erinnerungen*, p. 249; *Memoirs*, pp. 216-17.

10 'Schubert, Assmayr, Mozatti and I agreed to sing a new quartet for men's voices, of our own composition, every Thursday evening at Mozatti's, who kindly acted as host . . . Schubert attached very little importance to the small *pièces d'occasion* and scarcely six of them can still be in existence' (*Erinnerungen*, p. 206; *Memoirs*, pp. 179-80).

Nevertheless the great number of texts which Schubert set to music, and their variable quality from a modern viewpoint, repeatedly cause one to ask whether the reproach of a certain randomness or even bad luck in their choice[11] is not really justified. If one examines these texts more closely, leaving out Schubert's earliest years of song composition from the ages of thirteen to sixteen at the Vienna Stadtkonvikt (the City Seminary), they can be seen to fall into varied but clearly definable groups. They may be characterized by the names of Matthisson, Schlegel, Heine and Mayrhofer, with the addition of Goethe and Schiller; the latter, however, have a special place in Schubert's creative work.

During the very productive song-years 1814-16 the young composer turned with particular passion to the poems of Goethe, and to James Macpherson's 'Ossian' songs; besides these he set verse by Schiller, Matthisson, Klopstock, Kosegarten, Salis-Seewis, Hölty, Claudius and Mayrhofer. With the exception of the last-named these are poets who were generally popular at the time and whose importance was never questioned; Schubert had got to know their work in the circle of his student friends, and also probably at the Stadtkonvikt. He set the poems of these authors mostly in fairly large groups.[12] Thus thirteen songs to Matthisson's lyrics were written between April and October 1814[13] with a further six in April 1816, eleven by Hölty in May–June 1815 with another eight in May 1816, thirteen by Kosegarten in June–July 1815, nine by Klopstock in September–October 1815, seven by Salis in March–April 1816, and seven by Claudius in November 1816. Whilst Schubert selected poems by one author from a particular volume of poems,[14] he did not choose them indiscriminately; only very seldom did he set adjacent poems in a volume.

It is nevertheless clear that the inner relationship of many poems in an author's collected works strongly appealed to Schubert and led him to favour a somewhat cyclical approach to composition; in such groups of songs he sought to preserve a unified atmosphere. This led to the adoption of a definite plan. On 17 April 1816 Schubert sent Goethe a book of songs set to the

11 See Josef von Spaun, 'Some Observations on the Life of Schubert by Herr Ritter von Kreissle-Hellborn' (*Erinnerungen*, p. 420; *Memoirs*, p. 365): 'It is stated in the biography that Schubert was not successful in his choice of texts; now this may well be true as regards operettas and cantatas, in which he had no choice, but not as regards his songs . . .'

12 See the foreword to Maximilian Schochow and Lilly Schochow, *Franz Schubert. Die Texte seiner einstimmig komponierten Lieder und ihre Dichter*, 2 vols. (Hildesheim and New York, 1974).

13 The thirteen songs to texts by Matthisson appeared as a self-contained group (musical texts from the *NGA*) in *Franz Schubert. Ausgewählte Lieder (Matthisson, Hölty, Claudius, Schiller)*, ed. W. Dürr and P. Reinhard Van Hoorickx (Kassel etc., 1969).

14 See section entitled 'Textvorlage' in the Supplement *Quellen und Lesarten* to Franz Schubert, *Lieder*, vol. 7 (*NGA*, IV/7), edited by W. Dürr (Kassel, etc., 1979), p. 15.

latter's poems, and in a covering letter Schubert's friend Josef von Spaun explained on the composer's behalf:

The general acclamation accorded to the young artist [i.e. Schubert] for the present songs as well as for his other, already numerous compositions . . . [has] at last induced the modest youth to open his musical career by the publication of part of his compositions . . .

A beginning is now to be made with a selection of German songs, to be followed by sizeable instrumental works. It is to comprise eight books. The first two (of which the first is enclosed as a specimen) contain poems by Your Excellency, the third contains poems by Schiller, the fourth and fifth by Klopstock, the sixth by Matthisson, Hölty, Salis etc. etc., and the seventh and eighth contain songs from Ossian, these last excelling all the others.[15]

At that time Schubert clearly wished his songs to be printed in comprehensive volumes, arranged by poet. But the plan fell through: at this time he could not find a publisher. The principle of literary arrangement was nevertheless the same for the much smaller books of songs (a kind of collection then more customary) which he did publish later. Like the proposed first two volumes described in the letter, Schubert's first songs to appear in print – opp. 1-3 and 5 – were exclusively settings of poems by Goethe, and they were all songs from the book which Schubert had sent to Goethe in April 1816.

An entry in Schubert's diary of the same year also throws light on his relationship with Goethe. He writes of a musical gathering at which he had to play:

I played variations by Beethoven, sang Goethe's 'Rastlose Liebe' and Schiller's 'Amalia'. Unanimous applause for the former, less for the latter. Although I myself think my 'Rastlose Liebe' better than 'Amalia', I cannot deny that Goethe's musical poet's genius contributed much to the success. (*Dokumente*, p. 43; cf. *Documents*, p. 60)

This entry testifies not only to the extraordinary esteem in which Goethe was held by Schubert, but also to the powerful influence on and through music which his poetry possessed in Schubert's eyes; this is shown by the words 'musical poet's genius', as well as by the admission that it 'contributed much to the success'. In saying this Schubert was certainly not thinking of contemporary theories of song composition, as for example that the melody 'should arouse an enhanced attention . . . to the words of a good song-writer'[16] – such requirements held good for the strophic song, to which type Schubert's 'Rastlose Liebe' (D 138) is entirely opposed. Schubert was rather of the opinion that poetry has a direct influence on the musical impact of the song, which means that for him both music and poetry, perhaps in the sense already described, exert an influence upon each other.

15 See *Dokumente*, pp. 40-1; *Documents*, pp. 56-7 (here slightly revised).

16 Thus Johann Abraham Peter Schulz in the introduction to his *Lieder im Volkston* (1782); cf. H. W. Schwab, *Sangbarkeit, Popularität und Kunstlied* (Regensburg, 1965), p. 44.

In the succeeding years Schubert turned to other poets; he abandoned the fashionably sentimental Matthisson, Salis and Kosegarten for the poetry of the Schlegels, Novalis and Rückert, together with Tieck, Platen and Schulze. For this turn to Romantic poetry Schubert's friendship with Franz von Schober was probably decisive. Schober gathered around him a circle of literary enthusiasts who held regular evening readings. 'We hold readings at Schober's three times a week', wrote Schubert on 7 December 1822 to Josef von Spaun (*Dokumente*, p. 173; *Documents*, p. 248) – one must however assume that such gatherings had occurred much earlier, although informally and not as meetings of a society. In the autumn of 1816 Schubert first moved in with the Schobers;[17] Josef von Spaun describes it thus:

> Schober, with his mother's permission, repeatedly received Schubert into his home and gave him many proofs of his friendship and his care . . . The society of a young man so enthusiastic about art and of such refined culture as Schober, himself a successful poet, could clearly only have the most stimulating and favourable effect on Schubert. Schober's friends also became Schubert's friends, and I am convinced that living among this circle of people was far more advantageous to Schubert than if he had lived among a circle of musicians and professional colleagues, though he did not neglect these either. (*Erinnerungen*, p. 419; *Memoirs*, pp. 363-4)

On the subject of the meetings of the reading society proper, whose members were admitted at a formal ceremony and were nicknamed after well-known figures of the literary world, our first information comes from the year of Schubert's death, when Franz von Hartmann noted the titles in his diary. The readings were mainly taken up with the Novellen and dramas of Kleist, together with Tieck's Novellen;[18] among other works we hear of Heine's *Reisebilder* (*Dokumente*, p. 476; *Documents*, p. 709) and Friedrich Schlegel's group of poems entitled *Abendröte* (*Dokumente*, p. 494; *Documents*, p. 738). It therefore seems that these evenings gave Schubert no direct incentive for the composition of songs. He had in fact set various poems from Schlegel's *Abendröte*, but this was in 1819-20, and long before the reading described by Hartmann. Besides this Hartmann mentions only prose works and dramas. Whether discussion of literary theory followed upon such readings we do not know, but it can safely be assumed that it did.[19]

17 See Rudolf Klein, *Schubertstätten* (Vienna, 1972), p. 25.

18 The following works by Kleist were read: *Die Marquise von O...*, *Der Zweikampf*, *Der Findling*, *Der zerbrochene Krug*, *Die Verlobung in St. Domingo*, *Der Prinz von Homburg*, *Das Käthchen von Heilbronn* (*Dokumente*, pp. 474, 485, 489, 494, 496, 523, 525; *Documents*, pp. 706 and 709, 724, 730, 738, 742, 785 and 787, 790); and by Tieck: *Die Gemälde*, *Die Verlobung*, *Der Geheimnisvolle*, and *Der Aufruhr in den Cevennen* (*Dokumente*, pp. 499f, 506, 513; *Documents*, pp. 746, 759, 769).

19 Conversations are referred to only once, and in a negative way, in Schubert's letter to Schober of 30 November 1823, during a difficult period for the reading group: 'If Bruchmann is not there, or even ill, we go on for hours under the supreme direction of Mohn hearing nothing but eternal talk about riding, fencing, horses and hounds' (*Dokumente*, p. 207; *Documents*, pp. 300-1).

From the early 1820s there is occasional evidence to prove that Schubert by no means set every text that was put before him, and even that he could refuse texts that were strongly urged upon him. On 5 September 1821 Franz von Bruchmann wrote to August, Graf von Platen, with whom he had become friendly in Erlangen, saying that he was sending him 'Goethe Songs' by Schubert, and adding: 'Schubert has not yet received yours, as he is not here' (*Dokumente*, p. 135; *Documents*, p. 190). Evidently Platen, through their mutual friend, had asked Schubert to set some of his poems to music. On 8 November Bruchmann then wrote to Erlangen: 'Schubert is setting not only the little poem you sent me, but also several others of your *Lyrische Blätter*, including the two wintry songs' (*Dokumente*, p. 141; cf. *Documents*, p. 198). Not until 17 April 1822, however, was Bruchmann able to send his friend the song 'Die Liebe hat gelogen' (D 751), and the accompanying letter sounds resigned: 'Enclosed you will find your poem, set to music as requested. So I have done what I could' (*Dokumente*, p. 155; *Documents*, p. 221, here revised). He had not been able to persuade Schubert to set to music 'several' of Platen's poems. To be sure, he did set Platen's 'Du liebst mich nicht' (D 756) in the summer of 1822, but no more were to follow.

A similar case occurs in a letter from Anna Milder, the famous singer, who wrote to Schubert from Berlin on 12 December 1824:

> Allow me now to tell you in writing how very much your songs enchant me and what enthusiasm they call forth among the circles to whom I sing them. All this emboldens me to send you a poem which I would earnestly beg you to compose for me, if your Muse will permit it. (*Dokumente*, p. 267; *Documents*, p. 388)

Schubert, who was hoping that the singer might support his operatic plans, sent her in reply the score of *Alfonso und Estrella* (D 732), but did not set the poem, which was in all probability 'Der Jüngling und der Nachtschmetterling' by Karl Gottfried von Leitner.[20] In its place he sent her 'Suleika II' ('Ach um deine feuchten Schwingen', D 717), which had probably been composed in March 1821. Anna Milder replied on 8 March 1825:

> 'Zulaika's Second Song' is heavenly and moves me to tears every time . . . The only regrettable thing is that all these endless beauties cannot be sung to the public, since the crowd wants only treats for the ear. Should the 'Moth' ['Nachtschmetterling'] not be suited to the making of somewhat brilliant music for the voice, I would ask you to choose another poem in its place, if possible by Goethe; one which can be sung in various tempos, so that several emotions can be represented. (*Dokumente*, p. 280; *Documents*, p. 408, here slightly revised)

However important such contact with Berlin must have been to Schubert, he made no response at all to this suggestion. The reason for this is surely that

20 In the opinion of Otto Erich Deutsch: see *Dokumente*, p. 268; *Documents*, p. 389.

it was fundamentally opposed to his manner of composition. According to established custom, Schubert was to write a particular kind of piece for a particular singer, choosing a suitable text for it – yet in general Schubert looked to a text to inspire a certain type of composition. How this happened we can learn from Josef von Spaun's recollection of the origin of 'Der Erlkönig' (D 328):

One afternoon [in 1815] I went with Mayrhofer to see Schubert, who was then living with his father on the Himmelpfortgrund; we found Schubert all aglow, reading the 'Erlkönig' aloud from the book. He paced up and down several times with the book, suddenly he sat down and in no time at all (just as quickly as one can write) there was the glorious Ballad finished on the paper. (*Erinnerungen*, p. 153; *Memoirs*, p. 131)

Such an account – and a quite similar one dates from 1827[21] – makes it clear that Schubert first worked at his raw material, the language, by reading it aloud, and seizing upon the poetic significance; in this lay the genesis of the musical idea, which he afterwards elaborated as he wrote it down. That this was by no means the end of the work is shown by the four versions of the song which have come down to us, each with new alterations, until 'Der Erlkönig' was finally given to the printer six years after he first set it.[22]

In the later 1820s the Romantics again recede into the background among Schubert's authors. Schubert then turned principally to Wilhelm Müller and Heinrich Heine, but also to Ludwig Rellstab; he probably chose Heine and Müller, however, more for what they have in common with the Romantics than as their antithesis.[23] A reference to this perhaps occurs in Johann Mayrhofer's recollection of Schubert: 'The poet's irony, rooted in despair,' he says, with reference to *Winterreise*, 'appealed to him: he expressed it in cutting tones' (*Erinnerungen*, p. 20; *Memoirs*, p. 15). 'Irony' here must be understood in the structural sense peculiar to the Romantics; the expression 'rooted in despair' justifies this interpretation. The poet is not superior to his subject-matter, does not contemplate it with playful detachment as

21 Anna Fröhlich tells of the origin of Grillparzer's 'Ständchen' ('Zögernd leise', D 920): 'And when Schubert came to see us shortly afterwards, I said to him "Look, Schubert, you must set this to music for me." He: "Well, let's have a look at it." Leaning against the piano he read it through repeatedly, exclaiming over and over again "But how beautiful it is – it's so beautiful!" He looked thus at the sheet of paper for a while and finally said "There, it is finished now, I've got it already." And only three days later he really did bring it to me, finished . . .' (*Erinnerungen*, p. 288; *Memoirs*, p. 252, here slightly revised).

22 See W. Dürr, Preface to *NGA*, Series IV, *Lieder*, vol. 1 (Kassel etc., 1970), pp. XIXf.

23 It seems that it was from Beethoven that Schubert received the incentive to compose the Rellstab Lieder; Rellstab himself writes of it: 'Professor Schindler returned them [some scraps of paper with poems written on them] to me from Beethoven's estate years ago. Some had pencil marks in Beethoven's own handwriting; they were the ones he liked best and the ones he had given Schubert to compose . . .' (*Erinnerungen*, p. 348; *Memoirs*, p. 303).

though from a higher standpoint – by means of irony he seeks to come to terms with his own despair, using 'ever more intensified reflections'. 'In cutting tones' the musician plays a part in the same process.[24]

In these last years, which saw the birth of *Winterreise* and *Schwanengesang*, an especially warm friendship grew up between Schubert, the poet Eduard von Bauernfeld and the painter Moritz von Schwind. It is Bauernfeld who particularly strikingly describes Schubert's intimate feeling for literature:

> Moreover in literature, too, he was anything but unversed and the way he understood how to interpret, with inventiveness and vitality, the different poetic individualities, like Goethe, Schiller, Wilhelm Müller, J. G. Seidl, Mayrhofer, Walter Scott and Heine, how to transform them into new flesh and blood and how to render faithfully the nature of each one by beautiful and noble musical characterization – these recreations in song should alone be sufficient to demonstrate, merely by their own existence and without any further proof, from how deep a nature, from how sensitive a soul these creations sprang. A man who so understands the poets is himself a poet![25]

Of the poets here mentioned by Bauernfeld, two cannot easily be assigned to the poetic circles already referred to – that of fashionable sentiment, and the Romantic and post-Romantic circles; these are Johann Gabriel Seidl and Johann Mayrhofer. Both belonged to the more intimate group of Schubert's friends. It is Schubert's choice of these and similar authors that has brought upon him the reproach of lack of discrimination. In addition to Mayrhofer, a close friend of Schubert's from 1814, many of whose poems he set, and Seidl, whom he probably got to know only in 1824, we must mention not only other poetry-writing friends – Schober, Spaun, Senn, Bruchmann and of course Bauernfeld himself – but also other poets, such as Karl Gottfried von Leitner, whom Schubert did not know personally, but was made aware of through families he knew.[26] There is now no doubt that Schubert's re-

24 The extent to which Wilhelm Müller's *Winterreise* and Schubert's composition have been understood in a narrow Romantic sense is shown by a review of the first part of the song-cycle in the *Wiener Allgemeine Theaterzeitung* of 29 March 1828: 'Schubert's mind shows a bold sweep everywhere, whereby he carries every one away with him who approaches him, and he takes them through the immeasurable depth of the human heart into the far distance, where premonitions of the infinite dawn upon them longingly in a rosy radiance, but where at the same time the shuddering bliss of an inexpressible presentiment is companioned by the gentle pain of the constraining present which hems in the boundaries of human existence. Herein lies the nature of German romantic being and art, and in this sense Schubert is a German composer through and through, who does honour to our fatherland and our time' (*Dokumente*, p. 506; *Documents*, p. 758). The dialectic between the 'premonitions of the infinite' and the 'gentle pain of the constraining present' is a fundamental theme of the Romantics. It can only be portrayed through 'irony, rooted in despair'.

25 *Erinnerungen*, p. 263; *Memoirs*, p. 230. Bauernfeld published his memories of Schubert on 17 and 21 April 1869 in the Vienna newspaper *Die Presse*.

26 Leitner himself wrote to Heinrich Schubert on 24 December 1881: 'Then later,

lationship with these poets and their works was different from that with other writers whom he first came to know through reading and discussion. In the verses of his friends he could hear their own voices, their own delivery; he therefore knew what moved them to write. It is only natural that such texts had a direct and immediate appeal for him. These poems tell us little about his relationship to literature, but they tell us much about his relationship to their authors.

Schubert did not therefore indiscriminately choose the words of his songs from 'any volume of poems which happened to be at hand' – he set to music whatever had a special attraction for him, and rejected much that was put before him. His knowledge of the literature of his time was certainly no less comprehensive than that of his friends in the Schober circle. On the interaction of poetry and music in his songs he was answerable only to himself. 'A man who so understands the poets is himself a poet!' – Was Bauernfeld right when he thus summed up Schubert's relationship to literature? The 'understanding' referred to here excludes all such conditions of mind as 'clairvoyance or somnambulism'. Schubert's 'recreations in song' alone give us the answer.

III

There is hardly a work from Schubert's early years over which he took greater pains than the ballad 'Der Taucher' (D 77). It is not too much to say that this is the climax of his song-writing during this period (1811-13).[27] The first draft was begun on 17 September 1813 and completed on 5 April of the following year. He set to work immediately to make a thorough revision and finished this in August 1814. His work on the ballad was not yet at an end, however; various sketches exist from the following months of two important sections of the second version, which he then incorporated in a third version – the latter dating probably from the spring of 1815.

Schubert's revision is mainly concerned with three aspects of the composition: the relationship between recitative and arioso, the instrumental interlude, and details of the declamation. In each case he strove for a closer bond between the words and the music, primarily so that the musical setting should as far as possible grow out of the poetry. In Schubert's earliest ballads he largely kept to the older practice of attending first to the principles of musical form, even where this has no relation to the form of the poetry.

when Franz Schubert spent a few weeks in Graz as the honoured guest of my friends, the family of Dr. Karl Pachler . . ., I was unfortunately not here . . .; but Dr. Pachler's artistic wife, Marie Pachler . . ., drew Schubert's attention to the first edition of my poems, published in the summer of 1825, and presented him with a copy of this little volume . . .' (*Erinnerungen*, p. 227; *Memoirs*, p. 197).

27 See Alfred Einstein, *Schubert. Ein musikalisches Porträt* (Zurich, 1952), pp. 58-9.

In the later version of 'Der Taucher' Schubert therefore deletes arioso passages wherever they conflict with the total effect and bring too close an attention to bear on the details. For example, at the words 'Da zeigte mir Gott, zu dem ich rief, / In der höchsten, schrecklichen Not, / Aus der Tiefe ein ragend Felsenriff, / Das erfasst' ich behend und entrann dem Tod',[28] the first version has a separate section of 15 bars marked 'più presto', with a subtly differentiated piano accompaniment; in the later version this is condensed into eight bars of a kind of secco recitative.[29] Not until this later version does the climax make its effect like a significant caesura; the dramatic momentum is interrupted, the attention is no longer directed towards the roaring whirlpool, but towards the rocks which offer a hand-hold. The next words – 'Und da hing auch der Becher an spitzen Korallen'[30] – lead logically to a new rhythm and a new arioso.

The instrumental interlude before the last stanza is expanded by Schubert from six bars in the first version to 56 bars in the finished composition.[31] He wishes to give the listener time to feel the transition from the dramatic climax – 'Da treibt's ihn, den köstlichen Preis zu erwerben, / Und stürzt hinunter auf Leben und Sterben'[32] – to the epilogue – 'Wohl hört man die Brandung, wohl kehrt sie zurück . . .'[33] In a 'through-composed' ballad the listener is given no chance to imagine unspoken thoughts for himself. The poet demands a mental pause before the beginning of the last verse, but the impetus of the music gives the listener no opportunity to realize it. The composer must therefore supply what the poet does not need to say; he must make a pause for the listener. The six bars of the first version were clearly insufficient for this purpose.

Schubert's work on this ballad is most clearly seen in the various surviving drafts of a passage only six bars long. The stanza which follows the daughter's request 'Lass, Vater, genug sein das grausame Spiel'[34] was evidently seen by Schubert as the key to the whole ballad:

> Drauf der König greift nach dem Becher schnell,
> In den Strudel ihn schleudert hinein,
> Und schaffst du den Becher mir wieder zur Stell,
> So sollst du der trefflichste Ritter mir sein,
> Und sollst sie als Eh'gemahl heut noch umarmen,
> Die jetzt für dich bittet mit zartem Erbarmen.

28 'Then God, to whom I called in my greatest and most dire need, showed me a ledge of rock rearing up from the deep, which I clutched at nimbly and so escaped death.'

29 See *NGA*, Series IV, *Lieder*, vol. 6 (Kassel etc., 1969), pp. 99f (first version) and p. 134 (second version).

30 'And there on the pointed coral hung the goblet'.

31 *NGA*, Series IV, *Lieder*, vol. 6, pp. 110f and pp. 143-6.

32 'Driven to win the precious prize, he plunges down to life or death'.

33 'True, they hear the surf, true, it returns . . .'

34 'O father, let that be enough of this cruel game'.

This stanza[35] at the climax of the composition depicts the tyranny of the ruler who, acting on 'the desires of his heart', plays with the lives of his subjects as unscrupulously as with his daughter's future and happiness.

In the first rendering of the conclusion of this stanza, Schubert adopts the older practice of responding to the meaning of each individual word. The hitherto imperious tone of the king softens to a melodic flourish, particularly at the words 'mit zartem Erbarmen': Ex. 1. In the first revision Schubert deletes as inappropriate the little semiquaver melisma which had laid stress on the words 'mit zartem Erbarmen'; apart from this the gentle mood of the passage is retained: Ex. 2. On a page which contains sketches not only for these bars but also for the above-mentioned instrumental interlude, Schubert maintains the imperious tone almost to the end of the passage; the declamation is characterized by melodic leaps and strongly rhythmic accentuation. The most conspicuous change of character occurs in the dynamics: the *subito piano* in the second bar has disappeared, the *ff* is maintained throughout. Only in the chromatic appoggiatura on 'Erbarmen' can one still find a vestige of the original mildness: Ex. 3. On another page of sketches (written towards

Ex. 1

35 Thereupon the king quickly snatches the goblet
And hurls it back into the whirlpool:
'Bring back that goblet of mine to its place,
And you shall be the first of my knights;
Today as husband you shall embrace her
Who now begs for you with tender mercy.'

Ex. 2

sein, und sollst sie als Eh'-gemahl heut noch um - ar - men, die jetzt für dich
bit - tet mit zar - tem Er - bar-men

Ex. 3

sein, und sollst sie als Eh' - ge-mahl heut noch um - ar-men, die jetzt für dich bit -tet mit
zar - tem Er - bar-men.

Ex. 4

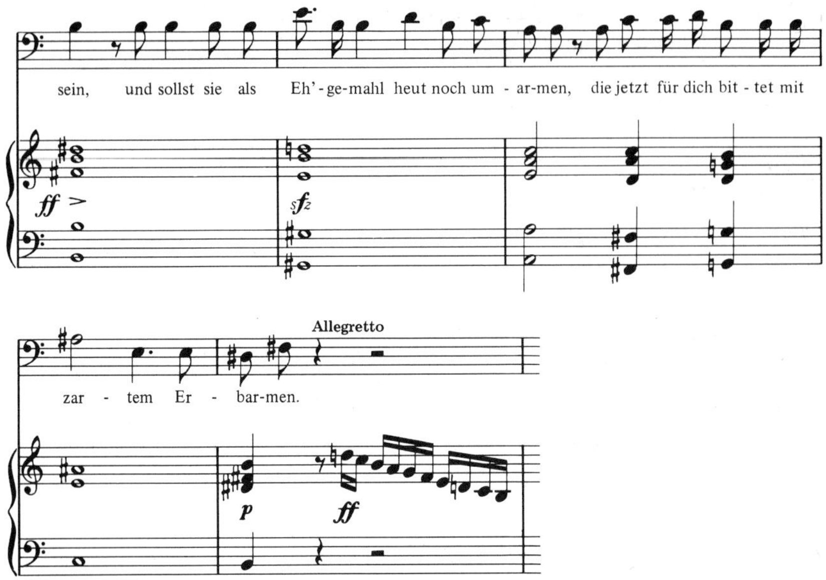

the close of 1814), and then in the second revision of the entire ballad, the definitive setting of this passage makes its eventual appearance: Ex. 4. The melodic and harmonic progressions are still stronger; the chromatic appoggiatura has disappeared, and in its place there occurs an unexpected modulation, which turns the leap of a fourth in the vocal part into a tritone: 'mit zartem Erbarmen' no longer sounds tender, but rather scornful – music and words now speak with the same tongue.[36]

Schubert's work on this early ballad shows clearly how very concerned he was not only to do justice to the details of the text – the linguistic medium – but also to give a just interpretation of the whole poem. We have here not a Romantic song in the sense already outlined – such are naturally to be found only later (see Schubert's own remarks on his 'Rastlose Liebe'), and above all in his settings of Goethe.

In September 1816 Schubert composed his first small song-cycle in the strict sense of the term – the 'Gesänge des Harfners aus *Wilhelm Meister*' (D 478), three songs which are closely linked in content and in musical style. Schubert thought very highly of them; he published them as his op. 12 in December

36 See W. Dürr, Preface to *NGA*, Series IV, *Lieder*, vol. 6, pp. XVIff.

1822, soon after he was first given the chance to see his works in print. Let us examine the first of these 'Gesänge':

Wer sich der Einsamkeit ergibt,
Ach, der ist bald allein,
Ein jeder lebt, ein jeder liebt,
Und lässt ihn seiner Pein.
Ja, lasst mich meiner Qual!
Und kann ich nur einmal
Recht einsam sein,
Dann bin ich nicht allein.

Es schleicht ein Liebender, lauschend sacht,
Ob seine Freundin allein?
So überschleicht bei Tag und Nacht
Mich Einsamen die Pein,
Mich Einsamen die Qual.
Ach werd ich erst einmal
Einsam im Grabe sein,
Da lässt sie mich allein.[37]

Who yields himself to solitude,
Ah, he is soon alone,
Everyone lives, everyone loves,
And leaves him to his pain.
Yes, leave me to my torment!
And if just once I can
Be quite lonely,
Then I am not alone.

A lover steals up, listening gently,
Is his girl alone?
Thus by day and night
Does pain steal upon me, the lonely one,
Does torment steal upon me.
Ah, when I am at last
Lonely in the grave,
Then it will leave me alone.

Each of the two eight-line stanzas, closely knit by the unusual rhyme-scheme ababccbb, is divided into two parts, or two successive steps. The first four lines of the first stanza provide the setting for the whole poem: Who yields himself to solitude is soon alone, for every man lives for himself. The next four lines convert the general into the particular, and also supply an antithesis: When I am truly lonely, I am not alone.

The second stanza gives the poet's reasoning and draws the conclusion from it. The stanza is irregularly divided into sections of five and three lines (the reasoning must be argued out, and this requires more space). As a lover stealthily watches his beloved, whose fidelity he suspects, so do pain and torment lie in wait for me. Hence: Only in the grave am I really alone.

37 The text – here given according to *NGA*, Series IV, *Lieder*, vol. 1, pp. 85-8 – follows Schubert's composition, not the text in Goethe's *Gedichte*.

How is this dialectical process realized in the music? Schubert begins with an arpeggiated prelude. 'The old man', Goethe says in *Wilhelm Meister*, 'looked at the strings, and after preluding softly, began his song.'[38] Schubert seizes gladly upon this stage direction: Ex. 5. The broken chords used throughout the song find their justification here. Schubert loves to create a kind of

Ex. 5

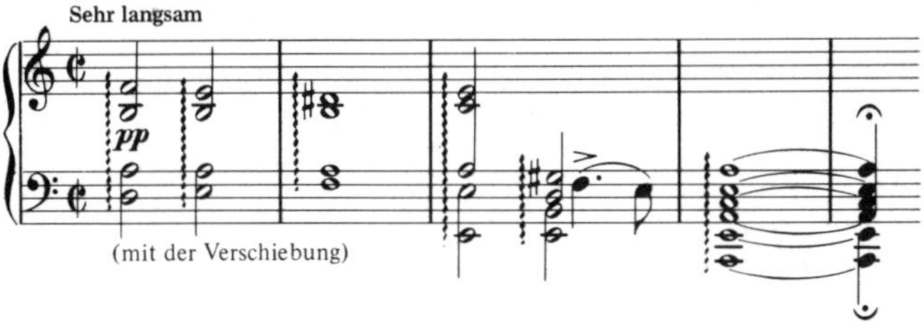

stage-set in this way, which helps unite the movement of the whole. The harp-like chords admittedly begin only with the second part of the first stanza – up to this point the song is rhapsodical. The first four lines are treated as it were in narrative style; the melody is clear, regular, almost neutral in character, and enriched by various ornaments, which show their flourishes all the more distinctly on repetition, while the piano merely supports and accompanies the voice. Schubert's writing corresponds to the contextual function of the four lines – viz., a universal statement which, treated by Schubert as a kind of broad cadence, sets the basic tone.

After a pause Schubert begins again: 'Ja, lasst mich meiner Qual!' The section opens with a transition to the submediant – it seems as though Schubert intends to make it a modulatory one. The listener is deceived, for it too closes in the tonic (which Schubert scarcely leaves again), yet through surprising turns of harmony the composer gives it colour and personal feeling. The change in the text to 'ich' is mirrored in the music, and at this point the piano is released from its merely subordinate role: it continues to accompany still, but takes on an insistent movement of its own; the instrument has become a partner.

At the beginning of the new stanza the piano gives up its subordinate role completely. While the voice sings a declamatory quasi-recitative, the keyboard part – inspired by the imagery of stealth ('schleicht') – develops its own independent line in the bass: Ex. 6. At this point the rhythms of voice and

38 As the text for his 'Gesänge des Harfners' Schubert used the version which Goethe had published in his *Gedichte* (see the Supplement *Quellen und Lesarten* to *NGA*, Series IV, *Lieder*, vol. 1 (Kassel etc., 1972), p. 28). Since Schubert set many songs from *Wilhelm Meister* at this time, it is to be assumed that he had read the novel and knew the introduction to the poem 'Wer sich der Einsamkeit ergibt'.

Ex. 6

Ex. 7

accompaniment, hitherto parallel, begin to diverge; while the voice declaims in basic 2/4 bars, the first being light, the second heavy, the piano keeps to the regular 4/4 time. The uneasiness of the poetic image, which reflects the strife in the mind of the harpist, a prey to self-inflicted pain and torment, thus finds its correlative in the music: Ex. 7.

It is interesting to observe how different are the interpretations of Schumann and Wolf in their settings of the poem.[39] Following the keyword 'Liebender' (lover) they conceive this passage as idyllic in tone, and the

39 See Paul Mies, 'Goethes Harfenspielergesang "Wer sich der Einsamkeit ergibt" in den Kompositionen Schuberts, Schumanns und H. Wolfs', in *Zeitschrift für Ästhetik und allgemeine Kunstwissenschaft*, XVI (1922), 383-90.

formal contrast thus provided is seen as musically desirable. Schubert on the other hand shuns this; he often likes to insert brighter middle sections of this type in which the tension is relaxed, but here it would have disturbed the inner logic of the composition.

The fourth section is the musical sequel to the preceding three. The instrument now leads the way, and marks it with descending chromatic progressions in the bass: Ex. 8. The vocal line sustains a kind of passionate

Ex. 8

arioso, in which the course of the melody – despite some violent outbursts – seems to be foreshadowed in the accompaniment. The declamation itself contributes to this effect. Goethe's irregular stresses ('Ach wèrd ich èrst einmàl / Éinsam im Grábe sèin') are forced by Schubert into a regular series of beats ('Ach wérd ich èrst einmál / Einsám (!) im Gràbe séin'). Here we see the effect not of language on music but of music on language.[40]

Musical laws also prevail in the formal construction. Of Goethe's three closing lines the third is repeated to make a group of four; only in this way does Schubert achieve a regular eight-bar period, which he immediately repeats and thus emphasizes. Nowhere else in the song does one find such repeats

40 Later attempts to 'correct' Schubert's declamation – as in a copy that probably goes back to Johann Michael Vogl, in the Witteczek–Spaun collection (Gesellschaft der Musikfreunde, Vienna) – are for that reason unsatisfactory (see *NGA*, Series IV, *Lieder*, vol. 1, Appendix, pp. 297f).

determined by purely musical needs – here too one feels the preponderance of the instrumental part.

Like the poet, the composer directs the song by a dialectical process towards one end: at first the voice predominates, while the piano merely accompanies and supports; later the instrument becomes a partner, then comes into open conflict with the vocal line, finally assuming the mastery. In the postlude the chromatic figure in the bass therefore has the last word. To be sure, while in his closing lines the poet speaks of death as a release for the individual from pain and torment, at the same time applying the concept of death to the harper in his solitude ('mich' is the next-to-last word of the song), the composer leads the song into a realm in which general musical principles predominate, and in which the personality of the tormented one, the singer, is subsumed. Out of this proceeds that partial incongruence of specifically musical and specifically poetic processes which run side by side, yet obey their own laws (as I argued at the beginning of this essay), leaving the song accessible to 'ever more intensified reflections'.

Am fernen Horizonte
Erscheint, wie ein Nebelbild,
Die Stadt mit ihren Türmen,
In Abenddämmrung gehüllt.

Ein feuchter Windzug kräuselt
Die graue Wasserbahn;
Mit traurigem Takte rudert
Der Schiffer in meinem Kahn.

Die Sonne hebt sich noch einmal
Leuchtend vom Boden empor,
Und zeigt mir jene Stelle,
Wo ich das Liebste verlor.[41]

On the far horizon
Appears, like a misty image,
The town with its towers,
Veiled in the evening light.

A moist breath of wind ripples
The grey waterway;
With mournful stroke
The boatman rows my boat.

The sun rises once again,
Glowing, from the land,
And shows me that place
Where I lost my dearest one.

41 Text and music are here reproduced from the autograph of *Schwanengesang* in the Pierpont Morgan Library, New York, and the first edition by Tobias Haslinger (Vienna, 1829): see *Schubert's Liederzyklen . . . In verkleinerter Nachbildung der Originalausgaben*, ed. and intr. Heinrich Kralik (Vienna, n.d.), pp. 308-10.

In August or September 1828 Schubert set Heine's poem as 'Die Stadt' (D 957/11) in a cycle of six Heine songs which later appeared together with settings of Rellstab and Seidl as his *Schwanengesang.* The poem could well be a model for a strophic song, in which the composer may 'seize upon every inflection of feeling, as though to make it a focal point, from which the melody shines forth'. The three identically constructed stanzas describe a condition, rather than a process; their effect makes itself felt in the last two lines, though the poem does not develop towards them. The first two stanzas could also be said to foreshadow these lines. Yet Schubert did not treat it as a strophic song. Why?

The uniform mood of the poem conceals an inner dialectic: on one side the singer in his boat, which the boatman moves along 'with mournful stroke'; on the other 'the town with its towers', to which the singer is attracted, where once his loved one was, but which now seems as unreal as a 'misty image'.[42] But the 'grey waterway', the 'moist breath of wind', the boatman and the boat are all real.

In the introductory bars Schubert paints this real world as a kind of backcloth, before which – as with the plucking of strings by the harpist – the actual song unfolds. In the scenario everything is susceptible of a 'poetic' interpretation: diminished-seventh arpeggios refer to the moist breath of wind, regularly accented chords to the strokes of the oars, tremolos in the bass to the unsteady gliding of the boat. All combine to form a musical movement of which the chief characteristic is uncertainty: uncertainty over the key – the whole prelude is harmonically built upon the diminished seventh C-E♭-F♯-A, in which the C is clearly to be heard, but which does not resolve to C minor, the key in the signature of which the song is written; uncertainty also over the metre – in the first two bars the tremolo, the first beat of a 3/4 bar, seems to be prominent, whilst in the following bars Schubert himself stresses the second and third beats. Finally, in the bars of the prelude no melody can be said to take definite shape: Ex. 9.

With the entry of the vocal part the musical conformation of the song is altered at a stroke. To the uncertain reality Schubert opposes an 'apparition' in clearly visible contours: a passage of eight bars in firmly related harmony (with the first pair closing on the dominant, the second on the subdominant, the third again on the dominant, and the last on the tonic – C minor), the use of 3/4 metre so constructed as to be clearly intended almost as a *ritmo alla francese* (with the first beat bearing the main stress), and a well-defined

42 That the singer in the following poems of the book *Die Heimkehr* in Heine's *Buch der Lieder* really enters the town is in this context of no importance ('So wandl ich wieder den alten Weg,/Die wohlbekannten Gassen'), nor is the fact that Schubert shows him in the town in the last poem of the song-cycle ('Still ist die Nacht, es ruhen die Gassen,/In diesem Hause wohnte mein Schatz'). If one looks at the songs in relation to each other, one can speak of a process of development in which 'Die Stadt' marks a stage.

Ex. 9

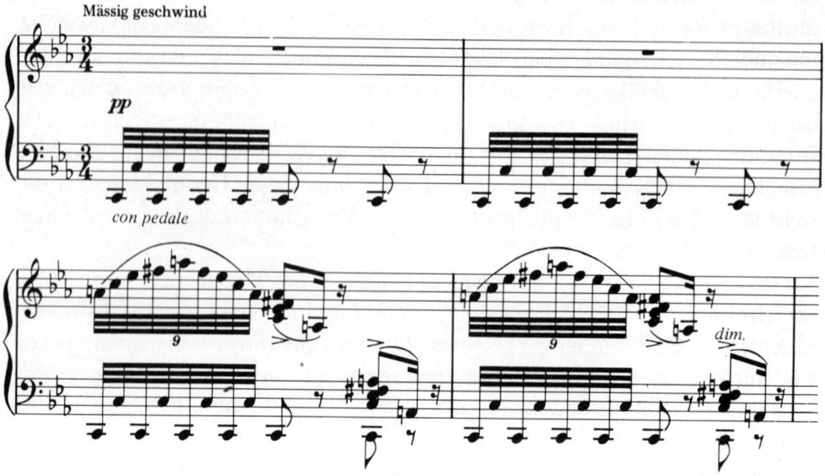

melodic line, in which however quasi-recitative (i.e. a declamatory passage derived from the text), as often in Schubert's later works, combines with genuine melodic material obeying purely musical dictates.

The apparition of the first stanza subsides suddenly; the very regular eight-bar period finds no regular response, nothing to balance it. The words of the second stanza first make this clear to the listener; it is not the town which has reality, but the grey waterway. In this stanza the poet first uses the lyric 'I'. Throughout it Schubert accompanies the slowly descending solo voice with an even and unbroken succession of the diminished sevenths heard in the introduction, here heard as broken chords to render the oar-strokes. The rhythmic content of the 3/4 bar has become established; the vocal part, the singer, articulates it clearly: Ex. 10. The metrical stress (the first beat) is at times followed by an emphatic stress (with a dotted rhythm drawing

Ex. 10

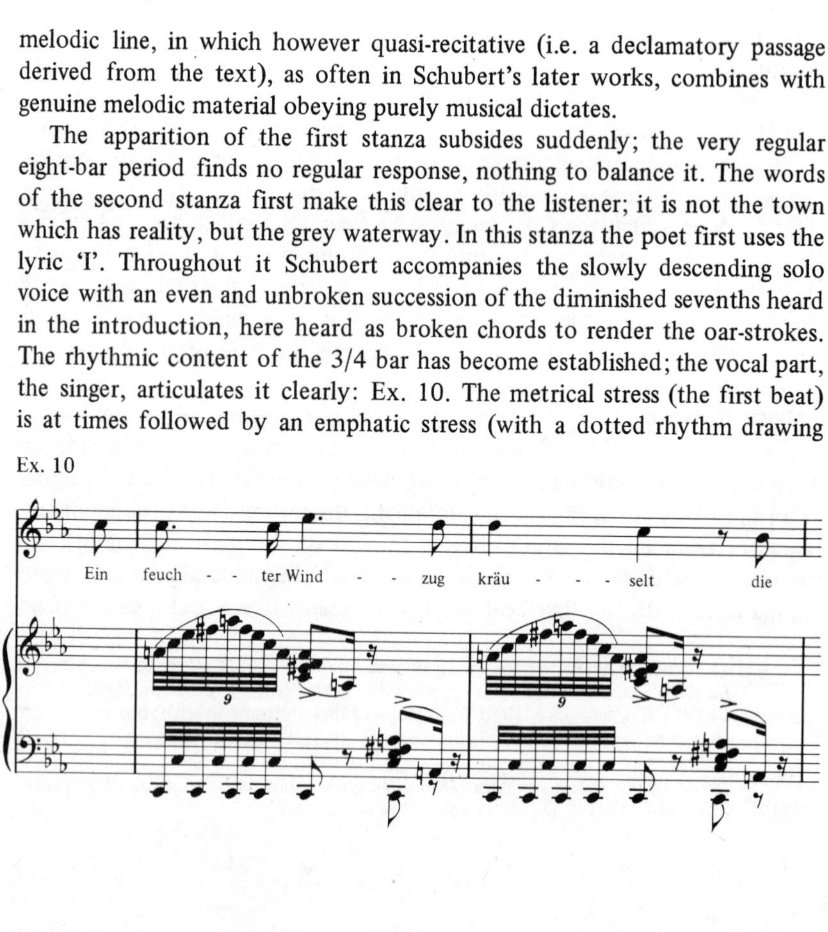

together the second and third beats); the latter is further reinforced by the oar-strokes in the keyboard part. Thus there emerges a kind of saraband rhythm, that 'mournful stroke' to which the boatman keeps time – clearly the only dependable element in a world of uncertainty.

The apparition however returns once more, again as a firmly related eight-bar phrase, yet altered. Just as Heine in the third stanza throws a bridge across from the apparition to the singer, who there 'lost his dearest one', thus bringing illusion and reality together, so in Schubert's second stanza the rhythm of the saraband has a retrospective effect on the *alla francese* of the first. The singer has become a character; he can no longer withdraw into the neutral role of the narrator. The piano on the other hand takes up unchanged the rhythms of the first stanza. The dialectic of reality and illusion is thus reflected in the conflict between voice and keyboard in the opening bars of the third stanza: Ex. 11. In the following bars the piano is obliged to come into line with the voice, to help throw the bridge across from both sides, as it were. At the words 'Und zeigt mir jene Stelle' the accompaniment also takes up the saraband rhythm – for the piano this almost has the effect of a change of time signature, which the composer marks with an accent – and it then shares in the singer's one great outburst at the words 'Wo ich das Liebste verlor'.

Ex. 11

(stark)
Die Sonne hebt sich noch ein - mal leuch-tend vom Bo - den em - por,
f

The apparition then subsides once again; the piano returns in the epilogue to the music of the opening bars. The song finishes, as it began, open. The dialectic of apparition and reality is not resolved in the music any more than in the text. The listener is left to pursue the reflections posed by the poem.

IV

These observations on the three songs 'Der Taucher', 'Wer sich der Einsamkeit ergibt' and 'Die Stadt' serve to show that even in his early years Schubert sought to find exact musical equivalents for language, the medium of poetry. In musical declamation he not only is faithful to the words, but paints characters and seizes upon relationships. Declamation in the style of recitative, on the other hand, reveals elements which properly belong to the arioso – and out of this there later develops Schubert's individual use of declamatory melody, in which recitative, springing mainly from the language, is fused with arioso, which tends to be fashioned according to the dictates of music.

It is not only on the plane of individual words that musical and poetic structures correspond – this holds true to a similar degree for larger relationships, for the whole conception of a poem as an amalgam of form and content. In this the musical equivalents are naturally not generated by the text – they are essentially musical means with which Schubert works: the interplay of rhythm and metre, the individual movement of voice and instrument in the manner of strict part-writing, musical *topoi* (such as a bass line falling a fourth by chromatic steps). Yet the musical relationships which arise correspond closely to the poetic, as only such media can correspond. What lies outside this leads to the phenomenon of partial incongruence, which I have already discussed more than once. There can be no doubt that 'Wer sich der Einsamkeit ergibt' and 'Die Stadt' are poetic in the Romantic sense, open. This is not unquestionably true for all of Schubert's songs, not even for the majority of them. Only poems which are 'Romantic' in the narrow sense can also be so in their music. The close interrelation between musical and poetic forms – or 'making the song literary' – is indeed surely characteristic of the Schubertian song in general.

A third element, to which I have often drawn attention, also plays an important part. Inspired mostly by the poetic images, Schubert frequently creates a scenario which holds for the entire song (here too the stimulus is poetic, though the means are musical); this allows him to keep the composition open and yet to place it within a framework, which has the effect of defining it – just as a play's plot can unfold against one permanent backcloth, and is yet open, free to move into the past or the future, while seemingly closed because of the permanent set. By means of a scenario of this sort a composer can bind together the separate parts of a song in open form, and make them relate to each other.

Schubert's 'Auf dem Strom' *

RUFUS HALLMARK

> It is a matter of fourteen pages. The voice bids passionate farewells, while the horn gives free imitations of the melodies, above the pianoforte's arpeggios. The music flows with animation, but the sentiment is really only formal. This sort of composition belongs to the 'copious' Schubert of the legend.[1]

With this uncharacteristic lack of sympathy, Richard Capell dismisses 'Auf dem Strom' as a facile composition of relatively little artistic value. Like most writers dealing with the songs of 1828, Capell appears anxious to proceed to *Schwanengesang.* While this attitude is understandable, the consequent neglect of other songs – by performers and scholars alike – is not always deserved. In particular, 'Auf dem Strom' merits reappraisal. Not only is it a better song than Capell gives it credit for being, but it is also one through which Schubert seems to have tried to project a special, personal message.

The song is a masterly setting for tenor, piano, and horn of a poem by Ludwig Rellstab.[2] A comparison of the poem with the song emphasizes the ingenuity of Schubert's treatment of formal and expressive elements of Rellstab's text. An examination of the composer's autograph manuscript, heretofore ignored, brings to light some telling compositional changes and divergences from the published editions. Finally, a consideration of the music and of the biographical context of its creation reveals the song's unnamed dedicatee.

* This article is based on a paper read at the national meeting of the American Musicological Society in Washington, D.C., November 1976.

1 Richard Capell, *Schubert's Songs*, rev. edn (London, 1957), p. 247.

2 D 943: *Schuberts Werke* (cited below as '*AGA*'), Series XX, ed. Eusebius Mandyczewski, vol. 10 (Leipzig, 1895), no. 568, pp. 2-15 (Dover reprint, New York, vol. 17). References to this score are made by citation of page and bar numbers.

I

Auf dem Strom

Nimm die letzten Abschiedsküsse
Und die wehenden, die Grüsse
Die ich noch ans Ufer sende,
Eh' Dein Fuss sich scheidend wende!
Schon wird von des Stromes Wogen
Rasch der Nachen fortgezogen,
Doch den tränendunklen Blick
Zieht die Sehnsucht stets zurück!

Und so trägt mich denn die Welle
Fort mit unerflehter Schnelle.
Ach, schon ist die Flur verschwunden,
Wo ich selig Sie gefunden!
Ewig hin, ihr Wonnetage!
Hoffnungsleer verhallt die Klage
Um das schöne Heimatland,
Wo ich ihre Liebe fand.

Sieh, wie flieht der Strand vorüber,
Und wie drängt es mich hinüber,
Zieht mit unnennbaren Banden,
An der Hütte dort zu landen,
In der Laube dort zu weilen;
Doch des Stromes Wellen eilen
Weiter ohne Rast und Ruh,
Führen mich dem Weltmeer zu!

Ach, vor jener dunklen Wüste,
Fern von jeder heitern Küste,
Wo kein Eiland zu erschauen,
O, wie fasst mich zitternd Grauen!
Wehmuthsthränen sanft zu bringen,
Kann kein Lied vom Ufer dringen;
Nur der Sturm weht kalt daher
Durch das grau gehobne Meer!

Kann des Auges sehnend Schweifen
Keine Ufer mehr ergreifen,
Nun so blick' ich zu den Sternen
Dort in jenen heil'gen Fernen!
Ach, bei ihrem milden Scheine
Nannt' ich sie zuerst die Meine;
Dort vielleicht, o tröstend Glück!
Dort begegn' ich ihrem Blick.

On the River

Take these last good-bye kisses
And my waving farewells
That I send shoreward
Before your steps turn away.
Already the skiff is hurriedly withdrawn
Before the river's current.
And yet, longing keeps drawing back
A tear-darkened gaze.

And so the waves carry me
Away with unmerciful speed.
Already the meadow has disappeared
Where I blessedly found her.
Gone forever, blissful days!
Hopelessly dies away my mourning
Over the beautiful homeland
Where I found her love.

See how the shoreline flies by,
And how it attracts me,
Draws me with inexpressible bonds
To land there at the cabin,
To linger there in the bower;
But the river's waves hurry on
Without rest or peace
And carry me to the ocean!

Alas, before that dark wilderness,
Far away from any bright coast,
Where no island can be seen,
O, how a trembling dread seizes me!
Tenderly to bring tears of melancholy
No song can penetrate from the shore;
Only the storm blows cold
Through the gray, tossing sea!

Since my eyes' yearning search
Reaches the shore no more,
Now I look to the stars
There in that holy, distant place.
O, by their soft light
I first called her mine;
There perhaps, consoling fortune,
There I meet her gaze.

Rellstab's poem[3] is grandiose in theme and scope. Five imposing eight-line stanzas depict in vigorous language the voyage of a ship from an inland harbour out to sea. The persona of the poem sails for an unstated destination, taking anguished leave of his beloved. Deeper metaphorical meaning urges itself on the reader and heightens the tone.[4] Schubert's equally grand song (209 bars) matches the drama of the poem and, as we shall see, treats the figurative meaning of the poem by musical allusion. As well as capturing its mood, Schubert skilfully translates literary features of the poem into music.

In their content the stanzas of Rellstab's poem alternate two viewpoints. Stanzas, I, III, and V dwell nostalgically on the woman and the country left behind; II and IV pessimistically contemplate the future. The odd-numbered stanzas tend to focus on the land (or, in V, on its substitute, the heavens), the even-numbered ones on the water. This distinction in content is paralleled by a difference in formal procedure. Stanzas I, III, and (to a lesser extent) V fall into contrasting half-stanzas; each begins reminiscently but is interrupted by the progress of events. In stanzas II and IV, on the other hand, the two halves are not contrasting and developmental, but reiterative and corroborative. For example, in stanza I, the first four lines describe the farewell as the ship stands in the harbour. This tableau is then broken by the departure of the skiff, signalling the ship's imminent leave-taking. In stanza II, both halves deplore the separation from the homeland 'where I blessedly found her' (line 4) and 'where I found her love' (line 8).

Schubert matched these distinctions in his music. He did not compose a strophic setting, but rather alternated sections of music in the same design as the poem, these sections preceded by and interspersed with horn music and followed by a coda. The odd-numbered stanzas are in E major, the even-numbered ones in the relative minor. Furthermore, Schubert heeded the internal structure of the stanzas. The music for I, III, and V is non-repetitive, and the second halves of I and III are in the contrasting tonic minor key.[5] In stanzas II and IV, with their similar half-stanzas, the music for lines 1-4 is repeated for lines 5-8:[6]

3 *Franz Schubert. Die Texte seiner einstimmig komponierten Lieder und ihre Dichter,* 2 vols., ed. Maximilian Schochow and Lilly Schochow (Hildesheim and New York, 1974), vol. 2, pp. 469-70 (as taken from *Gedichte von Ludwig Rellstab*, vol. 1 (Berlin, 1827), pp. 120-1).

4 The themes of departure, separation and loneliness also figure in the Rellstab poems Schubert set in *Schwanengesang*, a circumstance which is perhaps not purely coincidental. See further below, in section III.

5 In stanza V, the second half continues in E major, there being no interruption in the text to warrant the contrast that the modal change provided. Furthermore, the occurrence of the major key where one has heard the minor in two previous stanzas is an appropriate musical analogue to the new hopefulness of the text.

6 In stanza II, each half-stanza cadences in C♯ major, this momentary turn from the minor paralleling the fleeting reminiscence of the beloved. Stanza IV is unremittingly in the minor, each half-stanza of the text ending with despair.

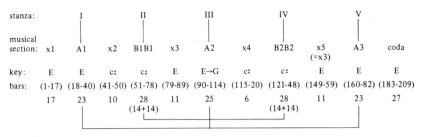

stanza:		I		II		III		IV		V	
musical section:	x1	A1	x2	B1B1	x3	A2	x4	B2B2	x5 (=x3)	A3	coda
key:	E	E	c♯	c♯	E	E→G	c♯	c♯	E	E	E
bars:	(1-17)	(18-40)	(41-50)	(51-78)	(79-89)	(90-114)	(115-20)	(121-48)	(149-59)	(160-82)	(183-209)
	17	23	10	28 (14+14)	11	25	6	28 (14+14)	11	23	27

In addition to the appropriate formal design of his song, Schubert created a masterful harmonic effect as an analogue for a textual detail. In stanza I, even as the skiff pulls away from the larger ship, longing draws back the lover's tearful gaze. With the boat's withdrawal, the song turns to E minor, and soon the G♮ momentarily becomes tonic and the song heads for a cadence in G major. At that cadential moment, however, the music is wrenched away by a D♯ in the bass and drawn back to E major, even as 'die Sehnsucht zieht den Blick zurück!' (see bars 34-40 = *AGA* Series XX, vol. 10 (no. 568), p. 4 bar 11 to p. 5 bar 1). Having introduced this feint toward another key as a musical analogue to the text in stanza I, Schubert used it in every stanza (in II and IV, E major is drawn back to C♯ minor in each half-stanza). Perhaps he did it for the sake of unity, but surely in order that he might play on the listener's expectation of it in stanza III (see further below).[7]

In the first part of stanza III, Rellstab accomplished a clever rhythmic feat which does what the words of the poem say. The traveller is drawn by inexpressible bonds to land near the cabin he spies and to linger in the bower there. The fifth line of the text ('In der Laube dort zu weilen') belongs syntactically to the first half-stanza, although in rhyme it is bound to the next couplet. The first half-stanza then is extended by one line, and the reader, in effect, 'lingers' beyond the first two couplets into the middle of the next. Schubert's musical response is analogous. To the music he used for lines 1-4 of the first stanza, Schubert sets the corresponding lines of stanza III and then adds an extra phrase for line 5 (cf. bars 17-26 and 89-101 = p. 3 bar 10 to p. 4 bar 3, and p. 8 bar 6 to p. 9 bar 2). By extending the original ten-bar period, Schubert directly translates Rellstab's rhythmic effect into music.

At this point, the verse says, 'But the river's waves hurry on without rest or peace', and Schubert, as in stanza I, turns to E minor and hints at G major. However, this time the poem does not speak of any turning back; rather, the waves carry the traveller from the river out into the ocean. Here Schubert turns to good account the listener's expectations. Instead of turning back to E major, as in stanza I, he proceeds to a full and repeated cadence in G (bars

7 The chromatic twist in the horn's prelude, moving momentarily from E major toward a cadence in G♯ minor (bars 7-9), foreshadows, while not literally introducing, the harmonic progression Schubert composed into the vocal stanza.

112-14). The new tonality, earlier approached but avoided, now arrives with full force (see bars 109-14 = p. 9 bar 10 to p. 10 bar 1). (The coincidence of the cadence in G with the traveller's being carried out to sea is not exact in Schubert's first draft of this passage, as we shall see below.)

For the two remaining stanzas of the poem, Schubert essentially repeats the music of stanzas II and I respectively, with some alterations. Among these, the most effective is the variation of the music for the ends of the two halves of stanza IV. At lines 4 and 8 (bars 129-34 and 143-8), the tenor and horn now sing together a melody derived from the piano bass of stanza III (bars 59-64 and 73-8), while the piano assumes the lines that earlier belonged to tenor and horn.[8] The expressiveness of horn and tenor sounding the bass line in octaves enhances the chilling quality of the text, which speaks of the traveller's dread and of a storm at sea (cf. bars 58-64 and 129-34 = p. 6 bars 4-10 and p. 11 bars 1-6).

Rellstab has woven into his poem of travel, as though it were a backdrop to the dramatic situation, the passage of time. The river flowing to the sea symbolizes time's passage, and between and within the stanzas there is an implicit progression from the daylight departure at the beginning through a storm to the clear, starlit night of the poem's conclusion. The posthorn is an aural symbol of travel and so an appropriate obbligato instrument. Moreover, the horn interludes afford a real time-lapse between the stanzas, suggesting the passage of time implicit in the poem.

II

The autograph manuscript of 'Auf dem Strom' is in the Houghton Library of Harvard University, MS Mus. 99.2.[9] It consists of six leaves of coarse, heavy paper ruled with twelve staves on each page, which Schubert set up as systems in the order of 'Voce', 'Corno in E', and 'Pianoforte'.[10] The manuscript is titled, signed, and dated 'März 1828'. Although relatively clean, the

8 This exchange of parts prefigures the more literal voice-swapping in the coda (bars 183-94).

9 The manuscript was formerly in the possession of George B. Weston, late professor of romance languages at Harvard University: O. E. Deutsch, *Schubert. Thematic Catalogue of All His Works in Chronological Order* (cited below as '*D1*') (London, 1951), p. 460; see also Craig Wright, 'Rare Music Manuscripts at Harvard', *Current Musicology*, no. 10 (1970), p. 31. I wish to thank the librarian of Houghton, W. H. Bond, the custodian of manuscripts, Rodney Dennis, and Marty Shaw for their assistance.

10 The manuscript is made up of three bifolia, gathered as two (one within the other) plus one, and stitched together. The leaves measure roughly 24.2 cm x 31.8 cm. The first two bifolia appear to have been cut from one sheet; folios 1 and 2 bear the matching halves of a fleur-de-lis countermark (quadrants 2 and 1), and faint traces of a 'W' can be seen on folios 3 and 4 (quadrants 4 and 3). Prof. Joshua Rifkin, to whom I am indebted for inspecting the manuscript with me, has identified the paper with that which Schubert used for Part II of

Figure 1. 'Auf dem Strom', p. 1 of the autograph (Harvard University, Houghton Library, MS Mus. 99.2)

manuscript contains a number of alterations of its original musical text. These corrections appear to have been entered after the complete song had been written out; i.e. the autograph is, in the strictest sense, not a composing manuscript. The final version of the song in this source, furthermore, differs in significant details from the published version.[11]

One can see on the first page (see Figure 1) that Schubert first wrote d♯′ and e′ (concert pitch) at the ends of the horn's opening phrases (bars 4 and 6) and then changed these notes to f♯′ and g♯′. The interlude after stanza I contains the same original and corrected readings (see Ex. 1), from which one infers that Schubert made the change only after he had written out the horn music twice in its original form. In their revised form, these first two phrases are part of a larger melodic sequence that continues (in longer note values) in the next phrase (bars 7-9). Since the melodic turn of the third phrase was present in Schubert's original conception, the sequential relation with the

Ex. 1 Houghton, MS Mus. 99.2, p. 3 bars 40-4 : first version of the first interlude

Winterreise (Pierpont Morgan Library, New York, Cary Collection), a Bohemian product by Welhartitz. Although he finds the watermarks too faint for absolute certainty, Rifkin believes folios 1-4 to be mould a, and folios 5 and 6 mould b. The manufacturer of the paper is confirmed by Robert Winter's separate identification of it as Welhartitz, type VIIb (see p. 249 below). All the staff rulings are alike: each staff is 0.75 cm wide; the space between staves is 0.85 cm; and the total staff span on each page is 18.5 cm.

11 The following discussion of the contents of Schubert's manuscript does not attempt to be exhaustive; the intent here is rather to present what I have considered the most significant aspects of the autograph.

preceding bars – a propelling feature of the prelude and subsequent interludes – is revealed to be the result of a creative afterthought.[12]

In the published song, the piano takes up the first phrase of the interlude after stanza I and is then answered by the horn playing the second. The same thing occurs after stanzas II and IV. In the manuscript, however, the horn originally played the whole tune (Ex. 1). Schubert modified this, as in his correction of the first interlude on p. 3 of the manuscript (see Figure 2), where he crossed out the first phrase in the horn and transferred it to the piano, sacrificing the bass figure in bar 42. The same correction was made after stanzas II and IV. The change adds a pleasing ensemble effect to the music and also serves an important practical need – a momentary respite for the hard-pressed horn-player.

Ex. 2 Houghton, MS Mus. 99.2, pp. 6–7 bars 109–14 : first version

12 Note, too, that the bass note in bar 4 was changed from f♯ to d♯ in response to the change in the horn part, and that the melody in bar 10 was changed from a dotted minim and two quavers on a♮′-b′-a′ (concert pitch).

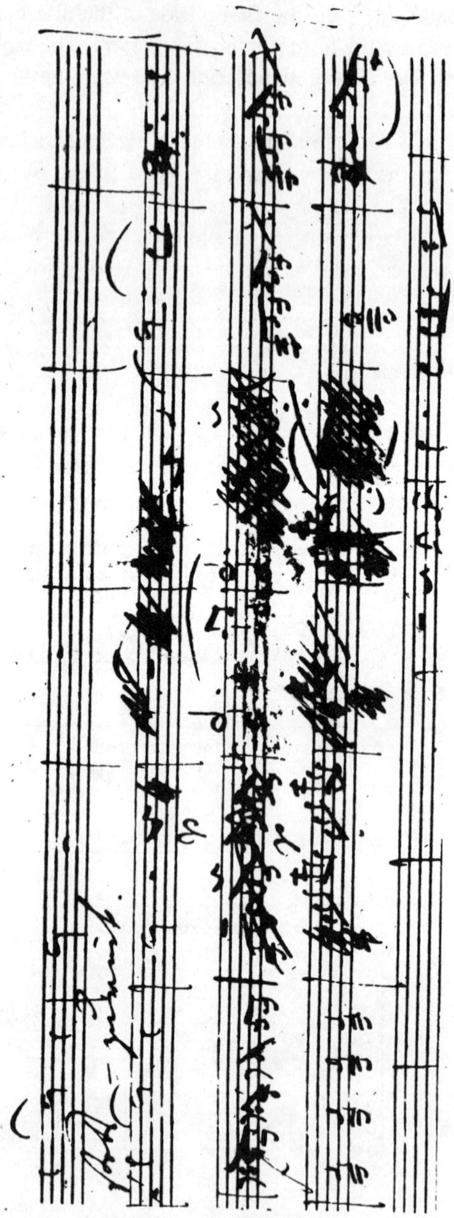

Figure 2. 'Auf dem Strom', p. 3 of the autograph (detail)

Figure 3. 'Auf dem Strom', part of pp. 6 and 7 of the autograph

The most extensive revision in the autograph involves the conclusion of stanza III. Schubert's compositional change there can be read as a partial confirmation of the interpretation given above of the G major cadence. In this stanza Schubert extended the E major section to accommodate line 5, as we have seen. Therefore, he was left with only three lines instead of four for the remainder of the music. To the first two E minor phrases he set lines 6 and 7 ('Doch des Stromes Wellen eilen / Weiter ohne Rast und Ruh'). He then set line 8 to the next musical phrase and simply repeated it in a single cadence: Ex. 2. In his revision of this passage (see Figure 3), Schubert fashioned a composite text from lines 6 and 7 ('Eilen ohne Rast und Ruh') and substituted this for the first statement of line 8. He also repeated the G major cadence in a marginal insertion, giving more weight to this musical rhetoric. One of the net effects of this emendation is to save line 8 ('Führen mich dem Weltmeer zu') for the very moment of the cadence in the alien key.[13]

On the last page of the manuscript one finds a small but not trivial change of the final cadence at the very end of the coda. The manuscript shows clearly that Schubert wrote a shorter ending (see Figure 4 and Ex. 3) but later changed his mind and added one more bar.[14] The longer vocal phrase is now closely related to the song's opening vocal melody. The tenor's first phrase is virtually a musical palindrome, a rising arpeggio g♯-b-e′ and a descending one with a turn around e′ in the middle. The closing phrase of the song, as modified, opens with the turn around e′ and follows this with an ornamented version of the descending arpeggio (Ex. 4). (The modification of the cadence and the resultant reference to the song's beginning may be due to Schubert's imitation of a famous model: see further below.)

13 In the first layer of the manuscript, the progression to G major in this passage is different. In all three stanzas where it occurs, Schubert first wrote triads on B (bars 34, 109, and 176), which he later changed to first-inversion G major chords. It is ambiguous whether the original chords on B were major or minor; the natural signs before the Ds could have been made at the first or second writing.

14 At first I imagined Schubert intended to close the song with the words 'ihrem Blicke', but Prof. Joshua Rifkin observed to me that the composer need not have added the 'e' to the dative and could easily have set 'Blick' to a minim with a quaver appoggiatura. Furthermore, Prof. Louise Litterick noted to me that the difference in handwriting between the words 'Dort begegn' ich' and 'ihrem Blick' suggests that Schubert had already written the former underneath his original ending, closing the song with the fragment of a sentence, and then completed the clause with the latter two words when he lengthened the cadential melody. The first three words seem to match the ink colour and pen pressure of the first musical writing, while 'ihrem Blick' has the more vigorous appearance of the musical emendation. I am also grateful to Prof. Lowell Lindgren for recalling to me the strong resemblance between Schubert's first ending and the close of the sixth song in Schumann's *Frauenliebe und -leben* ('Süsser Freund'), which ends with leading note and upper appoggiatura to the tonic on the words 'dein Bildnis!'.

Ex. 3 Houghton, MS Mus. 99.2, p. 11 bars 206-8 : first version

Ex. 4

'Auf dem Strom' was published as op. 119 in the autumn of 1829, nearly a year after Schubert's death, by Leidesdorf, and some time thereafter by Diabelli,[15] both issuing the obbligato part for horn or alternatively for cello.[16] Deutsch assumes that Schubert had made arrangements for publication before he died, and he construes a small monetary receipt recorded by Ferdinand

15 Publishers' plate-numbers are Leidesdorf 1161 and Diabelli 3550. Apart from different publishers' names and plate-numbers, the two editions appear to be identical and must have been printed from the same plates. (Leidesdorf edition: Wiener Stadt- und Landesbibliothek, M6478 Sch; Diabelli edition: Library of Congress, M3.3/.S37 case). Diabelli also issued an edition (VN 3551) in which the song is transposed to C major and the piano and horn parts are fused into a piano reduction (Wiener Stadt- und Landesbibliothek, M6478 Sch). It is clearly on this score that Friedländer based his Peters edition (*Schubert Gesänge*, vol. 3, pp. 100-9). I wish to thank Dr Franz Patzer of the Wiener Stadt- und Landesbibliothek for his help with bibliographical matters.

16 As it was performed by the cellist Linke at a private concert on 30 January 1829. See O. E. Deutsch, *Schubert. A Documentary Biography* (cited below as '*Documents*'), transl. E. Blom (London, 1946), p. 851; idem, 'The Schubert Catalogue. Corrections and Additions', *Music and Letters*, XXXIV (1953), 31; idem, *Schubert. Die Dokumente seines Lebens* (cited below as '*Dokumente*') (Kassel, etc., 1964), pp. 574-5.

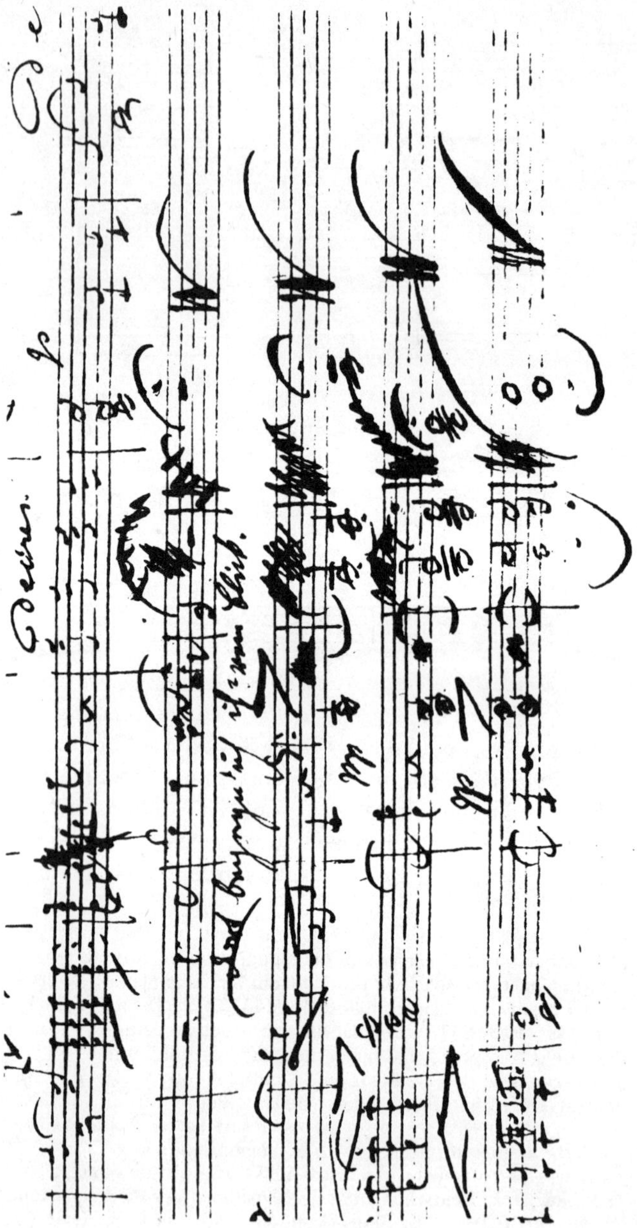

Figure 4. 'Auf dem Strom', p. 11 of the autograph (detail)

Schubert in May 1829 as payment by Leidesdorf for this and four other songs.[17] Mandyczewski's edition for the *AGA* in 1895 is based solely on these first prints.[18]

The autograph manuscript differs from the published version of the song in some prominent details. One can plainly see that the horn has no appoggiatura at the end of its opening solo (bar 17: see Figure 1) as it has in the published score. (It should be noted that the published version agrees with the manuscript in having no appoggiatura in the parallel passages at bars 89 and 159.) In bars 55, 57, 69, and 71 in stanza II, the horn melody is dotted in the manuscript like the voice in the same passage, although it plays even quavers in the published version. At the cadence of stanza III, in the manuscript, the horn's note in bar 114 is tied into bar 115; this tie is absent in the published version. At the end of stanza IV in the published version, neither the piano nor the horn has the first phrase of the interlude; in the manuscript the piano carried this melody, transferred from the horn, as elsewhere. In the final vocal phrase, the last three notes of bar 207 are written as triplet quavers in the manuscript, but as two semiquavers and a quaver in the first edition. There are numerous differences in dynamics and accents.

Some of these divergent readings seem preferable to the published ones, but one must entertain the possibility that the published version had Schubert's express approval. It is doubtful that the publishers used the present autograph as their model, for there are none of the usual indications in the manuscript of an engraver's use. As Maurice Brown warned in general about such a situation, we should consider two possibilities: that there was a fair copy for the publisher, which is lost, and that Schubert corrected proof sheets.[19] Although the latter may seem unlikely because of the time lag between Schubert's death and the song's publication, neither is impossible, and one cannot reach definite conclusions about editorial revisions without further information, which may never be forthcoming.[20]

17 *Documents*, pp. 898-9; *Dokumente*, pp. 579-80.

18 See Mandyczewski's short critical note in *AGA*, Series XX, *Revisionsbericht* (1897), p. 115 (Dover reprint vol. 19, p. 351).

19 'Schubert: Discoveries of the Last Decade', *Musical Quarterly*, XLVII (1961), p. 310.

20 I would urge that the tie in the horn part between bars 114 and 115 be restored. In copying from the present autograph, this tie could easily have been overlooked in the confusion of Schubert's extensive emendation of this passage. The tie is essential to Schubert's phrasing, which makes bar 115 an upbeat to the new phrase from bar 116. To play the crotchet b′ (concert pitch) on the downbeat of bar 115 makes little musical sense. I also suggest that performers restore the dotting of the horn melody to match the voice part (bars 55, 57, 69, 71, and 127) and reinstate the tune in the piano for the first phrase of the interlude following stanza IV (bars 149-50: dotted minim c♯′, two quavers d♯′ e′, dotted minim d♯′). The horn appoggiatura in the prelude (bar 17) presents a quandary. Horn-players are understandably reluctant to revert to the autograph reading and omit the appoggiatura, and although the documentary

III

In his Schubert biography, Alfred Einstein wrote of 'Auf dem Strom', 'If any of Schubert's songs was influenced by the spirit and "sentiment" of Beethoven's *An die ferne Geliebte*, it was this one.'[21] Einstein did not elaborate, but he was right. There is first of all a textual kinship. Both Jeitteles's lyrics and Rellstab's poem treat of the union of loved ones despite their separation. In Beethoven's cycle, the singer's songs reach his distant beloved; in Schubert's song, the beloved's face is beheld in the stars.

The similarity of 'sentiment' is not all; there are musical resemblances as well. The codas of the two pieces have so much in common that Schubert's appears to have been modelled on Beethoven's. Both composers created their codas as a concluding peroration based on the last four lines of their respective texts, the very lines which promise reunion.[22] Both composers made their codas of much melodic repetition and of climactic, high-register vocal writing. Beethoven's melodic repetition alternates between voice and piano; Schubert's begins as an exchange of two tunes among the three parts. Both pieces end by recalling their opening melodies and close on the third degree of the scale. In Beethoven's the piano concludes by playing the voice's opening phrase; in Schubert's the tenor sings a final phrase strongly reminiscent of his opening one.[23]

Schubert's indebtedness to Beethoven extends to another genre. The voyage away from the 'bright coast' and out into that 'dark wilderness', and the separation of the lovers, have strong overtones of death in Rellstab's poem. Whether the closing lines have a Classical heritage and suggest the absent lover's appearance as a starry constellation, or voice a more typically Christian expectation of heavenly reunion, does not matter. The crucial point is that a figurative reading is preferable to a literal one. A mere reminiscence

argument for it is not authoritative, I favour its inclusion. It is conceivable that the ornament in question was added to the separate horn part (either by Schubert or by the player with Schubert's approval) for the first performance and, furthermore, that the first edition of the horn part ultimately derived from this performance manuscript and not from Schubert's autograph. (The first edition does not include the horn in the piano/vocal score, but only as a separate part.)

21 *Schubert. A Musical Portrait* (New York, 1951), pp. 302-3 (also London edn, 1951, p. 346).

22 In the Jeitteles, 'Dann vor diesen Liedern weichet, / Was geschieden uns so weit, / Und ein liebend Herz erreichet / Was ein liebend Herz geweiht!'

23 The two codas have nearly the same proportion in relation to the whole works. Beethoven's coda (from the *Allegro molto con brio*) is 38 bars out of a total of 343 (11 per cent), and Schubert's is 27 out of 209 (13 per cent).

of the lovers' first meeting by starlight is too weak a conclusion for this grandiose poem. One may therefore construe the poem as a metaphorical depiction of death as a nautical journey, a journey on which an initial fear of the unknown gives way to a hopeful anticipation of reunion.

The melody of Schubert's second and fourth stanzas, the stanzas which deal with the physical cause of the separation (the rushing waves of the river, the dark wilderness) – hence, death – is a quotation of Beethoven's 'Marcia funebre' from the Third Symphony (see Ex. 5). The first two phrases are practically identical. After that, allowing for Schubert's side-step toward the relative major key, his song (in stanza II) retains the harmonic and melodic outline of Beethoven's march theme. In the first bar of stanza IV (bar 121), Schubert at first wrote a dotted rhythm on 'dunklen'; though later replaced

Ex. 5 (a) Beethoven, Symphony no. 3: second movement, 'Marcia funebre'

(b) 'Auf dem Strom', stanza II

by four even quavers, Schubert's first thought seems a tell-tale clue to the borrowing.[24]

One should distinguish between the two kinds of reference. The coda is a case of stylistic influence; Schubert copied the manner of *An die ferne Geliebte* to close his extended song. The melody of stanzas II and IV, on the other hand, is a direct quotation; Schubert used Beethoven's funeral march for its topical appropriateness.[25] Aside from finding the Beethoven pieces useful as model and source, respectively, did Schubert have any other reason for these musical references? To construct a hypothetical answer to this question one must turn to reported biographical information.

Schindler stated that in February 1827 he showed Beethoven some of Schubert's songs.

> I put in front of him a collection of Schubert's songs and vocal works, about 60 in all, many of which were then still in manuscript . . . The great master, who previously had not known five songs by Schubert, was . . . utterly astonished when he got to know their content . . . With delighted enthusiasm he cried out repeatedly: 'Truly, in Schubert there dwells a divine spark!' – 'If I had this poem I would have set it to music too!'[26]

The news of Beethoven's favourable reaction to his songs must have reached Schubert, for Josef von Spaun reported:

> it certainly made him extremely happy when he learned that, during his last days, Beethoven had derived great pleasure from his songs.[27]

And Schindler says,

> The success that rewarded my efforts to give Beethoven, though already on his deathbed, the opportunity of getting to know and appreciate Schubert's talent . . . earned me Schubert's gratitude and especially close friendship.[28]

24 In the second half of the first bar of stanza IV (bar 121), Schubert at first wrote dotted quavers and semiquavers, then rubbed this out and substituted four even quavers. It would appear that in a momentary lapse of concentration he had reverted to the dotted rhythm of his model. The original notes were unbeamed, suggesting either that Schubert had intended a different text underlay or that he jotted down the rhythm automatically without reference to specific words (one cannot assume that he had written the text 'dunklen' below the voice staff before he penned the notes).

25 The case is not unlike Schumann's quotation of the 'Marseillaise' in 'Die beiden Grenadiere' (op. 49/1). The Schubert song may be the first instance of such quotation in a Lied of known musical material for its reference value. Vesque von Puttlingen pertly quotes the beginning of Schumann's 'Ein Jüngling liebt ein Mädchen' (op. 48/11) in his setting of the same Heine poem (op. 41/1). In 'Nachtzauber' (*Eichendorff-Lieder* no. 8, bars 22-4 and 51-3) Hugo Wolf appropriately quotes the closing vocal phrase of Schumann's 'Mondnacht' (op. 39/5).

26 Deutsch, *Schubert. Memoirs by His Friends* (cited below as '*Memoirs*') (New York, 1958), p. 319.

27 Ibid., p. 366. Elsewhere Spaun similarly reported: 'Schubert had the joy of learning that Beethoven spoke appreciatively of him and that, although already ill, he had looked through several books of his songs with pleasure and had spoken very kindly of them' (ibid., p. 137).

28 Ibid., p. 319.

In 1828, Schubert set ten poems by Rellstab: 'Auf dem Strom', the seven songs of *Schwanengesang*, and two lesser lyrics.[29] It appears that it was because of Beethoven that Schubert came into possession of a group of poems by Rellstab. Schindler reported:

I frequently had the pleasure, in the summer of 1827, of seeing [Schubert] at my home . . . During these visits, certain portions of Beethoven's literary estate had engaged his very special attention, among them once more the lyric poems of all kinds which had been sent to the great master. A collection of perhaps twenty items absorbed his attention, because I was able to tell him that Beethoven had ear-marked several of them to compose himself. The question as to the poet of this collection – which still exists in its entirety – I could not answer with certainty; I thought it was Herr L. Rellstab or Varnhagen von Ense. Schubert put these poems in his pocket. Only two days later he brought me 'Liebesbotschaft', 'Kriegers Ahnung' and 'Aufenthalt' set to music. These, together with four others from that collection, form the major part of the contents of 'Schwanengesang', the name of 'Rellstab' being added.[30]

Rellstab confirms the outlines of this story and provides a fuller context in his memoirs. He visited Vienna in the spring of 1825 and, in hopes of collaborating with Beethoven, took an opera text with him.

I had taken with me not only manuscripts of my operatic poems, but also – since at that time almost nothing of mine was printed – those of my little lyrical products that I considered the best ones to lay before Beethoven . . . I did not yet send him the copies of the opera texts, but chose about eight or ten of the lyric poems, each neatly written on a separate sheet . . . The poems moved in different moods; perhaps one of theirs might happily coincide with his and inspire him to breathe into eternal tones the transitory emotion of his breast! . . .

So I carefully packed up the sheets of paper, wrote a few lines to Beethoven . . . and then carried both to his dwelling myself, for I would entrust such an important matter to no other hand.[31]

In a footnote to this passage, Rellstab added:

These scraps of paper have not been lost; Professor Schindler returned them to me from Beethoven's estate years ago. Some had pencil marks in Beethoven's own handwriting; they were the ones he liked best and the ones he had

29 'Lebensmut' (D 937) and 'Herbst' (D 945).

30 *Memoirs*, p. 319.

31 *Aus meinem Leben* (Berlin, 1861), pp. 244-5: 'Nicht nur Abschriften meiner Operngedichte, sondern auch – denn damals war noch fast nichts von mir gedruckt – derjenigen meiner kleinen lyrischen Erzeugnisse, die ich für die besten hielt, hatte ich mitgenommen, um sie Beethoven vorzulegen . . . durch alle diese Erwägungen bestimmt, sandte ich ihm die Abschriften der Operngedichte noch nicht, sondern wählte mir etwa acht oder zehn der lyrischen Gedichte aus, jedes auf ein besonderes Blättchen sauber geschrieben . . . die Gedichte bewegten sich in verschiedenen Stimmungen; vielleicht traf doch eins derselben ein mal mit der seinigen glücklich zusammen, und regte ihm die Lust an, die vorüberfliegende Bewegung seiner Brust in ewige Töne zu hauchen . . .

'So packte ich denn die Blättchen sorgfältig ein, schrieb einige Zeilen an Beethoven . . . und trug dann Beides selbst in seine Wohnung, weil ich die mir so wichtige Angelegenheit keiner fremden Hand anvertrauen mochte.'

given Schubert to compose at that time, because he himself felt too unwell. Moreover they are to be found among Schubert's vocal works and some of them have become generally well known.[32]

The stories differ in details, and the reliability of Schindler's testimony has frequently been called into question. It would be tenuous to erect an hypothesis that depended on the accuracy of details in his reporting; for example, we believe that Schubert composed the *Schwanengesang* Rellstab songs in August 1828, not 1827.[33] But in the present instance, all one needs is the general content of the story. Whether it was Schindler or, as Rellstab tantalizingly reports, Beethoven himself who gave Schubert the poems, and which poems were among them – these details are inessential to the simple, central point that Schubert became acquainted with Rellstab's poetry in a way that caused him to associate the poet with Beethoven.

There is one other piece of pertinent evidence. In his biography of Schubert, Kreissle von Hellborn printed a letter of Rellstab's that has no addressee or date, but that Thayer believed had been sent to Beethoven. The letter reads, in part:

Most honoured Sir

I send you herewith some songs which I have had copied fairly for you; some others, written in the same vein, will shortly follow. They have perhaps this novelty about them, that they form in themselves a connected series, and have reference to happiness, unity, separation, death, and hope on the other side of the grave, without pointing to any definite incidents.

I should wish that these poems might succeed so far in winning your approval as to move you to set them to music . . .

Day and night I am thinking of an opera for you . . .

With the deepest respect,
M. L. Rellstab.[34]

It is easy to believe, with Thayer's reported endorsement, that this was the covering letter for the sheaf of poems to which Schindler and Rellstab referred and which Schubert borrowed. The poet's terse characterization of them fits the poems of the *Schwanengesang* collection. Indeed, the statement that they refer to 'death, and hope on the other side of the grave' encourages one to think that 'Auf dem Strom' was among them as well. But of this, as well as of the letter's recipient, one cannot be certain.

32 Ibid., p. 245, as translated in *Memoirs*, p. 303.

33 *D1*, pp. 470-1. In the complete manuscript, songs 1 and 14 are dated August and October 1828 respectively. It is interesting to note, however, that sketches of songs 1-3 appear in an undated manuscript together with 'Lebensmut' (D 937), another Rellstab setting (see note 29 above). John Reed also accepts the outline of Schindler's testimony; see his discussion of Schubert's acquisition of Rellstab's poems (*Schubert. The Final Years* (New York, 1972), pp. 222-4).

34 'Herr Alexander W. Thayer, the musical biographer, thinks it certain that this letter was addressed to Beethoven' (Heinrich Kreissle von Hellborn, *The Life of Franz Schubert*, transl. A. D. Coleridge, 2 vols. (London, 1869), vol. 2, p. 134).

Deutsch states that Schubert composed 'Auf dem Strom' expressly for his concert in March 1828.[35] Deutsch does not explain the basis for his assertion, and one must assume he is following the circumstantial evidence: first, the manuscript is dated March 1828, and secondly, the piece received its first performance at that concert, with the horn-player Josef Rudolf Lewy, the amateur tenor Tietze, and the composer at the piano. The date of Schubert's concert, the only public concert devoted to his music during his lifetime, was 26 March 1828, one year to the day after Beethoven's death.

On the basis of the foregoing musical and biographical evidence, it looks as though Schubert may have composed 'Auf dem Strom' in memory of Beethoven. He wrote it for the concert on the anniversary of Beethoven's death, selected a genre which he knew had won Beethoven's hearty approval, chose an appropriate text by a writer whose poems had been intended for Beethoven to set, and paid homage to Beethoven by imitating and quoting his music.

Edward Cone has detailed borrowing by Schubert of thematic material and formal procedures from Beethoven:

> Although some of his quotations may have been unconscious . . . , it is hard to believe that others were not wholly intentional. Thus, when one finds in each of the last three piano sonatas, composed . . . during the summer of 1828, a reference to the music of the master, then one begins to suspect that Schubert may have been deliberately trying to pay a tribute to the memory of the illustrious colleague who had died only a short time before.[36]

To Cone's catalogue of Schubert's indebtedness and tribute to Beethoven may now possibly be added this special homage in 'Auf dem Strom'.

If one accepts this hypothesis, how does one interpret the poem? Should the song be understood as Beethoven speaking from the grave or as Schubert's own farewell to life? Either (or both) seems possible and acceptable, and in either case the persona is a composer.[37] This may explain a text discrepancy that might otherwise be construed as a copying error. In line 6 of stanza IV, the reading in Schubert's manuscript and in both first editions (bar 137) replaces 'vom' with 'zum', so that instead of reading 'No song can penetrate *from* the shore' it reads 'No song can penetrate *to* the shore'.[38] It seems likely that this was an intentional change.[39] Rellstab's poem is concerned

35 *Documents*, pp. 751-2; *Dokumente*, p. 502.

36 'Schubert's Beethoven', *Musical Quarterly*, LVI (1970), 779-80.

37 I am indebted to Prof. Cone, who read a draft of this article and in a private communication urged further speculation about the persona of the song. He also counselled that in the final analysis the 'private meaning' of the song for Schubert is irrelevant to its 'public meaning' as a work of art symbolizing a farewell to life.

38 Mandyczewski reinstated Rellstab's 'vom' in his edition of the song in *AGA* (see note 2 above).

39 Joseph Kerman, in his essay on *An die ferne Geliebte*, has similarly posited a deliberate alteration by Beethoven of Jeitteles's text. He argues that the com-

with the psyche of the traveller, not with that of the abandoned lover. Every statement in the poem tells of a new effect of the separation on the voyager. It is thus natural for the persona to say that no song reaches *from* the shore to bring *him* melancholy tears. It is unlikely that Schubert would switch the preposition and abruptly reverse the poem's tendency unless he had the intention of identifying the persona as the singer of the song, and thus as a composer whose creative life is at an end.[40]

poser added an extra stanza to the first poem (borrowing and adapting lines from the end of the last poem) in order to insinuate at that point the separation by time as well as by space. *Beethoven Studies*, ed. Alan Tyson (New York, 1973), pp. 126-9.

40 Since the present study was completed, three articles have appeared that have some bearing on it: Maynard Solomon's 'Schubert and Beethoven', *19th Century Music*, III (1979), pp. 114-25, and Charles Rosen, 'Influence, Plagiarism and Inspiration', *19th Century Music*, IV (1980), pp. 87-100. Solomon considers the testimony of Schindler and others regarding Schubert's actual encounters with Beethoven to be dubious; however, he does not deal specifically with the reported visit by Schubert to Beethoven's house after the latter's death. Rosen discusses musical allusions and the formal modelling of one composer's work on another's – the two kinds of derivation one finds in 'Auf dem Strom'. See also Walther Dürr, 'Wer vermag nach Beethoven noch etwas zu machen?', *Musik-Konzepte Sonderband Franz Schubert*, ed. Heinz-Klaus Metzger and Rainer Riehn (Munich, 1979), pp. 10-15.

Schubert and Sulzer revisited: a recapitulation of the events leading to Schubert's setting in Hebrew of Psalm XCII, D 953

ELAINE BRODY

In 1828, the year he composed some of his finest works, including the E flat major Mass, the Fantasy in F minor for Piano Duet, the String Quintet in C, and the last three piano sonatas, Schubert wrote several intensely moving sacred compositions, among them a little-known, rarely performed setting of Psalm XCII.[1] For several reasons, this piece is unique among his works. First, its language. Except for Latin sacred pieces and Italian songs, his vocal works are all in German. For his other psalm-settings, Psalm XII (D 663, June 1819) and Psalm XXIII (D 706, December 1820), the latter written for the pupils of Anna Fröhlich's singing class at the Vienna Conservatory, the composer chose to use Moses Mendelssohn's German translation.[2] With Psalm XCII, he apparently preferred to set the original Hebrew text, probably because of a commission, or perhaps even out of deference to Salomon Sulzer, the new young cantor of the Seitenstettengasse Temple. Secondly, this psalm, unlike Schubert's setting of Psalm XXIII, has no piano accompaniment. Instead, in keeping with the tradition of the synagogue, the composer wrote an *a cappella* setting, an antiphonal exchange between individual voices and mixed chorus with a baritone solo for the cantor in the middle section. Schubert may have been familiar with the Jewish service; we do not know for certain. But he must surely have had Sulzer's help in the matter of declamation: it would have been virtually impossible for him to set the Hebrew words properly without the assistance of a knowledgeable Hebrew scholar.[3] As it happens, his treatment

1 Sir George Grove's article on Sulzer in *Grove's Dictionary of Music and Musicians*, 5th edn (London, 1954), vol. 8, p. 185, incorrectly describes the setting of Psalm CXII as '(in Moses Mendelssohn's version) . . . for baritone solo and four men's voices'. The autograph, formerly in the possession of the Israelitische Kultusgemeinde of Vienna, must now be accounted lost (cf. O. E. Deutsch, *Schubert. Thematic Catalogue of All His Works in Chronological Order* (London, 1951), p. 468).

2 Mendelssohn's German translation of the Psalms appeared in 1783, three years before his death. During his lifetime, his translation of the Old Testament went through three printings. Schubert was obviously familiar with his translations, as he used them for his two other psalm-settings.

3 The Swiss composer Ernest Bloch (1880-1959), who wrote a *Sacred Service* for baritone (cantor), mixed chorus and SATB, described his difficulty in

of the verses, while not exceptionally beautiful, is nevertheless absolutely correct, as we shall see later.

Who was Sulzer? How did Schubert get to know him? Why and under what circumstances did the composer prepare this music? How well did he succeed? Who helped him with the text underlay in this foreign tongue? How frequently has this piece been performed? Can we be certain of its authenticity? Whereas the last question can definitely be answered in the affirmative, many of the others continue to present problems.

The events leading to the construction of the new Temple for which this music was composed have been reported elsewhere.[4] In addition, many of his contemporaries have described Sulzer's remarkable vocal facility, providing a fascinating account of the impression he made on non-Jews as well as on his congregants.[5] Much of the relevant material is inaccessible, however, and lies

learning the meanings of the individual words and then setting the Hebrew text; see Suzanne Bloch, *Ernest Bloch: Creative Spirit* (New York, 1976), pp. 11ff, particularly the plate on p. xii, showing how Bloch prepared a list of Hebrew words and their French equivalents. Alfred Einstein, in *Schubert: A Musical Portrait* (New York, 1951), p. 296, also assumed that Sulzer must have helped Schubert with the declamation.

4 The literature on this subject is vast. A selective list follows: L. A. Frankl, *Zur Geschichte der Juden in Wien* (Vienna, 1853); Heinrich Jaques, *Denkschrift über die Stellung der Juden in Österreich*, 4th enlarged edn (Vienna, 1859); Gerson Wolf, *Geschichte der israelitischen Kultusgemeinde in Wien 1820–1860* (Vienna, 1861); Sigmund Mayer, *Die Ökonomische Entstehung der Wiener Judenschaft* (Vienna, 1904); S. Husserl, *Gründungsgeschichte des Stadttempels der israelitischen Kultusgemeinde Wien* (Vienna, 1906); Sigmund Mayer, *Die Wiener Juden 1700–1900: Kommerz, Kultur, Politik* (Vienna and Berlin, 1917); A. F. Pribram, *Urkunden und Akten zur Geschichte der Juden in Wien* (Vienna, 1918); and Max Grunwald, *Vienna* (Philadelphia, 1936). Among the most recent contributions is the beautifully illustrated monograph commemorating the 150th anniversary of the founding of the Jewish Temple in Vienna: *Der Wiener Stadttempel 1826-1976*, Studia Judaica Austriaca, vol. 6 (Eisenstadt, 1978). Edited by Kurt Schubert for the Österreichisches Jüdisches Museum in Eisenstadt, this work includes valuable essays on the Jewish community in the nineteenth century and portraits of several persons mentioned in this article.

5 On the occasion of the hundredth anniversary of Sulzer's birth, one of his students, Cantor Eduard Birnbaum, wrote 'Zum Gedächtnis Salomon Sulzers: Ein Ehrenkranz zu seinem 100. Geburtstag' in the *Israelitische Wochenschrift*, XIII (1904), serialized in nos. 13-22. See also A. Friedmann, *Der Synagogale Gesang*, 2nd edn (Berlin, 1908); Eric Mandell, 'Salomon Sulzer 1804-1890' in *The Jews of Austria*, ed. Josef Fraenkel (London, 1967); Max Wohlberg, 'Salomon Sulzer and the Seitenstettengasse Temple', *Journal of Synagogue Music*, II/4 (April 1970); Eduard Birnbaum, 'Franz Schubert as a Composer of Synagogue Music' (also commemorating Sulzer's centenary in 1904), reprinted in *Contributions to a Historical Study of Jewish Music*, ed. Eric Werner (New York, 1976); and Eric Werner's most recent book, *A Voice Still Heard . . . The Sacred Songs of the Ashkenazic Jews* (Philadelphia, 1976), ch. 12. See also F. Trollope, *Vienna and the Austrians* (London, 1838), vol. 1, p. 373; Franz Liszt, *The Gipsy in Music*, transl. Edwin Evans (London, n.d.), pp. 52ff; and A. L. Ringer, 'Salomon Sulzer, Joseph Mainzer and the Romantic A Cappella Movement', *Studia Musicologica*, II (1969). The most recent scholarly dis-

buried in discontinued periodicals and privately printed memoirs and journals. The following essay is an attempt to organize the references to Schubert's setting of Psalm XCII, to indicate the known facts about the relationship of Schubert, Sulzer and the Jewish community in Vienna in the 1820s, and to describe the musical and textual setting of the psalm itself.

Salomon Sulzer (1804-1890) was born into an upper-middle-class Jewish family of Hohenems in West Austria, near Switzerland. Site of the oldest Jewish cemetery in the country, this town had been host to a small but thriving Jewish community since the seventeenth century. From the age of seven, when he narrowly escaped death by drowning in the swollen waters of the Emsbach, Sulzer's future was planned. His mother, grateful for his rescue, determined that he would enter the rabbinate. Sulzer was of a different mind. Passionately devoted to music, he compromised and studied instead to become a *chazzan* (cantor). Entrusted with portions of the musical service at his own synagogue from the time of his confirmation, he was obliged, following a directive from the Emperor to all religious leaders, first to complete his musical and secular education before receiving an official appointment.[6] Young Sulzer then embarked on several years of study at the musical centre of Karlsruhe, and also travelled through Switzerland, France and Swabia as an apprentice with several fine cantors in order to familiarize himself with current practice before returning to his post at his home town.

Meanwhile, in Vienna, as the walls of the ghetto began to crumble, many of the restrictive measures against the Jews were lifted.[7] By the time of Sulzer's birth, the inhabitants of the ghetto had already established a Hebrew printing press and a hospital they could call their own. Shortly afterwards, in 1811, through the efforts of two successful businessmen, Loew Hofmann and Lazar Biedermann, the Emperor approved plans for the purchase of a building to be used as a house of worship.[8] On 4 September 1812 the edifice was pro-

cussions of Sulzer and his activities took place in Vienna, 27-30 September 1980, at an international conference entitled 'Salomon Sulzer und seine Zeit'. The conference, arranged by Walter Pass, included Eric Werner and Alexander L. Ringer from the United States, Israel Adler, Hanoch Avenary and Herzl Shmueli from Israel, Manfred Angerer, Cornelia Knotik, Klaus Lohrmann and Nikolaus Vielmetti of Vienna, and others from elsewhere in Austria and from Germany and Switzerland.

6 Even today, the Austrian government regulates the appointment of religious officials, insisting that they be educated in philosophy and secular studies as well as religious matters.

7 Under Maria Theresa (reigned 1740-80) the Jews suffered excessively. Harshly taxed, forced to wear yellow arm badges, unable to own land, they were also refused permission to build a synagogue. Joseph II (reigned 1780-90), in a reversal of his mother's policies, abolished several of the more severe restrictions and, with his Edict of Toleration of 1781, became one of the first European monarchs to relax anti-Jewish legislation.

8 Because of restrictions, Jews customarily worshipped in private homes. Using their religious devotion as a source of income for the state, the Empress Maria

perly consecrated, with ceremonies for which the opera conductor Joseph Drechsler (1782-1852) composed the music. On Sunday 5 September 1813 a service was held in this building before the Austrian troops left to do battle with Napoleon. And nine months later, on Sunday 19 June 1814, a thanksgiving service was held there after the Emperor's victorious return to the city. This time Ignaz Moscheles (1794-1870) composed a cantata suitable for the occasion.[9] At the Congress of Vienna in the following year, many Jewish hostesses entertained the nobility along with prominent writers and musicians. Also, for the first time in history, a Jewish 'lobby' effectively campaigned to remove further restrictions against the Jews.[10] In 1821, nine Jews were ennobled by the Emperor; by 1835, the aforementioned Hofmann was made Edler von Hofmannsthal (grandfather of the writer and dramatist Hugo von Hofmannsthal). Modernized Jews like von Hofmannsthal and Biedermann sought to accelerate the *Heskalah*, the Jewish Enlightenment in Vienna. They endeavoured to emulate the Christian citizens of their country, and they hoped to build a new house of worship, one which they could be proud of, and not – as Biedermann complained – one that was as dirty and impoverished as a prison.

The reformers planned to do away with the Eastern style of cantillation; they intended to introduce an organ into the formerly *a cappella* musical service; they preferred to recite their prayers in German rather than in Hebrew. Seemingly unaware of the actual state of music in the Viennese

Theresa 'arranged that Jews should pay 24 florins for permission to conduct a service in a private residence and 50 florins if this service included reading from the Torah'. See Grunwald, op. cit., p. 144. Isaac Loew Hofmann (1759-1849), orphaned at thirteen, became a successful businessman who introduced the manufacture of silk to Austria, thus freeing the country from dependence on Italy. He was later permitted to acquire an estate in Lower Austria. Lazar Biedermann (1769-1843) was commissioned to engrave the imperial seal. In 1800 he opened a shop for jewellery and antiques, and in 1830 he became court jeweller. Later entering the woollen industry, he transferred the centre of that trade from Budapest to Vienna. Biedermann founded one of the first banks in Vienna and in 1816 gave the Emperor an interest-free loan to combat famine in the city.

Among the property-owners in the Jewish quarter in 1812 was Barouch Jeitteles. In 1826 when the new Temple was built, his widow Fannie, having sent two sons to medical school, was unable to bear her share of the costs of the Temple. One son, Alois, was the poet of Beethoven's *An die ferne Geliebte*.

9 See Eduard Birnbaum's article on Schubert in Werner (ed.), *Contributions*, p. 234, where he quotes a report of the ceremonies in the *Wiener Zeitung* of 21 June 1814.

10 For Jewish hostesses and their salons, see H. Arendt, *Rachel Varnhagen, The Life of a Jewess* (New York, 1957); M. Susman, *Frauen der Romantik* (Zurich, 1960); H. Spiel, *Fanny von Arnstein oder die Emanzipation* (Vienna, 1962); and H. Spiel, 'Jewish Women in Austrian Culture' in Fraenkel (ed.), *The Jews of Austria*. Among the politicians who favoured the Jews was the Prussian Wilhelm von Humboldt, brother of the scientist Alexander von Humboldt. At her salons, Fanny von Arnstein entertained the Varnhagens and Schlegels of Berlin, Madame de Staël, and the Austrian writer Franz Grillparzer, as well as the aristocracy, including the Emperor Joseph II.

churches of the time, they proposed a musical service analogous to that of the Christian Church.[11] By 1817, they had convinced the Emperor of the need for support for their synagogue, and as a result he directed that all the other small houses of worship be closed and that their congregants assemble at the main Temple.[12] The overcrowded, noisy service that resulted from this decree impelled Biedermann once again to approach the Emperor, this time for permission to tear down the older building and construct the first officially recognized synagogue since 1671.

A parcel of land at Dempfingerhof, later called Seitenstettengasse, was purchased through the assistance of twenty-eight members of the community who pledged funds. This committee hired the architect Joseph Kornhäusel, who designed an oval-shaped hall that accommodated about 550 persons with 200 additional standing places.[13] Kornhäusel moved the traditional *Bimah,* the raised platform where the Torah was read, from the centre of the hall to the east wall, under the Ark. He arranged for the ladies, formerly seated behind an opaque glass screen unable to see or hear the proceedings, to be housed in the upper gallery, from where they could now see and participate in the services. Having improved their physical surroundings, the elders now looked for ways to refine their liturgical service.

Before selecting a new rabbi, several were invited to preach a trial sermon before the congregation. One of these gentlemen, Isaak Noah Mannheimer (1793-1865), arrived from Copenhagen where he had been having difficulties with his parishioners because of his tendency to preach in Danish instead of in Hebrew. Mannheimer, who had travelled to Leipzig, Berlin and Hamburg, delivered his sermons in German and observed the modernized services, particularly that of the reform movement at Hamburg. The members of the Seitenstettengasse Temple, impressed with his three sermons in the summer of 1823, invited him to be their permanent rabbi with the title 'teacher of religion', owing to the imperial edict that still obtained against the appointment of a rabbi or the recognition of the Jews as a *Gemeinde*, a community.[14] Mannheimer, essentially a radical reformer, modified his demands for modernization in order to placate the older members of the Temple. Having heard

11 See A. L. Ringer, 'Salomon Sulzer, Joseph Mainzer . . .' for a description of the prevailing conditions in the musical service of the Church at that time. He cites not only Mainzer but Reichardt, Berlioz and Trollope, all of whom deplore the depths to which the Church service had fallen. [Edward Holmes], *A Ramble among the Musicians of Germany* (London, 1828, reprinted New York, 1969), p. 142, also criticizes the musical portion of the service in St Stephen's Cathedral at that time.

12 Grunwald, *Vienna*, p. 216.

13 See the photograph of the interior of the Temple in O. E. Deutsch's *Franz Schubert: Sein Leben in Bildern* (Munich and Leipzig, 1913), p. 373, and in Josef Pick, *Jüdisch-Geschichtliche Stätten in Wien und den österreichischen Bundesländern* (Vienna, 1935), pp. 26-7.

14 At that time the Jews were labelled the *Judenschaft* rather than the *Jüdische Gemeinde*; see Werner, *A Voice Still Heard*, p. 206.

the musical services at the synagogues he had visited in Germany, however, he determined to improve those portions of the service at the new Temple as well. As he was aware of Sulzer's reputation, it was perfectly natural for him to invite the younger man to become the cantor at the Temple.

Together, Sulzer and Mannheimer proved a fine team. The former, raised in an orthodox environment, wanted to refine the service, but hesitated to go as far as Mannheimer would have liked. So they compromised. They would continue the cantillation, and they would not have an organ (although in later years Sulzer approved the introduction of this instrument). They would have some prayers recited in German, but they would completely overhaul the musical service. Sulzer set out to determine which were the traditional melodies, to cleanse them of the accretions of several centuries, and to compose and commission from other composers appropriate music for the services. Sulzer himself was accustomed to the procedure whereby a cantor would sing his melodies while a boy soprano and a bass on either side of him provided the accompaniment for his solos. This trio of performers, the *meshorim*, achieved a fairly high level of competence in their rendering of the synagogue melodies.[15] It is highly unlikely that at the time of his arrival at the Temple Sulzer had attended Christian Church services. Yet he seems to have acquired a sense of the classical musical style of Mozart, Haydn and Beethoven, probably from having heard their secular music. Therefore, in his own music he followed their models, providing harmony and rhythm for some of the traditional melodies as well.

On the occasion of the inauguration of the Temple in 1826, Sulzer expected to celebrate with music by one of the more prominent composers resident in Vienna. Mannheimer reputedly approached Beethoven to compose a cantata for the consecration of the house. Sick and despondent in these last years of his life, the ailing master rejected the offer.[16] Sulzer invited Michael Umlauf (1781-1842), Seyfried (1776-1841), Schubert and Drechsler to contribute a musical offering. Drechsler, Kapellmeister at St Stephen's, accepted the commission and wrote a cantata for the ceremonies, which took place on 9 April 1826. Shortly thereafter, the cantor, eager to further his own musical education, became a student of Seyfried's. It was possibly

15 For the *meshorim* in the eighteenth century, see Charles Burney, *The Present State of Music in Germany, the Netherlands and United Provinces* (London, 1775), vol. 2, pp. 299-302. I am grateful to A. L. Ringer for calling my attention to this source.

16 See Hans Volkmann, 'Ein unausgeführt gebliebener Plan Beethovens' in *Beethoven-Jahrbuch*, I (Munich and Leipzig, 1908), pp. 51-7. Volkmann cites excerpts from the Conversation Books, *Hefte* 25, 41a and 43b. See also L. Nohl, *Beethovens Leben*, vol. 3 (Leipzig, 1877) p. 930 n. 243. I am indebted to Maynard Solomon for calling my attention to these sources.

G. Wolf, in *Geschichte der israelitischen Kultusgemeinde in Wien 1820-1860* (Vienna, 1861), does not mention the matter. Paul Nettl, however, in *Altjüdische Spielleute und Musiker* (Prague, 1923) p. 43, refers to Beethoven's invitation from the Jewish community, but cites no source. Later writers continue to quote Nettl.

through Seyfried, conductor, teacher, and composer of a considerable number of operas based on Old Testament subjects, that Sulzer met Schubert.[17]

In later years, Sulzer's codification of and contributions to the musical portions of the service appeared in two volumes, *Schir Zion*, the first of which was distributed in 1839, the second being published in 1865. Drechsler was responsible for fourteen items in the first volume; Umlauf and Seyfried also contributed works. Of 159 compositions in the first volume of *Schir Zion*, 122 were composed by Sulzer; thirty-six of these are based on traditional melodies. Generally he writes a five- or eight-part *a cappella* setting. Sulzer maintained that traditional melodies were more closely associated with the High Holidays than with the service on Friday night or Saturday. Consequently, for these latter occasions, he felt justified in including the works of non-Jewish composers. In approaching Schubert, he probably suggested that the composer set a psalm for the Sabbath.

Psalms appropriate to the day are recited or sung by the cantor and the congregation responsively each day of the week, beginning with Sunday, the first day. Psalm XCII, a psalm for the Sabbath, is a very special one. It is recited on Friday evening directly after the Sabbath is welcomed with the prayer *Lechoh Dodi*, immediately before the mourners of the congregation enter the Temple. According to Jewish tradition, during the first week of mourning, the bereaved remain at home, except on the Sabbath when, slightly before sunset on Friday evening, mourning is suspended as the mourners leave their homes for the synagogue. They remain in an anteroom until the conclusion of *Lechoh Dodi*, when they enter the Temple and recite with the congregants this special hymn. The expression of thanksgiving in this psalm is so universal that some rabbis claim it was written by Adam when he first saw the wonders of nature. Originally, when they were first composed (about 200 B.C.), this group of psalms (nos. XC-CVI) must have been sung by the Levites in the Temple.[18] Besides its appearance in the service on Friday evening, Psalm XCII is also included twice in the morning service on Saturday. Rabbis maintain that this Psalm implies that the Sabbath day offers a foretaste of Heaven and immortality. Perhaps for this reason, on Saturday morning, before the mourners declaim the *Kaddish*, the mourner's prayer, the psalm is again recited.

17 Friedmann, *Der Synagogale Gesang*, p. 125, states that Schubert was so impressed with Sulzer's fine tenor voice that he had him sing 'Der Wanderer' three times in succession for him. See also O. E. Deutsch's many references to Seyfried in *Schubert. A Documentary Biography*, transl. Eric Blom (cited below as '*Documents*') (New York, 1947), and *Schubert: Memoirs by his Friends*, transl. Rosamond Ley and John Nowell (London, 1958).

18 In the late eighteenth century, a family by the name of Levy left the village of Sulz, near Feldkirch, and journeyed north to settle in Hohenems. Once there, they became known by the name of Sulzer. It is interesting to learn that Salomon Sulzer was a Levite (Levy) on his father's side. Traditionally, the Levites concerned themselves with the musical portion of the service. See Mandell, 'Salomon Sulzer'.

Of the 150 psalms, about 100 include in their superscription the name of an individual, possibly the author, such as David, Asaph, Korah, Solomon, Heman, and Ethan.[19] Psalm XCII belongs among the others, the so-called 'orphan' Psalms. Whereas the leading genre is the hymn, basically the psalms represent different literary types. Many of the technical terms in the superscriptions, particularly those referring to performance practice, remain obscure, as for example, the word *mizmor* in the first verse of Psalm XCII (a verse omitted by Schubert: see the phonetic text below). The *zmr* root implies a song accompanied by instruments in contrast to a dance-song or one accompanied by hand-clapping or percussion instruments.[20] Singing with instruments is generally indicated in Hebrew by the preposition *be* or *bi* (with) and *al* (see verse 4).[21] Morning and evening services of the Sabbath are more elaborate, longer than those on weekdays. Hence those musical settings included instruments. Probably, in the days of the Temple, at the pouring of the libation, the Levites sang Psalm XCII divided into three sections with blasts of trumpets between them.[22]

It is well to remember that Hebrew poetry never appears in a ready-made frame. Every word, every sentence keeps its own metre. No regular sequence of dactyls or iambs or constant number of feet exists. Hebrew poetry consists of poetical prose. In contrast to classical, mechanical verse, Hebrew verse is dynamic.[23] Similarly, Hebrew music, which is non-metrical and flowing, proves impossible to notate in Western musical notation. Once a traditional Hebrew melody is harmonized and fitted into a precise rhythmic structure, it loses the essentially dynamic quality it had possessed.

Psalm XCII

[1. Miz-mor schir l'yom ha-sha-bos:]

2. Tov l'hō-dos l'A-do-noy.
Ul'zå-mer l'shim-cho ël-yon:

19 Seventy-three psalms are attributed to David; twelve to Asaph, eleven to the children of Korah, two to Solomon, and one each to Moses, Heman and Ethan. See Alfred Sendrey, *Music in Ancient Israel* (New York, 1969), pp. 95ff. See also James Thirtle, *The Titles of the Psalms* (London, 1904).

20 Sendrey, op. cit., p. 98.

21 Ibid., p. 119.

22 See Herbert G. May and Bruce M. Metzger, *The New Oxford Annotated Bible, Revised Standard Version* (New York, 1973), p. 728, for the separation of the sixteen verses of Psalm XCII into three strophes: verses 1-4, 5-9, 10-15. It is well to remember, however, that in ancient manuscripts the texts had no breaks, no divisions into paragraphs and chapters. (Not until the work of the Masoretes, about A.D. 600, were these verses separated.) For this reason, some scholars assign the superscriptions to the preceding psalm, instead of to the one they purportedly introduce. See also W. O. E. Oesterley, *A Fresh Approach to the Psalms* (New York, 1937), ch. VI.

23 See Elcanon Isaacs, 'The Metrical Basis of Hebrew Poetry', *American Journal of Semitic Languages and Literature*, XXXV (1918). For another point of view, see Oesterley, op. cit., p. 126 n. 1.

3. L'ha-gid ba-bo-ker chas-de-cho.
Ve-mu-nos'cho ba-le-los:

4. A-le o-sor va-a-le no-vel.
A-le hi-ga-yon b'chi-nor:

5. Ki si-mach-ta-ni A-do-noy b'fo-o-le-cho.
B'ma-a-se yo-de-cho a-ra-nen:

6. Mah go-d'lu ma-a-se-cho A-do-noy.
M'od om'-ku mach-sh'vo-se-cho:

7. Isch ba-ar lo ye-do.
U-ch'sil lo yo-vin es zos:

8. Bi-f'ro-ach r'sho-im k'mo e-sev.
Va-yo-tzi-tzu kol po-a-le o-ven
L'hi-schom'dom a-de ad:

9. V'a-toh mo-rom l'o-lom A-do-noy:
(l'o-lom l'o-lom.)

A Psalm, a Song for the Sabbath day.

It is a good thing to give thanks unto the Lord,
and to sing praises unto thy name, O most High:

To shew forth thy lovingkindness in the morning,
and thy faithfulness every night,

Upon an instrument of ten strings and upon the psaltery;
upon the harp with a solemn sound.

For thou, Lord, hast made me glad through thy work:
I will triumph in the works of thy hands.

O Lord, how great are thy works!
and thy thoughts are very deep.

A brutish man knoweth not;
neither doth a fool understand this.

When the wicked spring as the grass,
and when all the workers of iniquity do flourish;
it is that they shall be destroyed for ever:

But thou, Lord, art most high for evermore:
(for evermore for evermore.)

Explanation of signs: — = Sephardic accents; ○= Ashkenazic accents; >, >> = Schubert's accents; [ ] = omitted by Schubert; ( ) = added by him
Given the choice, Schubert seems to favour the Sephardic accents. However, there is some disagreement on this matter. A. L. Ringer, citing the variety of Jewish musical and verbal conventions, believes that Schubert–Sulzer employed the proper Central European accentuation. He cites Abraham Baer, *Baal T'Fillah oder 'Der practische Vorbeter'* as confirmation.

Exegetical commentary on the Psalms provides the following explanations. Psalm XCII is a song in praise of the Lord, rejoicing in the act of praising Him day and night with instrumental music (verses 2-4), wondering at the greatness of His divine works and thoughts, especially His permitting the righteous to flourish (verse 13; this portion is not included in Schubert's setting) and the wicked to perish (verses 8 and 10).[24] Observe the pairs: to give thanks and to sing praises (verse 2); loving-kindness and faithfulness, morning and night (verse 3);[25] upon an instrument of ten strings and upon the psaltery, upon the harp with a solemn sound (verse 4).[26] Some commentators discuss the specification of ten strings as if this number had special significance – which, of course, it has with regard to Jewish tradition. Ten men form a *minyan,* a quorum for prayers; ten men are necessary for a circumcision, a marriage service or a funeral. The contrast between 'a brutish man' and 'a fool' (verse 7) is sharper than the *New Oxford*'s 'the dull man' and 'the stupid'. This differentiation appears as well in the *Haggadah*, read at the Passover Seder. A fool does not know how to formulate his question; he does not even know that he should ask one. A brute sneers; it is beneath his dignity to pose a question.

Despite his abiding interest in the meaning of the texts he set, Schubert could hardly be expected to concern himself with minute details of the hermeneutics of Scripture. The commentary does, however, assist us when we examine his text underlay, the curve of his melody, his phrasing, his texture, and his use of text-reflection. Schubert omitted the first verse of the psalm (the superscription) and set the next eight verses (verses 2-9) for a group of soloists and chorus in alternation. He included a baritone solo in the middle for Sulzer. The entire piece consists of 87 bars. Cognizant of the meaning of the text, of the syllabification of the words and of their accents, he has properly emphasized *noy* and *yon,* for example (verse 2). In verse 3, he has provided a

24 A comparison of various translations, for example those of *The New Oxford Annotated Bible*, p. 728, *The Bible Designed to be Read as Living Literature*, arr. and ed. Ernest Sutherland Bates (New York, 1952), pp. 638-9, and *The Illustrated Jerusalem Bible*, English translation edited by M. Friedlander (a facsimile of the London edn of 1884), p. 1487, proves fascinating.

25 References to morning and evening also imply the sacrifices at those times.

26 Only three times does the Bible indicate the number of strings on specific instruments. In Psalm XCII verse 4, *Ale osor v'ale novel* presents an enigma to the translator because *osor* is usually considered to be derived from the root meaning 'ten'; it also generally appears along with references to a stringed instrument. Here it stands alone, as a ten-stringed instrument. Curt Sachs believed the *osor* was neither a lyre nor a harp, but a ten-stringed zither, a Phoenician zither (see his *History of Musical Instruments* (New York, 1940), pp. 117-18). It is certainly not a lute, as it is translated in *The New Oxford Annotated Bible*. In contemporary Hebrew usage, a lute is *kasros*, a harp is still *novel*, and *chinor* or *kinor* is a lyre. The word *higayon* often appears with the word *selah*, where it implies a sense of rest, an interlude. See Sendrey, *Music in Ancient Israel*, p. 157. Used with its musical connotation, as in *ale higayon b'chinor*, it may refer to the solemn sound of the lyre (or the harp, as some translators have indicated).

flourish for 'in the morning' (*baboker*) and has descended at 'night' (*balelos*). In bars 18 and 19, the initial stress on *le* is unnatural, but in bar 18, the added accent on *no* of *novel* shows that the composer must have recognized that *novel* was the more important word. *Higayon* usually appears with *selah* as an indication of a kind of fermata. Schubert actually writes a fermata at that point and then follows with the solo baritone entry, bar 29. Sulzer was meticulous in his text-setting; he must have advised Schubert on these matters. *Ki simachtani* suggests that the summit has been reached. Opening the fifth verse, it presents another concept, the awesome power of the Lord's works, followed by the depth of His thoughts (verse 6). Tension increases here, but the momentum slows temporarily in the music accompanying the 'brutish man', the 'fool', and later the 'wicked'. At *L'hischom'dom*, Schubert brings the music to a climax; the setting's highest pitch and *forte* dynamics combine to stress the meaning of the words here: 'It is that they shall be destroyed for ever.'

The ninth verse comprises but one line: 'But thou, Lord, art most high for evermore.' Schubert repeats the four-word Hebrew sentence six times and concludes with a simple repetition of the final word *l'olom* ('for ever': literally, 'to eternity') instead of *Adonoy* ('Lord'), the last word in the Hebrew.

This composition has not been heard often.[27] The first performance took place at the Temple shortly after the work was completed in July 1828.[28] It may not have been sung again until 1904 at the hundredth anniversary of Sulzer's birth when, under his son's direction, it was sung in the Musikverein in Vienna.[29] Stylistically it resembles church music more than synagogue music; it displays no characteristic Hebrew melody. The conclusion on *l'olom* instead of on *Adonoy* may also have militated against its performance. (Biblical texts have a sanctity. Alterations are – at least to the Orthodox – unacceptable.) Schubert probably stopped at that verse in order for Sulzer to chant the remaining verses in recitative. The cantor's own recitative, the one he used with no. 7 of his songs in *Schir Zion*, seems appropriate for this psalm-setting (which is no. 6 in *Schir Zion*).[30]

27 In recent years, a new ensemble of singers, the Cantica Hebraica, has performed the psalm several times. See *American Choral Review*, XVI (July 1974), pp. 25ff for more information on the ensemble and their repertoire. I am indebted to Cantor Paul Kwartin, a member of the group, who sent me a recording of their performance of Psalm XCII. In the summers of 1976 and 1977, Psalm XCII was performed at the Hermann Prey Schubert Festival at Hohenems, Sulzer's birthplace.

28 *Documents*, p. 93, in a list of first performances of works in Schubert's lifetime, indicates that Psalm XCII was performed first in the summer of 1828 at the Jewish Temple.

29 See Mandell, 'Salomon Sulzer' in Fraenkel (ed.), *Jews of Austria*, p. 221. It was sung '"On Thursday May 12, 1904 at 7 p.m. in the large hall of the Musikverein," according to the program for a concert arranged by the Society for the Collection and Preservation of Artistic and Historic Jewish Mementoes'.

30 See Birnbaum, 'Schubert as Composer of Synagogue Music' in Werner (ed.), *Contributions*, p. 230.

In the last two years of his life, Schubert demonstrated renewed interest in sacred music, conceivably with the hope of obtaining some much-needed remuneration. He composed several *geistliche Gesänge*, the Mass in E flat, and this setting of Psalm XCII within a few months of one another during the summer and autumn of 1828. As usual, Schubert chose his music carefully to reflect the essence of his text. A comfortable range and a simple rhythm help make the piece eminently singable. (See Ex. 1 for the resolute, declamatory opening phrase. The composer shifts from four-bar phrases to two-bar groups

Ex. 1

for bars 17-32 where, at the cantor's solo entry, the text demands greater expressiveness.) Aware of the pitfalls in choral singing, Schubert often started his chorus with a chord in the accompaniment to guide the singers. Because Psalm XCII is an *a cappella* setting, the singers get their cue from the cantor. Sulzer's group had a reputation for excellence; even so, Schubert saw to it that they generally entered on a downbeat. He reserved offbeat entries and syncopations for the soloists and for the midpoint of the piece, where the cantor's soaring tones provide additional support for the choristers. While melodic inventiveness is not a significant feature here, the harmonic progressions that surface in this brief work are more exceptional. (See Ex. 2, where Schubert prepares for the dramatic unison passage at bars 56-63.) Where the composer embarks on his typical tonal peregrinations, the changing tonalities usually parallel the alternation of solo and tutti forces. The music opens in C major and moves in turn to G, F, D minor, F, B♭, and B♭ minor before coming home to C. Such modulations, combined with his keen sense of phrasing, enabled Schubert to project a suitable mood in keeping with the dignity of the text. Through his customary harmonic and textural treatment of musical materials within the limitations imposed by the singers and the situation, the composer has crafted a remarkably subtle and exceptionally appropriate choral composition.

A final point concerns Schubert's use of Sephardic rather than Ashkenazic accents. (See pp. 54-5 above for indications of both types of accents as well as Schubert's accentuation.) There was evidently a Sephardic community within

Ex. 2

the ghetto in Vienna and they even had their own small house of worship.[31] After the Emperor had in 1817 abolished the smaller synagogues – the word 'synagogue' must be interpreted here as a meeting-hall for prayers – the Sephardim were forced to accommodate themselves to the Ashkenazic rite at the Seitenstettengasse Temple. This group of Greek and Turkish Jews has always been more clannish, less likely to borrow secular or operatic melodies for their services. Schubert could well have heard their Sephardic Hebrew as well as Sulzer's Ashkenazic accents.

Considerable evidence confirms the authenticity of this psalm as Schubert's setting. First, a manuscript copy, made from the autograph shortly after Schubert's death, is today in the Gesellschaft der Musikfreunde, Sammlung Witteczek–Spaun, vol. 31, pp. 77-90; it is dated July 1828.[32] Also, when Nottebohm prepared his Schubert catalogue, he said that the psalm was 'composed in July 1828 for the Jewish community of Vienna, which also has the autograph manuscript in its possession':[33] in other words, the manuscript itself still existed in 1874. Unfortunately, it has since disappeared. Nottebohm

31 N. B. Gelber, in a fascinating article, 'The Sephardic Community in Vienna', *Jewish Social Studies*, X/4 (1948), pp. 359-96, describes the organization of this community, and the various ordinances governing its members. At p. 367 n. 19 he writes: 'According to a statement of the police authorities of 1818, there were 45 Sephardic families in Vienna at that time (57 men, 42 women, 115 children, 24 non-Turkish servants and 2 Turkish servants). Landesarchiv Judenakten K. ca. 1818. Liste der tuerkischen Juden in Wien.' For an illustration of the Turkish temple in Wien II, Zirkusgasse, see Pick, *Jüdisch-Geschichtliche Stätten in Wien*, p. 21. In 1817, this congregation was abolished by the Emperor (cf. note 12 above).

32 I am indebted to the late Christa Landon for this information.

33 G. Nottebohm, *Thematisches Verzeichniss der im Druck erschienenen Werke von Franz Schubert* (Vienna, 1874), p. 229.

also explains that the psalm was published first in *Schir Zion* and then in 1870, in German, by J. P. Gotthard.

For the Jews, the *Tehillim*, the Book of Psalms, has been a source of consolation over the millennia. While Christians use the title 'Psalter' from the Greek word *Psalmoi*, which describes its contents, Jews prefer to stress the function of the poems: praise and thanksgiving to the Lord. Notice the root *HLL* from *Hallel* ('to praise'), as it appears in the word *Tehillim.* The exclamation *Hallelujah* or *Alleluia* also derives from this root. Although printed with the masoretic accents, the psalms cannot be sung to the same cantillation as either the Pentateuch or the other sacred texts. Their original melodies have disappeared with time, but more than any other group of prayers they have accumulated a store of tunes that have sprung from the community in which they are sung.

After his unsuccessful attempt to obtain a composition from Beethoven for the temple, it is fitting that Sulzer should next have turned to Schubert, perhaps even offering a commission. In 1828 Schubert was not an unknown composer; rather was he on the threshold of fame. A letter from Schott, the publisher of Beethoven's Ninth Symphony, clearly indicates that he had begun to establish his reputation.[34] Engaged in work on the E flat Mass and the Quintet in C, Schubert nevertheless found time to write this Hebrew psalm. He could have used the German text; it would have been considerably easier and acceptable as well to Sulzer.[35] Instead, in a remarkably generous gesture to the small community of Jews in Vienna, he presented a gift of his extraordinary lyrical talents.

34 See ***Documents***, p. 736, for item no. 1037, a letter of 9 February 1828 from B. Schott's Sons to

Franz Schubert, Esq.
Famous Composer in
Vienna

35 See p. 52 above.

For assistance in the preparation of this article, I should like to thank the staff of the Leo Baeck Institute, the Yivo, and the Hebrew Union College Library in New York; Professor Don Harrán of Israel, Nitza Weisgras of New York and once again, the late Christa Landon of Vienna.

Schubert revises Schubert *

MARIUS FLOTHUIS

Among those compositions of Schubert which are known to exist in more than one version is the famous 'Ständchen', D 920/921. Gerhard von Breuning has transmitted the story of its origin as told by Anna Fröhlich:

Another time Anna told me: 'Whenever the birthday or nameday of [Fräulein] Gosmar . . . was approaching I always went to Grillparzer and asked him to write something for the occasion and I did this once more as her birthday drew near. I said to him 'Look, my dear Grillparzer, there is nothing I can do about it. You simply must write me a poem for [Fräulein] Gosmar's birthday.' He replied, 'Very well, if I can think of something!' But I said, 'Then see to it that you do think of something.' In a few days he gave me the 'Ständchen', 'Leise klopf' ich mit gekrümmtem Finger . . . ' And when Schubert came to see us shortly afterwards, I said to him 'Look, Schubert, you must set this to music for me.' He: 'Well, let's have a look at it.' Leaning against the piano he read it through repeatedly, exclaiming over and over again 'But how beautiful it is – it's so beautiful!' He looked thus at the sheet of paper for a while and finally said 'There, it is finished now, I've got it already.' And only three days later he really did bring it to me, finished, set for mezzo-soprano (that is, for my sister Pepi) and four men's voices. At this I said to him 'No, Schubert, I can't use it like this, it's meant to be a tribute from [Fräulein] Gosmar's women friends only. You must write me the chorus for women's voices.' I remember quite clearly saying this to him; he was sitting over there in the right-hand window recess of the ante-room. – And soon afterwards he brought it to me, set for Pepi's voice and women's chorus, as it is now.[1]

This story probably helped create the widespread opinion that Schubert was

* The following abbreviations are used in this article:
NGA = *Franz Schubert. Neue Ausgabe sämtlicher Werke* (Kassel, etc., 1964-); references in the form 'IV/7' mean 'Series IV, vol. 7'.
AGA = *Schubert Werke. Kritisch durchgesehene Gesammtausgabe* (Leipzig, 1884-97).
D1 = O. E. Deutsch, *Schubert. Thematic Catalogue of All His Works in Chronological Order* (London, 1951).
D2 = Deutsch, *Franz Schubert. Thematisches Verzeichnis seiner Werke in chronologischer Folge*, ed. by the Editorial Board of the *NGA* and Werner Aderhold (Kassel, etc., 1978).

1 O. E. Deutsch, *Schubert. Memoirs by His Friends* (London, 1958). pp. 251-2 (here slightly revised).

a composer who wrote easily and quickly. Certainly, Schubert could compose with amazing rapidity; but the adverb 'easily' should be questioned, and should indeed be rejected if anyone connects with it implications of 'lightweight' – or, worse, of 'superficial'. Schubert was a hard-working composer, never neglecting quality or opting for a facile solution to a problem. When he received Anna Fröhlich's message that the work was to be performed by female choir, he set to work with the utmost care in order to comply with this request. Thus, he did not simply transpose the four male voices an octave higher but wrote a new score in which the five voice parts (solo alto; first and second soprano, first and second contralto) were interwoven in a new manner.

The two versions of 'Ständchen' provide one of numerous instances of Schubert rewriting an already finished work. It is a special case in that it was a commissioned work, and the change was not brought about on his own initiative. Schubert often transposed songs, though we usually lack evidence that he did so at anyone else's request. The user of O. E. Deutsch's thematic catalogue (*D1, D2*) soon becomes aware that Schubert frequently wrote two, three or more versions of the same song. It should be taken into account, however, that Deutsch sometimes used the word 'version', and only one catalogue number, for what had better been labelled 'new setting' or 'new composition', e.g. the 'Harfner-Gesänge' (this error has however been corrected in the new complete edition (*NGA*) and in *D2*). Schubert also often wrote new versions of earlier compositions, especially songs; moreover, he not only felt compelled to revise an earlier composition but frequently set the same poetic text to totally new music. In the latter case especially, he displayed a critical attitude towards his own work.

In this essay an attempt will be made to trace some of the factors that caused Schubert to write a second or third version, or even an entirely new setting, of a poem, and to compare the quality of earlier and later settings. Several scholars have already presented attempts of this kind.[2] When considering possible reasons for Schubert's inclination to revise or rewrite a song, the phenomenon immediately confronting and puzzling us is the relation between the subconscious and the conscious in the creative process. The influence of the subconscious has not yet been thoroughly investigated, and it is quite likely that the very nature of this phenomenon will prevent its ever being fathomed.[3] But as soon as the composer intervenes in his own work – striking out notes, bars or even larger units, or replacing them with others – we observe a visible,

2 E.g. Friedrich Blume, who dealt with this subject as early as 1928, criticizing the current views on Schubert's method of composing ('Schubert's "Mondlied"', *Der Bär* (Leipzig, 1928), pp. 31-58). Blume rightly applauds Dahms, who as long ago as 1912 dismissed these views in his Schubert biography. But in 1976 an intelligent musician like Alfred Brendel could still write that Schubert composed 'like a sleepwalker' (*Musical Thoughts and Afterthoughts* (London, 1976), p. 42).

3 See on this subject the correspondence between Goethe and Schiller: Schiller's letter of 27 March 1801, and Goethe's reply of 3 April 1801.

conscious activity (which in itself may be the result of an unconscious incentive). Analysis of it may widen our insight into the creative process.

Why did Schubert often feel compelled to revise his songs? We may consider as an answer to this intriguing question a multitude of possible reasons. He may have felt, for example, that for a forthcoming printed edition he should strive to find a definitive form, since printing meant that the song would be distributed in a large number of copies. He may then have started to look at his work with a new and rather critical attitude, for instance adding a keyboard introduction or altering some of the word-setting (e.g. in strophic forms where previously he had not taken carefully into account the verses of later stanzas of a poem). Sometimes a performance of a song may have made him aware of just one passage that needed revision. However, as we may see from the following investigations, it seems that Schubert often felt inclined to write another version of a song simply because of a particular performance with a singer whose voice necessitated a transposition or an alteration to the compass of the voice part; or that the singer wanted some embellishments ('Kolorierungen', as Schubert once called them in a sketch),[4] to which Schubert in some cases may have agreed.[5] We may ponder whether a version owing its existence to such a cause should be considered more 'authentic' than an earlier one. In his general preface to the Lieder volumes of *NGA*, Series IV (e.g. vol. 1a p. XIV) Walther Dürr draws attention to the practice of such additional little embellishments.

From a multitude of possible examples of Schubert's different versions and settings we have chosen ten for analysis and grouped them in the following way ('A' and 'B' are used for ease of reference and do not indicate separate D numbers):

Group A: Different versions of the same song	
Szene aus *Faust* (Goethe)	D 126A and B
'Der Sänger' (Goethe)	D 149A and B
'Nähe des Geliebten' (Goethe)	D 162A and B
'Laura am Klavier' (Schiller)	D 388A and B
'Orpheus' (Jacobi)	D 474A and B
'Auf dem See' (Goethe)	D 543A and B
Group B: New settings of the same text	
'Jägers Abendlied'	D 215 and D 368
'An den Mond'	D 259 and D 296
'Am Flusse'	D 160 and D 766
Group C: Combination of A and B (new setting incorporating some revisions)	
'Sehnsucht'	D 52 and D 636

4 See the sketch for the E flat Trio, D 929, second movement, bars 86-8.

5 See W. Dürr, 'Schubert and Johann Michael Vogl: A Reappraisal', *19th Century Music*, III (1979), pp. 126-40.

A. Different versions of the same song

Szene aus Faust, *D 126A and B*

The two versions of the cathedral scene from *Faust* both date from December 1814, and must therefore have been written not long after 'Gretchen am Spinnrade'. Whereas it seems that the latter was composed at a single sitting, and hardly presented a problem to its author, the two versions of the cathedral scene give a completely different impression. Here Schubert did not use a closed lyrical form but worked on a dramatic scene interpreted by two voices and a choir.

Schubert may originally have intended this scene for dramatic realization, with two solo singers and chorus. In the first version he notated indications for instrumentation ('Tromboni', 'Orgelton'). In my opinion this indicates that he imagined a dramatic scena accompanied by an orchestra. In spite of the fact that for the second version he apparently altered his intention, and therefore most of these indications as to instrumentation are missing, it could still be performed by a female voice (Gretchen), a male voice (Böser Geist) and a choir in unison. (Deutsch states in a note to *D2* (p. 189) that the indications as to instrumentation 'were in part also taken into the second version, as is shown by the copies'.)

How are the two versions related? The *NGA* (IV/7, p. 196) rightly adds to the heading 'Erste Fassung' the phrase written on one of the two manuscripts, 'Sketch for later completion' ('Skizze zu einer weitern Ausführung'). Of the first 18 bars, for instance, only the bass in the piano part has been written out, and the harmonies are filled in only in four places. Do the arpeggios in D 126A point to the intended co-operation of a harp? In bars 68-9 and 85-8 the harmonies are also missing. Since Schubert was not a Baroque composer, what we have before us amounts more to an elaborate sketch than to a completed composition; in this state it cannot be performed. The only complete sections are those for the choir.

What could be meant by 'Orgelton'? Did Schubert want to include the organ in his orchestration, or was it an organ-like effect he wished to create by some other instrumental means? It was evidently not a piano that he had in mind. The completion of the composition from the first sketch presented a good deal more work for Schubert than just the insertion of missing chords. The most salient revisions concern:

1. The two opening bars, which in the second version are apparently more conventional but also more logical than in the first one: Ex. 1 (opposite).
2. The way in which the opening motif of the second version is incorporated

Ex. 1 (a) D 126A

(b) D 126B

into bars 15ff (it does not occur at all in D 126A).

3. The melodic structure of the recitatives: see bars 12-18 in A and 15-23 in B. In B some vocal appoggiaturas are written out and there is also more arioso (therefore more variety of texture) as well as a higher range. Cf. A/40-5 and B/45-50; and especially A/85-91 and B/90-4.

4. The length: though the second version is two bars longer, some episodes are actually more condensed.

The principal similarities occur in:

1. The choir sections. They obviously presented no problems to Schubert, since he copied them almost unchanged into version B.

2. Some accompanying motifs: cf. A/19-23 and B/24-8 ('quillend').

3. Some chromatic turns: cf. A/24-7 and B/29-32; and A/46-9 and B/51-4.

Both versions contain an unexpected bar in 3/4 time (A/47 and B/52); this suggests less that it was an error on Schubert's part than that he forgot to change the time-signature.

D 126A bar	words	D 126B bar	
1-(11)	Böser Geist: Wie anders . . . Missetat	1-14: more articulate and longer than in A	
(12)-18	Bet'st . . . Blut	15-23	
19-23	Und unter . . . Gegenwart	24-8	NB bars 24-32 almost form one unit
24-7	Gretchen: Weh . . . wider mich	29-32	
28-39	Chorus	33-44	
40-5	B. G.: Grimm . . . bebt auf	45-50	
46-9	Gr.: Wär ich . . . löste	51-4	
50-63	Chorus	55-68	
64-7	Gr.: Mir . . . Luft	69-72	NB bars 69-76 form one unit
68-71	B. G.: Verbirg dich . . . wehe dir	73-6	
72-84	Chorus	77-89	
85-91	B. G.: Ihr Antlitz . . . Weh	90-3: more concise	
92-8	Chorus	94-100	

In its elaborate definitive form, the second version, this song is one of Schubert's most revolutionary compositions; it is one of the very few examples in his *oeuvre* of a song which, apart from the choral interruptions, is conceived wholly as a recitative (a familiar comparable example is 'Prometheus', D 674). Harmonically it is also a bold venture in its utterly unstable tonality (there is, of course, no disruption of tonality, rather of tonal unity).

'Der Sänger', D 149A and B

It is tempting to investigate the whole group of *Wilhelm Meister* compositions, as they offer plenty of opportunities to study different 'versions' as well as 'new compositions' of a poem. However, Hans Holländer has dealt with them,[6] and I myself have devoted a long study to these songs.[7] I shall confine myself here to the discussion of one song which was mentioned but briefly in my article of 1974: the ballad 'Der Sänger'.

The two versions of 'Der Sänger' offer some rather intriguing riddles. In the first place, one is puzzled by the order in which they occur. The *AGA* (1894) presents as an 'Erste Bearbeitung' (first version) what is called a second version by the *NGA*, and vice versa. *D1* (1951) adheres to the *AGA* order, while *D2* (1978) corresponds to the *NGA*. In the following paragraphs, 'A' and 'B' indicate the versions as they are designated in the *NGA* and *D2*.

D2 describes D 149A as a 'fair copy in the second volume of songs for Goethe'. If this is true, then there can hardly be any doubt as to its being the

6 'Franz Schubert's Repeated Settings of the Same Song-Texts', *Musical Quarterly*, XIV (1928), pp. 563-74.

7 'Franz Schubert's Compositions to Poems from Goethe's *Wilhelm Meisters Lehrjahre*' in *Notes on Notes* (Amsterdam, 1974), pp. 87-138.

second version, because if D 149B were to be the second version – as is claimed in the *NGA* and in *D2* – it must have been written some time after the copy which was sent to Goethe. If one version came into being only shortly after the other, Schubert would surely have sent to Goethe the one he regarded as 'definitive'.

The differences between the two versions are more or less analogous to those between the two versions of 'Auf dem See', D 543A and B (but without the transposition); both are identical in the opening bars (a characterization of the singer playing on his harp) with one exception: in the instrumental introduction the dynamic indication in D 149A in bar 1 is *pp* instead of the *fp* in D 149B; and the words 'in der Ferne' ('from afar') are added in A to the opening bar of the piano part.

Some details are musically more convincing in version A than in B:
bar 17: the rhythm in the piano part
bar 29: the harmony is more interesting
bars 36-41: the melodic line of the voice part is more interesting
bars 41-3: more concise in A than bars 41-7 of B (four somehow superfluous bars omitted)
bar 48: in comparison with bar B/52 this is far more convincing.

However, the repetition of the words 'Die Ritter schauten mutig drein / Und in den Schoss die Schönen' (bars 56-60 in A) is not an improvement; here, version B is preferable (see Ex. 2). On the other hand, bar B/66 (c♯″ in the voice against d″ with ∾ in the piano) is surely not as good as bar A/62. The shortened interlude (A/64-9, B/68-83) is also an improvement; there is little point in a literal repetition of the opening ritornello.

Then follows the most important revision. In A the narrating text is treated as a recitative ('Der König . . . holen', bars 69-72) and the singer's reactions in arioso ('Die goldne Kette' etc., bars 73ff); B has recitative for this passage until 'Ich singe'. The following arioso is practically identical in both versions (A/88-99, B/99-110).

The last section (from 'Er setzt . . .') contains the hardest nut to crack for the investigator who wants to clarify the question of which version is the earlier and which is the revision. The major difference is of length: 27 bars in A and 38 bars in B. The longer version contains some striking modulations and is by no means inferior to the shorter one. On the other hand, the final bar (129) in A contains an interesting detail: the arpeggio chord of B♭, which does not occur in B, might symbolize the singer taking leave of his audience with a single chord on his instrument.

So long as no additional documentary evidence comes to light, such as a dated manuscript or copy, the problem of the order of these two versions will remain unsolved.

Ex. 2 (a) D 149B (second version, according to *NGA*)

'Nähe des Geliebten', D 162A and B

Two versions of the same song can differ in many ways, which becomes clear when we compare the versions of 'Nähe des Geliebten' with those of, say, 'Laura am Klavier' (see below).

In both versions of 'Nähe des Geliebten' the vocal part is essentially the same, whereas the piano part appears in a completely different light. From the almost unchanged vocal part we might guess that the difference in metre (6/8 instead of 12/8) is less important than the replacement of semiquavers by quavers and the enlargement of the first bar which results in twice the

Ex. 2 (b) D 149A (first version, according to *NGA*)

length of time for the opening harmonies. (The whole introduction might be called a 'deceptive beginning', on the analogy of a 'deceptive cadence'.) Changes in the vocal part are restricted to a rhythmic change in bar 1 (♩. ♩ ♪ instead of ♩. ♪♪. ♬), and one in the ending (first ♩. ♩ then ♩ ♪); the held final d ″ of the first version is replaced by a falling fifth in the second version, after Schubert had tried a falling third.

Obviously this is a vital change to a definitive, finished composition. The song's conception had been outlined from the start. By the way, both versions are dated 27 February 1815. Schubert must have realized almost immediately that the external excitement of the semiquaver accompaniment went beyond the scope of the poem's emotional context. The autograph of the first version, rightly called a 'sketch' by Maurice Brown, was crossed out by Schubert and marked as invalid ('Gilt nicht'). The second version exists in two autographs with only minor discrepancies (see the *Revisionsbericht* of *AGA*, and *Quellen und Lesarten* to *NGA* IV/1 (1972), pp. 14f).

'Laura am Klavier', D 388A and B

Schubert composed two versions of this poem by Schiller in March 1816. Only the last three bars of the autograph of the first version, D 388A, are known. As a source for his edition of this version for the *AGA*, Mandyczewski used a manuscript copy made by Schubert's friend Witteczek, and for version B a copy by Albert Stadler.

Schiller's poem, rather long for a Lied and full of metaphors and romantic expressions, praises enthusiastically the magic power of Laura's piano-playing, through which the soul of the poet is carried away to the Elysian fields. Two names used by Schiller may need explanation today: Philadelphia was a famous magician, in Schiller's day apparently a household name; and Cocytus was one of the three rivers of Hades.

Schiller revised his poem, leaving out the last ten lines from the original version, for the new edition of his poems which appeared in 1800-3. It seems that Schubert used this edition, or one based on it.

In literary circles, the name Laura immediately brings Petrarch to mind. But in Schiller's case, the thought-association is less simple. Friedrich Förster in his memoirs transmits reminiscences of Minna Körner, who had known Schiller well:

When Schiller – which happened quite often – spoke of a most beautiful girl, whom he felt he must get to know more closely, and whose piano-playing entranced him, with other such expressions which to him were everyday language, we would remind him of his 'Entzückungen' and of 'Laura am Klavier'. When we teased him once again about this, he made an admission which I would never have believed, had I not known Schiller to be the most fundamentally honest of men.

'That Laura,' he said, 'when I made myself her Petrarch, was a captain's widow, in whose house I lived when I was in Mannheim [actually Stuttgart]. It was her good nature, far more than her mental qualities, which attracted me, and least of all her beauty. She played the piano extremely well, and could make an excellent bowl of punch. She had no idea that it was herself whom I had chosen for my Laura, and of whom I sang so rapturously. Even then I thought that a poem should live only in an ideal world, and if at that time I had needed another bridge, to take me into the world of ideals and out of the wretched reality of everyday life, my good landlady would have provided a very acceptable one. I should think, though, that the reader must have seen that my poems were not to be taken too seriously, for with such "extravagances" [Überschwenglichkeiten]' – that was the word he used – 'no sensible girl, least of all a Swabian, would have attached herself to me.' Frau von Kalb assured us that from what she remembered hearing from Schiller in Mannheim, Laura was the talented daughter of a *Konzertmeister*; she was neither young nor pretty, but her playing gave Schiller, who was living in the same house, a great deal of pleasure.[8]

It seems that Schubert wrote the second version rather soon after having composed the first. The most striking difference between the two versions concerns their tonality: it is remarkable that the first version begins in E major but ends in B♭ major, whereas the second version of the song begins and ends in A major. Schubert certainly was not averse to the use of progressive tonality; why then did he return to the conventional custom of starting and ending the song in the same key? Obviously, there must have been a reason. But let us consider first the differences in structure between the two versions:

D 388A	key	words	D 388B	key
introd. 1-6 (the girl playing) goes into	E		introd. 1-13	A
recit. 6-10	modul. to C	Wenn dein Finger . . .	recit. 13-17	modul. to G
instr. interlude 11-14	E		instr. interlude 18-21	modul. to e
recit. 14-17	modul. to A	Du gebietest	recit. 21-5	c♯
instr. transition 18-19		. . .	instr. transition 26-7	modul. to A
arioso 20-46	A, modul. to A♭	Ehrerbietig . . .	arioso 28-54	A–B♭ (new music)
recit. 46-50	modul. to G♭	wie, des Chaos . . .	recit. 55-8	d, modul. to c
arioso 50-3			arioso 58-61	modul. to A♭
arioso 54-80	D . . D	Lieblich itzt . . .	arioso 62-88	E . . . E
recit. 81-5	B♭	Mädchen, sprich . . .	recit. 89-93	A (ending on dom.)
postlude 86-7	B♭		repeat of introd. 94-106	A

Most obvious is the difference in length between the two versions (the first consists of 87 bars, the second of 106). This is partly accounted for by the expansion of the instrumental introduction from 5½ bars to 12½ bars. The first four bars of each setting are similar though not identical; even if we do not consider the fact that Schubert transposed the second version a fifth

8 *Friedrich Schiller*, ed. Bodo Lecke (Dichter über ihre Dichtungen, ed. R. Hirsch and W. Vordtriede), vol. 1 (Munich, 1969), pp. 48-9.

Ex. 3 (a) D 388A

down, there is a notable difference: for one thing, the second version is easier to play (Ex. 3).

It seems that Schubert intended to give a musical portrait of Laura at the piano, and this he achieved more convincingly in the second version than in the first. In the revised version he ends the song with a complete repeat of the introduction, which has been extended. The last lines of the poem – 'Ist's die Sprache, lüg mir nicht, / Die man in Elysen spricht?' – are answered not with words, but with Laura's playing: hence the return of the instrumental introduction at the end.

In both versions the same lines of the poem are treated as recitative. There are some slight rhythmic alterations, but overall the melodic divergences are greater than the rhythmic ones. An obvious improvement is the altered declamation (as a result of a completely new melodic line) in Ex. 4.

In the second version the number of tonal centres has decreased: A major can be felt throughout as the central key. Although the episode with the farthest-reaching modulations (from the words 'Lieblich itzt . . .' to '. . . Thränenwellen der Cocytus schleift') is only slightly altered, the second version shows a greater integration of the different elements.

To summarize: the second version is evidently a conscious revision of the first; it is certainly an improvement, especially in view of the fact that Schubert composed new music to the words from 'Ehrerbietig' onwards, thus

Ex. 3 (b) D 388B

Ex. 4 (a) D 388A

Ehr - er - bie - tig lei - ser rau- schen dann die Lüf - te, dir___ zu lauschen;

(b) D 388B

Ehr - er - bie - tig lei - ser rau - schen dann die Lüf - te, dir zu lau - schen;

reserving the melody of the piano introduction for the beginning and the end. The effect of the closing bars as an answer to the last question of the poem is thus musically intensified.

'Lied des Orpheus, als er in die Hölle ging'
('Orpheus'), D 474A and B

Schubert's second version of this song apparently owes its existence to a purely practical problem: the range of the voice part, just over two octaves, was probably found uncomfortable by singers. The structure of the song is nearly identical in the two versions. The modulatory scheme differs, however, owing to Schubert's changes in the compass of the voice part. In the first version the range goes from a♭ (below middle c′) to a″, and both extremes demand *f* or *ff* singing. In the second version the lower and upper limits are a♭ (it seems that Schubert did not wish to give up the low register) and f″; in this way the song is made suitable for baritone (or mezzo-soprano), whereas the first version could be mastered only by a voice with a quite exceptional range.

An outline will show how Schubert altered the range of the voice part whilst modifying the song's key scheme:

D 474A bar	key	words	D 474B	key
1-6	G♭	(introduction)	1-6	G♭
7-21	G♭	Wälze dich . . .	7-21	G♭
21-30	f♯–A	. . . fürchterliche Schatten	21-30	f♯–A
31-51	A–E	Von der Erde . . .	31-51	A–E
51-67	E–B	Meine Klage . . .	51-68	E
67-70		(interlude)	68-73	
71-81	B–D	O, ich sehe . . .	74-84	G–B♭
81-90	D–B♭–D	. . . ewig büssen . . .	84-93	B♭–G♭–B♭
91-132	D	Götter, die für euch	94-133	B♭

As one can see, instead of modulating into the dominant key (in bars 51-67), Schubert stayed in E major in the second version (bars 67ff) and then modulated into G major. Afterwards, instead of moving to B and D major he moved to G and B♭. Both versions are examples of progressive tonality, in that they end in a different key from the one in which they start.

In the second version Schubert changed the tempo indication right at the beginning by adding 'alla breve', which of course, does not mean that it should be sung twice as fast, but only that he was aware that 4/4 together with 'mässig, mit Kraft' could lead to too slow a tempo.

Bars 1-30 are almost identical in both versions. The most important of the altogether rather small-scale changes occur in the following places:

D 474 A bar		D 474B bar
43	change in melody	43
51	change in modulation	51
59	one bar added, rests for voice part, change in dynamics	59-60
63	change in declamation	64
67-70	interlude is extended. Here the second version is already 3 bars longer; music remains essentially unchanged until bar 126/129	68-73
126-32	essential change: 2 bars suppressed; *ff* instead of *p*	129-33

Unlike the other changes, the one essential difference in the closing bars of the two versions – the dynamic change from *p* to *ff* – has nothing to do with questions of vocal range. Evidently Schubert wished to retain in the postlude the glimpse of hope, the positive feeling of 'Hoffnung' ('Durch die Finsternisse bricht ein Strahl von Hoffnung').

'Auf dem See', D 543A and B

Of the two versions of this song, composed in March 1817, it may be said that the second is certainly more intriguing than the first. However, the first is by no means a rough draft or a mere sketch – on the contrary, had Schubert not written a revision of it, we would have been willing to accept the first as a successful sample of his musical adaptation of a text by Goethe.

Apart from the transposition from E to E♭, the two versions differ considerably. They give an especially fascinating insight into Schubert's critical attitude towards his own work. Right at the outset we have four bars of piano introduction in the first version as against five bars in the second. (In both cases the voice enters on the last quaver of the bar.) In the E major version there is a regular alternation between tonic and dominant; in the second version a first inversion of the supertonic is inserted in bar 4, anticipating the same harmony in bars 7 and 14. The first vocal section is metrically unusual –

2 x 7 bars – and this may have moved Schubert to break up the metrical scheme of the ritornello as well. To a certain degree the first version is still a kind of sketch: the tempo is indicated, but no dynamic markings are given before bar 23. (For other small modifications see: voice part D 543A/10, B/11; piano part A/10-11, B/11-12.) The part from 'Die Welle wieget' to 'Begegnen unserm Lauf' proceeds on essentially analogous lines, if we do not count minimal variations (voice part A/22, B/23).

Extremely significant is the sudden full bar's rest inserted after the next transition section at bar 34, before 'Aug', mein Aug'' – a literal holding of the breath. The canon between voice and piano part (A/36-40, B/38-42) is completed; the 'double melody' (two interwoven melodic lines) at 'Weg, du Traum' is elaborated in a more logical manner (no melisma on 'bist' at B/44); the harmonization of 'Hier auch Lieb' und Leben ist' becomes more interesting (deceptive cadence on E♭ VI in bar 46); the melody is rhythmically better profiled, the piano's interjections more expressive. The fermata on the last quaver before the change to 2/4 time functions as a counterpart to the silence of bar 34.

The revision is even more radiantly successful in the second section (in 2/4 time) than in the first section (in 6/8 time). It creates the impression of having been put down in rough outline in the first version, awaiting further elaboration. There are quite essential modifications; the voice part undergoes many small but very expressive changes. In the first version the melody used for the line 'Auf der Welle blinken / Tausend schwebende Sterne', which occurs twice, is unchanged: Ex. 5. In the second version, the melody is slightly simplified the first time and varied the second time: Ex. 6. In bars B/58-65 the melodic

Ex. 5 D 543A, bars 47ff and 63ff

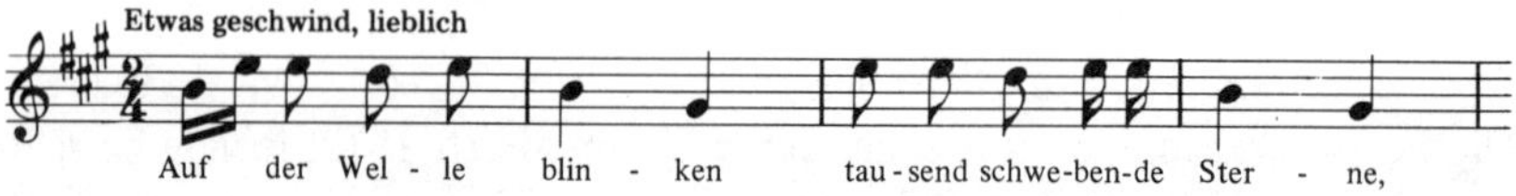

Ex. 6 (a) D 543B, bars 50ff

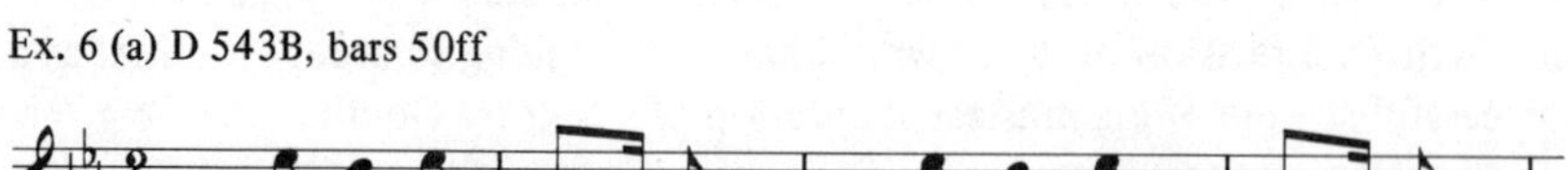

(b) D 543B, bars 66ff

lines of voice and piano (right hand) are interchanged as compared with the first version; the four final bars of the voice part (A/75-8) are extended to nine bars (B/78-86), the postlude accordingly to six bars instead of three (B/86-91 corresponding to A/78-80).

Survey of the structure of the two versions:

D 543A bar	words	D 543B bar
1–4 (6/8 metre)	(introduction)	1–5 (6/8 metre)
5(with upbeat)–18 (7+7)	Und frische Nahrung . . .	6(with upbeat)–19 (7+7)
19–30 (4+4+4)	Die Welle wieget . . .	20–31 (4+4+4)
30–2	(interlude)	31–4
33–46 (3+4+6+1)	Aug', mein Aug' . . .	35–49 (3+5+6+1)
47–62 (2/4 metre, 4+4)	Auf der Welle . . .	50–65 (2/4 metre, 4+4)
63–78 (4+4)	(repeats of words)	66–86 (4+4+4+4+5): last bar of last group coincides with first bar of
78–80	(epilogue)	86–91

B. Different settings of the same text

It may be hard – and in some cases even impossible – to explain why Schubert occasionally wrote different compositions to the same words, even if we take into account that a composer who wrote so many songs in such a short space of time may simply have forgotten, when charmed by any given text, that he had already written music to it several years before. The anecdote in which Schubert heard a song, judged it favourably, and then inquired about the composer and was told that he had composed it himself[9] may be nothing more than a legend; the fact that the story exists at all seems significant. If the incident did indeed happen, it makes this group particularly interesting. We should try to assess differences in quality by other than just subjective standards. Again, we are obliged to confine ourselves to just a few examples.

'Jägers Abendlied', D 215 and D 368

We know that Goethe – if he considered a musical setting of his poems at all – preferred strophic composition. But we also know that the contents of his poems did not often admit of strophic setting, in spite of the metrical unity of the stanzas. Reichardt struggled with this problem,[10] and even Goethe's close friend Zelter abandoned strophic composition when setting Goethe's poems to music.

9 Related by Kunigunde Vogl: see Deutsch, *Memoirs*, pp. 216-17.
10 W. Salmen, *J. F. Reichardt* (Freiburg im Breisgau, 1963), p. 309.

The four stanzas of 'Jägers Abendlied' are indeed metrically identical, with regularly alternating lines of four and three accents. The third stanza, however, is grammatically intelligible only in connection with the second, because 'Des Menschen' must be linked with 'mein verrauschend Bild'. In the musical sense the second stanza would have to form a unity with the third, and the fourth possibly with the first.

Neither in his first nor in his second attempt can Schubert be said to have been wholly successful. In the first setting (20 June 1815) he combines two stanzas into a unity; this is in itself a wonderful musical whole, and the prodigality of modulatory possibilities so characteristic of his early songs is in evidence. But this joining of the first two stanzas blocks the path to the third. The *NGA* prints the words of the third and fourth stanzas in italics, which indicates that they do not occur in the sources (Schubert's manuscript and the first edition). Metrically they could be sung to the same music, but the grammatical coherence between the second and third stanzas is lost through the layout of the composition.

In the second composition (early 1816 (?)) this is also the case, though the problem is less obvious since it is possible to sing all the stanzas to the same melody (some copies dating from Schubert's lifetime give all four stanzas; the copy that was sent to Goethe on 17 April 1816, however, omitted the third stanza, which the poet would hardly have appreciated). The compositions differ considerably in their treatment of the words. The first, though of high quality, is not entirely free from 'operatic' elements. In the later one this facet is less marked. Here Schubert constantly employs a repeated motif in the accompaniment, probably symbolizing the idea of 'schleichen' ('creeping'), thereby achieving a strong sense of unity:

'An den Mond', D 259 and D 296

In this poem lyrical expression and philosophical reflection are wonderfully interwoven; it has been called 'impossible to set . . . to music'[11] for this very reason. However, according to Schuh no fewer than forty-six composers have tried their hand at it (including Reichardt, Zelter, Tomášek and Pfitzner).[12] Among the successful ones was certainly Schubert, at least in his second setting; not unjustly, Richard Capell says 'The song is unduly neglected.'

Goethe's poem, written during the winter of 1777-8, seems at first sight to be a little piece of nature poetry; but on closer study it proves to be packed

of the moonlit river scene evokes echoes of joy and sorrow; the rushing of the

11 Alfred Einstein, *Schubert. A Musical Portrait* (London, 1951), p. 108. R. Capell, *Schubert's Songs* (London, 1928; 2nd edn 1957), p. 103, speaks of a 'hopeless task'.

12 W. Schuh, *Goethe-Vertonungen* (Zurich, 1952), pp. 33-4.

stream becomes symbolic of the irretrievable past; but the flowing water, after winter has given way to spring, is also a symbol of new life: its creative forces awake the inner forces in man himself, his faculty for friendship and for cultivation of the emotions, but vaguely realized, that move the soul on such a moonlit night. The images of 'friend' and 'night' recur at the end, thus rounding off the poem by alluding to its initial lines.

Schubert's second setting, D 296, bears no date: *D1* suggests 'autumn 1815 (?)', *D2* '1815 or 1816 (?)'.[13] There is certainly good reason for the assumption that it was composed later than D 259, which contains a basic compositional error that does not occur in D 296. It is not likely that Schubert would first write a 'correct' composition and then another to the same words which contains a disturbing error. The poem consists of nine stanzas of four lines each; in D 259 Schubert combines two stanzas within one melodic unit. This leaves one odd stanza, and as a result the song cannot be performed without a distorting deletion from the poem. The *AGA* solves the problem by printing the first four stanzas with the music, placing the fifth in brackets, and giving the sixth to the ninth separately.

The second composition (D 296) also begins with four stanzas set two by two to the same music. The introduction is very unusual in that it establishes the main key only in bars 4 and 5. Should we perhaps assume that the opening bars symbolize the poet's feelings at the overwhelming sight of the moonlit landscape? Schubert arrives in the key of A♭ major 'out of the blue', so to speak, and does not modulate conventionally from one key to another. The fifth stanza takes its music from the first and third. In the sixth and seventh a new development sets in: via A♭ minor Schubert modulates to C♭ major, and with the murmuring ('rauschen') of the river he introduces a semiquaver figure in the piano part. In the last two stanzas the initial music returns, now containing some important new elements. In the eighth stanza the main melody is played in double octaves together with the voice part (symbolizing the twofold unity of the friends, foreshadowed by similar octave-doubling in the first stanza).[14] But in the ninth stanza both poet and composer turn entirely inwards; from the third beat of bar 50, the voice part follows now the bass line, now the middle voice – an example of astonishing technical skill. Only the last words of this last stanza are repeated; the repetition, one octave higher than the preceding phrase, functions as a codetta.

As in the first version of 'Orpheus', the range of the voice part presents a problem (a♭–g♭″), but Schubert was evidently unconcerned, and an important difference is that neither the lowest nor the highest note is to be sung *forte.*

13 Einstein, *Schubert*, p. 108, specifies (without giving a source) that it was composed shortly before 'Erlkönig'; similarly Blume, 'Schubert's "Mondlied"', p. 35, mentions 'November 1815'.

14 The explanations for the unison effects given by P. Mies ('Die Bedeutung des Unisono im Schubertschen Liede', *Zeitschrift für Musikwissenschaft*, XI (1928-9), p. 96) are not satisfactory.

Nevertheless, the a♭ is rather difficult for a tenor; the sixth stanza on the other hand is inconvenient for a baritone; the only voice really suited to the song is a mezzo-soprano; yet the text makes this unmistakably a man's song.

Let us once more turn our attention to the first composition (D 259). The song belongs to a group sent to Goethe by Spaun on 17 November 1816, accompanied by a long letter of recommendation. The possiblity that this song should be considered unfinished must therefore be excluded. It still seems inexplicable that Spaun sent to Goethe a song which on the one hand was to the poet's taste with regard to its strophic setting, but which on the other hand could hardly have been to his liking since it could not be performed at all without cutting one stanza.

This first composition shows another shortcoming. The poem's lines alternate regularly between seven and five syllables. As a result of his very strict treatment, intensified by the somewhat monotonous bass, Schubert was obliged to lengthen the syllables at the ends of the even-numbered lines, thereby causing a somewhat dragging effect. (The only other possibility would have been to write only one note and a rest.) Blume held the opinion that both settings provide enough material to tell us why Schubert set a given text to music as he did and not in any other way.[15] This is only partly true: it is of course quite possible to infer from the second composition what he found unsatisfactory in the first; but then, why did he treat the text as he did the first time in D 259? Blume also criticized Schubert for combining the fourth stanza with the first three. 'Fliesse, fliesse, lieber Fluss!' does indeed suggest a new element; but the words 'nimmer werd' ich froh' are clearly related to the third stanza ('Jeden Nachklang . . . / Froh- und trüber Zeit'). The emotional caesura is much more intense at 'Ich besass es doch einmal'. Starting with the melody of the beginning Schubert unites three stanzas into a musical whole, and for the sake of the melodic line adds the word 'ohne' before 'Ruh'' (stanza six, line two). One might speculate about Goethe's reaction if he ever noticed Schubert's alteration. The poem's metre is disturbed, though this is hidden by the music. (The alterations made by Goethe in those poems of Marianne von Willemer which he included in his *West-Östlicher Divan* are more important, but they never change the metre.)

From Schubert's alterations to Goethe's verse one might conclude that within a few decades the German Lied had indeed developed into an independent art, made up of three components: words, voice part and piano part. The liberties that composers allowed themselves with regard to the poems (and Schubert certainly is not the only one who altered texts) are closely interwoven with this evolution.

15 Blume, 'Schubert's "Mondlied"', pp. 32f.

'Am Flusse', D 160 and D 766

These two settings of Goethe's poem differ so widely, both in date and in character, that it is quite likely that Schubert wrote the second without having any recollection of the first.

The poem dates from Goethe's early youth (1768) and may owe its origin to a personal experience. To Schubert it was just a literary theme – or was it? We do not know how deeply he was in love with Therese Grob, who sang the soprano part in his Mass in F major on 16 October 1814, and whose father would not consent to her marrying Schubert. In 1820 Therese married a baker; in 1821 Schubert related the story of his unrequited love to Anselm Hüttenbrenner. And in 1822 he wrote the second setting of 'Am Flusse'. Any connection remains pure guesswork, of course.

As in 'An den Mond', the flowing water is symbolic of the transient, the irretrievable – but this time it is no more than that, which after all is hardly surprising with a poet not yet twenty. Still, the poem, simple and direct as it is, surpasses those of Uz, Gleim or Hölty. It was written during the period of Goethe's relationship with Käthchen Schönkopf, and perhaps – in its mixture of melancholy and resignation – it is connected with the unhappy ending of that relationship. The poem itself allows more than one interpretation. That it tells about a lost love, that the girl only laughs at the faithful lover, that the verses dedicated to her are 'written in water' – these are facts. Their interpretation depends on the emphasis given to certain lines. If one lays the stress on the words 'spricht sie meiner Treue Hohn', the accent falls on bitterness; if the stress falls on 'fliesst mit ihm davon', we are aware of resignation.

Schubert's compositions represent both aspects. The first setting (1815) stresses the bitterness. It is in D minor in 3/8 time throughout, and in three-part form; disregarding the strophic structure, it reverts to the beginning in the third line of the second stanza. The climax comes at the above-mentioned line 'Nun spricht sie meiner Treue Hohn': the highest note in the melody, the strongest dynamic degree and a fermata. Instead of a tempo indication Schubert indicates the character of the song: 'Wehmütig' ('with melancholy').

In the second setting the emphasis is on resignation. Strophic structure is respected (the second stanza is a variant of the first), dynamic contrasts are small (*pp* with a few crescendos and decrescendos). The accompaniment contains a barely concealed tribute to Beethoven: a quotation from the scherzo of his Seventh Symphony (second horn part). Only the last line is repeated, unlike the first composition, where the last two lines are repeated. It is noteworthy that both songs begin with the interval of a fourth, a′–d″; could this be a symbol for a final parting? The German 'Ade' stands in folk poetry for 'adieu' and traditionally was sung on a rising fourth. (Cf. also Schubert's song 'Abschied', D 957/7, which starts with the word 'Ade', sung on a rising fourth.)

C. Combinations of A and B (new setting incorporating some revisions)

'Sehnsucht', D 52 and D 636

The evidence given by two settings of Schiller's 'Sehnsucht' is in flat contradiction to the assumption that Schubert might have 'forgotten' after a number of years that he had set a certain text to music. The later composition, D 636, may be labelled partly a revision of the earlier song, D 52, and partly a new composition. Three versions of D 636 are known, two in the bass clef (one of which is incomplete) and one in the treble clef; we refer to the latter, the one published in 1826 as op. 39. *D2* dates it 'early 1821 (?)', as the first performance took place on 8 February 1821. This means that nearly eight years may have elapsed between D 52 and D 636.

D 52 (15–17 April 1813) was conceived entirely as a dramatic scena and contains frequent changes of tempo and metre as well as changes from arioso to recitative. Especially from 'Frisch hinein' until the end, the style is rather operatic, not unlike the last section of Beethoven's 'Adelaïde'. It is noteworthy that this same section recurs almost entire in D 636 (but notated differently); however, minor alterations in the piano part have practically removed the theatricality. Furthermore, there are no changes in metre, nor are there recitatives proper; and there is only one tempo change ('Ziemlich geschwind' at the beginning, 'Schnell' at 'Frisch hinein'). New motifs and new keys reflect the various moods of the poem, but these elements are well integrated into the overall structure. Thus, D 636 is indeed more balanced than D 52. It owes its impression of being a very successful rendering of the poem to its concise conception. It is little short of astonishing that Schubert found some motifs from D 52 still useful.

Survey of the structure of the two songs:

D 52	words	D 636
a Allegretto, d	Ach, aus dieses Tales Gründen . . .	a Ziemlich geschwind, b
b^{1} Recit., F	Dort erblick' ich . . .	b G
b^{2} Allegretto, d–F	Hätt' ich Schwingen . . .	
	Harmonien . . .	c^{1} B♭–E♭
c Recit., C	Ach, wie schön . . .	c^{2} B♭–F modulating interlude
d Andante, C	Doch mir wehrt . . .	d g–B (= dom. of E)
e Allegro agitato ma non troppo, f	Einen Nachen . . .	
f Più allegro, F	Frisch hinein . . .	e Schnell, E

Summarizing, it can be stated that the study and comparison of different versions of the same Lied make us well aware of Schubert's critical attitude towards his own work. Out of all the poem-settings mentioned, only one was little more than a rough sketch in its first version (the Szene aus *Faust*, D 126A). It seems that whenever Schubert revised or altered a song, the later composition is superior to the earlier one – with the exception of 'Der Sänger', D 149, where in both versions some few shortcomings are to be found, and where in any event the chronology is uncertain. The later setting is also superior in those cases where there was an extrinsic reason for an alteration, such as the request of a singer for a different vocal range as in 'Ständchen', D 920, or (possibly) in 'Orpheus', D 474. Transpositions to another key may have been made on request, but Schubert always took the opportunity to alter at least some few details. It seems, however, that Schubert sometimes felt inclined to transpose a song without having a singer's convenience in mind (as in 'Auf dem See', D 543B). In his essay 'Drafting the Masterpiece', Maurice Brown called the song 'Nähe des Geliebten' in its first version (D 162A) a 'sketch'[16] – probably because Schubert cancelled this version with the words 'Gilt nicht' ('invalid'), and wrote the second version the same day, apparently having realized immediately (after a first run-through?) that a less excited accompaniment would better fit the emotional content of the poem. We may accept the term 'sketch', or we may propose 'draft' as more appropriate – it does not really matter. There are many possible terminological categorizations. Whether we call a version sketch, draft, revision, last version or fair copy – it was a characteristic habit of Schubert's to write out his songs in considerable detail, even when they have some characteristics of a sketch; and we shall never know for certain whether the intention to revise and rewrite a song was already forming in his mind before he finished a first version, or whether the motivation for a revision came to him only after he had finished a composition, perhaps after he had heard it sung through. Sometimes a new version may have been brought about by the fact that Schubert was too poor to afford a copyist when wanting to meet the request of a friend for a copy of a song. Andreas Holschneider convincingly deduced that one of the four autograph manuscripts of the song 'Frühlingsglaube' (D 686) owes its existence to such a request,[17] since one of the holograph copies contains besides a few alterations some copying mistakes which indicate an otherwise inexplicable lack of concentration on Schubert's part.

Where Schubert wrote different compositions of the same poem, in the examples discussed the second setting usually is musically superior to the first. This is especially obvious in those cases where a span of several years with symbolism and allusions. 'Moon' is compared to 'friend'; the desolation

16 M. J. E. Brown, *Essays on Schubert* (London, 1966), p. 4.

17 A. Holschneider, 'Zu Schuberts "Frühlingsglaube"' in *Festschrift Otto Erich Deutsch zum 80. Geburtstag* (Kassel, 1963), pp. 240-4.

separates the two compositions. A different understanding of the poem's emotional content may have motivated Schubert to re-set the text of, for example, 'Am Flusse' (D 160 and D 766). Tradition has it that Goethe was of the opinion that all good poetry is susceptible of more than one interpretation. One wonders, then, whether music as compared with poetry is not the poorer art, since it took Schubert two compositions to find the musical equivalent of the two aspects of the poem. One could also quote in this connection Mendelssohn's letter of 15 October 1842 to Marc André Souchay. Mendelssohn too considered words to be ambiguous and music clear; but, starting from the same premiss, he reached the opposite conclusion. He definitely preferred musical to verbal art, as for him it was completely clear what message music conveyed. Perhaps we may reconcile the two viewpoints in this way: Schubert could not express the two aspects of a poem in one song, but in composing two settings he found the equivalent of what he wanted to express.

Schubert as a composer of operas

ELIZABETH NORMAN McKAY

It is now common knowledge that Schubert wrote a large amount of music for the theatre. In the last decade or two we have witnessed a great upsurge of interest in forgotten operas, and this has resulted in revivals of works once popular in opera houses all over Europe, and of others that were less successful in their day. Schubert's theatrical contributions have not been overlooked in the search for interesting 'new' works; operatic companies (although for the most part amateur or semi-professional) and broadcasting and recording companies have given us some authentic performances of several of the stage works. But if we are to be honest we must own that, while we find a great deal in Schubert's theatre music that is inspired or inspiring, the music is of inconsistent quality. We must also admit that Schubert frequently showed a complete lack of understanding of the requirements of dramatic situation and timing. In his Lieder and ballads he could be intensely dramatic, but the dramatic response here is to a situation which is timeless. When watching a stage production the audience is always aware of the time-scale which controls dramatic action, and of the possibility of dramatic interruption. Above all else, good opera must be theatrical. In the following discussion I shall endeavour to come to some understanding of the sources of Schubert's style in his mature compositions for the theatre, and to explain both his own part in the failures and the part played by his musical and theatrical environment. I have restricted my discussion almost entirely to the completed works of 1818 to 1823.

The two composers who had most influence on the style of Schubert's theatre music up until 1821 were Joseph Weigl (1766–1846) and Adalbert Gyrowetz (1763–1850), both of whom were very successful and highly esteemed composers in their day. *Die Freunde von Salamanka*, D 32 (1815), dramatically weak but musically often very striking, is a Singspiel written in the same Viennese pastoral style as Weigl's very popular Singspiele *Das Waisenhaus* (1807) and *Die Schweizerfamilie* (1808). In these idyllic Romantic pieces, in which Weigl was returning to the spirit of innocence and gentle gaiety of Rousseau's early opéra-comique, scenes frequently start with charming village choruses describing the joys of the country and of country life.

The arias and ensembles are on a small and fairly intimate scale, without the larger-than-life emotional range of grand opera. In an article on Josef Weigl published in the London *Harmonicon* of June 1825 (p. 92) Weber, who closely shared Schubert's operatic heritage, is quoted as referring to Weigl's operatic style as 'ingenious, yet effeminate velvet painting'. He also credited Weigl with 'uncommon richness in the most pleasing musical ideas' and, above all, with the same 'soundness and purity of style which has become so predominant in the Viennese school through the works of Mozart and Haydn'. But 'For serious dramatic music he does not seem to possess a congenial talent.' In spite of Weigl's preference for the sentimental rather than brilliant intrigue, he was a great lover of Mozart's stage works, some of which he had heard the composer conduct. Frequently in his operas there are indications of his intimate knowledge of the music of the older composer.

Weigl's admiration for Mozart was shared by Gyrowetz, a prolific Bohemian composer who finally settled in Vienna in 1804. Gyrowetz wrote the grand festival opera for the Congress of Vienna in 1815 – *Agnes Sorel*, a patriotic piece with a libretto by Sonnleithner, who had earlier provided Beethoven with the first version of the *Fidelio* libretto. Gyrowetz had studied in Naples where he developed his somewhat Italianate tastes. Apart from his Italian training and his admiration for Mozart's operatic music, his theatre music shows that he was steeped in the traditions of Viennese taste. His influence on Schubert is especially evident in some of the younger composer's earlier Singspiele, and is therefore less relevant to this discussion; but a few instances of his influence on Schubert are pertinent. Gyrowetz wrote a sentimental two-act Singspiel in 1811, *Der Augenarzt*, on the then-popular theme of medical cures. In this piece the Quintet, no. 3, has a guitar-like accompaniment in a style which Schubert was to adopt for the boy Philipp's 'Romance' in his 1815 Singspiel *Fernando*, D 220. (It is worth noting that the boy, one of two blind children in *Der Augenarzt*, is called Philippe (sic), and his mother Leonore, the same names for son and mother that Schubert was to use in *Fernando*.)[1] The 'Romance', no. 4, sung by the two blind children, may also be compared to the music of the two children in Schubert's *Die Bürgschaft*, D 435 (1816). There are several similar reflections of Gyrowetz's music and ideas in Schubert's early stage music. Yet of all the composers of his day, it is Weigl to whom Schubert and his librettists were most indebted, especially in the works up to and including *Alfonso und Estrella*, D 732 (1821-2). The same sincerity is to be found, and often, alas, the same lack of truly dramatic

1 It is also interesting to note that *Fernando* and Beethoven's *Fidelio* share some roots in Kotzebue's five-act romantic tragedy *Die Spanier in Peru oder Rollas Tod*. Stadler's libretto for Schubert corresponds almost exactly to Act V, scene 1 of Kotzebue's play. Another scene in the same play takes place in a dungeon where the hero, like Florestan, is about to die. Pizarro appears in Kotzebue's piece, and it was this name that Sheridan chose as his title for his adaptation of Kotzebue's play for a performance at the Theatre Royal, Drury Lane, London, in 1804.

music. Of course, Schubert moved on from the Weigl style, and was in turn further influenced, especially by Mozart, Beethoven and Rossini,[2] and it is the influence of these composers which becomes more apparent in Schubert's last works for the theatre.

Early Singspiele

The influence of Weigl's Singspiel style on the text and music of *Die Zwillingsbrüder,* D 647, was strong. Schubert was commissioned to compose this light-weight one-act piece at the end of 1818; the libretto was by Georg von Hofmann, an experienced but mediocre librettist (he was later to succeed Treitschke, author of the revised version of the *Fidelio* text, as resident librettist at the Kärntnertor-Theater in Vienna). The village background presented Schubert with the familiar format of friendly choruses and idyllic romance of country lovers. The music has much charm, and the quartet, a crisp and clean ensemble suggesting Mozart's influence, is especially delightful.

Schubert's next Singspiel, completed in 1823, was *Die Verschworenen,* D 787, a more sophisticated piece than *Die Zwillingsbrüder,* thanks to the libretto of Ignaz Franz Castelli (1781-1862), who wrote the play as a challenge to German composers who were bitterly complaining at the dearth of good opera librettos. This complaint is relevant and significant in our discussion of Schubert's stage music. The early decades of the nineteenth century were difficult times for German opera, a period of transition and experimentation for librettists and composers, and of searching for a new national theatrical identity. In the preface to his play, Castelli wrote:

> The German composer's complaint is usually this: 'Indeed, we should gladly set operas to music, if only you would supply us with books!' Here is one, gentlemen! If you wish to set it to music, I would ask you to give my words some respect, and not to spoil the comprehensibility of the plot by preferring roulades to musical characterization. I believe the opera must be a dramatic action accompanied by music, not music with an added text; and the total impression, in my opinion, is more important than giving an individual singer the opportunity to show off the agility of his vocal cords. Let us do something for real German opera, gentlemen![3]

As well as being a reputable government official, Castelli was a prolific and successful author and translator of plays. He had written the libretto of *Die Schweizerfamilie* for Weigl, and helped to spread the fashion for Austrian poems in dialect. The story of *Die Verschworenen* was an adaptation of Aristophanes' *Lysistrata,* transferred to a background of Vienna at the time

2 See my article 'Rossinis Einfluss auf Schubert', *Österreichische Musikzeitschrift,* XVIII/1 (1963), pp. 17-22.

3 *Die Verschworenen,* Textbuch Nr. 60, Tagblatt-Bibliothek Nr. 695 (Vienna, n.d.), p. 7.

of the Crusades. This Singspiel, with a well-constructed and lively libretto, has been the most frequently performed of all Schubert's music for the theatre. For a twentieth-century audience the obvious humour of the libretto makes rather heavy going, and the music, while charming and melodious, becomes at times repetitive. *Die Verschworenen* is of some historical interest, however, both as being an attempt to resolve a crisis in the operatic field in Vienna, and also by virtue of the kind of libretto Castelli invented for his purpose. A short survey of the state of the musical theatre in Vienna between 1819 and 1823 will throw some light on the crisis, and on the problems and attitudes of the pro-German school of writers and composers in the city.

Vienna heard its first Rossini opera, *L'inganno felice*, on 26 November 1816 at the Kärntnertor-Theater, and after this his operas became increasingly popular. Edward Holmes, who visited Vienna in 1827, wrote: 'It has been said that the people of Vienna are Rossini mad, but they are not only mad for him, but mad for his worst imitations.'[4] He continued with an account of the frivolous fashion in the city for everything Italian, not only for the music, but for language, dress and behaviour. Between 1819 and 1823, when Schubert was engaged in writing his mature operas, Viennese enthusiasm for Rossini's operas had not reached its peak, and was not yet virtually exclusive.

The fashionable attitude amongst members of the highly theatre-conscious Viennese society became increasingly that anything foreign was best, whether by Rossini, Cherubini, Boieldieu or Hérold. At the same time, a conflict developed between the supporters of Rossini and the Italian opera on the one hand and the smaller number of supporters of Weber and German opera on the other, a conflict which was an echo of that in Paris of the previous century between admirers of Gluck and Piccinni. There is, however, one other important feature of the repertory of the Kärntnertor-Theater: the great increase in the number of performances of Mozart's operas. In 1819, for example, there were forty performances of Mozart's operas (all sung in German) as compared with only thirty-four Rossini performances (also in German). Even so, it is Boieldieu's operas which head the list for frequency, with some forty-two performances. There was a steady and proportionate decline in the number of performances of works by living German or Austrian composers, as represented by the single appearance of a Weigl opera, *Die Schweizerfamilie*, whereas there had been twenty-three performances of the popular *Das Waisenhaus* and *Die Schweizerfamilie* only four years previously. Remembering that Castelli was the author of *Die Schweizerfamilie* and that he was a keen advocate of Viennese culture, we can well understand his concern for German opera.

Weigl refused in his later years to write operas for Vienna as he objected to the frivolous tastes of the audiences, and his concern at deteriorating standards of taste is certainly confirmed by a study of the repertory lists of the first

4 [Edward Holmes] *A Ramble among the Musicians of Germany*, by 'A Musical Professor' (London, 1828), p. 116.

three decades of the century.[5] There was a marked increase in light, popular, easy entertainment which made few demands on the audiences. A bright scene, topical humour, a colourful personality and a gay and easily remembered tune was all that the public in Biedermeier Vienna wanted. The post-1815 political repression is significant in this context, for Metternich's censorship laws could be ludicrously inhibiting. Deprived of all semblance of free expression of opinion and serious experimentation, writers opted for an unreal world of social conviviality and witty triviality; burlesque and light satire were characteristic of this artistic mood. It was a proper complement to the restricted, staid daily life of the Viennese people existing in the police state of Prince Metternich. In the first fifteen years of the century, Weigl's worthy and sentimental Singspiele, and serious operas by his contemporary Ignaz Ritter von Seyfried, had alternated with French operas by Méhul, Spontini, Isouard and Paer; but by 1819, it is clear from the repertory lists that there was little encouragement to serious young Austrian composers or their librettists to write German operas, for the chances of their works receiving performances at the Kärntnertor-Theater or the Theater an der Wien were very small indeed; and if they were performed, they fell quickly from the repertory.

When Castelli produced his play *Die Verschworenen* (*The Conspirators*), the censors left it intact except for the title, which they presumably felt to be dangerous and liable to incite the audience to rebellion or revolution. The name was therefore changed to *Der häusliche Krieg* (*Domestic Warfare*). In this Singspiel Castelli created a comic play with the high spirits and humour expected and desired by Viennese Biedermeier audiences, but he added to these qualities considerable sensitivity and tenderness which lift it far above the other comic Singspiele of its day. Eduard Hanslick attended the first night of a new production of Schubert's setting of the play at the Court Opera on 30 January 1897. On the following day he wrote in his review in the *feuilleton* section of *Die Neue Freie Presse*:

> About the opera itself there is nothing new we can say; who does not already know and love it? Chivalrous courage, tender devotion, amorous teasing, roguish humour – all live and sparkle in this music, which, with its naive geniality and cordiality, is stronger and more lasting than many music dramas of recent times.

Johann Herbeck had 'discovered' the work, which had never until then had a public hearing, and performed it with great success in 1861, after which *Die Verschworenen* became a firm favourite for several decades, and was performed in many countries. In fact, in 1897 it was the only German comic opera writ-

5 This deterioration in taste coincided with that of the concert audiences. The general Viennese concert-going public, at the few concerts given in the early decades of the century, increasingly demanded virtuoso brilliance rather than musical excellence. The cult of the artist was developing rapidly, and it was in this atmosphere that concert-giving infant prodigies, and in 1828 the phenomenally gifted Paganini, throve.

ten between those of Mozart and Lortzing still in the repertory. The roles are well defined and sympathetic, and the choruses of knights and of their ladies are well characterized and play an important part in the story. Indeed, it is very sad that this operetta was never performed during Schubert's lifetime, owing quite clearly to the adverse conditions for German operas in the Vienna of 1823. It is hard to imagine how this very Austrian piece could have been performed by the Italian singers of the Kärntnertor-Theater; and the Theater an der Wien, then in serious financial difficulties, could hardly afford a new production of such a work, demanding, as it does, a fairly large cast of soloists and chorus. *Die Verschworenen* could have been a great success had it been given a chance in 1823; for Schubert's charming music admirably emphasizes the virtues of the libretto – as Castelli himself, hearing the music for the first time as an old man, readily and enthusiastically agreed.

Alfonso und Estrella

In *Die Zwillingsbrüder* (1818-19) and *Die Verschworenen* (1823) Schubert endeavoured to portray characters by musical means. In this he succeeded only partially, and it is perhaps his failure to characterize that represents one of the greatest weaknesses of *Alfonso und Estrella*, D 732, the first of his two grand operas. The libretto of this opera, written by his friend Franz von Schober, bears many similarities to Shakespeare's *As You Like It.* The usurped King Troila lives in exile in an idyllic valley surrounded by his adoring followers (courtiers) and his loving son Alfonso. Alfonso and Estrella, the daughter of the usurping King Mauregato, fall in love at their first meeting, and after an insurrection by Mauregato's army chief, Adolfo, has finally been quelled by the exiled King Troila's army led by Alfonso, all ends happily amidst repentance and forgiveness as the young couple are blessed, and their respective fathers abdicate the throne in their favour. *Alfonso und Estrella* is the result of a collaboration between poet and composer unique in Schubert's creative writing for the theatre. Schober and Schubert left Vienna to spend the autumn of 1821 in nearby St Pölten, much of the time as the guests of the Bishop of that town in his country residence at Ochsenberg. Here the young men spent a comfortable, peaceful and happy few weeks, Schober writing the text of one act of the opera while Schubert was composing the music to the previous act. Together they discussed the work as it was created, so that *Alfonso und Estrella* – like *Der Freischütz* of Weber and Kind written a few years earlier – was the result of constant collaboration. Unfortunately, it was a collaboration between two dramatic novices, and Schubert cannot be exonerated from blame for the unsatisfactory aspects of the opera. Had Schubert, the musical genius, been a natural composer of theatre music he would surely have spotted some of the blatant errors and deficiencies in his friend's libretto. And it is these errors which make it almost impossible to stage *Alfonso und Estrella* satisfactorily, if at all, despite the variety of scene and colour in a not unimaginative story. Probably the only virtually complete stage version of the opera since Liszt performed it at the Hoftheater in Weimar in 1854 was a largely amateur production by the Reading University Opera Club in February 1977. Liszt thought that Schubert had welcomed the libretto for its lyrical possibilities, and lacked understanding of the requisites of good theatre.[6] He further objected that *Alfonso und Estrella*, designed as an opera with Italian pretensions of grandeur, consistently reverted to the style of Singspiel, with light and broadly melodic numbers; and that the music was insufficiently strong for the drama and emotions it was supposed to represent. Liszt felt that some of the most beautiful music of the opera was written for the exiled King Troila, a part intended for the great baritone Michael Vogl; throughout, Troila's music was gracious and noble, its only failings being dramatic ones.

In comparison with the great operatic composers of the past two hundred years – Mozart, Rossini, Wagner, Verdi, Richard Strauss and Puccini – Schubert had not only little understanding of the essentials of a good libretto, but even less of theatrical effects. The method of building up tension over a considerable period and releasing it at the moment of climax eluded him. In *Alfonso und Estrella* he wrote instinctively and often quickly, setting each number to music as it occurred or appealed to him, and frequently forgetting the overall shape of the entire scene or of the opera as a whole. As a result, there are long meditative sections in which a singer looks on the beauties of the scenery around him; the action is stopped, and nothing is learned about the behaviour or character of the singer except that he is not blind to the beauties of nature. In the faithful Reading production of *Alfonso* these weaknesses were very evident. The first scene of the first act is the weakest dramatically, although it possesses considerable Weigl-like charm. The young hero, Alfonso, has to stand on the stage during long respectful choruses and expressions of noble sentiments before he is allowed to utter a sound, let alone express the restlessness he is supposed to feel, and his desire to escape into a wider and more adventurous world. When he at last does this, it is in a lyrical, romantic aria in which his appreciation of the beautiful country, its dawns and sunsets, its streams and night skies, seems to outweigh his supposed restless spirit. The action has indeed stopped before it has properly started, and the true character of the hero is masked, misrepresented, by the lyricism. Eventually, at the end of a long first scene with no dramatic action of any significance, Troila's followers leave the stage and are replaced by Estrella and her female attendants out for a day's hunting. Estrella's spirit is restless, like Alfonso's, but she is also deeply distressed by the expressions of love and cruel deter-

6 F. Liszt, 'Schuberts *Alfonso und Estrella*', *Neue Zeitschrift für Musik*, XLI/10 (1 September 1854), pp. 101-5.

mination to win her hand uttered by Adolfo, the usurping King Mauregato's captain of arms. In this opera Adolfo is perhaps the most successful musical characterization. He first boasts his prowess in a blustering energetic aria, then pleads in a lyrical romantic duet of great charm, and finally bursts forth in a triumphantly threatening section of considerable power which culminates, like many of the set pieces in this opera, in a fiery Italianate *più mosso allegro* section. After a quick change of scene to Mauregato's court, an eventful if occasionally too slow-moving and unconvincing finale closes the act. The high point of the finale is the impressive *adagio* for solo trio later joined by the four-part chorus. Each principal character expresses his own feelings and fears. However, when at the height of the tension Mauregato suddenly and surprisingly remembers that Estrella can only marry the suitor who brings back the ancient Chain of Eurich, credibility is somewhat weakened.

The second act opens lyrically with Troila's ancient ballad of the Sky Maiden, in which we hear music that Schubert was to use again in the song 'Täuschung' in *Winterreise.* It has a dramatic point in that, when soon afterwards the beautiful Estrella appears alone, Alfonso first believes her to be the lovely Sky Maiden of the ballad. The scene between the young people is idyllic and romantic, and contains some delightful music. Unfortunately, there is as little action and drama in this extended scene as in the first scene of the first act. The next scene, with Adolfo and the conspirators, consists of one ensemble, a lively and well-characterized number in which Schubert came near to real operatic music in the realistic Italian style. Then, back again to extended lack-of-action: Estrella is lost, Mauregato is distraught until father and daughter are eventually reunited (a popular theme of early-nineteenth-century German operas and Singspiele which we have already experienced in Weigl and Gyrowetz, and in Schubert's *Fernando*). Estrella's aria, no. 21, though delightful, is indistinguishable from similar lyrical arias sung by Troila, Alfonso or Estrella herself, and these interchangeable solo expressions become tedious, presenting no clear picture of a character or a situation. The finale to the second act is again undramatic: 'Flee!', Mauregato is advised as the rebel Adolfo and his army approach the court. It takes an improbably long time – *allegro, allegro agitato, allegro vivace* and final *più mosso* – before the king finally reacts. Surely the authors could have dispensed with this scene more quickly and with far greater dramatic effect! Mauregato, Estrella and their friends, supposedly fleeing from the rebels, should not stand poised for flight for some ten minutes during which nothing happens. Again, credibility is lost, and the audience is bound to react with some loss of faith even if it can resist boredom.

The last act begins promisingly with the Introduction, no. 23, depicting the onslaught on Mauregato's kingdom by Adolfo and his rebellious forces. But as the scene lengthens, all the impetus of fleeing armies and terrified citizens is lost in a static scene which again offends the rules of theatrical timing. The cleverest production could do little for this scene, and when Mauregato and his daughter embark on a long 'I'll stay' – 'you must go' duet, the opera virtually stops. A prolonged love-scene between Alfonso and Estrella does nothing to raise the dramatic temperature. It is doubtful whether Alfonso's hunting friends, inexperienced in war, summoned by the special horn given to him by Troila in the first scene, and appearing to the customary *allegro* 6/8 huntsmen's music, could do much against a fully armed and experienced force led by General Adolfo, but they go off confidently to do what they can – and they actually succeed. We have explanations and introductions between royal fathers and their children, a scene which should surely have been postponed until after the end of the battle. But Schubert and Schober continued on their muddled way. However, in this scene there is a short and convincing episode when the villain Adolfo arrives, intent on capturing Estrella. It is a pity he did not take quicker advantage of having her to himself, for his music does illustrate some villainous intent, and is correspondingly exciting. The audience is prepared for action. But he goes on too long, indeed long enough for the hero Alfonso to rush in to his beloved's rescue, and to defeat the villain in a fight. Finally, everything is sorted out and the finale begins and ends with a hearty Singspiel-type chorus in the style of Weigl.

Perhaps I have been too hard on this opera, which Schubert himself thought his best work for the stage. I have not seriously criticized the music – and much of this is very fine – but I have tried to indicate the ineptitude of the libretto, and Schubert's lack of theatrical understanding, especially of dramatic timing and characterization. Most of the successful composers of opera have played an important, active and interested part in the first productions of their works, often selecting and making demands on producers, singers and designers. But there are no records of Schubert attending any rehearsals of his several works performed at the Kärntnertor-Theater or the Theater an der Wien, and if he did, it seems unlikely that the young and inexperienced composer was given any say in the productions. He had certain singers in mind when he composed some of his works, notably Michael Vogl as the twin brothers in *Die Zwillingsbrüder* and as Troila in *Alfonso und Estrella,* and possibly Anna Milder-Hauptmann as Estrella in the latter opera, but this is probably as far as his practical involvement went. (In fact neither Vogl nor Milder-Hauptmann thought very much of *Alfonso* as theatre music, and as they were both highly experienced and fine singers of opera, we cannot be surprised at their decided reservations about the theatrical qualities and possibilities of *Alfonso und Estrella,* or their lack of enthusiasm to perform it.) Weber, on the other hand, was a man of the theatre, born and bred to it, with a natural feeling for the stage, and he was active in the productions of his new operatic works. It is interesting to compare the operatic successes and failures of these contemporaries. With *Alfonso und Estrella* Schubert composed probably the first complete German opera without spoken dialogue, thus anticipating by a year or two Weber's *Euryanthe. Alfonso* was written shortly after Weber had completed *Der Freischütz*, but before the first Viennese performance, which Schubert attended, on 3 November 1821. The two operas have much is common in elements drawn from the late-eighteenth-century Singspiel. Each has a rural background, a pure and innocent heroine, a worthless villain who finally falls into his own trap, and a noble and magnanimous prince or king as ruler. To these attributes Schubert added some elements characteristic of contemporary Italian operas, such as battles and conspirators' scenes. Weber, on the other hand, contributed magical elements with satanic influences (as Schubert had in his melodrama *Die Zauberharfe*), both elements associated with German Romantic opera, with whose initiation he is usually credited. Weber's success lies in the excitement aroused by the precariously poised battle between the forces of good and evil, and by the very real characters enacting the drama. The action and the characters in Schubert's opera, conversely, fail to capture our imagination, and we tend to remain uninvolved: we may be moved frequently by the beauty and charm of the music, but any excitement which is built up is only too quickly dissipated in long-winded (sung) conversations. For the most part, *Alfonso* is not a good theatrical work.

Fierrabras

Schubert's only other completed grand opera, *Fierrabras* (D 796), written between 23 May and 2 October 1823, presents a very different picture from that of *Alfonso.* It was commissioned as a German opera to be written by a native Viennese librettist and composer for the Kärntnertor-Theater, whose management had become increasingly embarrassed by the superabundance of works by foreign composers in the repertory. *Fierrabras* is a 'heroic–romantic' opera, like *Euryanthe*, written at about the same time and performed at the Kärntnertor-Theater on 25 October 1823. The libretto of *Fierrabras*, written as an opera with spoken dialogue (unlike *Alfonso*), was by Josef Kupelwieser, elder brother of Schubert's friend, the artist Leopold, and at that time (1821-3) secretary at the Court Opera. The first performance was to have taken place at the end of 1823, but in fact the opera never was performed. Perhaps the failure of *Euryanthe* was partly responsible for this: the management must have been loath to risk another German grand opera of a similar kind so soon after the failure of Weber's work.[7] At the Kärntnertor-Theater there were internal managerial disruptions, and Kupelwieser resigned from his position there on 9 October. This was only a week or two after Schubert had completed the composition of the opera. The author's resignation was evidently in protest against the arrogance of the Italian singers who had replaced

7 To the best of my knowledge the only fully staged production of *Fierrabras* was in 1897 at the Grossherzögliches Hoftheater in Karlsruhe.

the dismissed German singers, including Schubert's friend and patron, the distinguished baritone Michael Vogl. This theatre and the Theater an der Wien were then under the same management, and both were in financial difficulties. The first performance of *Fierrabras*, which (as will be seen) would have been an expensive opera to stage, was postponed repeatedly until finally, by March 1824, Schubert had given up all hope. He was probably so disheartened after coming so near to seeing a major work of his own on the stage that he never completed any other theatrical composition except for the incidental music to *Rosamunde*, D 797. And he never received a fee for *Fierrabras,* despite the fact that it had been commissioned by the theatre.

The artistic significance of the dates of composition of the opera will be discussed later, but it is interesting to note at this point that Schubert had carefully dated and autographed the beginning and end of each act.

Act I: 25 May – 30 May 1823
Act II: 31 May – 5 June 1823
Act III: 7 June – 26 September 1823

The discrepancy between the time taken to write the first two acts and the last is immediately striking. Schubert was ill during this year, and went to convalesce during the summer in Upper Austria. Thus the writing of the third act was extended over several months, whereas each of the first acts was written in a mere six days. In a letter to Schober of 14 August, Schubert wrote from Steyr: 'Here I live very simply in every respect, go for walks regularly, work much at my opera and read Walter Scott.'[8] With what obsession and enthusiasm he must have worked to complete each of the earlier acts in less than a week!

At a time when originality in operatic texts was very rare indeed, the story of this opera combines the old French romance *Fierabrás* (the name means 'boaster' or 'swaggerer' in Spanish) and the legend of Eginhard and Emma. The first is an imaginative story of Charlemagne's wars in the Pyrenees against the heathen Saracens and their king's son, Fierabrás; and the second is the story of Charlemagne's minstrel knight, Eginhard, and how he wins the emperor's consent to the hand in marriage of his daughter, Emma. Here was good theatrical material with interesting and varied characters and exciting action, and Schubert had a librettist who, although no genius, knew what was needed for a good operatic text. The opera is dramatic and spectacular, and contains many of the elements of successful operas of the later nineteenth century. The German Romantic feeling, which found its definitive expression in Wagner, is strong: and the influence of the realistic Italian operas of Rossini is also present.

It has been claimed that Weber's *Euryanthe* contains some of this composer's finest operatic music, and yet it has been condemned as a whole. The grandeur of the conception of much of the music cannot be denied, and the

8 O. E. Deutsch, *Schubert. A Documentary Biography* (London, 1946), p. 286.

work has been acclaimed a landmark in the history of German Romantic opera between *Der Freischütz* and *Lohengrin.* To my mind, *Fierrabras* should be coupled with *Euryanthe* in this context although, lacking a contemporary production, it had no influence on the development of Romantic opera. Both works were based on medieval French romances, and both were trying to incorporate within a larger format the elements of German operatic Romanticism inherited from the earlier Singspiele. In both operas there are powerful arias and scenas on a large scale, and the chorus is used to great effect in both musical and dramatic senses. Each composer used reminiscence-motifs to create unity in his opera, and used themes from the main body of the work in the overture. *Euryanthe* contains no spoken dialogue, while Schubert reverted from the continuous song of *Alfonso* to the use of the spoken word between musical numbers in *Fierrabras.* However, despite the German-ness of much of the conception, the Austrian Schubert was closer to the Italian realism of Rossini than the German Weber, who incorporated a magic ring, a restless spectre and a mysterious serpent in his *Euryanthe*, thus combining elements of magic and chivalry in the manner of the German Romantics. In Schubert's *Fierrabras* there is no room for the supernatural, and the forces of good have to defeat the forces of evil by natural means. But both these operas reflect in no uncertain terms the transition between the old and new nineteenth-century German theatre music, and indeed they deserve to be heard and seen in their entirety.

For the sake of clarity in the argument, it is necessary at this point to summarize the rather complicated plot of *Fierrabras.*

Act I takes place at the court of King Karl (Charlemagne), whose daughter, Emma, and the minstrel knight, Eginhard, have fallen in love, but with little hope. The Frankish knights, led by their captain, Roland, return victorious from battle with the Moors, bringing prisoners who include Fierrabras, the son of the Moorish Prince Boland. The king now hopes for peace, and determines on sending a deputation to Boland's camp to negotiate the end of war, on condition that the Moors become Christians. Meanwhile, the prisoners are freed, not yet to return to their homeland, but to wander as they will in France. Only proud Fierrabras angers the king by refusing to bow before him or to co-operate; but Roland pleads for him, describing his former enemy's great heroism in the battle that has just taken place. The scene ends with general pomp and rejoicing. Left alone with Roland, Fierrabras confesses that four years previously he was in Rome where not only were his sympathies for Christianity aroused, but he also fell in love with a girl whom he now recognizes as the king's daughter, Emma. Roland also learns that the girl with whom he fell in love at the same time was Fierrabras's sister, Florinda, who also loves him. The two determine to do all they can to help each other. That evening Emma slips away from the court, and welcomes her lover, Eginhard, to her rooms. Fierrabras overhears their protestations of love (during a balcony scene) with horror, but rather than betray them to the king, he renounces his own claim to Emma's affections and helps to cover up the lovers' illicit meeting. In doing this, he is accused by the furious king of attempting to seduce Emma, and Eginhard is commanded to take the Moor to the dungeons – to the dismay of both Emma and Eginhard, who react with stupefied silence. The peace deputation, including Roland and Eginhard, prepares to depart for the Moorish camp.

In Act II, Eginhard is left on watch at the frontier as the other Frankish knights head for Boland's court. He is surprised and overpowered by a troop of Moorish soldiers, who escort him as a prisoner back to Boland's camp. When the Moorish prince hears that his son, Fierrabras, has been betrayed by Eginhard and is now imprisoned in King Karl's dungeons, Eginhard is condemned. The other knights arrive and present their terms for peace, announcing that Fierrabras has already accepted the Christian faith. Prince Boland is furious, and condemns all the Frankish knights to imprisonment in a tower until such time as he is ready to execute them. Meanwhile, his daughter, Florinda, who has already admitted her love for Roland to her companion Maragond, sees and is immediately in turn recognized by her lover. She determines to help the Frankish knights, fights her way into the tower and opens the door to an armoury where they find weapons. Roland and Eginhard attempt to fight their way out to freedom in order to return to France to get assistance to free their comrades, but only Eginhard succeeds. Roland is overpowered.

In Act III, Eginhard arrives back at King Karl's court to find that Emma has already confessed to her father her own and Eginhard's love, and their guilt over Fierrabras's undeserved imprisonment. The angry king has released Fierrabras and rebuked his daughter. Eginhard is ordered to lead the rescuing force, which Fierrabras begs to be allowed to join. Back at Prince Boland's castle, they arrive just in time to rescue Florinda, Roland and the other knights from immediate death. All ends happily, with the two pairs of lovers united and everyone forgiven. For his reward, Fierrabras chooses to fight under the king's flag.

Fierrabras is far superior in theatrical terms to *Alfonso und Estrella*. Of course it would be an expensive opera to produce, owing to the large cast of soloists and chorus, and to the elaborate scenic demands especially of Acts II and III; but its plot is well conceived, and there is much dramatic tension and characterization in the text and in the music. When he had a good libretto, Schubert could write theatrically. The first act is colourful and varied, with victorious armies and miserable prisoners, charming spinning-girls, an alternately magnanimous and outraged noble monarch, and the hero Fierrabras becoming deeply entangled in events. The second act is full of action, always dramatically powerful, often compelling, and it contains some fine musical characterization. The third act is adequate – at times much more, at times rather less. The principal roles, with one exception, are particularly well defined and contrasted: the gentle, fallible, lyrical pair of lovers Emma and Eginhard (lyric soprano and tenor) contrast with the fiery, romantic Moorish Florinda (dramatic soprano) and her dignified if duller lover, the Frankish knight Roland (baritone). The noble King Karl (bass) is a typical Romantic father and monarch (as was Troila in *Alfonso*) and his counterpart is the villainous Moor, Prince Boland (also bass). The title role is the exception. It is written for a dramatic tenor of some heroic pretensions, but here Kupelwieser and Schubert were less successful than with the other leading characters. Fierrabras has two sides to his personality – the proud prince and impetuous Moorish general, and the sympathetic friend and generous lover. (He is also in love with Emma, but does not pursue his suit on seeing the depth of mutual affection between her and Eginhard.) His refusal to bow before King Karl, when first led in as a captive with the other prisoners, shows his royal pride: his offer to fight in the Frankish army against his own people, albeit to rescue Roland and his friends, smacks of disloyalty and treachery. True, in the heat of this battle, during which his sister, Florinda, is saved, Fierrabras rescues his father from Eginhard's sword, but overall the character does not come out sufficiently strongly, and he is certainly not the braggart pictured in the original French romance. At his first appearance, in Act I, his outstanding bravery in battle and his skill as a fighter are described by Roland, and at the end of the opera his final wish expressed to the king, as his reward for his services, is to fight under the latter's flag; but, except for the brief rescue scene in Boland's camp, for the rest of the opera he remains very quiet, unwarlike and inactive. Kupelwieser and Schubert were more successful with Florinda, and she is admirably depicted as a brave and fiery young woman who is not above the occasional swoon expected of many a nineteenth-century heroine.

Schubert's part in the characterization of the principal roles in this opera is on the whole impressive. For example, the lyrical duets and ensembles for the young lovers, Emma and Eginhard, are ideally charming, and contrast finely with the brilliant music of the Moorish Princess Florinda. Both in her fine Aria no. 13, in Act II, and in the following melodramas her music illustrates a brave, impetuous and determined character. Her father, Prince Boland, is the villain of the piece, and his power and vigour are depicted in some strong and highly chromatic music. King Karl's music is more noble and dignified, and focuses attention on him at the centre of the stage. With no help from the libretto, Schubert was less successful with Fierrabras's music. True, he gave the tenor a fine recitative and aria to sing in the finale of Act I, composed with a somewhat Mozartian flavour but with some pure Schubertian orchestration and ornamentation. The aria is written in two sections, both of which are then repeated: the first, with a soft murmuring accompaniment, depicts the thoughtful lover; the second, strongly rhythmic and loud and vigorous, depicts the fighter. Schubert tried to underline his hero's importance by using a motif, or variation of it, at every appearance or mention of Fierrabras throughout the opera – this is an easily recognizable rhythmic figure (Ex. 1). On two

Ex. 1

occasions (in the first-act finale and in Act III) the hero joins the young lovers, Emma and Eginhard, in a trio. In each of these trios Schubert was at pains to make Fierrabras's music dominate that of the other two, and in this he was successful: in the second trio Fierrabras sings the melody while the lovers sing in simple harmony above it. However, these instances do not add up to total musical characterization, and although the main fault lies with the libretto, some of the hero's music is too static, insufficiently heroic.

The role of the chorus in *Fierrabras* is very important, and we find in it some strong manifestations of German Romanticism. Each act begins, as in the old Singspiele, with an innocent chorus of the 'good' characters. The first is a delightful spinning-chorus of girls weaving love-tokens for the returning soldiers, anticipating a similar scene in Wagner's *Der fliegende Holländer.* The chorus is written in the German folk-song style, clearly an expanded version of the simple Singspiel chorus, but not yet fully developed into the dimensions of grand opera. Later in the same act the girls present a crown of flowers to King Karl in a manner reminiscent of the first act of *Alfonso und Estrella* and some of Schubert's own early Singspiele; but the music is now more sophisticated, with some enchanting accompanying figures of rhythmic complexity in the orchestra, and the whole is incorporated in an extended, continuous operatic scene. Act II, like Act I, opens with a folk-song-like 'Lied mit Chor' in the Singspiel style, for the Frankish knights. On this occasion Eginhard is supposed to be accompanying himself in troubadour fashion ('nach Art der Troubadours' as the text demands) on a harp, and Schubert composed music with a charming, dancing lilt to it as the knights prepare with confidence to leave France for the uncertainties and dangers of the enemy court. One of the finest choruses (no. 11) is set at the Moorish court; in it the lively expression of Moorish patriotism balances well with similar patriotic scenes for King Karl and his court, especially in the first act (ensembles nos. 3 and 4), and later the *a cappella* chorus 'O theures Vaterland' (no. 14).

During the second and third decades of the nineteenth century both Schubert and Weber were experimenting in their German operas with the use of a recurring motif in a manner which was to reach perfection, later in the century, as the leitmotif in Wagner's operas. The most outstanding instance of the use of motif in Fierrabras has already been quoted (Ex. 1). Another example of a recurring theme is the march which is played at every entrance or exit of King Karl and his court. I have argued elsewhere[9] that Schubert had developed his use of motif with considerable skill in his impressive melodrama *Die Zauberharfe* (D 644) of 1820, and he was undoubtedly drawing on this experience in *Fierrabras*.

In 1823 Schubert worked on three stage pieces. These were *Die Verschworenen* (spring), sketches for another opera, *Rüdiger* (May), based on the second part of the Nibelungen saga, and *Fierrabras*. Thus, in each of his operas of 1823, Schubert was concerned with medieval chivalry. The mood of each opera was entirely different: the first was comic, the second in the romantic and supernatural vein, the last more realistic and dramatic. In most respects the last contains the best theatre music. Being on a serious subject treated realistically, this opera readily arouses our sympathies. Since completing *Die Zauberharfe*, Schubert had composed the extensive sketches of *Sakuntala* (D 701) and the grand opera *Alfonso und Estrella*, each an ambitious dramatic work for the theatre. He had also composed two masterpieces, the 'Quartettsatz' (D 703) and the 'Unfinished' Symphony (D 759), and in August 1821 sketched the E major Symphony (D 729). He was now a mature composer who could draw on his own past experiences as well as develop to his own ends the forms and styles which he had inherited. The Italianate influence on the music of *Fierrabras* is not as great as we might expect, although it is evident in some of the ensembles where Schubert moved on from the simple Singspiel style to one perhaps closer to Mozart in his Italian operas than to Rossini. The voices no longer move in parallel thirds or sixths, or in straight imitation, but are blended into something grander and richer in extended operatic writing. We find this in the exciting trio section of the Finale to Act I, in the Quintet no. 10 in Act II (in which the bass trombone doubles with cellos and basses for much of the time), and in Act III in the Quartet no. 19 and the final section of the Ensemble no. 22. The dramatic element so sadly lacking in *Alfonso* is very much present in this opera, both in the action and in human relationships. King Karl remains the same dignified figure throughout, but the characters of Eginhard and Fierrabras, along with Florinda, are developed sufficiently for the audience to become involved in their fates. For dramatic action the first- and second-act finales are particularly memorable. In this context, Schubert's use of melodrama must be mentioned, remembering that this was an accepted form in early-nineteenth-century theatre, and one which was often used at the most dramatic moments in serious musical theatre, as for example in *Der Freischütz*. The vocal demands on Florinda are considerable in this opera, but when in addition she is required

9 See my paper 'Schubert's Music for the Theatre', *Proceedings of the Royal Musical Association*, XCIII (1967), pp. 51-66.

to describe in speech the attempted escape of Eginhard and her lover, Roland, and this above the full orchestra, then one realizes that hers is no easy role: its interpreter should be a fine actress as well as singer. There are other melodramatic scenes in which the Frankish knights declaim, and each presents some problems; but none is as great as that for the princess at the end of Act II. Schubert composed these melodramas skilfully, if demandingly, benefiting from his experience in this form in the large-scale *Die Zauberharfe.*

There are moments when the opera sags somewhat. In the first-act finale, for example, the soldiers sent by King Karl to search for his daughter take too long to arrive. The first scene in the second act, when the Frankish soldiers return to aid Eginhard after he has blown his horn for help, is misconceived and untidy; groups of soldiers of opposing factions move on and off the stage in an ill-managed manner and to rather mediocre music. The opening of the otherwise impressive second-act finale could be faulted similarly for an uninteresting four-square 'farewell and good luck' ensemble which adds little to the drama: the words are repeated too often, thus spinning out a scene which would have been better dismissed quickly with a few well-chosen phrases rather than with a full ensemble. Yet the most important failure occurs in the last act, which Schubert completed under some pressure several months after the first two acts were dashed off, each in the space of a few days. For once, too much happens far too quickly – an unwonted fault in a Schubert opera. The Frankish soldiers, led by Eginhard and Fierrabras, hurry in and are just in time to rescue their companions and Florinda from death. At this point King Karl marches in, apparently accompanied by his daughter and courtiers. Should he not first have run in with soldiers to confirm the well-being of his knights, and left the womenfolk at a safe distance behind? All ends are agreeably tied up, the two sides united, like the two pairs of lovers, and all this in the space of a few minutes of fairly effective music. This is not an ideal end to a grand opera: the work in its entirety is unbalanced by the speed at which a happy conclusion is achieved in the last scene. It seems probable that the composer finished the opera in too much of a rush, and this resulted both in the imbalance and also in a somewhat lower standard of music in Act III. Sections of nos. 19 and 20 (both of which, incidentally, Schubert wrote out in his manuscript a tone higher than he wanted, indicating in the score that they should be transposed down) and the end of no. 21 are decidedly inferior to some of the best music in the opera.

It is worth noting that Schubert began the composition of *Die schöne Müllerin* in August 1823 before he had completed *Fierrabras*, and there are two pointers in the opera to the coincidence of the compositions. The first occurs in the second act when the Frankish emissaries, led by Roland, return to look for Eginhard to a 6/8 *allegro molto vivace* movement reminiscent of 'Der Jäger' (Ex. 2). The second occurs in the Aria and Chorus no. 21, in which Florinda longs to die with her lover, Roland, whom she believes to be already

Ex. 2 (a) *Fierrabras*

Allegro molto vivace
Chorus: Wir fol-gen den Spu-ren im has-ti-gen Lauf, in Thä-lern und Flu-ren wir fin-den ihn auf.

(b) 'Der Jäger'

Geschwind
Was sucht denn der Jä-ger am Mühl-bach hier? Bleib, trot-zi-ger Jä-ger, in dei-nem Re-vier!

Ex. 3 (a) *Fierrabras*

Andante con moto
Florinda: Des Jam-mers her-be Qua-len er-fül-len die-ses Herz,
pp

(b) 'Des Baches Wiegenlied'

Mässig
Gu-te Ruh, gu-te Ruh! tu die Au-gen zu! gu-te Ruh, gu-te Ruh! tu die Au-gen zu!
p

dead, and is comforted by the Frankish knights. There are definite suggestions in the textures of the melody and gentle, rocking accompaniment of the final song of *Die schöne Müllerin*, 'Des Baches Wiegenlied', when the brook accepts the unhappy young lover and comforts him (Ex. 3). Surely Schubert was influenced by his operatic music in writing this final song of the cycle (which was probably not completed until March 1824). In the opera Florinda's aria comes as a wonderful and beautiful release from the tension built up in previous scenes; and in *Die schöne Müllerin* the cradle-song provides a miraculous, soothing end for the broken-hearted young lover.

Conclusion

At the beginning of this study I claimed that Schubert failed in most of his theatre works on two counts: namely, that he lacked true understanding of theatricality, and that he lived at a time when German composers and librettists were necessarily experimenting in their efforts to create a new kind of opera. The creators' tasks were formidable: they had to develop an acceptable operatic form and style, and at the same time choose subjects capable of passing the ludicrously crippling official censorship: they then had to persuade impoverished theatres to risk performing their works, and win the enthusiasm of audiences on a more serious level than the frivolous one they seemed to prefer. Schubert's limited success in the theatre during his lifetime was to a great extent due to the state of the theatres and the preferences of theatrical audiences of that time. His operatic achievement, on the other hand, depended more on the professional expertise of his librettists than on the particular style of the actual librettos. He had little critical idea of what was needed, and if his text was poor and undramatic he followed it slavishly to the last. The results could be correspondingly feeble. If the text was good, he followed it equally faithfully, and in responding to the drama he frequently succeeded in creating some fine theatre music. Those works in which he collaborated with his intimate friends, such as *Alfonso und Estrella*, could be nearly disastrous from a dramatic viewpoint, even though much of the music is fine. Those works which were commissioned, like *Fierrabras*, were generally the most successful, as their librettos were by professional writers for the theatre. Basically, the *Fierrabras* text is good, imaginative and carefully planned, and Schubert showed that he could respond to the drama of such a libretto in a way that he had promised already some eight years earlier in the remarkably accomplished finales and ensembles of *Die Freunde von Salamanka*, altogether a very interesting work. *Fierrabras* is no disaster. It is the fascinating and ambitious work of a mature composer writing, through no fault of his own, in an incompletely formed idiom. The demands of casting, scenery and staging are very considerable, and this is therefore no piece for an amateur or low-budget production; but if it were superbly performed and produced, Schubert's *Fierrabras* might be vindicated.

In this study only a few of Schubert's works for the theatre have been examined, and attention has been confined to completed scores. Perhaps careful study of his last theatre score, the unfinished sketches of *Der Graf von Gleichen*, written to a libretto by his dramatist friend Bauernfeld, would have been revealing.[10] I do not believe that it would have altered my judgements or conclusions. Schubert was not a great composer of opera owing to his inability to grasp the essentials of good theatrical drama, and, allied to this, his uncritical attitude to his librettos. He was also the victim of circumstances in that he was writing at a period which produced little stage music of lasting appeal. *Fierrabras*, his final completed opera, is a very considerable achievement. In it, with its mixture of medieval legend, romance and high moral tone, he was moving towards the opera of the future. But he lacked the literary flair and the intellectual powers and training which might have led him to discover the further dimensions of expression, apart from mere story-telling and description, which great opera must contain. Yet Schubert's works for the theatre at their best are fine, movingly expressive and entertaining, and they do not deserve to be overlooked.

10 I was not able to examine the manuscript score of this unpublished opera as it was reserved by a Viennese librarian for his own use.

Schubert and the melodrama

PETER BRANSCOMBE

The links between music and the theatre were particularly close in Vienna in the late eighteenth and early nineteenth centuries. In his autobiography Franz Grillparzer discusses his family's amateur theatricals, and indicates the interest their performances aroused because of the accompanying free keyboard extemporizations of their music teacher, Johann Mederitsch-Gallus: 'These improvisations, to which, when the action became more significant, he even added melodramatic accompaniments, obtained for our absurdities a certain celebrity . . .'[1] This is only one of the more familiar instances of music being used to accompany amateur dramatics in Austria; others range from the full-scale performances of Eberl's melodrama *Pyramus und Thisbe* and Benda's *Medea* given at Count Franz von Stockhammer's private theatre at Hütteldorf[2] to dramatic tableaux at Eisenstadt for which on occasion Haydn provided organ accompaniment.[3]

At the end of the eighteenth century, melodrama was primarily an adjunct of the professional musical theatre; in the course of the nineteenth century and in the early years of the twentieth, it tended to become a feature of salon music-making, with piano accompaniment. The purpose of this article, to study Schubert's examples of and connexions with melodrama, will require a consideration of both the public and the domestic aspects of melodrama, though the emphasis will be laid firmly upon melodrama in the theatre.

The use of the spoken voice against a musical accompaniment is probably almost as old as the use of music in drama and worship, but it is generally accepted that in its modern application the form was 'invented' by Jean-Jacques Rousseau, with his *Pygmalion* (subtitled 'scène lyrique'). The text was probably written in 1762, though it was Easter 1770 before Rousseau invited Horace Coignet to set it to music; two numbers were composed by the poet himself. The libretto, which was more influential than the music, was published in at least three editions in 1771; further French printings, and

1 F. Grillparzer, *Selbstbiographie* in *Sämtliche Werke*, 4 vols., ed. P. Frank and K. Pörnbacher (Munich, 1965), vol. 4, p. 29.

2 *Theater-Kalender, auf das Jahr 1793* (Gotha), pp. 73 and 76.

3 *Journal of a Nobleman at Vienna, during the Congress*, 2 vols. (London, 1831), vol. 2, pp. 105-6.

translations into foreign languages, were not slow to follow. *Pygmalion* may have been given in Paris in 1772; certainly from 1775 onwards it enjoyed great popularity for some three decades. Baron Melchior von Grimm wrote of the 'effet surprenant'[4] that the work made. It was soon imitated, and the libretto was made the model for treatment of the same story by various German composers. It is clear from Rousseau's theoretical reflections on the relationship between the French language and music that his views on recitative run parallel to his experiments with melodrama, though the exact chronology is difficult to establish.

Rousseau's own achievement in the melodrama was modest – only two of the twenty-six *ritournelles* in the score of *Pygmalion* are by him, and influential as the libretto was, it differed in no essential feature from a short spoken play. But his realization of the value of musical accompaniment to preface and accompany the speaking voice was of a significance that transcended the characteristics of the French language which he had in mind. It is hardly going too far to say that his views on the virtues of increasing the effect of words and music by presenting them successively rather than simultaneously, as expounded in 'Fragments d'observations sur l'Alceste italien de M. le Chevalier Gluck',[5] drawing on the practical experience which he and Coignet had gained from their collaboration on *Pygmalion,* hold good for the entire later development of the genre.

The early history of melodrama in German lands is mainly concerned with the works of Georg Benda. However, his examples were preceded by Franz Aspelmayr's setting of Rousseau's *Pygmalion* text, which was given at the Court Theatre, Vienna, as early as February 1772;[6] and Anton Schweitzer's setting of the same story (often considered to be the earliest German melodrama) was heard at Weimar later in 1772. By the time that Benda's *Pygmalion* was staged in 1779, his most celebrated melodramas, *Ariadne auf Naxos* and *Medea* (both first performed at Gotha in 1775), had begun their triumphal progress through Europe's theatres. 1775 also witnessed the première of Benda's only other melodrama of importance, *Theone*. This work, later revised and renamed *Almansor und Nadine*, was comparatively unsuccessful; its interest lies mainly in the fact that in it Benda used the singing voice (solo and chorus) in addition to the speaking voice – an early example of the kind of mixed-medium work we shall examine later with Schubert's *Die Zauberharfe*.

Many German composers took up the example of Benda's melodramas –

4 *Correspondance littéraire, philosophique et critique par Grimm, Diderot, Raynal, Meister, etc.*, 16 vols., ed. M. Tourneux, vol. 11 (Paris, 1879), p. 139.

5 *Oeuvres complètes de J. J. Rousseau*, 27 vols., ed. P. R. Auguis, vol. 15 (Paris, 1825), pp. 304-9 (here especially pp. 307-8).

6 The libretto survives: *Pygmalion de M. J.-J. Rousseau, scène lyrique exécutée sur le Théâtre Impérial de Vienne avec la musique du Sieur Aspelmayer* (Vienna: Kurzböck, 1772).

among them Neefe, Reichardt, Zumsteeg and a number of the Mannheim musicians. We shall concentrate, however, on the rise of the melodrama in Vienna. The Viennese melodrama took many different forms, of both a public and a domestic nature, and on a large and a small scale. It is noteworthy that here, as in other forms of music, the Viennese showed a marked disinclination to welcome north or central German works. Though there had been earlier attempts to stage Hiller Singspiele in Vienna, with the benefit of hindsight we may see 1776 as the crucial year in the attempt to acclimatize north German stage works in the Austrian capital; during 1776 at least three Singspiele by Hiller and one each by Benda, Holly and Baumgarten were staged, yet none of them gained any popularity.[7] Benda alone of musicians from the north made a strong and lasting impact on the Viennese scene. His *Pygmalion* made only a belated and brief appearance in Vienna, with two performances in the Kärntnertor-Theater in June 1801 – but he had established his fame there as elsewhere with *Medea* (performed forty-four times in the court theatres between 5 December 1788 and 1816, and given in at least three other theatres; a parody version by Paul Wranitzky survives[8]) and *Ariadne auf Naxos.* The latter was performed in the Bauernfeindscher Saal in the Josefstadt suburb in 1779,[9] and on 4 January 1780 it received the first of thirty-four performances in the Burgtheater. It too was given in three other Viennese theatres and suffered at least three parodies: *Ariadne auf Naxos,* 'eine musikalische Laune', with text and music by Friedrich Satzenhofen, had the rare distinction of having both its words and its music published;[10] on 27 October 1803 Perinet's *Ariadne auf Naxos travestirt,* which was written to accommodate Satzenhofen's music, and also pillaged his text, was performed in the Theater in der Leopoldstadt; and Kotzebue's 'tragi-komisches Triodrama' *Ariadne auf Naxos* was published in Vienna in 1804. The continued familiarity of Benda's score is indicated by Kotzebue's introductory note: 'If this travesty is to achieve its entire intended comic effect, someone must play Benda's solemn music to it at the piano.'[11]

Benda dominated the Viennese scene in melodrama from the early 1780s

7 Details of repertory are derived mainly from the following sources: A. Loewenberg, *Annals of Opera 1597-1940*, 2nd edn, repr. (New York, 1970); A. Bauer, *Opern und Operetten in Wien* (Graz and Cologne, 1955); idem, *150 Jahre Theater an der Wien* (Zurich, Leipzig and Vienna, 1952); F. Hadamowsky, *Das Theater in der Wiener Leopoldstadt 1781-1860* (Vienna, 1934); idem, *Die Wiener Hoftheater (Staatstheater)*, part 1, *1776-1810* (Vienna, 1966), and part 2, *Die Wiener Hofoper (Staatsoper) 1811-1974* (Vienna, 1975).

8 Vienna, Österreichische Nationalbibliothek, Musiksammlung, S.m. 10230, 1 and 2; Archiv der Gesellschaft der Musikfreunde, IV, 26383.

9 E. K. Blümml and G. Gugitz, *Alt-Wiener Thespiskarren* (Vienna, 1925), pp. 281 and 483-90.

10 The text was published by J. G. Binz in 1799, and a copy of the vocal score survives in the Musiksammlung of the Nationalbibliothek, M.s. 38951, dated 1801.

11 A. von Kotzebue, *Theater*, vol. 24 (Prague, 1819), p. 234.

until well into the nineteenth century. But numerous native or naturalized Austrian composers also wrote melodramatic works – among them Mozart, the first great composer to take up melodrama.[12] Although nothing survives of the full-length *Semiramis* (K 315e, begun November 1778) that he was widely reported to be working on with Gemmingen, there are two striking instances in the incomplete *Zaide* (K 336b, 1779-80), and one in the incidental music to *Thamos, König in Ägypten* (K 336a, 1779). Mozart did not use melodrama in the works written for Vienna, however, and it is very unlikely that his early works including melodramas were known there in Schubert's day. By then too the full-length melodramas written with limited popular success by such composers as Maria Theresia von Paradies, Winter and Eberl had disappeared from the repertory.

The *loci classici* of melodrama are for us the dungeon scene in Act II of *Fidelio* and the Wolf's Glen scene in *Der Freischütz.* However, in the summer of 1820, when Schubert was writing *Die Zauberharfe, Der Freischütz* was still a year away from its Berlin première, and *Fidelio* had slipped from the repertory of the Kärntnertor-Theater a year before, after some sixty performances in five years. Schubert knew *Fidelio* well, but he is unlikely to have known Beethoven's other works which include melodramas. He may have attended one of the performances of Goethe's *Egmont* (first performed at the court theatres in May 1810), the penultimate number in Beethoven's score for which is a melodrama, but he probably knew nothing of the scores Beethoven wrote for Kotzebue's festival plays written for Pest in 1811, *Die Ruinen von Athen* and *König Stephan*, which contain respectively three and four melodramas, or of the Beethoven music for the projected but abandoned production of Duncker's *Leonore Prohaska* (1815) – none of these works was staged or published in Vienna until many years after Schubert's death, and they are not obviously suited to amateur performance. About Schubert's admiration for *Fidelio* we are informed by several sources – he heard it at least twice (the première of the revised version in May 1814, and the revival of November 1822); and Schindler reports that 'Shortly after Beethoven's death he [Schubert] wished to examine the manuscript of *Fidelio.*'[13]

There were numerous other German stage works with melodramas that were performed in Vienna during the years of Schubert's youth and maturity, particularly by Joseph Weigl, whom Schubert much admired. There is a simple, touching example in the middle of the last act of Weigl's *Die Schweizerfamilie*, already an established favourite at the court theatres when Schubert heard it, probably in July 1811 (see Table 1, p. 110 below). This melodrama, in which the heroine, Emmeline, expresses her confused emotions at the sight of her

12 His enthusiastic comments to his father about the Benda examples he heard may be found in his letters from Mannheim of 12 November and 3 December 1778, and from Kaisheim on 18 December 1778.

13 O. E. Deutsch, *Schubert. Memoirs by His Friends* (cited below as '*Memoirs*') (London, 1958), p. 315.

parents' cottage and her own neglected flowers in the garden, contains seventeen mainly short spoken phrases in the course of 87 bars. Weigl included very impressive melodramas at the start of both the second and third acts of *Der Bergsturz* (performed at the court theatres between 1812 and 1816), and less striking examples in *Adrian von Ostade*, which was frequently given between 1807 and 1822. Although Schubert is not recorded as having heard either *Der Bergsturz* or *Ostade*, his admiration for Weigl makes it likely that he heard as many of his works as he could. The main centres of melodramatic activity during these years, however, were the Theater an der Wien and the Theater in der Leopoldstadt; to them we shall shortly turn our attention.

By the early years of the nineteenth century the influence of Benda's melodramas was being replaced by that of examples from French operas imported from Paris. Here a firm word of caution is needed – it is dangerous to assume that all the passages spoken against a musical accompaniment in the French-language original were actually present in the German-language adaptations used in Vienna; and conversely, one should not overlook the possibility that in Vienna extra melodramatic passages may sometimes have been introduced. For instance, Cherubini's celebrated opéra-comique *Les deux journées* (variously known in German lands as *Die Tage der Gefahr*, *Graf Armand* and *Der Wasserträger*) has several melodramatic passages; the production first mounted at the Kärntnertor-Theater on 14 August 1802, with libretto adapted and translated by Treitschke, had the melodramas substantially cut and altered.[14] In the case of melodramas even more than recitatives or sung solo numbers, it was easy for adapters to omit spoken phrases to suit local conditions or performers, or to add them. Other French operas with prominent melodramas that were popular in Vienna include Grétry's *Richard Coeur-de-Lion* (first mounted in the Kärntnertor-Theater on 7 January 1788, and given 115 times in the Theater an der Wien from 1802 until 1822, and also staged in the Theater auf der Wieden and the Theater in der Josefstadt), Isouard's *Cendrillon* (which, as *Aschenbrödel*, was given 107 times in the Theater an der Wien between 2 April 1811 and 1823, and also in the Theater in der Josefstadt), Cherubini's *Médée* (which, with its brilliant use of melodrama to convey the temporary defeat of the heroine during the ceremony of Jason's second marriage (II, 6) before her spirit reasserts itself and she returns to singing, was given in the court theatres from 6 November 1802, with a new production in 1812), and Méhul's *Uthal* (performed in the court theatres in 1810-11). There are briefer passages of melodrama in a large number of French operas staged in Vienna, including Cherubini's *Lodoiska* (III, 6), Boieldieu's *Jean de Paris* (no. 12) and Paer's *Le maître de chapelle* (no. 1). Cherubini's *Faniska*, which was written for the Kärntnertor-Theater and is his only German Singspiel (in fact it was composed to an Italian text before

14 Information kindly supplied by Carolyn A. Martin on the basis of the MS score used at the performances, Nationalbibliothek, Musiksammlung, S.m. 32291.

Table 1. *Theatrical performances which Schubert is reported to have attended*

(All performances in the Kärntnertor-Theater (= KTh) unless otherwise indicated – adW = Theater an der Wien, JTh = Theater in der Josefstadt, LTh = Theater in der Leopoldstadt. Sources: *Docs* = Deutsch, *Schubert. A Documentary Biography* (London, 1946); *Mems* = Deutsch, *Schubert. Memoirs by His Friends* (London, 1958).)

Composer	*Title of work*	*Date of Schubert's reported attendance at a performance*	*Work contains melodrama*	*Source*
Weigl	*Das Waisenhaus*	*c.* 1812 and/or 12(?) Dec. 1810 (there were performances on 13 and 15 Dec. 1810, but not on 12)	No	*Docs* 20, 869; *Mems* 21
Weigl	*Die Schweizerfamilie*	8 July 1811 (?)	Yes	*Docs* 20, 870; *Mems* 21
		May 1826 (there were performances on 22, 24, 28 and 30 May, the first for more than four years)		*Mems* 129
Boieldieu	*Jean de Paris (Johann von Paris)*	*c.* 1812	Yes	*Docs* 28; *Mems* 129
Cherubini	*Médée (Medea)*	*c.* 1812	Yes	*Docs* 28; *Mems* 129
Isouard	*Cendrillon (Aschenbrödel)*	*c.* 1812, adW	Yes	*Docs* 28; *Mems* 129
Spontini	*La vestale (Die Vestalin)*	1 Oct. 1812 (?) (there were performances on 10 and 13 Oct. 1812, but not on 1)	No	*Docs* 28, 870; *Mems* 21
Mozart	*Die Zauberflöte*	*c.* 1812	No	*Docs* 28; *Mems* 129
		May 1826, adW		*Docs* 528
Gluck	*Iphigénie en Tauride (Iphigenia in Tauris)*	1813 (the only performances in 1813 were on 5 and 23 Jan.)	No	*Docs* 32, 870; *Mems* 21, 129, 305, 307
Beethoven	*Fidelio*	23 May 1814 (?)	Yes	*Docs* 42; *Mems* 299-300
		3 Nov. 1822		*Docs* 241; *Mems* 331-2 (see also *Mems* 315 for Schubert's interest in Beethoven's autograph score)

Rossini	*Tancredi (Tancred)*	? (performed in Italian at KTh in 1816–17, and in German from 1818; also given adW in summer 1817)	Yes	*Docs* 117-18
Rossini	*Otello (Othello, der Mohr von Venedig)*	April/May 1819 (*Othello*, in German, was in the repertory of KTh and adW at this time)	No	*Docs* 117-18; *Mems* 155
Schubert	*Die Zwillingsbrüder*	14 June 1820	No	*Mems* 23, 181
Wenzel Müller (text: Bäuerle)	*Aline, oder Wien in einem andern Weltteil*	19 Oct. 1822, LTh	Yes	*Docs* 236
Kreutzer	*Libussa*	early Dec. 1822	No	*Docs* 248
Weber	*Euryanthe*	25 Oct. 1823	No	*Docs* 293-4, 892; *Mems* 27, 137, 259, 366
Schubert	*Rosamunde, Fürstin von Cypern*	20 (?) Dec. 1823, adW	No	*Docs* 313
Weber	*Der Freischütz*	May 1826 (and probably first in or shortly after Nov. 1821)	Yes	*Docs* 294, 892, (1823), 528 (1826); *Mems* 27, 137, 259, 366, 377 (1823)
Wenzel Müller (text: Gleich)	*Herr Jacob [*recte *Josef] und Frau Baberl*	May 1826, LTh	No	*Docs* 528, 530
Meyerbeer	*Il crociato in Egitto*	5 Sep. 1827, Graz	No	*Docs* 664; *Mems* 68, 183-4

Sonnleithner wrote its definitive German book), contains two melodramas (nos. 9 and 15). Melodrama is rare in Italian opera, yet there are instances in Paer's *Agnese* (Act I finale) and Rossini's *Tancredi* (Arginio's reading of the fateful letter in the Act I finale), both of which were performed in Vienna.

There remain three areas of theatrical activity that cannot be disregarded in an examination of Schubert's relationship with melodrama: the biblical drama, the grand Romantic play, and the magic play (which often has a parodistic colouring). The genre of biblical drama, clearly derived from the eighteenth-century Lenten oratorio, and also from operas like Méhul's *Joseph* (1807; frequently performed in Vienna from 1809), was very popular, especially in the Theater an der Wien. Tuczek's setting of J. A. Schuster's *Samson, Richter in Israel,* staged in the Leopoldstadt on 13 August 1808 and popular for some years in several theatres, must be considered one of the earliest Viennese examples of the genre; the score[15] contains several choruses and a few sung solos, but it consists mainly of accompaniment to spoken melodramas. Another early example is *Saul, König von Israel,* adapted from the French of Caigniez by Joseph, Ritter von Seyfried, and set by his brother Ignaz. It had thirty-eight performances in the Theater an der Wien between 7 April 1810 and March 1816.[16] The eleven musical numbers include six marches, some of them choral, and three melodramas with chorus; the closing scene in the final act includes a monologue accompanied by three cellos and one double-bass. Klingemann's *Moses,* also with music by Seyfried, was given thirty-three performances between 24 April 1813 and August 1817; a sequel in the following month, *Moses' Errettung,* was a failure, as was Johann Fuss's opera *Judith, oder Die Belagerung von Bethulien* in 1814. Moses also provided the subject-matter for operas by Süssmayr and Rossini, and for *Moses in Egypten,* which with text by Gleich and music by Tuczek was given in the Theater in der Leopoldstadt in 1810 and in the Theater in der Josefstadt in 1813. Among other biblical dramas and operas that remained in the repertory for a shorter time are *Abraham* (Theater an der Wien, 1817-18) and *Noah* (Theater an der Wien, 1819-20), both with scores by Seyfried, and Weigl's opera *Baals Sturz,* produced at the Kärntnertor-Theater in 1820.

Among the large-scale Romantic plays which made use of melodrama are Klingemann's *Faust,* which with a score by Seyfried was first performed in the Theater an der Wien on 14 March 1816; it kept its place in the repertory for almost four decades. Most of its eighteen musical numbers are choral or purely instrumental, but it does include two melodramas.[17] Spohr's opera

15 Studied in the MS score preserved in the Musiksammlung of the Bayerische Staatsbibliothek, Munich, St. Th. 434.

16 Vocal score published by the Chemische Druckerey, Vienna, n.d. Copy in the Archiv der Gesellschaft der Musikfreunde, IV, 6299 R. The MS score preserved in the Musiksammlung of the Bayerische Staatsbibliothek, St. Th. 354 (Acts II and III only), consists almost entirely of melodramas, though David has sung solos.

17 Studied in the MS score in the Archiv der Musikfreunde, IV, 28525.

Faust, which also makes use of melodrama, was given at the same theatre in 1818. Other once-familiar works of a grand Romantic kind are Kotzebue's *Die kluge Frau im Walde, oder Der stumme Ritter* (Theater an der Wien, 1813), and *Adelheit von Italien, oder Der Schutzgeist* (Theater an der Wien, 1815), both with scores by Seyfried, and a large number of translations from the French of the kind of melodrama that sets more store by sensational happenings and the ultimate triumph of Good over Evil than by musical accompaniment. Examples of this kind of play are *Der Hund des Aubri de Mont Didier, oder Der Wald bei Bondy*, translated by Castelli from the French of Pixérécourt, again with music by Seyfried (it enjoyed great popularity between September 1815 and 1833), *Timur, der Tartar-Chan*, a product adapted from the English of M. G. Lewis by the brothers Seyfried (fifty-five performances in the Theater an der Wien between 14 September 1822 and July 1841), and *Ein Uhr*, also from the English of Lewis, translated by P. W. Vogel and performed in the Theater an der Wien with music by Lannoy (seventy-two performances between 21 November 1822 and September 1837). Most of the twenty-six numbers in the score of *Ein Uhr*[18] are mainly or entirely melodramatic. It is an apt comment on the highly charged emotional character of these French-style melodramas that almost all of those here mentioned were parodied in Vienna.

Although the biblical drama was not unknown in the Theater in der Leopoldstadt, as we have seen from the example of *Samson, Richter in Israel*, melodrama in that theatre tended to be used either as an accompaniment to necromantic and other supernatural happenings,[19] or – more typically, in Vienna's principal home of popular comedy – for comic purposes. Although the melodramas in Ferdinand Raimund's own plays postdate Schubert's in his stage works, it is quite possible that the latter was favourably impressed by works he saw in the Theater in der Leopoldstadt in which Raimund enjoyed some of his greatest successes as a comic actor. We know, for instance, that on 19 October 1822 Schubert attended one of the early performances of a work containing two melodramas, *Aline, oder Wien in einem andern Weltteil* (text by Bäuerle, music by Wenzel Müller),[20] and saw Raimund as Bims, one of his most celebrated assumptions; and Schubert returned to this theatre in May 1826 for a performance of *Herr Josef und Frau Baberl* (text by Gleich, music by Wenzel Müller).[21] *Aline* is the best-known example of a 'parodistisches Zauberspiel' – a convenient modern term to designate a work which began life as a parody, usually of an older operatic work, and rapidly gained in-

18 Studied in the MS score preserved in the Musiksammlung of the Bayerische Staatsbibliothek, St. Th. 433.

19 E.g. *Johann Faust, der Erfinder der Buchdruckerkunst*, 'ein romantisches Schauspiel mit Musikbegleitung', by J.F. Kringsteiner, with music by F. Volkert, given thirteen times in 1811-16.

20 See Table 1, and F. Hadamowsky, *Raimund als Schauspieler* (Vienna, 1925) = Ferdinand Raimund, *Sämtliche Werke*, vol. 5, parts 1-2, pp. 189 and 919.

21 See Table 1.

dependent existence. One of the most interesting works of this kind is Bäuerle's *Der verwunschene Prinz*, a version of the tale of Beauty and the Beast, which took as its starting-point Grétry's opera *Zémire et Azor. Der verwunschene Prinz* was first performed on 3 March 1818. It was the most successful of the sequels to *Zémire et Azor* – others were by Seyfried and Spohr, and both contained melodramas. Müller's score contains no fewer than five melodramas in Act II, two of them comic. None is very extensive, but they have an important structural role in the act, and between them have links with aria, vocal ensemble, dance, recitative and incidental music. Varied and striking as are the melodramas, the most interesting number for the Schubertian is the chorus that closes Act I. An unseen chorus sings 'Wandle auf Rosen, schöne Zemire' as the heroine walks towards her goal, guided by genii, while flowers open at her feet. The comparable 'pantomimische Scene' in Seyfried's revision of the Grétry opera was warmly praised by contemporary critics;[22] yet it is clear that this scene was even more effective in the Bäuerle/Müller work in the Theater in der Leopoldstadt.[23] This scene is far closer to the 'Chor der Genien' which closes Act II of Schubert's *Die Zauberharfe* than is the final scene of Kotzebue's *Sultan Wampun*, with its one *genius ex machina*, which Elizabeth Norman McKay, in her analysis of Schubert's stage works, considers to be the forerunner of Schubert's second finale.[24]

There is no documentary evidence that Schubert knew any of these works other than *Aline.* As can readily be seen from Table 1, he is recorded as having attended only slightly more than twenty theatrical performances in all. In addition he is reported to have known, either from attending performances on unrecorded dates or from study of the scores, some eight or ten additional operas, plus 'all Gluck's operas' and those of Handel (see Table 2). It is impossible to hazard more than a guess at the proportion of his actual visits to the theatre that the list in Table 1 represents. There is likely to be some substance behind Anselm Hüttenbrenner's reminiscence of an aspect of Schubert's daily life:

> In the evening he went to one or other of the theatres. Good actors interested him just as much as good operas. Lange, Ochsenheimer, Madame Schröder, Anschütz, Koberwein, Korn, Heurteur and so forth absorbed his attention every bit as much as the sonorous voice of a Wild, Jäger, Rauscher, Haizinger, Vogl, Weinmüller, Siboni, Tacchinardi, of a Milder, Wranitzky, Waldmüller, Schechner, Borgondio, etc.[25]

22 See e.g. *Wiener Theaterzeitung*, 13 January 1818, pp. 23-4. For further details about the relationship between the *Zemire und Azor* operas of Seyfried and Spohr, and Bäuerle's *Der verwunschene Prinz*, see P. Branscombe, 'An Old Viennese Opera Parody and a New Nestroy Manuscript', *German Life and Letters*, n.s., XXVIII (April 1975), pp. 210-17, especially p. 212.

23 See e.g. *Der Sammler*, 14 March 1818, p. 132.

24 Elizabeth McKay, 'The Stage-Works of Schubert, Considered in the Framework of Austrian Biedermeier Society', unpublished D.Phil. thesis, Oxford 1963, p. 364.

25 *Memoirs*, p. 183.

Table 2. *Theatrical works which Schubert is reported to have known, but not necessarily to have seen*

(Abbreviations as in Table 1)

Composer	*Title of work*	*Notes on performances in Vienna in Schubert's time*	*Work contains melodrama*	*Source*
Catel	*Sémiramis*	Schubert knew the opera before its revival on 22 May 1819.	No	*Docs* 117-18
Gluck	*Orfeo*; 'all Gluck's operas'	*Alceste* had four performances in the court theatres in April/May 1810; Schubert is not known to have begun going to the theatre by this time. *Iphigénie en Tauride* was performed KTh 1807–15, and 1817–19 (and adW 9 Jan. 1810). No other Gluck opera was given in Vienna during Schubert's years of theatre-going, so his knowledge of 'all Gluck's operas' must have been derived from the scores.	No	*Docs* 870; *Mems* 21, 59, 363
Handel	oratorios and operas	None of Handel's stage works was given in Vienna during Schubert's years of theatre-going.	No	*Mems* 114, 177, 180, 255
Mozart	*Don Giovanni*; *Le nozze di Figaro*; *Idomeneo*	*Don Giovanni* was in the repertory of adW from 1802 and of KTh from 1817; *Figaro* was in the repertory of KTh from 1814, and *Idomeneo* from 1819. Of Mozart's other operas, *Die Zauberflöte* was performed frequently: KTh 1812–14, 1818–23, 1827–8, adW from 1802, LTh 1810–11; *Die Entführung* was given six times adW 1803–24, *Così fan tutte* (as *Die Zauberprobe*) in 1814 (seven performances) and *Der Schauspieldirektor* in 1814 (six performances).	No	*Mems* 180, 365
Rossini	*Il barbiere di Siviglia*; *Zelmira*; *Elisabetta, regina d'Inghilterra, etc.*	*Il barbiere* was performed adW from 28 Sep. 1819, KTh from 16 Dec. 1820, JTh from 5 Nov. 1825; *Zelmira* was performed KTh from 13 April 1822; *Elisabetta* was performed adW from 3 Sep. 1818, and KTh from 30 May 1822.	No	*Mems* 11, 135, 183, 367
Salieri	*Axur, rè d'Ormus*; *Les Danaïdes*	*Les Danaïdes* was not performed in Vienna; the last performance of *Axur* was in 1805, before Schubert's theatre-going began.	No	*Docs* 868

However, if frequent, let alone daily, visits to the theatre and opera were a feature of Schubert's life, it is perhaps surprising both that more such visits are not documentarily attested and that these experiences are not reflected in a more marked and consistent development of his own skills as a musical dramatist.

Schubert used melodrama in five works,[26] the earliest dating from 1813, the last from 1826. There are two instances in *Des Teufels Lustschloss* (D 84, 1813-14), one in *Der vierjährige Posten* (D 190, 1815), five in *Die Zauberharfe* (D 644, probably summer 1820), four in *Fierrabras* (D 796, 1823); the final instance is 'Abschied' (D 829), written for a private performance on 17 February 1826.

I had hoped, when embarking on this investigation, that a clear picture would emerge, revealing that Schubert's own widely spaced attempts at melodrama were sparked off by his own experience of particular theatrical works which included melodramas. In fact no such claim can be sustained. Nor, in the absence of adequate manuscript evidence, can one even be sure in a number of cases whether in writing a particular passage as a melodrama, Schubert was following his own instinct, or obeying the behest of his librettist.[27] Schubert's melodramas will now be examined in chronological order.

It is not surprising that Schubert used melodrama in *Des Teufels Lustschloss*, his first completed opera – Kotzebue's text, with its spooky happenings in the bowels of the earth, positively encourages the composer to make use of every

26 A. Hyatt King has invited me to correct a small error in his account of Schubert's 'Music for the Stage' in *Schubert. A Symposium*, ed. Gerald Abraham (London, 1946), p. 209. In footnote 1, referring to Schubert's skilful use of bass trombone and bassoon, King cites 'the melodrama in *Adrast*'; the passage in question is in fact an accompanied recitative and aria (no. 5).

27 In the case of the two works containing melodramas for which it is reasonable to assume that Schubert was working from the printed editions then available, namely *Des Teufels Lustschloss* and *Der vierjährige Posten*, the melodramas are marked as such in the text; in the case of *Die Zauberharfe*, the libretto of which was not printed, no text survives; for the pianoforte-accompanied melodrama 'Abschied', see pp. 139-40 below. The remaining Schubert work containing melodramas, *Fierrabras*, is probably the most revealing of all. Josef Kupelwieser's libretto survives in a fair copy (Vienna, Stadt- und Landesbibliothek, Sammlung Ignaz Weinmann, 171942 Ja); it contains some alterations and indications in Schubert's hand, from which it can be seen that, for instance, Schubert reversed Kupelwieser's decision to end Act II with Florinda's cry 'Gefangen!'; Schubert concluded the act with the choral 'Mut und Besinnung schwinden', etc.

Kupelwieser used different ways of indicating melodrama. The melodramatic passage in no. 8 is preceded in the MS libretto (Act II, scene 3) by the direction '*Folgendes wird noch unterm Marsch gesprochen*'. In the Act II finale (no. 17) Kupelwieser indicates that Florinda is to speak rather than sing her passage beginning 'Schützt ihn, Ihr ew'gen Mächte!' with the words '*Melodramatisch unter Musik:*' And in Act III, scene 6 the melodrama during the 'Marcia funebre' (no. 21) is in the libretto marked '*Das Folgende unter dem Marsch gesprochen*'. (I wish to express my gratitude to Dr Eva Badura-Skoda for examining Kupelwieser's manuscript and supplying me with Xerox copies of specimen pages.)

Romantic device. Late in Act I, Ritter Oswald tries in vain to convince his timorous servant Robert that he could not have seen ghosts in the deserted castle. A brief exchange between them in spoken prose is interrupted by a short, strikingly impressive 'Trauermusik' (no. 10): Ex. 1. Schubert's *Grave* in C minor, a mere 14 bars in length, clearly takes up Kotzebue's stage direction ('*Eine dumpfe Musik lässt sich in der Ferne hören*').[28] The knight's commonsense dimissal of his servant's fears is at a musical stroke cast into a very

Ex. 1 *Des Teufels Lustschloss*

Grave
sempre pp
Cl.
Fag.
Tbn.
pp
ppp
Robert: Hört ihr, Herr Ritter, hört ihr? Oswald: (stutzt) Still, was ist das?
Robert: Nun bin ich noch betrunken? Oswald: Dumpfe Trauertöne.
Robert: Unter uns bebt der Boden. Gott steh' uns bei!

28 A. von Kotzebue, *Theater*, vol. 19 (Prague, 1819), p. 153.

different light – 'D'you hear, Sir Knight, d'you hear?' asks Robert, during the music, and Oswald, taken aback, admits his uncertainty. The scoring, for pairs of clarinets and bassoons and three trombones, is economical; in a stage performance the effect would surely be highly effective. The dynamic level is throughout *pp* or *ppp*, with crescendos, decrescendos and, especially, accents. By the end of the opera we have learnt that its subtitle 'Eine natürliche Zauber-Oper' indicates that there is a natural explanation for the seemingly supernatural events; but no. 10, which immediately precedes the Act I finale, comes at a time when melodramatic utterances punctuating the mysterious musical texture carry real conviction.

Melodrama is used again in Act II. Oswald, chained to a rock in a dismal cave, is awaiting sentence. In a two-part aria he laments his separation from his wife. A brief spoken monologue ('Oh, may you never learn, beloved wife, what a cruel fate has struck your Oswald!') leads into no. 14, 'Melodram und Marsch', a 19-bar *Andante con moto* in F major, scored for wind octet (oboes, clarinets, bassoons and horns), during which Oswald speaks: 'What do I hear? What sounds! – Do they announce my death?' There follows a *forte* enunciation of a Marcia in F, with a 'Turkish' flavour. During its first section a chorus of richly dressed maidens enters, led by a mysterious Amazon; with the orchestra briefly reduced to triangle and quiet wind or string figuration, Oswald asks: 'What is this new apparition! Do you come to mock me? – With what magic light do these rocks shimmer?' He receives no other answer than the choral dance of the maidens. After this scene the remainder of the action unfolds in dialogue and closed musical numbers; there is no further use of melodrama.

There is an often unremarked melodrama in Schubert's second completed stage work, *Der vierjährige Posten* (D 190), which was composed between 8 and 19 May 1815. It occurs during the Marcia no. 6 which leads into the soldiers' chorus 'Lustig in den Kampf'. The dialogue is a brief exchange in rhymed doggerel between Duval, the deserter whose domestic bliss is threatened by the sudden return of the army, and his wife Käthchen, for whose sake he became a deserter four years before. The march (B♭, scored for oboes, clarinets, bassoons, horns and trumpets) begins in the distance ('*Marsch in der Ferne*' is the direction in Theodor Körner's libretto, 'Marcia (*in der Ferne beginnend und immer näher kommend*)' is the entry in Schubert's score[29]). As the band approaches, Duval tells his wife he must hasten back to his sentry-post – he was not relieved when the army departed four years before, and he intends to bluff his way into being taken for an unusually resolute man of duty. The ten lines of dialogue spoken during the march are not in the strictest sense melodrama, in that the words are not set to be spoken against precise

29 Libretto: *Körners sämtliche Werke* (Stuttgart, n.d.), vol. 4, p. 137. Score: *Schuberts Werke* (cited below as '*AGA*'), Series XV, vol. 2 (Leipzig, 1888), p. 69.

musical phrases, or in gaps between musical phrases. However, the combination of spoken dialogue with otherwise independent music is a valid and useful device for the dramatic composer: in this way he can condense the action in the interests of verisimilitude and dramatic tension. The exchanges spoken during the march could perfectly well have formed part of the block of dialogue succeeding the Aria no. 5, but librettist and composer saw the advantage to be gained from having the march – the clear evidence of the army's return – break urgently in on the dialogue. Since a military march is by its nature an accompaniment to a non-musical activity, Schubert was doubly justified in combining his jaunty yet urgent tune with the hurried dialogue of the hero and heroine.

Schubert's most extensive experiment in the field of melodrama, *Die Zauberharfe* (D 644), was probably composed in the summer of 1820. The stage works of the five years which had elapsed since *Der vierjährige Posten* consist of four Singspiele and the unfinished opera *Die Bürgschaft*; but in many ways the most interesting product of these years is the unfinished 'Scenic Oratorio' *Lazarus, oder Die Feier der Auferstehung* (D 689, February 1820.)[30] As Maurice J. E. Brown has pointed out, it is in *Lazarus* that Schubert first used orchestrally the 'short, modulating figures in the orchestra' that had been a feature of a number of the longer dramatic songs,[31] and were to occur with striking effect in *Die Zauberharfe* and the later operas.

Of all Schubert's completed stage works, *Die Zauberharfe* is the least accessible – despite the fact that it was the first such work to be published in the new complete edition.[32] The greatest obstacle to performance is the loss of the libretto. Attempts to provide the score with a replacement libretto have been at best only partially successful. Moreover, the genre of 'Zauberspiel' or 'Melodram'[33] is so foreign to modern taste and experience that even a much better example than Georg von Hofmann's text would have no chance of establishing itself in the repertoire.

Schubert's score consists of: Overture; in Act I: two choruses, melodrama and finale; in Act II: chorus, melodrama, chorus, melodrama and finale; and in Act III: overture, three melodramas and finale. Apart from the chorus – variously required to represent troubadours, knights, pages, genii and spirits – the only singing role is Palmerin, who has solos in two of the choruses, and a

30 Despite the implication of the Deutsch numbers, *Lazarus* was written some months before *Die Zauberharfe*, which should properly have been given the number D 697 rather than 644.

31 M. J. E. Brown, '"Lazarus, or the Feast of Resurrection"' in *Essays on Schubert* (London, 1966), pp. 107-9 (especially p. 109). Brown cites the second subject of the first movement of the 'Unfinished' Symphony (bars 44-53) as 'the most famous example', and in his music examples 76 and 77 he quotes instances from *Lazarus*.

32 *Franz Schubert. Neue Ausgabe sämtlicher Werke*, Series II, vol. 4 (Kassel, etc., 1975), ed. Rossana Dalmonte: cited below as '*NGA*, II/4'.

33 The various appellations may be found in O. E. Deutsch, *Schubert. Die Dokumente seines Lebens* (Kassel, etc., 1964), pp. 100-9.

Romanze towards the end of the second act. All eight of the named characters, and three unnamed knights, take part in the various melodramas. Since only short spoken comments or cues survive in the score, it is impossible to reconstruct the story in any detail.

Typical of the dramatic ineptitude of the work – the bare essentials of the story may be extrapolated from the score and from contemporary reviews – is the fact that the knights, who in the opening choral scene (nos. 1 and 2) sing of their projected assault on Melinde's castle, are discovered at the beginning of the second act still drinking and singing rather than undertaking their mission – which they finally attempt in the last act. The story concerns the unhappy marriage between a tyrant, Arnulf, and his still-loving wife, Melinde, a fairy; he suspects her of having killed their son. To the man who vanquishes Melinde he will give the hand of his niece, Ida, heiress to Brabant. Melinde is implicated with Sutur, a fire-demon, and swears to him that she will never be reunited with her husband. Ida nevertheless tries to reconcile the estranged couple. When Arnulf finally yields to the arguments of Melinde, a happy ending is postponed by the reappearance of Sutur, who is finally vanquished by Palmerin's magic harp.

The six melodramatic numbers differ widely in character and size. Two of them are short and quite simple: no. 8, during which Ida sees the knights set out to attack Arnulf's castle, laments her captivity, and contrasts her loneliness with the beauty of nature; and no. 11, during which Melinde describes Ida and Arnulf in her castle as her prisoners, with Ida kneeling in vain supplication, beseeching Arnulf to be reconciled with his wife. Both these numbers are accompanied only by wind instruments – full wind ensemble (plus timpani) in the earlier, pairs of oboes, clarinets, bassoons and horns and one bass trombone in the later. In no. 8 Ida speaks in irregular iambic rhymed verse; Melinde in no. 11 speaks in prose. In neither number is the speaker required to speak through the music, though strict adherence to the musical phrasing and the rest-values would at least twice require Ida to begin or end a phrase during lightly scored, *piano* woodwind phrases. No. 8 (64 bars at *allegro moderato*) is dominated by four-bar phrases which only during and following the depiction of the chirping of the crickets and the singing of the nightingales become less rigid: Ex. 2. Melinde's no. 11 (21 bars at *andante*) is metrically more free, with a six-bar opening period followed by a series of single bars or pairs of bars separated from each other by a spoken phrase, and then a five-bar conclusion.

The other four melodramas are more ambitious and longer. No. 3, with 431 bars easily the most extensive of all, opens with the *allegro vivace* sequence of held chords familiar from the so-called *Rosamunde* Overture. The turbulent, dramatic C minor music is punctuated by phrases (in many cases all that survive are their last words, cues for the conductor) spoken by Sutur. He summons Melinde (to whom he is nevertheless subject) and attempts to persuade

Ex. 2 *Die Zauberharfe*

Ex. 2 (contd)

Fl.
Ob.
Cl. (B♭)
Fag.
Hn. (B♭)
Tpt. (B♭)
Tbn.
Timp.
fp
In Büschen tönt
der Nachtigallen
Chor,

Der süssen
Liebe darf
sich Alles
weihen,

Ex. 2 (contd)

her to renounce her love for Arnulf. So far, all but one of the spoken phrases have fallen in silent bars; when the tempo drops to *molto moderato* (bar 135) for Melinde's reflections on her relationship with Sutur, she speaks through the music (mainly quiet string tremolos). The brief *andante* (bars 162-5) with its prominent harp might be thought to be connected with Palmerin, with whom the harp has from the first been associated; but it is to Arnulf that she refers after bar 131 ('mein Feind') and after bar 273 ('Ungeheuer'). It is surely quite possible – and would make good musical sense – that Melinde does call up a vision of Palmerin (bar 155: 'Doch schauen will ich ihn, im Bilde sehen!'; bar 160: 'Erscheinen soll der Heissgeliebte!'), before commanding Sutur to bring Arnulf before her, the more so since the clarinet melody at bar 199 (*larghetto*) – Ex. 3a – recurs in Palmerin's Romanze at the beginning of no. 9 (where it is given to the oboe) – Ex. 3b – and the harp figuration of the *larghetto* has already been used in the *andante* at bars 162ff – Ex. 3c. Palmerin, furthermore, will later be revealed to be the son of Melinde and Arnulf.

Be that as it may, the gentle *larghetto* in no. 3 gives way to a powerful *allegro vivace* (bar 274), during the pauses in which Melinde swears that she will never be reconciled with her cruel husband, on pain of surrendering herself to Sutur should she ever weaken. A brief hunting flourish (bar 321) heralds the next scene; Sutur agrees to Melinde's conditions, and then the sequence of chords that opened the Overture and this melodrama suggests the disappearance of Sutur. A double-bar is then immediately followed (bar 362) by an urgent *allegro agitato ma moderato* before Ida is discovered, separated from her hunting companions, anxious and lost. She protects a dove which

Ex. 3 *Die Zauberharfe* (a)

Ex. 3 (contd)

(b)

(c)

she sees attacked by an eagle. Most of the phrases of her running commentary are spoken during rests in the music, but the depiction of the eagle's flight (accented falling quaver figuration) is declaimed against a continuous, rapidly moving musical texture. After a *fortissimo* climax (bars 415-17) the music dies away to a quiet conclusion.

The melodrama no. 6 opens with a D minor *allegro,* in the very first bar of which Arnulf is evidently challenging Melinde ('Furie bebe!'). His rage turns to exhaustion in the course of 27 bars, and then a powerful tutti passage (with the bass line growling out a variant of the chordal motif), rich in sforzatos and syncopations, presumably covers the scene-change (bars 30-2: '(*Arnulf spricht fort bis zur Verwandlung.*)') from Arnulf's castle to Melinde's. In bar 82, Melinde (speaking in rhymed iambic pentameters, whereas Arnulf uses prose) bids her spirits bring Arnulf to her. At bar 118 (*andante,* F♯ minor) she invokes Arnulf, then questions him (speaking now in prose) about his intentions with regard to Ida and the throne of Brabant. Virtually the whole of their dialogue is carried out above a chromatically changing string tremolo accompaniment, punctuated by mainly brief woodwind figures, though after the tempo-change to *allegro* (bar 177), when strong dynamic contrasts are introduced, their exchanges are carried out in the silent bars that punctuate the texture. Arnulf cries for revenge, and a very powerful climax leads into an *allegro furioso* (bar 193, D minor). It must be at this point that a second transformation transports Arnulf back to his own castle (bar 238: 'Ha! wo bin ich? . . .'). He reflects angrily on what he has been through, and on his foiled plans for his son's ascendancy; several of his exclamations need to be projected strongly, since the full orchestra is employed.

The melodrama no. 10 (*allegro,* E♭ major/C minor), which features an inversion of the chords associated with Melinde and Sutur, is the number during which the assault on Melinde's castle at last begins. During the opening bars, Arnulf and his companions make their way towards their objective, but by bar 54 the castle has disappeared, to be seen now on a distant and unscaleable height; their bewilderment is underlined by a brief, jerky motif on the strings. To a variant of the by now familiar chords, Arnulf bids Melinde show herself. After a tutti characterized by rushing wind semiquavers and held string chords she appears (following bar 107). Seven further bars bring the number to an end; the confrontation between husband and wife takes places in a lost spoken scene. The musical action continues with the melodrama no. 11 (already described), during which Melinde is presumably showing Arnulf's companions by means of a magic tableau[34] that Arnulf and Ida are secure in her castle.

No. 12, the final melodrama in *Die Zauberharfe,* opens softly with an extended *allegro* (C minor) during which Arnulf admits that Melinde's power is greater than his; all of their exchanges, some of which are quite long, fall in silent bars or rests. The musical phrases between speeches are rarely longer than two bars (phrases of five, eight and four bars are the only exceptions in over forty exchanges), which helps create a feeling of tension – though inevitably there is little sense of musical continuity. When at bars 107ff Melinde speaks through a quiet string accompaniment, telling Arnulf that their son is still alive and well, the contrast with what has gone before is marked and effective. At bar 137 the tempo changes to *andante,* 12/8, and Ida's right to choose her own husband is confirmed. When reconciliation between Melinde and Arnulf is close, Melinde recalls her oath to Sutur (bar 145), and the music is plunged into an agitated C minor *allegro.* Sutur appears, remorseless; the choral support of his minions is the only instance in the work of a melodrama

34 A feature of Baroque opera given new popularity by scenes such as the tableau vivant in Grétry's *Zémire et Azor* (Act III, no. 19) and its various Viennese sequels; see note 22 above.

including singing. It is then that Ida bids Palmerin appear; he does so (bar 236, *andantino*), silent but for his magic harp, the arpeggios of which overpower and expel Sutur. The melodrama (271 bars long) moves very softly, *attacca,* into the brief final chorus, during which not only Melinde and Arnulf, but perhaps also Ida and Palmerin too, are united.

The *NGA* score includes in an appendix an 'Entwurf eines Melodrams' (pp. 355-8); Rossana Dalmonte, the editor, argues plausibly that this sketch, notated on two staves and bound in with the autograph score, was intended for *Die Zauberharfe.*[35] Though no textual phrases occur, and it is not headed 'Melodram', the suggestion that this sketch (which breaks off after 188 bars) was intended as a melodrama seems reasonable, though it would be idle to speculate on its possible function within the work.

Die Zauberharfe was written at the end of a period of considerable theatrical activity for Schubert. It was followed in the autumn of 1820 with work on the sketches for the projected *Sakuntala,* but it was not until the autumn of 1821 that Schubert embarked on a second period of intensive work for the stage. The two main works of this period, the grand operas *Alfonso und Estrella* (D 732) and *Fierrabras* (D 796), may have a broad general similarity in their serious, archaistically Romantic stories, but in musical treatment they are sharply contrasted. *Alfonso,* written between September 1821 and February 1822, is a carefully integrated score; it contains no spoken dialogue or melodrama, and the recitatives and choruses, and most of the arias, are incorporated within extended musical forms. If *Alfonso* tends to be centripetal, *Fierrabras* is centrifugal; although it has few separable arias, its scope ranges from spoken verse dialogue through melodrama in verse and prose, recitative, arioso, Lied, solo and ensemble numbers, to choral scenes of various kinds.

Despite the fact that in *Fierrabras* the use of melodrama is only incidental, whereas in *Die Zauberharfe* it lies at the heart of the score, the examples in *Fierrabras* are the most interesting, and in musical and theatrical terms probably the finest, that Schubert created. He took particular care to integrate within the overall musical pattern the passages of spoken dialogue. Effective as are isolated examples of melodrama in opera – be it the dialogue between Rocco and Leonore in *Fidelio,* or the reading of the letter in Verdi's *La traviata* or Smetana's *Two Widows* – the impact is even greater when the composer has taken care to hint at the possibility of extended melodrama to come, by introducing snatches of dialogue earlier in the opera – Weber does this in *Der Freischütz* by incorporating spoken comments from the peasants in the opening scene of the shooting-match, and from Caspar during the stanzas of his drinking-song, in anticipation of the extended melodrama of the Act II finale.

This is Schubert's method in *Fierrabras*. By comparison there is something fortuitous about the use of melodrama in *Des Teufels Lustschloss* and *Der*

35 *NGA*, II/4, 'Quellen und Lesarten', p. 378.

vierjährige Posten; in his last completed opera he uses melodrama quite extensively in the second act, having paved the way with a short example in the first act; he also makes use of the device in the last act.

The first melodramatic passage is built into the big ensemble no. 4. Roland reveals that his prisoner, overcome in single combat, is the son of the Moorish king. Emma, the king's daughter, watches maidens present Roland with a wreath; she is recognized by Fierrabras, though only Roland and Emma of those present detect Fierrabras's reaction. As the music of the maidens' chorus dies away (*andantino,* 6/8, A major), important information is put across in the following brief dialogue:

> *Fierrabras* [with an involuntary cry]: Ha!
> *Roland:* What is it?
> *Fierrabras:* It is she!
> *Roland:* The Princess? yes! The daughter of our lord.
> *Fierrabras:* And my beloved!
> *Roland:* Be silent, madman! You are lost!
> *Fierrabras:* You gods!

The music then moves into an F major chorus and ensemble.

There is a rather longer melodramatic exchange in the second number of Act II (no. 8), at the confrontation between the Frankish knight Eginhard and Brutomonte, a Moorish captain. Schubert lightens the texture of the march-like orchestral interlude – woodwinds, horns and double-bass accompany the (irregularly rhymed) speeches. Eginhard reveals that he has been chosen by the king to offer peace to the Moors; when Brutomonte proves suspicious, threatening, Eginhard sounds his horn to summon his knights.

The principal melodrama in *Fierrabras* is the climax and conclusion of Act II. Eginhard, Roland and their comrades have been imprisoned by the Moors. Scene 11 opens with the noble and expressive *a cappella* chorus 'O teures Vaterland' (no. 14) – in this way Schubert widens the expressive range of his musical vocabulary, perhaps in conscious anticipation of the extended combination in the following number of sung, melodramatic and purely instrumental music. The unaccompanied chorus is followed by dialogue between the knights, and then by the melodrama no. 15. Ogier, one of the knights, manages to climb to a window from which he can give his companions some account of the action outside the prison. The music opens quietly, with scurrying staccato strings and held low wind chords (*allegro molto*, A minor); Ogier makes out a Moorish guard fleeing wounded from outside their prison-tower; to mounting excitement (*cresc. poco a poco*) the door of the tower is opened, and Florinda – daughter of the Moorish king, and Roland's beloved – bursts in. In ecstatic song (rather than the spoken dialogue that the heading 'Melodram' would lead us to expect) she seeks out Roland. She faints, Roland and the knights bring her round, and the number continues as a recitative followed by a sung duet with chorus.

After a brief spoken dialogue, in which Florinda throws in her lot with Roland and his companions, no. 16 ('Chor und Melodram') opens with a brief choral passage in which the knights thank Florinda for the chance she has given them. In an initially unaccompanied choral passage (with strong rhythmic wind support at the end of each period) they pray to God for deliverance. Trumpet-calls and side-drums without indicate that Florinda and the knights have lingered too long (her spoken exclamation 'We are betrayed! . . .' is melodramatic in two senses). But she remembers that weapons are stored near at hand, so the Moors (whose trumpets and drums draw nearer during the scene) will not have it all their own way. Roland and Eginhard will try to escape through a postern and bring a relieving force before the Moors can storm the tower. Ten mainly brief spoken exchanges have imparted the essential information, against a turbulent, rapidly moving and motivic orchestral texture. No. 16 and no. 17 (Act II finale) are separated by spoken dialogue in the course of which Roland and Eginhard prepare to depart; however, as the stage direction indicates a continuous and growing clangour of Moorish trumpets and drums, the effect is of melodrama.[36]

The finale opens with the sung farewells of Roland and Eginhard as they take leave of Florinda and the knights. Florinda, left alone on stage, relates in a series of twenty-five brief spoken utterances (only five of them in silent bars or rests) the events which she can see through the window (Ex. 4). At first she believes that Roland has broken through to safety, but he is finally overcome – to the (sung) grief of the returning Frankish knights. Florinda collapses again, and the act ends with a 'silent tableau of horror and despair'.

There is also one melodrama in Act III, scene 6. The first group of scenes has shown that Eginhard did win through to Karl's court; an expedition to try and rescue his comrades is hastily mounted. Back in the beleaguered tower, Florinda has recovered, and in an aria with chorus (no. 21) she laments that Roland's death is certain, her father being a man of firm and speedy resolve. The aria leads without a break into a Marcia funebre (*andante*, B minor) played by wind instruments on stage. During it, Florinda and the knights again resort to melodrama. Olivier, at the vantage-point by the window, reports the advent of a procession in the courtyard outside; at the naming of the victim about to be burnt on a pyre – 'Roland!' – the march gives way to an agitated orchestral outburst, and Florinda sings of her determination to die with Roland if she cannot save him. Then, in a pause following a *fortissimo* outburst from full orchestra, she resorts effectively to speaking voice to cry: 'Release him! The tower shall be surrendered!' A brief *più moto*, during which Florinda and the knights make their way down to the courtyard, closes the scene. No further melodrama occurs in the final scene, in which Karl and the

36 The stage direction at the close of no. 16 which calls for the persistent sound of trumpets and side-drums is not found in Kupelwieser's libretto (see note 27 above).

Ex. 4 *Fierrabras*

a2
Sie stehen staunend–
Jetzt öffnet sich
das Thor –

Ex. 4 (contd)

Fl.
Ob.
Cl. (B♭)
Fag.
Hn. (E♭)
Hn. (D)
3. Tbn.
Mit blankem Schwert stürzt Roland mit dem Jüngling durch die Schaaren!

Sie brechen durch!
Dank euch, ew'ge Götter!

Ex. 4 (contd)

Fl.
Ob.
Cl. (B♭)
Fag.
Hn. (E♭)
Hn. (D)
3. Tbn.
p
stacc.
f
Er stösst auf
neue Schaaren –

a2
in C
kann er entfliehn?
Rings mäht sein Stahl!

Ex. 4 (contd)

Franks arrive in time to save Roland and his companions, and to bless the forthcoming union of Roland and Florinda, Eginhard and Emma.

Schubert's last melodrama (D 829), the only one with piano accompaniment, is generally referred to by the title 'Abschied von der Erde' which it bears in the *AGA* (XX, 603) and in the first edition of O. E. Deutsch's Schubert thematic catalogue. The revised thematic catalogue, which indicates that Schubert's autograph is untitled (and undated), reasonably prefers the plain title 'Abschied'.[37] The earliest published reference to this melodrama seems to be in H. Kreissle von Hellborn's *Franz Schubert.* In view of the fact that Kreissle became the brother-in-law of the author of the text of 'Abschied', it is tantalizing that he says nothing of the circumstances of the composition or first performance of the little piece. Near the end of the chapter for the year 1825 Kreissle says:

> Finally, we must mention a pianoforte accompaniment by Schubert which is combined with the final strophe of a dramatic poem entitled 'Der Falke' to form a melodrama, bringing it to a declamatory–musical conclusion.[38]

Kreissle appends a footnote which indicates that these final words are spoken by Ritter Hugo before his death, and that Schubert wrote the keyboard accompaniment at the request of the author, Adolf von Pratobevera, 'in which form the verses were recited during the scenic representation of the poem'.

As Clemens Höslinger has recently shown,[39] the words for which Schubert composed his musical accompaniment, which begin 'Leb wohl, du schöne Erde', are the final five stanzas of Pratobevera's one-act play *Der Falke*, which was performed in the poet's home on 17 February 1826 in celebration of the birthday of his father, the lawyer Karl Josef von Pratobevera.

These closing verses, all that has been published of the play, are valedictory. The speaker bids farewell to 'Master Grief' in the second stanza,[40] confident

37 *Schubert. Thematic Catalogue of All His Works in Chronological Order* (London, 1951); and *Franz Schubert. Thematisches Verzeichnis seiner Werke in chronologischer Folge*, ed. by the Editorial Board of *NGA* and Werner Aderhold (Kassel, etc., 1978), cited below as '*D2*'.

The heading of the copy in the Witteczek–Spaun collection is 'Abschied. Melodramatisch': *D2*, p. 523.

38 *Franz Schubert* (Vienna, 1865), p. 375.

39 'Aus den Aufzeichnungen des Freiherrn von Pratobevera' in *Schubert-Studien. Festgabe der Österreichischen Akademie der Wissenschaften zum Schubert-Jahr 1978*, ed. Franz Grasberger and Othmar Wessely (Vienna, 1978), pp. 119-29.

40 Höslinger misses the opportunity to explain the curious 'Leb wohl du Meister Kummer!' of the second stanza of Schubert's setting, though it is to his summary of the rest of the play that I owe the information that 'Meister Kummer' is the nickname of the hero's squire, Kuno. Höslinger also fails to point out an interesting change of plan at the end of the play. Kreissle's brief summary attributes the closing lines to the old knight, Hugo. Höslinger's summary of the version of *Der Falke* completed in 1825 (pp. 123-6) gives these lines to Kuno's daughter, Mechtild, and the stage direction requires them to be sung.

that he is taking Joy with him. Schubert's composition is 33 bars long, in 4/4 time, and is marked *langsam* and 'Con pedale, appassionato'. It is basically in F major, though it modulates quite freely. The five bars of piano introduction introduce the  rhythm which, with variation, dominates the texture almost throughout. The voice enters in the sixth bar, and the pattern is regular: one line of text per bar, with one bar's interlude after each stanza, and finally a four-bar postlude. The iambic metre (the lines rhyme abcb) might well encourage the reciter to speak the unstressed initial syllable of each line against the fourth beat of the previous bar; but Schubert's choice of common time for the reciting of lines each of which has only three stressed syllables, and three unstressed syllables (four in the first and third lines of the stanzas), is an obvious warning against imposing a strict rhythmical pattern on the recitation. The broken chordal textures, the frequent use of triplet rhythms, the predominantly *pp* dynamics and the direction *appassionato* all suggest that Schubert saw his task as being to provide and sustain a musical atmosphere against which the spoken voice could project the simple yet not ineffective words.

There is nothing in the tone of the lines that Schubert set to substantiate Deutsch's comment that Pratobevera's *Der Falke* is a parody.[41] In view of the popularity of parodies in Vienna at that time, there would in itself be nothing surprising about the choice of a parody even for a respected father's birthday; but the dignified if slightly maudlin tone of the play's closing lines seems to suggest sincere if hardly talented poetic endeavour.

Although Schubert did not set any further melodramas after he completed his composition of the last lines of *Der Falke*, he did receive an invitation from Friedrich Rochlitz twenty-one months later to set his poem 'Der erste Ton' as a melodrama. Rochlitz's letter of 7 November 1827[42] was presumably prompted by Schubert's three Rochlitz song-settings of January 1827 (D 903-905), which were announced as op. 81 by the publisher Tobias Haslinger in the *Wiener Zeitung* of 28 May 1827, and dedicated to the poet himself, 'that author deserving so well of music and the polite sciences'.)[43]

'Der erste Ton: Eine Phantasie', first published anonymously in the *Allgemeine Musikalische Zeitung* of 2 October 1805, had been set by Weber in 1808,

In the absence of any information about the performance on 17 February 1826 it is permissible to speculate whether the poet's sister Franziska (Fanni) von Pratobevera, mentioned in family correspondence (see O. E. Deutsch, *Schubert. A Documentary Biography* (London, 1946: cited below as '*Documents*'), pp. 708, 716 and 779) as an excellent singer of Schubert's songs, was not available for the performance on her father's birthday, that in consequence the closing lines were transferred to the actor taking Hugo, presumably not an accomplished singer, and that Schubert was accordingly asked to set them as a melodrama.

41 *Documents*, p. 509.

42 *Documents*, pp. 686-8.

43 *Documents*, pp. 646-7.

and was offered to Beethoven in 1822.[44] In his letter to Schubert of 7 November 1827 Rochlitz set out in some detail the manner of composition which he envisaged for his poem. He took care, however, to make it clear that he was not attempting to impose his views on Schubert. The latter indicated politely but firmly in his reply (undated, but presumed by Deutsch to be of the same month) that he felt unable to accept the invitation:

Your proposal concerning the poem 'Der erste Ton' I have carefully considered, and it is true that I believe your suggested treatment of it to be capable of making an admirable effect. But as in this way it would be a melodrama rather than an oratorio or cantata, and the former being no longer favoured (perhaps with good reason), I must openly confess that I should very much prefer a poem that may be treated as an oratorio, not only because an orator like Anschütz [whom Rochlitz had suggested] is not always to be had, but also because it is my most ardent wish to furnish a purely musical work, without any extraneous matter apart from the elevating idea of a long poem to be set wholly to music. I need hardly say that I recognize in you the poet for such a work and that I should devote all my powers and diligence to composing it in a manner worthy of the poetry.

'Der erste Ton' really being such a glorious poem, I should be glad to try it, should you wish me to set it to music, but I should let the music (i.e. song) enter at the words 'Da vernahm' [line 30 of the 66-line poem], if you agree.[45]

As Deutsch comments, 'This brought the correspondence between Schubert and Rochlitz to an end.' And it also marks the last known occasion on which Schubert considered using melodrama.

As we have seen, Schubert's interest in the melodrama extended over most of his career as a composer, from *Des Teufels Lustschloss*, his first completed opera, written when he was sixteen, to *Fierrabras*, his last completed opera, ten years later; and in 1826, probably bound by the conditions of a commission, he wrote his last melodrama. Throughout, he shows a lively appreciation of the expressive and dramatic potential of the combination and juxtaposition of speaking voice and orchestral (in one case keyboard) accompaniment. Indeed, no other composer of Schubert's stature has written as many melodramas. If the precedent of the dungeon scene in *Fidelio* (and of examples in the works of Weigl and others) occupied his mind, he established his credentials in the genre before Weber wrote his best-known examples in *Der Freischütz* and, later, *Preciosa.* One could argue that from first to last Schubert showed a surer hand in controlling melodrama than he did in most aspects of his operatic writing.

44 *Documents*, p. 688.
45 *Documents*, pp. 688-9 (here slightly revised).

Hausmusik (Schubert making music with Josephine Fröhlich and Johann Michael Vogl), pencil drawing by Ferdinand Georg Waldmüller, 1827: discovered in 1978 by Otto Biba in a sketchbook of Waldmüller's (Albertina, Vienna)

Schubert's 'Der Tod und das Mädchen': analytical and explanatory notes on the song D 531 and the quartet D 810

CHRISTOPH WOLFF

Singling out a composition for analytical discussion presents just as many problems as it provides advantages and opportunities. Of course, a musical opus – regardless of its dimensions and significance – should not be considered solely as a work of art in its own right; it reveals its intrinsic qualities, characteristic properties and aesthetic value first and foremost by being brought into focus by both performance and analytical reflection. As for the problems, isolating individual works from their narrower and wider contexts necessarily results in restricted perception and appraisal of styles and ideas. The following analytical and explanatory notes on Schubert's song and quartet 'Death and the Maiden' recognize the twilight of an unbalanced discussion. Therefore, it seems only appropriate to stress the fragmentary nature of this study, which aims at a contributory rather than a definitive approach in furthering the understanding of the two compositions in question.

I

Matthias Claudius (1740-1815) figures among the principal poets whose texts Schubert selected for setting as Lieder in the crucial years 1815 to 1817, which were the most formative ones in regard to the emergence of a truly personal style of song-writing. After Goethe (who clearly predominates), Hölty, Kosegarten, Matthisson, Mayrhofer, Salis-Seewis and Schiller, we find Claudius represented with fourteen songs.[1] The north German Claudius had earned his literary reputation mainly by editing a newspaper (*Der Wandsbecker Bothe*) to which he contributed a large number of prose essays and poems. Most of these he republished in a widely disseminated series of collected writings under the Latin–German double title *Asmus omnia sua secum portans, oder Sämmt-*

1 The poets are listed in descending order of the number of texts by each composed by Schubert in 1815-17. For the exact details see O. E. Deutsch, *Franz Schubert. Thematisches Verzeichnis seiner Werke in chronologischer Folge* (cited below as '*D2*'), ed. by the Editorial Board of the *Neue Schubert-Ausgabe* and Werner Aderhold (Kassel, etc., 1978), pp. 687-9. (The trio 'Klage um Ali Bey' D 140 is not counted among the fourteen Claudius songs.)

liche Werke des Wandsbecker Bothen, which appeared in eight volumes from 1775 to 1812.[2] His poems appealed very much to the popular taste of the time and ranged in character from the humoresque and burlesque to quiet meditation and solemn sentiment.[3] The latter kind was favoured by Schubert, as one can see from his selection of texts. Eight of the Claudius songs were composed in November 1816[4] and four in February 1817.[5] This apparent concentration of the Claudius songs in the winter months of 1816-17 is not without its stylistic implications. Indeed, the simplicity, purity and clarity of Claudius's poetic language had an immediate and direct impact on Schubert's melodic–rhythmic phrasing, especially in setting lyric verses: the effect is most noticeable in the strophic songs such as 'Das Lied vom Reifen' D 532 and 'Täglich zu singen' D 533 of February 1817.[6]

In content as well as in terms of lyric quality 'Der Tod und das Mädchen' stands on a slightly higher level than the other Claudius texts set by Schubert, and his composition seems to mirror this fact. Together with three other Claudius poems it was composed in February 1817.[7] Schubert published the piece about four and a half years later as the third and concluding song of his op. 7.[8]

The poem represents an imaginary dialogue with the two stanzas assigned to two speakers identified in the headings as 'Das Mädchen' and 'Der Tod'. In its fundamentally positive portrayal of death the poem fulfils a moral–didactic function very typical of much of Claudius's writing, although it lacks the Protestant–pietistic touch ordinarily to be found in his works. In his treat-

2 The new critical edition of the *Sämtliche Werke*, ed. Jost Perfahl (Munich, 1968), includes extensive bibliography on Claudius, pp. 1057-67.

3 Cf. J. Karl Ernst Sommer, *Studien zu den Gedichten des Wandsbecker Boten* (Frankfurt am Main, 1935). For a catalogue of Claudius's poems set to music by various composers see Max Friedländer, *Das deutsche Lied im 18. Jahrhundert*, vol. 2 (Leipzig, 1902), pp. 244-59.

4 'Bei dem Grabe meines Vaters' D 496; 'Klage um Ali Bey' D 496A; 'An die Nachtigall' D 497; 'Wiegenlied' D 498 (Claudius's authorship questionable; not in *Asmus*); 'Abendlied' D 499; 'Phidile' D 500; 'Zufriedenheit' D 501; 'Am Grabe Anselmos' D 504.

5 'An eine Quelle' D 530; 'Der Tod und das Mädchen' D 531; 'Das Lied vom Reifen' D 532; 'Täglich zu singen' D 533.

6 During the month of February 1817, or in March 1817 at the very latest, Schubert's close association with the singer Johann Michael Vogl began; see O. E. Deutsch, *Schubert. A Documentary Biography* (London, 1946), p. 75 – cited below as '*Documents*'.

7 The autograph manuscript is dated. Andreas Schubert, Franz's stepbrother, appears to have cut the autograph into eleven pieces in order to present them to some of his students as awards. Only eight of these pieces have come to light so far. A facsimile of the fragment in the Archiv der Gesellschaft der Musikfreunde in Vienna (A 223) may be found in *Franz Schubert. Neue Ausgabe sämtlicher Werke* ('*NGA*'), Series IV, vol. 1a (Kassel, etc., 1970), p. xxxi, and in the catalogue *Franz Schubert – Ausstellung der Wiener Stadt- und Landesbibliothek zum 150. Todestag des Komponisten*, ed. Ernst Hilmar and Otto Brusatti (Vienna, 1978), p. 167. See also *D2*, p. 310.

8 Together with 'Die abgeblühte Linde' D 514, and 'Der Flug der Zeit' D 515; published by Cappi & Diabelli, Vienna.

ment of the death theme, a favourite subject of classical and Romantic poetry, he was greatly indebted to the thoughts of Gotthold Ephraim Lessing and Johann Gottfried von Herder. Both, in corresponding and identically entitled critical theological–philosophical essays,[9] had discussed the question of 'how the ancients represented death' and contrasted the medieval picture of death as repulsive skeleton with the Classical Greek image of death as beautiful youth, as spirit (*Genius*) and symbol of sleep. They distinguished sharply between the understanding of 'death as punishment', which they saw as typical of 'misunderstood religion' and the 'superstitious' aspects of Christianity, and, on the other hand, the concept of death as 'gentle and consoling', death as the symbol of sleep, which they deemed more worthy of the 'Christianity of reason' in an enlightened age.[10]

It is interesting that Claudius, despite the obvious influence of Herder in particular, does not give up the traditional image of the skeleton. On the contrary, the first volume of *Asmus*[11] shows as frontispiece an engraving of the dreadful skeleton with the scythe (Figure 1). The caption, however, reads 'Freund Hain'[12] and thus defines death as a friend. It is this 'Freund Hain' to whom Claudius dedicates the entire volume. In the dedication he reflects upon the ancient representations of death. He considers the Greek young *Genius* with inverted torch as allegory of sleep but prefers the medieval skeleton. 'So he appears in our church,' he writes; 'as such I've always pictured him from childhood on . . . This way, I believe, he is quite beautiful, and if only one gazes at him long enough, he'll finally look entirely friendly.'[13]

This helps us to understand the poem where the Maiden is frightened by the appearance of the 'savage skeleton', which she later addresses as 'dear'. She first panics and puts up fierce resistance against death, begs him 'pass by, do not touch me'. But death calms her down by referring to her physical

9 *Wie die Alten den Tod gebildet*. Lessing's essay appeared in 1769, that of Herder in 1774. For a detailed discussion see Ludwig Uhlig, *Der Todesgenius in der deutschen Literatur von Winckelmann bis Thomas Mann* (Tübingen, 1975), with extended chapters on both Lessing (pp. 9-19) and Herder (pp. 19-29); Uhlig also considers specifically Herder's influence on Claudius, pp. 51f, with reference to 'Der Tod und das Mädchen'.

10 Quotations from Lessing. See the critical analysis by Henry Hatfield in his chapter 'The Ancient Image of Death: Lessing and His Impact' in *Aesthetic Paganism in German Literature from Winckelmann to the Death of Goethe* (Cambridge Mass., 1964), pp. 24-32. Reinhold Hammerstein, *Tanz und Musik des Todes. Die mittelalterlichen Totentänze und ihr Nachleben* (Berne and Munich, 1980), discusses the Claudius poem and Schubert's setting in the context of the tradition of the medieval dance of death (pp. 12f).

11 (Hamburg, 1775). This was Schubert's text source for D 140, 344, 362, 496A, 497, 500, 501, 504, 530 and 531.

12 This euphemistic name for death may stem from the vernacular in north Germany, but was introduced in literature first by Claudius in his review of Goethe's *Werther* (*Wandsbecker Bothe*, 1774); cf. Grimm, *Deutsches Wörterbuch*, vol. 4, part 2 (1868), col. 885.

13 Claudius, *Sämtliche Werke*, p. 12.

beauty and explaining that he does not 'come to punish', that he is 'not savage'. Claudius here transforms the abstract Greek image of death as genius and brother of sleep into a more concrete scene that would be much better understood by most of his readers: a benevolent death takes away a beautiful girl, not to punish her but to offer her – by sleeping in his arms – eternal peace.

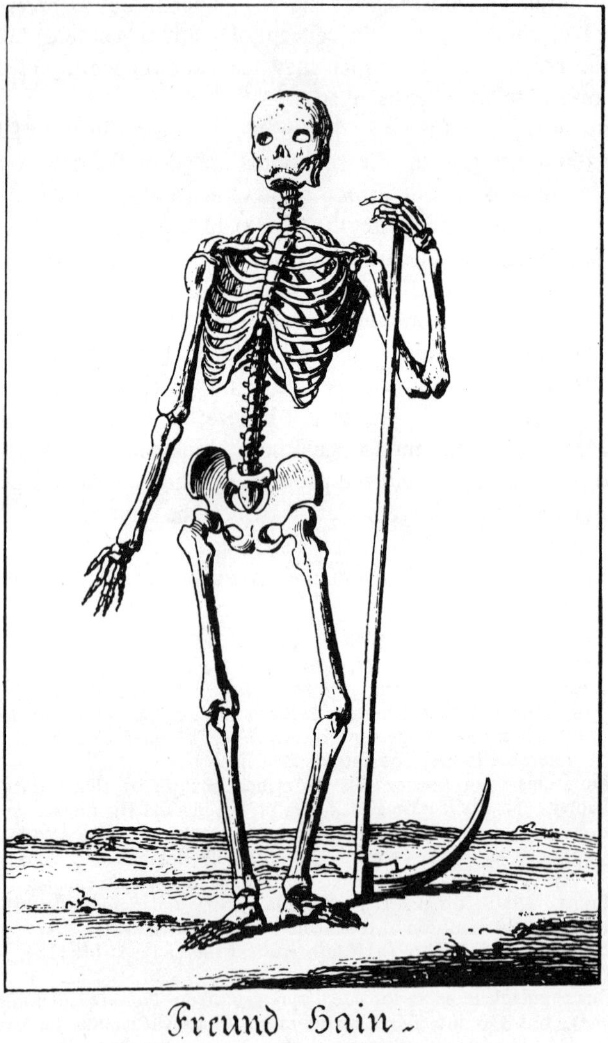

Figure 1. *Freund Hain*, engraving: frontispiece to M. Claudius, *Asmus omnia sua secum portans* . . . (Hamburg, 1775)

The dialogue partners of this lyric miniature scene could not represent more strongly contrasting personae:[14]

	(1)	(2)	(3)
[*A*] Das Mädchen.			
Vorüber! Ach, vorüber!	7	a	f
Geh, wilder Knochenmann!	6	b	m
Ich bin noch jung, geh Lieber!	7	a	f
Und rühre mich nicht an.	6	b	m
[*B*] Der Tod.			
Gib deine Hand, Du schön und zart Gebild!	10	c	m
Bin Freund, und komme nicht, zu strafen.	9	d	f
Sei gutes Muts! Ich bin nicht wild,	8	c	m
Sollst sanft in meinen Armen schlafen!	9	d	f

The design of the poem stresses those contrasts. They take shape particularly in the uneven lengths of the lines (short lines metrically paired in stanza *A*: 7–6–7–6, correspondingly rhyming abab; considerably longer lines with irregular syllable-counts in stanza *B*: 10–9–8–9), in the reverse order of line endings (feminine–masculine in stanza *A*, masculine–feminine in stanza *B*), and in the absence of any rhyme common to the two stanzas. At the same time, these contrasts are balanced by various unifying devices, primarily the stable iambic metre and the uniform rhyme-scheme of four interlocking pairs. After all, the poem is supposed to be one whole and not two pieces, which is underscored by the subtle symmetry of the feminine–masculine / masculine–feminine line-endings, binding the two stanzas together.

II

Ex. 1

14 Text (including orthography and punctuation) according to the original edition in *Asmus I/II*. The variants in Schubert's song are very minor.

Ex. 1 (contd)

Etwas geschwinder
Das Mädchen
7
Vor - ü - ber, ach vor - ü - ber, geh
p
11
wil - der Kno - chen-mann! Ich bin noch jung, geh
cresc.
15
Lie - ber und rüh - re mich nicht an, und rüh - re mich nicht
19
Das erste Zeitmass
Der Tod
an. Gib dei - ne Hand, du
pp dim.
pp

24
schön und zart Ge - bild, bin Freund und kom - me nicht zu stra -
29
fen. Sei gu - tes Muts! ich bin nicht wild, sollst
34
sanft in mei - nen Ar - men schla - - fen.

Schubert's composition follows the prosody as well as the structure and form of the text quite closely. First of all, he clearly differentiates between the two stanzas and the two dialogue partners, respectively, by firmly establishing and intensifying the element of contrast in various terms: tempo (*A*: 'Etwas geschwinder'; *B*: 'Mässig'[15]), tessitura (*A*: e′ to e♭″; *B*: d[16] to f′), declamatory gestures (*A*: short, disjunct phrases; *B*: long, conjunct phrases), dynamics (*A*: *piano*, *pianissimo*, crescendo, diminuendo, sforzato; *B*: *pianissimo*), diastematic activity of the melodic lines (Ex. 2), prevailing rhythmic patterns (Ex. 3), and harmonic layout (*A*: open-ended, from D minor via G minor to A major in fast harmonic rhythm; *B*: closed, from D minor via F major to D major in slow harmonic rhythm).

Ex. 2

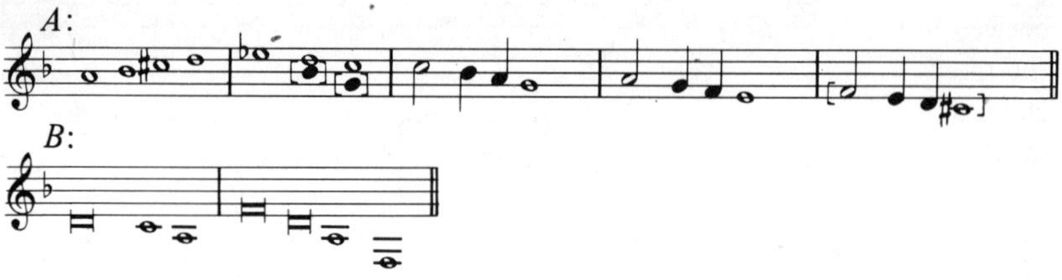

Ex. 3

The parallels in declamatory style between the poem and the song are quite striking. For instance, Schubert strictly observes the grammatical structure by translating the punctuation of the text into rhythmic caesuras and differentiating between the various functions of these caesuras (cf. 'Vorüber!' and 'Knochenmann!', for example). He shapes the musical phrase-endings according to the poetic line-endings and metric scheme:

. . . vorüber,
. . . Knochenmann!
. . . geh Lieber!
. . . nicht an.

. . . Gebild,
. . . strafen.
. . . nicht wild,
. . . schlafen.

Parallels also govern the prosody and the corresponding musical flow (*A*: short, interrupted lines and phrases; *B*: long, coherent lines and phrases). There are

15 The metronome indication 𝅗𝅥 =54 appears in the first edition (1821).
16 Schubert obviously preferred the lower d, but provided d′ as an alternative since it fits the normal voice range much better.

further structural details in which Schubert leans on Claudius. For instance, he imitates exactly the rhyme-scheme of *B* by placing cadential points in the voice part accordingly (see the cadences in bars 25 and 33 on 'Gebild' and 'wild', in bars 29 and 37 on 'strafen' and 'schlafen'). Schubert also underscores the intensifying word-repetition at the beginning ('Vorüber, ach vorüber') by turning it into a sequential repetition of emphatic appoggiaturas (b♭–a, c–b♭).[17] This emphatic opening to stanza *A* on paired motives is balanced by an anticlimactic concluding pair ('Und rühre mich nicht an': c–b♭–a–g, a–g–f–e). At this conclusion the text repeat does not stem from the original text – Schubert's only textual departure from Claudius.

Overemphasizing the similarities between the poet's and the composer's approaches would be misleading, for Schubert follows his own rules in a great number of significant points. For instance, in order to intensify the contrast between stanzas *A* and *B*, between the Maiden's and Death's voices, he changes the metric scheme by starting lines 1 and 3 of *B* in dactylic metre – 'Gib deine Hand'; 'Sei gutes Muts' – while stanza *A* remains iambic throughout. At a musically more significant level, Schubert also alters the entire phraseological concept of the poem. In contrast to Claudius, Schubert's musical periodization of the *B* stanza is extremely symmetrical: two eight-bar periods, each consisting of four-bar antecedent and consequent. Stanza *A*, on the other hand, accentuates its asymmetry (as opposed to the poem) by introducing irregular phrasing (cf. bars 9-16 in particular) or, where it appears regular (bars 16-21), by turning it into a threefold division (2+2+2 bars).

Schubert furthermore develops Claudius's simple bipartite format into a more complex and rounded overall form. The opening eight-bar ritornello is compositionally derived from stanza *B*, anticipates material from *B* before the presentation of stanza *A*, and is almost literally repeated at the end of the song. This results in a well-planned sectional organization where the principal bodies of contrast, the stanzas *A* and *B*, are framed and motivically bound together by the *b* ritornellos:

form scheme	*b*	:	*A* ⟷	:	*B*	:	*b*
harmonic plan	d–d	:	d–g–A	:	d–F–D	:	D–D

This overall form as well as the inner structures reflect the composer's interpretation of the poem to a considerable degree. The following attempts to paraphrase Schubert's musical exegesis are made in the knowledge that such things are actually inexpressible in words. The *B* material that opens the piece does not just function as a unifying device but primarily introduces the shadow of death at the beginning. Hence the Maiden's voice from the initial panic outcry on appears to be reacting to a real and frightening vision. The original title of the poem, 'Der Tod und das Mädchen' – in this order, despite the reverse order of the dialogue stanzas – already hints at the presence

17 The corresponding rhyme 'geh Lieber' (bar 15) is also set to an appoggiatura.

of death, before the opening words of the first stanza. Schubert's *A* stanza then characterizes the Maiden in her desperate resistance by a combination of musical means: climactically ascending melodic line, gradually approaching the high point of e♭″; underscored by animated rhythmic pulse and chromatically shifting harmonies. The culminating point of the *A* stanza is sustained for quite a while, bars 13-15, by a delay of the melodic high point of the bass line (g in bar 14, one bar after the e♭″ of the voice) and by a diastematic differentiation between the intervallically leaping voice and the stepwise progression of the accompaniment: Ex. 4. This is quite different from the parallel progression of the voice and the upper part of the accompaniment in the immediately preceding passage: Ex. 5. But the extended culmination point in

Ex. 4

Ex. 5

bars 13-15 represents a turning-point as well, since it marks the beginning of a descending direction in the melodic drive and the corresponding harmonic structure. Together with the slowing down of the rhythmic pulse this indicates that the Maiden is giving up resistance, gradually, with a final gesture of withstanding at the beginning of the last 'Und rühre mich nicht an', accented by the sforzato in the accompaniment. The words 'do not touch me' seem to coincide with the physical encounter of the Maiden and Death since (beginning with the accompaniment in bar 16) the *B* material reaches into the *A* stanza. This overlap of *A* and *B* provides, together with the half-cadence at the end of *A*, a smooth transition from one stanza to the other. But this transitional passage is also meaningful in terms of the content of the poem: death strikes at the end of stanza *A*, the Maiden ceases to speak, her voice is carried on only in the accompaniment (note the *pianissimo* diminuendo at this moment, bar 20). Meaningful too is the sudden predominance of the major mode in the concluding six bars of stanza *A* leading towards A major. While the minor mode prevails from the beginning until bar 14, the Maiden's recognition of Death as a dear friend ('geh Lieber', bar 15) brings about a modal change, the modulation to F and C major in bars 16-17.

This change in modal orientation has its parallel in the *B* stanza, which also starts out in the minor mode but rather quickly approaches the major. The modulation from D minor (bar 25) via G and C major (bars 27-8) to F major coincides with Death's reference to his friendly character ('bin Freund'). In their modal direction (minor–major), then, the two stanzas are quite similar:

stanza:	*A*		*B*	
lines:	1		1	minor modality
	2	minor modality	2	↓
	3	↓	3	major modality
	4	major modality	4	

In nearly every other respect, however, the musical differences between them prevail. This appears most strikingly in the solemn, psalmody-like declamatory style of the vocal part in *B*. Also the relative inactivity on both harmonic and rhythmic levels characterizes the voice of Death as the voice of the supernatural, strongly contrasting with the genuinely human, very active voice part in *A*. The words of Death aim at consolation, and the concluding ritornello functions as an extension of the comforting role of 'Freund Hain'. Another formal parallel between *A* and *B*: at the end of both stanzas the accompaniment carries on the material of the voice, in *A* for just two bars (20-1), in *B* for seven (the asymmetrically abridged reminiscence of the eight-bar piano introduction). But more important than the parallels between *A* and *B* is the relationship of the prelude and the postlude. The formal function of the ritornello has already been pointed out; but beyond this the D minor version of the ritornello represents the prelude to the vision of the hideous 'Knochenmann', the skeleton image of death, while the D major version stands for 'Freund Hain', the allegory of sleep. Schubert's song in both large-scale structural design and small-scale compositional detail delineates the metamorphosis of the image of death from the frightening to the consoling, thereby expanding, intensifying and deepening the scope of the Claudius poem.

The masterful short Lied received a counterpart only a few weeks after its completion. The Claudius poem stimulated Joseph von Spaun, one of Schubert's closest friends, to write the poem 'Der Jüngling und der Tod' in imitation of it. This happened primarily, without a doubt, as a result of the deep impression Schubert's composition must have made on his friends as soon as they heard it. Spaun wrote a very similar dialogue, although he gave the Youth a proportionately much longer part than Death. But the most significant difference between Spaun and Claudius – apart from the quality of the poetic language – lies in the fact that the Youth approaches Death with the express desire to die: 'Come and do touch me' are his last words.[18] While in Schubert's composition, D 545 (dated March 1817), the stanza of the Youth

18 For a discussion of this piece see Erdmute Schwarmath, *Musikalischer Bau und Sprachvertonung in Schuberts Liedern*, Münchner Veröffentlichungen zur Musikgeschichte, vol. 17 (Tutzing, 1969), p. 115.

(26 bars) shows no connection at all with 'Der Tod und das Mädchen', the Death stanza (seven bars) clearly borrows from the earlier work. Apparently Schubert first tried to avoid too close references to 'Der Tod und das Mädchen', as can be gathered from the extant early version of the piece (which was planned for two singers). But in the final version the general declamatory and expressive style of the Death stanza are clearly indebted to the Claudius song: Ex. 6.

Ex. 6

dei - ner Qual er - bar - - - - men.
fzp
pp
24 Version 2 :
Der Tod.
komm! Es ruht sich kühl und
p
f
sanft in meinen Ar - men, du rufst, ich will mich dei - ner Qual er -
bar - - - - men!
pp

The most striking discrepancy between the two pieces lies in the nature of the dialogue. Spaun's dialogue takes place between quasi-congenial partners, thereby eliminating the need for expressive contrast, whereas Claudius focuses on the sharp polarity of the dialogue partners in order to bring about the metamorphosis of Death's image. As a result Spaun's poem lacks the strong dramatic impetus of the Claudius text that inspired Schubert to build up an imaginary scene which is as forceful as it is brief.

III

Claudius's choice of the dialogue format implies that his intentions were genuinely dramatic. And Schubert's decision to neglect the original distribution of roles between the Maiden and Death by not assigning the stanzas to two different voices (as in the first version of D 545) must not be interpreted as an anti-dramatic one but rather as good judgement. In the interest of a unified composition of such small dimensions he utilized inner musical rather than external means in order to make the dramatic dialogue work.

The technical vocabulary of the music is taken from opera. The *A* stanza follows in its design the traditional pattern of an *accompagnato* recitative. The principal features displayed are: well-placed appoggiaturas (bars 8-10: 'Vorüber, ach vorüber'; bars 14-15: 'geh Lieber'), chordal accompanimental figuration in tremolo style (i.e. the traditional illustrative formula of 'trembling'), the freer tempo approach in combination with a more flexible dynamic treatment, and finally the use of harmonic intensity to build up suspense in preparation for a dramatic high point.

For the voice of Death Schubert then employs another operatic element, the oracle *topos* of eighteenth-century *opera seria.* Oracle speech belongs to the technical repertory of Greek tragedy, either as inception of dramatic developments or as conclusion of a dramatic climax. When the gods predict the inevitable – and this is frequently a death sentence – the solemn voice of the oracle pronounces the verdict in a liturgical recitation-tone. A most characteristic example of a musical oracle scene – whose origin goes back to French Baroque opera, specifically to Rameau – can be found in Gluck's *Alceste* of 1776.[19] The oracle there is preceded by an *accompagnato* recitative in tremolo style, ending with the words 'bow your head to the ground, listen and tremble'. The text of the subsequent oracle reads: 'The king will die unless another dies for him': Ex. 7.

The direct relationship with 'Der Tod und das Mädchen' cannot be overlooked. The solemn, quasi-psalmodic pitch-repetition; the trombone-like low-register accompaniment so uncharacteristic of pianoforte writing;[20] the strictly

19 Premièred in the Burgtheater at Vienna.

20 The graphic significance of the empty upper staff of the piano part (to be found in both the autograph and the first edition) as emphasis of the unusual range should not be overlooked.

Ex. 7

Le Grand - Prêtre
Sai - si de crain - te et de res - pect, peu-ple, ob - ser-ve un pro-fond si -
pp
len - ce! Rei - ne, dé - po-se à son as -
f
pect le vain or - gueil de la puis - san - ce,
p
trem - - - - ble.
Sans lenteur
L'Oracle
Le roi doit mou -

regulated rhythmic declamation and the cadential formulas; the preparation of the oracle by an *accompagnato* recitative – all those very characteristic elements of the Schubert song find their logical explanation in their connection with the scene from *Alceste.*[21] A similarly striking musical parallel appears in the cemetery scene of Mozart's *Don Giovanni* of 1787, where the oracle *topos* occurs outside the sphere of the *opera seria* proper[22] in order to endow the voice of the statue of the Commendatore with the aura of the supernatural: Ex. 8. A more stylized, intensified and dramatically integrated

Ex. 8

See also bars 59-63: 'Ribaldo, audace, lascia a' morti la pace.'

oracle style characterizes the voice of the 'stone guest' within the ensemble at the beginning of the second finale of *Don Giovanni*. Pitch-repetition with

21 At the time when Schubert had become an opera-goer *Alceste* was presented four times in 1810 (Burgtheater, Vienna) with Anna Milder in the title role. (I am indebted to Dr Clemens Höslinger of the Haus-, Hof- und Staatsarchiv, Vienna, for this information.) Anna Milder's association with Schubert (he later dedicated his op. 31 (D 717) to her) began no later than 1812; see *Documents*, p. 22.

22 A prominent occurrence of the oracle *topos* is to be found in Mozart's *Idomeneo* of 1781 (no. 28: La Voce). There are four versions of this passage extant (cf. *Neue Mozart-Ausgabe* II/5:11, ed. Daniel Heartz (Kassel etc., 1972), preface pp. xivf).

psalmodic cadential formula together with a stable rhythmic pattern serve to establish the theatrical contrast between Don Giovanni/Leporello and the voice of death represented by the Commendatore who announces the end of the 'giovane cavaliere estremamente licenzioso'.

Although the topic 'Schubert and opera' with its many facets still remains on the list of desiderata of modern Schubert research, there can be little doubt that Schubert was intimately familiar with the world of opera and its musical–dramatic resources. 'Der Tod und das Mädchen' demonstrates his virtuoso application of the operatic vocabulary, making significant means of musical expression, characterization and imagery available to the genre of art song.

IV

As operatic elements infiltrate Schubert's song style, so his instrumental works gain from his experience as a composer of Lieder. The instrumental pieces which incorporate songs mainly in the form of a variation movement play a particularly important role in this respect. One finds a rather high concentration of those works in the spring of 1824, and among them the Quartet in D minor, D 810.[23] This quartet, completed in March 1824,[24] bases its second movement on the song 'Der Tod und das Mädchen' of 1817. This variation movement isolates the *B* material of the song from the material of the *A* stanza and transforms it into a rounded binary musical setting. Schubert organizes the 24 bars of the piece in three absolutely symmetrical eight-bar phrases, the first and last of which are taken directly from the piano part of the song:[25]

D 531	bars	1–8		30–7
D 810	bars	1–8	9–16	17–24
harmonic layout		‖: g–g :‖:	E♭–B♭	E♭–g :‖

The inserted, newly composed section (bars 9-16) provides the necessary link between the outer periods with the appropriate harmonic transition.[26]

One understands why Schubert had to omit the *A* material, i.e. the entire first stanza of the song, because as a recitative-like piece it lacks the qualities of

23 Variations in E minor for Flute and Piano, D 802 (January 1824); Octet in F major, D 803 (February 1824); Variations in A flat major, D 813 (May–July 1824).

24 The autograph score (Pierpont Morgan Library, New York: The Mary Flagler Cary Music Collection) is dated March 1824 (the second half of the autograph, movement II bars 143ff and movements III and IV, has not survived). The autograph shows a number of rather revealing compositional corrections, but no trace of the alleged revision of February 1826 mentioned in *Documents*, p. 506.

25 Only the piano part in stanza *B* possesses, of course, melodic qualities that would lend themselves to variation treatment.

26 The newly composed section stands out also by reason of its forceful dynamics (crescendo – *forte* – decrescendo).

a variation tune. Furthermore, a combination of the two stanzas in whatever form would hardly have made sense owing to the extreme contrast of style between *A* and *B*. But while Schubert deliberately excluded the *A* material from the variation setting,[27] it is legitimate to question whether he rejected this material for the entire quartet, particularly in view of the fact that the dramatic correlation of *A* and *B* figures so prominently in the song.

This brings up the issue of cyclical planning in the four-movement work, whose key structure is restricted entirely to minor modes: D minor, G minor, and twice again D minor – a most unusual and apparently unprecedented tonal design. The original D minor of the song occurs in all movements except the one that draws its material directly from the song. Were the D minor movements of the quartet meant to have no connection at all with the song? Indeed, the fact that the key of the song is the key of the quartet, regardless of the 'transposition' of the variation movement, seems to imply that Schubert thought of a deliberate association of the song and quartet in terms of key relationship. A closer examination of the first movement reveals further aspects which suggest specific ties between the first and the second movements and, beyond this, between the others as well.

The principal thematic complex of the first movement has to be divided into two parts. The core part, which unfolds with a repeated opening section, after bar 14 states from the outset two main motivic elements: first, a gradually ascending melodic line incorporating chromatic steps D-E-F-F♯-G-G♯-A, and secondly, an obbligato accompaniment in the form of an imitatively treated triplet figure ♩ ♪♪♪ (3) 𝅗𝅥 , which provides a strong motoric force. Both elements can be directly related to the *A* material of the song if the essence of *A* is to be defined as strong melodic (primarily ascending) chromatic–harmonic drive underscored by a forceful rhythmic pulse (cf. Exx. 2 and 3, above). The introductory part (bars 1-14) of the principal thematic complex points in a different direction. Though the accompanimental triplet motif is first introduced here (bar 1) – and the tremolo manner recalls the *accompagnato* tremolo of the *A* stanza – the prevailing declamatory gesture and the diastematic and harmonic qualities of bars 7-14 in particular recall the *B* material if the substance of *B* is to be defined as diastematic and harmonic repose: Ex. 9. The *B* connection is also supported by the fact that the autograph score of the quartet at bars 9-10, before Schubert revised it, used the dactylic rhythm typical of *B*. (The corrections at bars 5-6 in the first violin further strengthen the *B* qualities in that they reduce the original ascending melodic gesture to a more static repetition.) If the core part of the principal thematic complex indeed relates to the *A* stanza of the song, the function of the in-

27 Schubert clearly avoids any noticeable chromaticism, which appears as a characteristic element of *A* (c♯–d–e♭, bars 11-13). However, the overall *B* qualities of the second movement are stressed by an accumulation of pitch-repetitions which gain motivic–thematic prominence in variations 3–5 (bars 73ff, 97ff, 121ff).

Ex. 9

* Version before revision

Ex. 9 (contd)

troductory part (bars 1-14) might be explained in terms of the function of the opening ritornello of the song as preparation for the dramatic entry of the voice.

While the core part (bars 15ff) is immediately followed by extension and further elaboration (bars 25ff) and undergoes permutations and developments later on in the movement,[28] the 14-bar introduction recurs only once more during the course of the entire movement, namely as the opening of the coda: Ex. 10. In the process of development the principal melodic line as well as the individual parts are more narrowly restricted in range, and in the context of sustained notes in the first violin and cello this has the effect of emphasizing the *B*-related character of the passage. The subsequent *A*-derived core part of the thematic material develops into a fully chromatic ascending scale portion, incidentally, for the first time in the movement (bars 318ff). It appears that the beginning of the exposition of the quartet and, correspondingly, the beginning of the coda extend the first half of the song – i.e. the *b* ritornello and the *A* stanza – into an elaborate and quite sophisticated instrumental format. Schubert transforms here the heterogeneous structure of the song, where *A* and *B* stand in juxtaposition, into a homogeneous thematic complex in which *A* and *B* form a dialectical partnership.

Regarding the general relationship of the first two movements of the quartet, however, the *A*-related principal theme of the first movement[29] predetermines the dramatic drive of the entire first movement, and the structural relationship of the two song stanzas (*A*:*B*) thereby appears stylized in the juxtaposition of the two quartet movements (*A*:*B*).

28 The 'principle of variation', which Carl Dahlhaus ('Die Sonatenform bei Schubert. Der erste Satz des G-dur-Quartetts D 887', *Musica*, XXXII (1978), pp. 125-30) identifies as one of the decisive forces in Schubert's thematic procedures in his late sonata-form compositions, also governs the development of the principal thematic complex in the D minor Quartet.

29 The subsidiary theme (see below for its *B* relation) is intentionally kept in the shadow of the predominant first theme.

Ex. 10

299
pp
pp
pp
pp
[B] →
fp
fp
fp
fp
pp
pp
pp
pp
più mosso
p
più mosso
p
più mosso
p
più mosso
p [A] →

If the first two movements do indeed form a specific correlation, questions persist concerning more comprehensive cyclical intentions on the part of the composer. Various hypotheses which have been proposed pertain specifically to the possibility that the quartet as a whole, and not just the second movement, deals with the subject of death. And references range from the dance of death to the Dies irae.[30] Maurice Brown sharply and rightly rejects any speculation about programmatic elements in the quartet.[31] Alfred Einstein had already remarked that Schubert 'does not write "program" music, nor do we need to know the song, but we feel unmistakeably in this music the symbols of inevitability and consolation'.[32] But what 'we feel unmistakeably' belongs all too clearly to the vague sphere of the listener's psychology.[33]

Leaving aside merely speculative hypotheses the following points might be considered. First, in pursuing the analytical approach applied to the first two movements, the role of *A*- and *B*-related materials for the last two movements can be determined and concretized. The thematic basis of the scherzo consists of a chromatically descending line which appears first in the bass, later in the top voice (bars 23ff): Ex. 11.[34] Note that the bass line of bars 1-4 constitutes the exact retrograde version of the ascending outline of the Maiden's stanza in the song (bars 9-12: see Ex. 2). Bars 5-8 then state the chromatically descending tetrachord, the traditional *lamento* bass. In further defining the chromatic nature of the *A* material the occurrence of the *lamento topos* here suggests a connection with the musical tradition of that figure, particularly in opera and church music. The *lamento* bass appears, for example, in Schubert's Mass in A flat major, D 678, of 1822, where it functions very prominently in the 'Crucifixus' and the subsequent 'judicare vivos et mortuos' sections of the Credo.[35]

30 Konrad Huschke, 'Franz Schuberts "Todesquartett". Eine Huldigung zum 100. Geburtstag des Werkes', *Der Türmer*, XXVIII (1926), pp. 61-4; Harold Truscott, 'Schubert's D minor String Quartet', *Music Review*, XIX (1958), pp. 27-36; Hans Holländer, 'Stil und poetische Idee in Schuberts d-Moll-Streichquartett', *Neue Zeitschrift für Musik*, CXXXI (1970), pp. 239-41.

31 *Schubert. A Critical Biography* (London, 1958), p. 180.

32 *Schubert. A Musical Portrait* (New York, 1951), p. 254.

33 Einstein (ibid., pp. 254f) sees a unifying device in a rhythmic pattern derived from what he calls the 'march of "inevitability"': movement II $\frac{2}{2}$ 𝅗𝅥 ♩♩| 𝅗𝅥 , movement I $\frac{6}{8}$ ♫♪ | ♩. ; movement III $\frac{3}{4}$ ♩.♪♩ | ♩.♪♩ ; movement IV $\frac{6}{8}$ ♩♪| ♩. . Martin Chusid ('Schubert's Cyclic Compositions of 1824', *Acta Musicologica*, XXXVI (1964), p. 41) also supports this view, but the derivation of rhythmic formulas from the clearly dactylic metre of the variation movement is nevertheless open to question.

34 This figure, the '*passus duriusculus*', is historically linked with requiems and elegies, and has a particular association with D minor (*tonus primus*): see Peter Williams, 'Figurenlehre from Monteverdi to Wagner' (parts 1-2), *Musical Times*, CXX (1979), pp. 476-9, 571-3; and Ellen Rosand, 'The Descending Tetrachord: An Emblem of Lament', *Musical Quarterly*, LXV (1979), pp. 346-59.

35 See Erdmute Schwarmath (cited note 18 above), in the chapter 'Über den Quartbass in Schuberts Liedern', pp. 105-18, where she discusses numerous occurrences of the *lamento* bass in songs and other vocal compositions of Schu-

Ex. 11 (a)

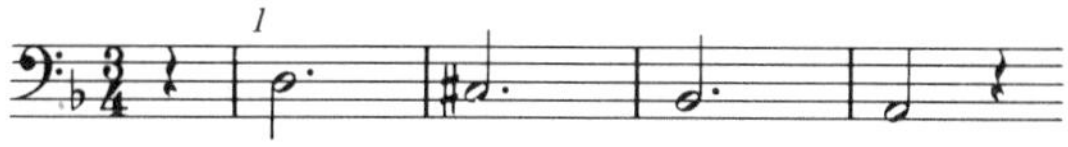

(b)

(c)

Ex. 12

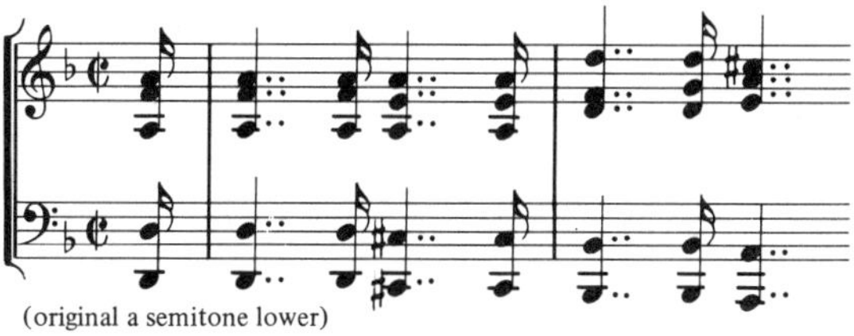

(original a semitone lower)

It is interesting to see that the frequent pitch-repetitions as accompanimental figures form some kind of a melodic–rhythmic counterpoint throughout the scherzo, that indeed they take on a thematic function in the trio: Ex. 13. Again, the dialectical relationship of *A* and *B* prevails, this time on yet another level of compositional integration.

The finale opens quite similar perspectives. The tarantella-style rondo does not show, initially, any apparent significant links with either the *A* or *B*

bert. She also notes (pp. 113f) that the opening of 'Der Jüngling und der Tod', D 545, is based on the *lamento* bass – Ex. 12 – without mentioning that this represents the retrograde version of the opening vocal line of 'Der Tod und das Mädchen'.

Ex. 13

material. However, three extended motivically controlled complexes in bars 217ff, 236ff, 575ff and 725ff feature the juxtaposition of *A*- and *B*-related materials very clearly: Ex. 14. The *prestissimo* coda (bars 707ff) is particularly revealing in this connection, because Schubert demonstrates there that the finale theme itself, in its de-colorated form, represents the quintessence of *B*: Ex. 15.

Ex. 14

Ex. 15

In further exploring the motivic interrelationship of the quartet movements we should take a closer look at the second theme of the first movement, which has so far been left out of the discussion. Even at first glance, its *B*-related qualities become quite obvious. It features an open-fifth bass drone which contributes significantly to its musical peculiarity within the context of the first quartet movement: Ex. 16 (cf. the static harmonic character of *B*, as indicated in Ex. 2 above). In addition, a very similar drone passage of subsidiary thematic value appears within the finale (bars 252-82, 610-37), thereby linking the framing quartet movements in quite a strong way: Ex. 17. In both

Ex. 16

Ex. 17

Ex. 17 (contd)

instances the short-winded, edgy and repetitive melodic phrases on top of the drone bass suggest that Schubert is here imitating the hurdy-gurdy in a stylized manner. This relates directly to the concluding song of *Winterreise*, 'Der Leiermann': Ex. 18. In the iconographic tradition since the middle ages[36] the hurdy-gurdy-player frequently serves as an image of death. This is certainly the case with 'Der Leiermann', marking the end point of *Winterreise*. Since

Ex. 18

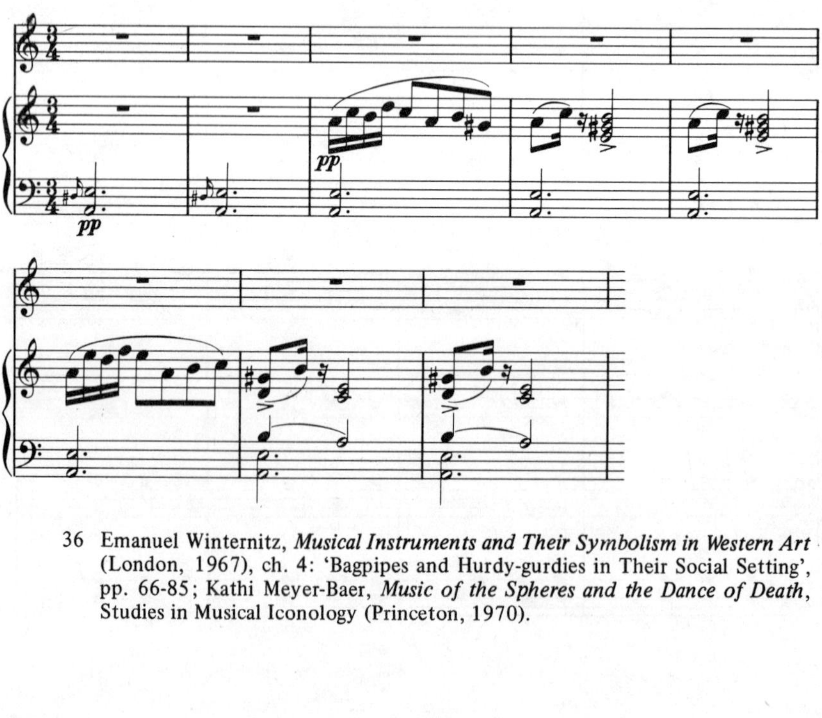

36 Emanuel Winternitz, *Musical Instruments and Their Symbolism in Western Art* (London, 1967), ch. 4: 'Bagpipes and Hurdy-gurdies in Their Social Setting', pp. 66-85; Kathi Meyer-Baer, *Music of the Spheres and the Dance of Death*, Studies in Musical Iconology (Princeton, 1970).

Schubert had decided to give the voice of death, the oracle *topos*, such a prominent place in the variation movement of the quartet, he may well have considered balancing the 'vocal' voice of death with the 'instrumental' voice of the hurdy-gurdy-player as an image of death.[37]

In conjunction with the iconographic tradition mentioned above, a reference must be made to a cycle of sixty-six pen-and-ink drawings by one of Schubert's closest and most faithful friends, Moritz von Schwind, under the title *Gräber oder Todesgedanken*[38] ('Graves or Thoughts on Death'), dated 1823, i.e. immediately preceding the year of the D Minor Quartet (figures 2-4). This certainly sheds some light on the wider context and significance of visual, literary and musical themes of death in the Schubert circle at about that time.

This is not to suggest any kind of concrete 'death programme' for the quartet. But one has to recognize that Schubert's use of musical *topoi* and imagery plays a rather decisive role in this quartet of such enormous and unprecedented dimensions,[39] particularly with respect to the extremely high degree of cyclical coherence. In this way the quartet could be related to the type of 'sinfonia characteristica' as represented in Beethoven's 'Pastoral' Symphony.[40] Musical characterization in late-eighteenth- and early-nineteenth-century musical aesthetics[41] does not aim – in contrast to the later ideals of programme music – at illustrations or depictions of narrative extra-musical events, but rather at the immediate effect and impact of 'characteristic' extra-

37 As a third traditional element the motivic integration of the *lamento* figure and the *passus duriusculus* in movements I, III and IV must also be considered in this connection.

38 Complete reproduction in *Schwind. Des Meisters Werke in 1265 Abbildungen*, ed. Otto Weigmann (Stuttgart and Leipzig, 1906), pp. 15-23.

Another *topos* may be relevant here, that of death as a frightening figure on horseback (cf. Figure 2, and the imagery of 'Erlkönig' D 328): in the Quartet D 810, 'galloping' rhythms figure prominently in every movement (see e.g. movement I bars 42ff, 160ff; movement II bars 73ff; movements III and IV throughout).

39 Movement I: 341 bars, movement II: 172 bars, movement III: 68 plus 96 bars, movement IV: 754 bars. Beethoven's op. 127, the first of his late quartets (completed in 1825), is considerably shorter.

40 In the original edition of 1809 the work is entitled 'Sinfonie / Pastorale'; the title 'sinfonia characteristica' appears in the principal sketchbook for the 'Pastoral' Symphony. Augustus F. C. Kollmann (*An Essay on Practical Musical Composition* (London, 1799)) differentiates between free and characteristic symphonies and, with reference to Haydn's *Seven Last Words*, denotes specifically 'those Symphonies, which are calculated to express a prescribed general character, but without pointing out its particular characteristics, or the places where they are to appear' (p. 16).

41 See in particular Christian Gottfried Körner, *Ueber Charakterdarstellung in der Musik* (Leipzig, 1795). Cf. Wolfgang Seifert, *Christian Gottfried Körner und seine Musikästhetik*, Jenaer Beiträge zur Musikforschung, vol. 3 (Leipzig, 1957), also Carl Dahlhaus, *Die Idee der absoluten Musik* (Kassel etc., 1978), pp. 7-23, and the article 'Charakterstück' in *Riemann Musik Lexikon: Sachteil* (Mainz, 1967).

Figures 2-4. Drawings by Moritz von Schwind, from the series *Gräber oder Todesgedanken*, 1823

musical elements on human sentiment. Seen in this light, the appearance of a set of variations in the two major works of February–March 1824, the D minor Quartet and the Octet in F major, D 803, means entirely different things. While in the octet the variation movement represents just one of the possible choices for a slow movement, the variations on the song 'Der Tod und das Mädchen' affect all other movements of the work in so far as the song material largely determines the overall subject-matter, cyclical concept and, above all, thematic and expressive coherence.

It may not be at all coincidental that Schubert, in the often-cited letter to Kupelwieser of 31 March 1824, refers to the two quartets in A minor and D minor (D 804, 810) and the Octet (D 803) in a very specific context: '. . . I intend to pave my way towards grand symphony in that manner'.[42] And Schubert's options concerning symphonic projects included, of course, the type of 'sinfonia characteristica'.[43] The D Minor Quartet could then, perhaps, be understood – at least in part – as a quite adventurous experiment in exploring not only dimensions of symphonic format[44] but, especially, new concepts of cyclical form and expressive content with a view towards grand-scale symphonic style.

42 *Documents*, pp. 338-40.

43 For references to the rather peripheral type of programme quartet in the late eighteenth and early nineteenth centuries (relatively popular in Bohemia, for instance) see Ludwig Finscher, article 'Streichquartett' *MGG*, vol. 12 (Kassel, etc., 1965), col. 1579.

44 The symphonic work of yet more unprecedented dimensions that followed the D minor Quartet rather soon (according to the new chronological findings of Robert Winter, see pp. 257-68 below) is the C major Symphony, D 944, of 1825.
Concerning the vertical dimensions of the score of the D minor Quartet, the unusually high frequency of multiple-stopping (not to be found to such a degree in the earlier A minor Quartet) appears as a significant feature of 'orchestral' quartet texture.

In what respect a quintet? On the disposition of instruments in the String Quintet D 956

PETER GÜLKE

'Why he chose so unusual a combination is a mystery.'[1] These words of M. J. E. Brown might refer primarily to an external stimulus which caused Schubert to write a quintet. Such an interpretation would, however, disregard any 'inner compulsion' such as apparently developed increasingly while Schubert was composing his last three string quartets, particularly the one in G major, and urged him to move beyond the confines of the quartet ensemble. Explanations, frequently found in the literature, which merely refer to Schubert's 'orchestral . . . conception and feeling' simply do not suffice.[2] Related to this idea is Einstein's desire to have the parts in the quintet doubled and the second cello replaced by a double bass,[3] a view which reveals the false conclusions which are possible if one conceives the taut relationship between intention and realization (found in so many great works within the orbit of Viennese classicism) in terms of a conflict which must be resolved as far as possible for the sake of euphony. Bearing in mind that sharp contrasts, richly coloured nuances of timbre, or the distinction between foreground and background sonorities should not *a priori* be regarded as the exclusive preserve of the orchestra (for such a view would be unfair to the majority of demanding works for chamber ensemble), one should remember that in the quintet Schubert increased the quartet by only one instrument. Thus he remains so close to the quartet that one can almost regard his choice of the quintet medium as merely a deviation from the norm. If certain broadly conceived passages still seem somewhat inhibited even in the quintet, this is no reason to seek potentially more suitable performing media: it provides rather an opportunity to acknowledge the contrast between concord and conflict in the relationship of structure and scoring as an important element of the composition. This contrast is considered to be a matter of course in Beethoven,[4] but in Schubert it

1 M. J. E. Brown, *Schubert. A Critical Biography* (London, 1958), p. 292.
2 A. Einstein, *Schubert. A Musical Portrait* (London, 1951), p. 333; A. A. Abert, 'Rhythmus und Klang in Schuberts Streichquintett' in *Festschrift Karl Gustav Fellerer zum sechzigsten Geburtstag* (Regensburg, 1962), pp. 10-11.
3 Einstein, loc. cit.
4 P. Gülke, 'Zum Verhältnis von Intention und Realisierung bei Beethoven' in *Bericht über den internationalen Beethoven-Kongress 10.–12. Dezember 1970 in Berlin* (Berlin, 1971), pp. 517-32.

has hardly been noticed until now. For far too long it has been assumed that Schubert naively and unprotestingly adopted all the compositional and aesthetic formulas which Viennese classicism offered him. In point of fact we may ask whether Schubert in his last works was not about to explore for himself this very Beethovenian structural and psychological level – in the G major String Quartet, *Winterreise* and the Heine songs, as well as in the String Quintet. Seen in the light of such a new departure, and bearing in mind that the Romantic continuation of classical traditions, as developed by Spohr or Mendelssohn, at first ignored Beethoven as a 'special case', the early death of Schubert appears as one of the great catastrophes of musical history.

The beginning of the quintet offers a striking example of Schubert's work in this new realm of composition. Neither the texture nor the ensemble is complete at the beginning: the relationship of the five instruments and the musical structure must first emerge from their mutual efforts. They approach each other by way of the quartet combination; not until bar 23 do all five instruments play together. At the beginning[5] there is a C major chord which gradually increases in intensity – at first this sounds unmeasured, because the bar-lines appear irrelevant in view of the concentration on the crescendo. A long fermata would probably serve as well; at the outset the music has no bars in the strict sense, but must find its own pace, subject-matter and structure. The example set by the opening bars as a development *ex uno* is followed by Schubert in what ensues; the swelling of the C major chord gives way to a diminished chord, out of which grow the first bars that have any melodic character. This does not last for long; they end as though with a questioning gesture, and a kind of echo in a higher register, against which the gloomy depths of the following harmonies stand out with particular plasticity. The gradual imparting of a sense of movement, followed by a loss of momentum, might well be illustrated thus:

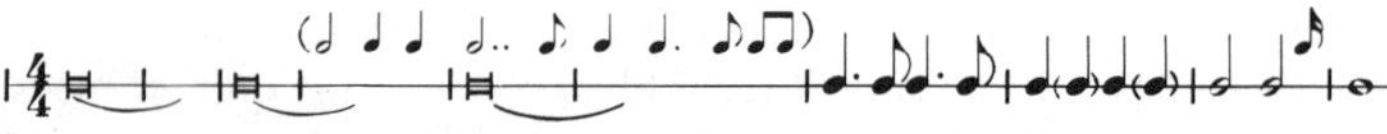

Schubert repeats this opening, but now in the minor and with a different and lower-lying instrumental combination, and introduces the first cello as the most important melodic instrument after the first violin. Against a background of considerable uniformity, bars 1-10 and 11-20 are seen as two pithy

5 For other descriptions of this beginning see T. Georgiades, *Schubert. Musik und Lyrik* (Göttingen, 1967), pp. 154ff; W. Riezler, *Schuberts Instrumentalmusik. Werkanalysen* (Zurich, 1967), pp. 117ff; P. Gülke, 'Zum Bilde des späten Schubert. Vorwiegend analytische Betrachtungen zum Streichquintett op. 163' in *Deutsches Jahrbuch der Musikwissenschaft für 1973/74* (Leipzig, 1978), pp. 5-58, and in *Musik-Konzepte, Sonderband Franz Schubert* (Munich, 1979), pp. 107-66. The present study selects some points of view from this comprehensive study and pursues them in greater detail.

but opposing statements, embodying all the symbolic contrast between the heights and the depths which is frequently to be found in this composition – in the jubilant high registers of the third and fourth movements, the funereal descent of the trio, or the first violin in the first movement which almost disappears into the heights (bars 188ff and 224ff). In bar 23 the whole ensemble unites in a concerted drive towards the main theme. What seems in bar 33 to be a theme – without a change of tempo, yet with all the signs of being the beginning of a main movement – appears on closer inspection to be the superstructure of the preceding 'introduction', if not merely a second version of it, especially when one thinks of the lyrical second subject which is to follow. Out of the tentative gropings of the beginning an arresting *appassionato* has indeed emerged, which seems to fit the category of a first subject in every respect. The interplay between the upper parts, with their vigorously leaping quavers, and the resounding unison of the cellos, playing the treble phrases of the introduction, reveals itself as an explosive combination. The two groups of instruments are widely separated, and each takes the initiative in turn. This seems at first to belong entirely to the higher of the two groups, while the lower calmly keeps to its long sustained notes. The latter, however, after its second appearance, now in D minor (bars 40ff), furiously increases speed by diminution (Ex. 1), thus forcing the upper group into passive yet still rapid

Ex. 1

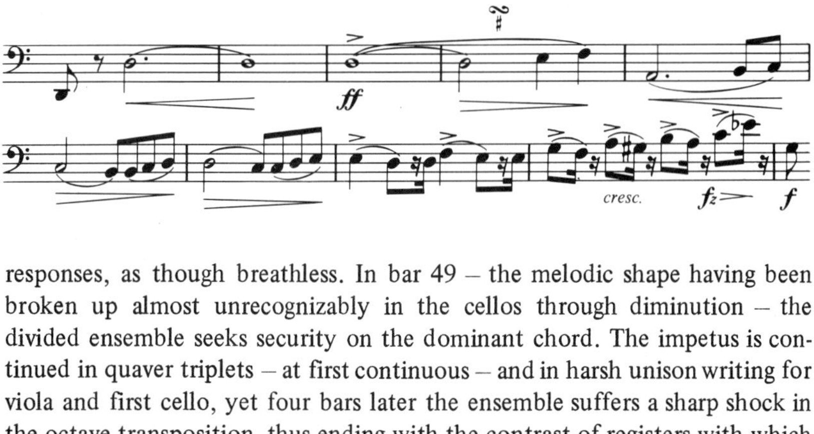

responses, as though breathless. In bar 49 – the melodic shape having been broken up almost unrecognizably in the cellos through diminution – the divided ensemble seeks security on the dominant chord. The impetus is continued in quaver triplets – at first continuous – and in harsh unison writing for viola and first cello, yet four bars later the ensemble suffers a sharp shock in the octave transposition, thus ending with the contrast of registers with which the movement began.

The general effect is that of a striving which fails to achieve its object. This impression is confirmed by what follows: the dominant which succeeds the agitation and is so vigorously approached and established proves to be a misleading achievement. It is disavowed at the entrance of the melody with its magical yet destructive composure, as though Schubert wished to say – with Schiller – that 'All that is highest comes as a gift from the gods' and is not to be achieved by the established rules of sonata form. The melody begins in E♭ major, with an air of naturalness, just as if this key had really been reached by modulation. Especially in view of the fact that sonata form, both traditionally and inherently, relies for its motivation upon the careful observance of key-relationships, Schubert's radiantly 'illegal' departure from the sonata norm needs no justification and creates a beauty that transcends normative categories. Here too the listener perceives that the music, and with it the ensemble, has found itself at last; it has also found (in a sense that cannot be pursued here[6]) its own momentum and timbre,[7] since here for the first time all the disruptions of tone, rhythm and content disappear, as do abrupt changes to new conceptions of ensemble. In the above-mentioned sense of the interrelationship between form and ensemble one may also say that here too the quintet first truly comes into being.

In one respect at least the second subject and the preceding material are alike; the ensemble remains divided into two groups[8] – here it is the two cellos with accompaniment for violins and viola. In part, this disposition is a matter of priorities, as in every cantabile passage it results from the focusing of attention upon the melody. There are particularly striking examples of this elsewhere in the quintet: in the E major sections of the *Adagio* and in the melody of the second subject's closing section in the finale, which appears like a *fata morgana* (bars 127ff); it is not by chance that both passages are closely connected with the lyrical second subject of the first movement. Inevitably and logically, the string quartet has become enlarged, inasmuch as division into instrumental groups plays a great part in the string quartets in A minor, D minor and G major. In the string-quartet medium this is all the more noticeable, since by its very nature it presents a homogeneous but many-sided ensemble – the realization in instrumental terms of Kirnberger's concept of pure composition ('reiner Satz') in four parts. The combination of four similar yet independent instruments sets a limit beyond which integration according to the principles of pure composition is not possible, and within which – exceptions aside – independence, equality and homogeneity may be manifested. To the classicists, five- or six-part counterpoint seemed too preoccupied with itself, always artificial and irreconcilable with the seemingly candid and improvisational character of, for example, the 'Romantic' counterpoint of Schubert's second subject. The quintet, exceeding the number of parts that was considered the ideal in Viennese classicism, could be said to expand beyond a certain 'critical mass': at this point it is inevitable that the ensemble will normally break up into various groupings and give the impression of fragmenting into strata of primary and secondary material, foreground and background, melody and ac-

6 See Gülke, 'Zum Bilde des späten Schubert'.

7 H. H. Eggebrecht, 'Der "Ton" als ein Prinzip des Schubert-Liedes' in *Musik und Wort. Kolloquium Brno 1969: Musikwissenschaftliche Kolloquien der Internationalen Musikfestivale in Brno 4* (Brno, 1973), pp. 243-58.

8 See in particular Abert, 'Rhythmus und Klang in Schuberts Streichquintett'.

companiment. But in this way the criteria of canonic precedence are set aside in favour of one of the supreme tests of composing, since the exemplar of 'pure composition' assumed a clear allotment of tasks and strict rules of performance, in which the string quartet by its very nature sets high standards. A badly composed string quartet is bound to represent something much worse than, for example, a badly composed solo concerto. While the quartet had a clearly defined character from the beginning, for composers of secondary importance (such as Pleyel) a stylistic norm was necessary. As a part of that 'ideal combination' the single instrument is but one voice in the whole ensemble and sacrifices to it something of its individuality. The more strict the structure and the more parts it has, the more it claims attention for itself and forces its dependence upon the nature of the instrument into the background, absorbing into superimposed contexts its independence of utterance. In opposition to this is the fact that when bringing out a solo part the spontaneity of the ensemble preserves some directness, since the standardizing effect of the whole is reduced when two players share one part. Further, absorption into the whole is also limited by a fact which must to a great extent have forced Schubert to determine upon an enlargement of the quartet – namely, that in the string quartet the balance of the ensemble is not as good as in the archetypal model for 'pure composition', the four-part *a cappella* choir; experiments with other instruments for the middle parts, such as the tenor and treble viols, have confirmed this. The tenor register causes difficulties, because the viola is here a deep-toned instrument, whereas the cello, which has at its disposal the luminous quality of its top string, must also play the part of providing a bass. But the tenor range was of special interest to Schubert.

This is clearly allied to his tendency to burst asunder the accepted procedures of the string quartet, as mentioned above, and to create a new directness of musical utterance; the disruption of form in Beethoven's late quartets and Schubert's extension of the medium to a quintet seem almost to be similar manifestations, even if in certain particulars Beethoven's String Quartet op. 59 no. 2 may have played a special part as a point of reference.[9] This comparison

9 See for example the subjects of the slow movements, the *all'ongharese* character of the finales, the arpeggios of Beethoven's second subject and the final section of Schubert's exposition (first time in bars 118ff), or details such as the chromatic episodes which suddenly break into both finales (Schubert, bars 253ff).

Light is cast on Haydn's attitude towards extension of the string-quartet medium in an anecdote related in F. G. Wegeler and Ferdinand Ries, *Biographische Notizen über Ludwig van Beethoven* (Coblenz, 1838), p. 103: 'On the same occasion I asked Haydn why he had never written a string quintet and received the laconic answer that he had always found four voices sufficient. I had in fact been told that Haydn had been asked for three quintets but that he could never compose them because he had become so accustomed to the quartet style that he could not find the fifth voice. He had started them, but one attempt turned into a quartet, another into a sonata.'

might well seem surprising, since the Romantic expansion of classical tone-colours, the opening-up of hitherto unusual instrumental combinations and qualities, has always been ascribed mainly to newly awakened consciousness of the need for a richer palette. This explanation views the facts too much from the outside, if not from below; for a wider range of colours is rather the result of the composer's intention to break with the preoccupation with definite characteristics and purposes which is present in numerous masterpieces, and to put in its place a new directness of utterance, to emphasize strongly the simple elements in music-making as opposed to the monopoly of the high spiritual claims of compositional structure, and thus to bring back among other things the 'archaic remains' of the nature of music as 'the property of a sonorous object set in motion'.[10] In the unaccustomed treatment of instruments such as the use of extreme registers, the material nature of the instrument (the 'sonorous object') comes necessarily to the fore, and the same is true for dispositions whose departure from the norm is obvious, as for example with the song of the two cellos in the tenor register in the quintet. The second subject of the first movement at its first appearance could well be imagined as being played by a quartet, since the second melodic voice is also within the range of a violin and the part of the second violin could if necessary be omitted. If this were done, the uniqueness, the overriding impression of the breaking of established rules, would be lost, and the change of instrumentation would lose its associated change of harmony to E♭, so that if one wished to make it completely banal, bars 58-60 would show not a descent into E♭ major but an ascent into G major (by the melodic progression a′-a♯′-b′), which would be much more in keeping with the textbook scheme of a sonata-form movement. The bowdlerizing cannot be carried much further, of course, since in its very unclassical way this theme is nowhere identified with one harmonic position. Over its E♭ major lies the shadow of the preceding G – just established, yet so lightly thrown away – and if we can talk of a particular tonality for this theme, then it must be in terms of the harmonic tension between the poles of E♭ and G, of which the latter finally prevails.[11]

10 E. Bloch, 'Zauberrassel und Menschenharfe' in *Zur Philosophie der Musik* (Frankfurt am Main, 1974), pp. 202-7.

11 In this context we must remember that this 'highly unclassical' procedure, as it has been called, not only presupposes the classical, but rests upon classical precedent – especially in Mozart; for various examples of this I am indebted to Eva and Paul Badura-Skoda. The 'violence' of the G major preceding the lyrical theme is accounted for by the fact that it is nowhere cadentially established and therefore serves as a temporary keynote, a kind of 'emergency landing-strip'. It would therefore be unthinkable for the following theme to enter in C major. To take another example, the A major of the bridge passage in the first movement of Mozart's 'Coronation' Concerto K 537 is likewise un-established, contrary to the textbook, and in addition seems 'premature'; only before the entry of the second subject does it become clearly established by modulation. A similar procedure is observable in the Sonata K 381/123a. An example that is even more compelling because of its similarity to Schubert occurs in the Piano Concerto K 503. In the first movement (bars 146ff and

Taking as our starting-point the starkly positive nature of the musical texture, there are many passages, other than this cantabile second subject, that could serve as examples of writing properly playable only by a quintet – such, among many others, are the whole of the *Adagio*, the trio, the *fata morgana* in the finale (bars 127ff, 320ff), or details like the shrill octave-doubling just before the second subject in the first movement, and in the middle section of the *Adagio* (where the expansively dramatic style would test to the limit an even larger ensemble, because the sense of extreme effort is deliberate). Against all positive proof, however, it weighs more strongly that here for the first time Schubert allows the quintet disposition to make its peace with the musical procedure – in a combination which would have been just possible for a string quartet. The explosive configuration of voices in the first subject has aroused expectations, and at the end has created the outlet for a new musical event, in which the music finds its own momentum, stability and lyrical 'mean', although both tonality and instrumentation seem to come from without. The taking-over of the subject by the two violins seems on the other hand to bring it into the ensemble, almost like an appropriation, which is then finally completed by the arrival at G major in bar 100. Schubert underlines these stages with a stereotyped accompaniment – quavers from bar 60,

324ff) G major – albeit arrived at plagally – is followed by a theme in E♭, which (as in the Schubert example) fails to establish itself and compensates for its deviation into the subdominant by moving firmly towards the dominant in the recapitulation. As a special harmonic effect the possibilities of the mediant relationship (which in earlier composers is more often found between an introduction and the first movement proper) are however fully exploited by Schubert – and particularly when introducing the second subjects of sonata movements. In this respect the Trio op. 99 (D 898) seems to be the last stage in his handling of it before the quintet: in the first movement Schubert makes the second subject enter in the mediant, not only in the exposition but also in the recapitulation (bars 59ff and 244ff); the keynote A (D in the recapitulation) which is left sounding is seen as the mediant of F major (or B♭ major) – a reinterpretation which must be regarded as more than merely dictated by the nature of the themes, since the preceding temporary tonality of A (or D) was fully established, and the continuation could easily have entered in D major (or G major) and not in the mediant. Beyond this point the device is best illustrated in the quintet, where the conclusion in G major lacks cadential definition, which would have made it into a kind of 'colon' on the dominant before the formulation of the new idea or the introduction of the new tonic, and would establish it as a keynote. Schubert here shows what is impossible, rather than what is possible. Even when little more was available to him than a sudden modulation to the key of the mediant, the feeling of deviation and of breaking the rules remains – this sudden transition is not made to seem necessary or expected. In the quintet the note left sounding, unlike that in the trio, is given an audible change of function; in the trio, after being left to sound alone, it is suddenly heard in its new meaning. In the development section of the trio (bars 137ff) the descending bass (c-B♭-A♭) accomplishes this change of function with a weightiness which makes it seem almost inevitable, whereas the 'slight' difference from the quintet, the chromatic passage, has a lingering quality, a lack of resolution, so that the new keynote of E♭ seems to have been discovered, rather than arrived at ineluctably.

triplets from bar 81, semiquavers from bar 100. When the music arrives at the appropriate key of G major the theme is lost, although it may be heard shimmering through, deep in dominant territory, which balances the modulation to the subdominant on its first appearance. The classical conception of the sonata, which does not permit the second subject to enter in the tonic key, seems to be thought out in a very specific way in Schubert's theme, which, though unusual, makes a triumphant entry, and which, in coming to terms with the medium and its formal requirements, loses more and more of its own individuality. In contrast to classical custom, tonality and theme fail to come together in the recapitulation too, and do not coalesce until the coda (bars 429ff) – a point at which the melody can only be remembered.

No less clearly does Schubert abandon the reconciliatory purpose and function of the classical recapitulation (we should regard it as the presentation of a musical event, or synthesis, or perhaps – reversing classical premisses – as the 'conjuration of a static identity in a development process'[12]), whilst – again utilizing the specific potential of the quintet – he increases the disparity of the complexes. The formal need to have a 'development process' is at a great remove from Schubert's assertive presentation of the themes, expecially when lyrical, a fact which enhances their uniqueness. In the section (bars 267-320) which includes the 'introduction' and first theme, he increases the sense of division: the former (bars 267ff) is in C major, the latter (bars 295ff) in F major, and compared with the exposition they are now a further octave apart. The contours thus stand out more sharply, and this is even more true of the second subject. If in the recapitulation the first subject is more harshly highlighted, the second (bars 322ff) is in even darker shadow, and here its lyrical self-sufficiency acquires a special forcefulness. Its A♭ major lies a fifth below the E♭ of the exposition, and the viola playing it at the bottom of its range gives the melody not only the rough sonority of its C string, but also a dark subterranean quality. One would dearly like to know how Schubert arrived at such a combination. The fact that the viola plays as far down as its lowest open string, even though in relation to the exposition nothing has been altered, seems to indicate that it was decided upon at an early stage, and that when the exposition was being written, the recapitulation was already planned. On the other hand Schubert had no choice but to keep this disposition if he wished to retain the predominance of the cello, as he needed the second cello for the pizzicato bass. Here one sees with exemplary clarity how Schubert's recapitulations, unlike those in the classical idiom, go against the modifying influences of the time-flow, of the need for a summary and a reconciliation of opposing ideas, as is demanded by tradition. We also see how the generally extensive quotation of the exposition[13] is connected with an attitude of obstinate insistence upon lyrical singing and its unique sound-quality.

12 T. W. Adorno, *Einleitung in die Musiksoziologie* (Frankfurt am Main, 1962), p. 223.

13 On this difficulty see especially H. Gál, *Franz Schubert oder die Melodie* (Frankfurt am Main, 1970), pp. 131ff.

From this unique sound one thing is inseparable – and the second subject of the first movement, the lyrical middle voices of the *Adagio*, the *fata morgana* of the finale (bars 127ff and 320ff), and in particular the lyrical characteristics of the G major String Quartet, all have it in common – the use of the tenor register. Schubert the lyricist sings most freely in the tenor; at any rate, he constantly begins in the tenor. Therein lies another obvious reason for the enlargement of the quartet to a quintet – the establishment of the tenor register as the fount of musical invention. Too much attention may have been paid to it as peculiar to the song; yet organically it is undoubtedly a mid-point, not only because its harmonics are especially pleasing to the ear, but even more because no sense of strain at reaching a particular register is associated with it. The melody can best be itself when it is neither too high nor too low; nowhere else can the natural calm of its appearance be so great, or can it give so firm and individual an impression of undisturbed composure. Not least, the melody can here be best surrounded by the accompanying voices. The cleavage into two groups at the beginning of the quintet can be described as leaving an intentional gap in the middle range, which, when given over to the lyrical second subject, in many respects causes the ensemble to sound complete; and it is not only in the quintet that deviations or passages involving great effort are constantly associated with the use of extreme registers. This is in great measure true also of the tempos; with these too Schubert tends to avoid extremes. One rarely finds a wild *presto* in his music; in this respect the exceptional finales of the string quartets in D minor and G major seem to be impelled by a feeling of hectic activity rather than of untroubled naturalness; and it is almost surprising, with a melodist of his rank, to find so rarely an *Adagio* like that in the quintet.

Here one might almost speak of a 'programmatic' intention, for in the *Adagio* Schubert has transcended the lyrical theme of the first movement and its particular configuration; that its vast melodic breadth should exceed everything that has gone before is part of the design. The long notes of the sonorous middle register endow the lyricism with an idealistic quality, which turns the subtle melodic current into the musical equivalent of a Platonic idea; this requires no formal realization, nor would one be possible, but it hovers like a perpetual promise over the actual notes. The quavers which recur mostly at the end of the bar therefore have the effect of a promise that the listener is at last to feel that he has grasped the melody, which nevertheless constantly withdraws anew into the repose of unmoving sound. Just as the tempo is remote from normal singing, so the key too points towards transcendental rapture; E major is with Schubert the key of almost unreal, dreamt-of promise. It is the key of 'Der Lindenbaum', of 'Dann Blümlein alle, heraus, heraus . . .' ('Trockne Blumen'), which is almost drunk with hope, of the all-consoling last song of *Die schöne Müllerin*, and of the second movement of the 'Unfinished' Symphony. The never-ending melody in the middle parts, with their long note-values seeming to be 'up there in the light' (Friedrich Hölderlin, 'Hyperions Schicksalslied'), cannot do without the harmonic and rhythmic support of the first violin and the second cello, yet can also convey the impression of being independent of such support. This ambivalence cannot be understood apart from the three-part layout, and gives the melodic fabric the possibility of complex harmonic changes but not of total freedom, as is evident from the frequent lack of bass notes. Again and again that melodic fabric rises and falls above the sound of the outer parts and becomes significantly more condensed at the pre-cadential bars (8, 12, 14, 23 etc.). In the lucid and restrained decoration of the transitions from one essential note to the next, the melody descends somewhat from its transcendental heights to the ordinary level of comprehensibility and appears like a consummation which is perpetually promised but never realized. The contributions of the first violin and the second cello are by no means simply decorative (in bars 24ff the violin begins to take the lead); and at the same time the listener's efforts to grasp the melody seem to become articulate – in the metrical framework, and in the urgent search for definition, for participation in the music, wherever this is possible.

It would be wrong to describe this by no means insignificant sound-stratum as a mere accompaniment, just as it would be wrong to say this about the second subject in the first movement. Schubert always found ways and means of protecting and nurturing his lyrical gift; he makes it possible by finding channels for it which, from the outset, create a safe environment by virtue of their stereotyped character as well as by a particular kind of natural motion, whose regularity contrasts with the delicate variety of the melodies which they protectively support. Therefore the melodies appear to be guarded in a way that is almost impermissible within the sonata cycle, which as it was understood by the classical era seeks the interdependence of manifold musical devices. Only in this way do Schubert's melodic structures become possible: in these parts serving as 'channels', a sheltered harbour is created for the melodies, a device with which the older classical composers did not need to concern themselves. For with them, tempo and metre were settled as if in an axiomatic relationship right from the first melodic coinage, and thus formed a clear system of co-ordinates, valid also – until explicitly cancelled – at those places where the music seems to be metrically free and not dependent on the ticking of an imagined metronome. As suggested above when discussing the opening bars of the quintet, Schubert's music must find its own pace and gain its own momentum, or, in the cantilena passages, simply receive it. Since with Schubert musical time is not governed by rules, it can move rapidly, come to a halt, or go calmly on its way (we are only at the very beginning of an understanding of these matters);[14] he can bring the introduction and the

14 See D. Schnebel, 'Schubert: Auf der Suche nach der verlorenen Zeit' in *Denkbare Musik* (Cologne, 1972), pp. 116-29; U. Schreiber, 'Schicksal und Versöhnung. Zum Spätstil Schuberts', *Musica*, XXX (1976), pp. 289-94.

tempo giusto of the opening of a first movement together under the same roof, i.e. within the same tempo; but he cannot leave the musical effect to take care of itself, and be carried along by a time-flow established at the outset. The measures he adopts to express his lyricism give to the latter an added expressiveness, and this also was a factor in the enlargement of the quartet, since with the minimum of two instruments for the accompaniment there would remain only two for the melodic parts. A constellation such as that in the *Andante un poco moto* of the G major String Quartet, with the viola acting as intermediary between the solitary cantabile cello and the stereotyped rhythmic figures of the violins, may in this sense be regarded as a compromise, even if it is also a very successful solution. A melodic structure such as that in the *Adagio* of the quintet, in which melodic and harmonic processes are continually intertwined and give each other support, was (as explained above) impossible for a string quartet.

A connection appears here between the canonic character of the quartet medium and the axiomatic character of the time-flow of classical music: both presuppose that an aesthetic structure can by reason of its inner logic be transmuted without difficulty into the world of physical sound. Here, too, Schubert's textural enlargement to a quintet reveals how the distance between intention and realization has increased. This is not to say that a structure designed for a string quartet can from now onwards only be realized on a grander scale – as a quintet, say, among other possibilities. Nevertheless, the thought does not appear in principle misleading, since in the quartet the objectification of the structural basis – the four parts – by reason of the physical nature of instruments seems to make the dialectic of the transmission of idea into sound superfluous. Such a 'spiritual' approach, which has been claimed for Schubert above, demands that in a philosophical sense instruments be regarded purely as instruments, a conception which evidently did not satisfy him in the preceding quartets, if it could ever have satisfied him. This problem only affected him when he first entered upon the highest level of composition.

Without more careful consideration of the most important points, the preceding discussion might be suspected of being contradictory. On the one hand mention was made of the inevitable way in which the quintet can be divided into sound groups, while the quartet is clearly organized according to the principles of pure composition; on the other hand in a case such as the delineation of the 'channels' the expansion into a quintet was explained by the challenge which the form then offered. The validity of both explanations becomes especially evident with the help of works which make it clear that the latter – or historical – argument is unconvincing, and that Schubert found his models in Mozart. How close the beginning of the recapitulation sounds in Schubert's first movement to the opening of Mozart's Quintet K 515 has often been remarked upon, when it has not been regarded merely as a sign of homage. Moreover in the regular semiquaver movement of the inner parts a melodic structure is also to be found, as also in the *Adagio* of the Quintet K 593, or the *Adagio* introduction to the finale of the G minor Quintet K 516. In general, Schubert seems to have learnt a great deal from Mozart about the change of sonorities and instrumental combinations; it was in Mozart that he found a copious inventory of what was possible in a quintet, from the almost uninterrupted note-against-note movement of the *Adagio* introduction in K 516 to the many-stranded counterpoint of the first movement of K 593. In its contrast of a group of high instruments with a group of low ones, Schubert's work could clearly be considered as modelled on Mozart's Quintet in G minor. As suggested above, Schubert creates for himself, in what may be taken as an introduction, the possibility of making the upper and lower parts reflect each other, whereas Mozart uses simple repetition for the most part in presenting his first subject. With Mozart such procedures are displayed more as readily available possibilities than as necessary consequences of quintet writing, as is the case with Schubert. To this extent the contemporary state of the art of composition clearly plays its part in his expansion of the quartet medium. This is borne out not least by the fact that Mozart's quintets stand strangely alone in their claims upon our attention; for Beethoven's quintets (and sextets) make demands that are very different from those made by his string quartets. Since the quartet is governed by strict premisses, it cannot be a matter of 'indifference' that such closely related works are composed as Schubert's String Quintet, in which intentions are realized that spring quite unmistakably from within the quartet's own province. Such are the almost quartet-like lyrical second subject of the first movement, with a new directness of utterance which a quartet cannot command, or the wildly sobbing lamentation of the middle section of the *Adagio*, the awesome sounds of the catacomb in the trio, and the 'unrefined' subterranean effects in the finale – realms of expression now thrown together which for the most part were kept comfortably apart. Since the last quartets of Beethoven point in other directions, Schubert accomplishes in the quintet that enlargement of accepted ideas about the string-quartet medium which is so markedly true of the Rasumovsky Quartets.[15] The question now arises whether after this crossing of the frontier a deliberately chosen restriction (and an element of retreat) would not be involved in the return to the established quartet model – which can be both limiting and stimulating. An investigation into the chamber music of Brahms might be enlightening. In Schubert's case the conjecture cannot be entirely dismissed as to whether, if he had lived to write another string quartet after the quintet, he would have been able to follow up the innovations of the latter, any more than in the C major Symphony, for all its greatness, he was able to follow up those of the 'Unfinished'.

15 P. Gülke, 'Zur musikalischen Konzeption der Rasumowski-Quartette op. 59 von Beethoven' in *Sozialistische Musikkultur* (Berlin and Moscow, 1977), pp. 397-430.

Precisely because its rank and its claims threaten to establish a new genre of composition, the quintet belongs to the history of the string quartet. Accordingly, Brown's remark quoted at the beginning of this essay – suggesting that Schubert could have chosen a different ensemble for the same purpose – can hardly stand up to a practical analysis.

Portrait bust of Schubert, unsigned (most probably by Anton Dietrich), *c.* 1830 (private collection, Vienna)

This hitherto unknown bust seems to be the lost portrait of Schubert of which Moritz von Schwind wrote in 1865 (when approached by the Wiener Männergesangverein regarding portraits of Schubert):

> Your Honour,
>
> Here, as fast as I could manage it, is the information you requested, to the best of my knowledge . . . You must inquire of Rieder where the original miniature is to be found. We have always held this to be the best portrait. A lithograph by Teltscher was more *en face* and should be taken note of by sculptors. There is a useful drawing by Kuppelwieser which I saw only last winter in a folder which his wife has; there is also a superb head in profile by him after his coloured drawing in the possession of Herr von Schober in Dresden. The bust by Dietrich, who knew Schubert very well, delights us all, and I only wish that one of your competitors could achieve something like this work. Those are all the portraits known to me . . .

Possibilities and limitations of stylistic criticism in the dating of Schubert's 'Great' C major Symphony

PAUL BADURA-SKODA

One of the most precious manuscripts belonging to the Gesellschaft der Musikfreunde in Vienna is the autograph score of Schubert's C major Symphony D 944, which the Society received from Schubert shortly after its completion. On the top right-hand side of the first page of the score is Schubert's usual signature, and a date which until December 1977[1] was unquestioningly taken to read 'March 1828'. In the process of binding, the upper edge of the manuscript has been cut in such a way that a small part of the date has been removed. Schubert's date on this autograph has repeatedly given rise to extensive discussion, since he was in the habit of dating his compositions when he began them rather than after they were completed.[2] If in this case he followed his usual practice, then he began it in 1828, the year of his death – assuming that he made no mistake and that '1828' is the correct reading, as has been supposed for many decades. From Winter's investigations into paper types (see pp. 232-7, 257-67 below) and Otto Biba's archival researches,[3] we now know that Schubert's last complete symphony was in fact written before 1828. The symphony was written on paper made in 1825-6 and must have been revised for the last time before August 1827, when the orchestral parts were copied.

1 On 14 December 1977 Ernst Hilmar gave a lecture at the Musikwissenschaftliches Institut of the University of Vienna, and here for the first time he propounded the thesis that the reading of the date as '1828' on the autograph manuscript of the C major Symphony was mistaken, the actual year written being '1825'. See Ernst Hilmar, 'Neue Funde, Daten und Dokumente zum symphonischen Werk Franz Schuberts', *Österreichische Musikzeitschrift*, XXXIII (1978), pp. 266-76.

2 If we leave out the many undated works, which in the main are youthful creations, there are very few cases of doubtful or incorrect dating by Schubert. Unlike the present problematic case most of those are easily accounted for, as for example when Schubert once, at the beginning of January, put the year which had just ended – an error which we are all liable to make.

3 The results of these researches were made known by Otto Biba in the course of a lecture entitled 'Franz Schubert und die Gesellschaft der Musikfreunde in Wien', delivered at the Schubert Congress in Vienna organized by the Österreichische Gesellschaft für Musikwissenschaft and held between 4 and 10 June 1978: Biba's paper is published in *Schubert-Kongress Wien 1978. Bericht*, ed. O. Brusatti (Graz, 1979), pp. 23-36.

In recent decades there has been an abundance of literature on the subject of the date of composition of the symphony.[4] It was John Reed's *Schubert. The Final Years* (published in 1972) that prompted the present article; Reed, like Feigl in his earlier and almost unknown study, came out decisively in favour of an early date for the symphony, without of course knowing the results of more recent scientific and documentary research. When Reed sought on stylistic grounds to prove its identity with the 'Gastein Symphony', which was certainly begun in 1825, it was precisely these stylistic arguments that from a musical point of view seemed questionable, at times even false, and therefore provoked opposition; if however the 'identity thesis' was sound – and in the meantime we have become virtually certain that the C major Symphony was indeed written before 1828 – then the result of Reed's researches must be regarded as correct.

An analysis of the style of Schubert's works would seem to us to require especial care, for the stylistic idiosyncrasies of different periods are less clearly defined with Schubert than with other composers. One repeatedly finds almost inexplicable anticipations and reversions. Does not the 'Quartettsatz' in C minor D 703 seem closely related to the C minor Sonata D 958, which was written over eight years later? Should not one regard the song 'Suleika I' D 720 as having been written more or less at the same time as the first movement of the 'Unfinished' Symphony D 759, to which it is so closely related in respect of key and motivic impulse, rather than one and a half years earlier? The tarantella finales of the D minor String Quartet, the G major String Quartet and the C minor Piano Sonata show a similar interconnection, although they belong to three different creative periods. The last movements of the 'Trout' Quintet (1819), the Grand Duo (1824), and the last piano sonata (1828) all begin with similar thematic material; likewise, the trio of the minuet in the first keyboard sonata (1815) is linked with the trio of the D major Sonata (1825), and the second movement of the Sonata in A minor D 537 (1817) with the finale of the A major Sonata D 959 (1828). Between the middle and last stylistic periods it is especially difficult to make any hard and fast distinctions, there is, rather, a gradual change of style. Therefore, in seeking to date a composition it would be a mistake to assign to a

4 Out of the abundant literature on this subject, and in addition to the relevant passages in O. E. Deutsch, *Schubert. Memoirs by His Friends* (London, 1958) and *Schubert. A Documentary Biography* (London, 1951), and M. J. E. Brown's *Schubert. A Critical Biography* (London, 1958), Appendix I, the following are the most important and comprehensive: Rudolf Feigl, *Klar um Schubert, Beseitigungen von Irrmeinungen, Fehlangaben usw.* (Linz, 1936), which deserves attention because it anticipates the theories of Brown and Reed (see below); Maurice Brown's article 'The Genesis of the Great C Major Symphony' in *Essays on Schubert* (London, 1966), pp. 29-58; John Reed, *Schubert. The Final Years* (London, 1972); also Reed's article 'How the "Great" C Major Was Written', *Music and Letters*, LVI (1975), pp. 18-25; and L. M. Griffel, 'Schubert's Approach to the Symphony', Ph. D. diss., Columbia University 1976.

particular period idiosyncrasies of style which are found throughout Schubert's *oeuvre,* or at least which extend beyond a single period. It was this mistake that John Reed made when, for instance, he related the rising third in bar 1 of the introductory theme of the C major Symphony (Ex. 1) to the beginning of the song 'Die Allmacht' D 852, which was written in 1825 (Ex. 2). The rising third in each is certainly unmistakable, but apart from this the two themes have nothing whatever in common. Such three-note motives are indeed more frequent in the works of Schubert's last year than before 1825, as in the finale of the Fantasia for Violin and Piano D 934 (December 1827) – Ex. 3 – which is closer to the opening of the symphony than is the song 'Die Allmacht' of 1825.

Ex. 1

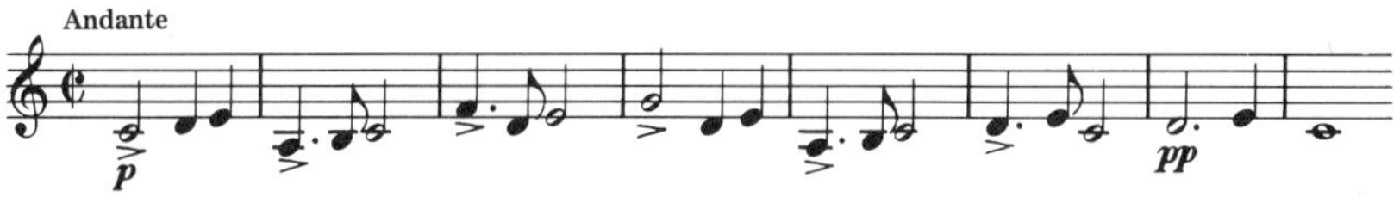

Ex. 2

Ex. 3

Other examples of a rising third above the tonic at the beginning of a movement may be found in the Gloria of the E flat major Mass D 950 (where it occurs frequently), in the first subject of the String Quintet D 956, in the B flat major Sonata D 960 (at the beginning of the first movement and in the middle section of the second), in the song 'Am Meer' D 957, and in the Benedictus D 961 – all of these could therefore equally be quoted as 'proof' of the correctness of 1828 as the date of the symphony. The same applies to the other signs of affinity which Reed mentions:

And the many references in the symphony to the other compositions of 1825 – the four-times rhythmically repeated notes, the 'run-up to the wicket' in triplet rhythm before a cadence back to the tonic, the ambiguous use of chromatically adjacent sevenths and sixths, these fingerprints of the years

1824 and 1825, and many others, leave no doubt where the internal evidence points on the question of the symphony's origin.[5]

The 'four-times rhythmically repeated notes' evidently refers to a passage in the last movement of the Sonata in A minor D 845 of 1825 (bars 181-91) – Ex. 4 – which indeed bears a certain resemblance to the second subject of the finale of the symphony – Ex. 5 – as well as to the last two bars of 'Mirjam's Siegesgesang' D 942 of 1828 (see the end of Ex. 27, below). However, since similar motives consisting of repeated notes are more often to be found in works composed in 1828, such as the Mass in E flat major D 950 (in the Quoniam and Dona nobis pacem: Ex. 6) or the three Klavierstücke D 946, this comparison also proves nothing. One could on the other hand indeed ask whether the sequence in bars 17-24 of the first of these pieces – Ex. 7 – does not more closely resemble the symphonic theme than any phrase dating from 1825 (see also Ex. 16 from the third of these pieces).

Ex. 4

Ex. 5

Ex. 6

5 *Schubert. The Final Years*, p. 97.

Ex. 7

In the second of these piano pieces the transitions which precede and follow the middle section in C minor are based upon the same technical principle as is the *Andante con moto* of the symphony (bars 89-92). The upper part remains stationary, while the bass descends a third to the new key-note (submediant). Yet this characteristically Schubertian procedure is found in several works, and not only between 1824 and 1828;[6] no stylistic conclusions can therefore be drawn from it. The triplet passages or the harmonic idioms cited by Reed, which resemble passages in the symphony more in feeling than in form, are likewise representative of no particular period, but are to be found in works that are early, middle or late.[7]

In his essay on the C major Symphony Maurice Brown also refers to other works, and rightly draws our attention to the resemblance between the opening bars of the second movement of the symphony and the song 'Der Wegweiser' in *Winterreise* (1827): 'The processional music of this song must have been in Schubert's mind during the composition of the symphonic A minor movement.'[8] He then rightly likens the trio of the scherzo to another *Winterreise* song, 'Die Nebensonnen', and to the trio from the String Quartet 'Der Tod und das Mädchen'.[9] At that time Brown was still thinking of 1828 as the date of origin. Do these similarities perhaps speak for the simultaneous conception of these songs, the D minor String Quartet, and the second movement of the symphony? The music paper allows the conjecture that the A minor movement was written earlier than 'Der Wegweiser', in the spring of 1827, but may have been revised; a direct connection is therefore possible but cannot be proved. (Brown's remarks (p. 32) concerning the bars afterwards inserted into

6 See the C major Fantasy D 760 ('Wanderer'), first movement, bars 66-7; the Sonata for four hands in C major ('Grand Duo') D 812 of 1824, fourth movement, bars 403-5; the Piano Trio in B flat major op. 99, D 898, first movement, bars 137-9; and the String Quintet in C major D 956, first movement, bars 58-60.

7 Reed has also drawn a false conclusion from one of Schubert's corrections in the finale: after bar 163 Schubert struck out the rest of the page, on which there was originally another draft of the second subject. If the rejected theme had first been written in 1828, as Reed supposes, Schubert would in 1826 have had to leave the other side of the sheet free, in order to be able to sketch out a finale in 'contrapuntal' style. Moreover, this rejected theme was in no way a 'fugue-like subject', as Reed (p. 201) and L. M. Griffel ('A Reappraisal of Schubert's Methods of Composition', *Musical Quarterly*, LXIII (1977), pp. 186-218, esp. p. 208) assert; rather is it a homophonic idea consisting of two eight-bar phrases.

8 Brown, 'Genesis of the Great C Major Symphony', p. 39.

9 Ibid., pp. 44-5.

the theme of the introduction are moreover untenable and were often corrected by him later.[10])

Let us now examine those technical peculiarities of the symphony which are of a more specific nature and can be found in few other works, and consider whether any cautious conclusions can be drawn from them. It is astonishing that to my knowledge no attention has been given to the fact that in the first, third and fourth movements Schubert uses a new harmonic formula, of which no trace appears in his work before the end of 1826. He places the German augmented sixth with the bass not on the submediant, as is usually the case, but on the subdominant, and resolves it on to the $^6_3$ of the tonic chord: Ex. 8. In the Viennese classical style one would normally expect this to resolve on to the major or minor $^6_4$ of the submediant: Ex. 9. This highly original turn of harmony, one of Schubert's discoveries, makes it possible for him to avoid the somewhat conventional resolutions which appear in his earlier works. It is to be found in the coda of the first movement, bars 632-7 (on an extra sheet of music paper which he subsequently added), in the trio of the scherzo, bars 378-83 (Ex. 10), and several times in the finale, bars 190-7, 246-53, 330-7, 778-85, 834-41, 918-25, and 1046-53 (Ex. 11).

Ex. 8

Ex. 9

10 In a letter dated 19 December 1967 Brown wrote to me, 'This error caused me never-ending distress.' At his request later copies of the *Essays* were provided with an erratum slip. Unfortunately this error was repeated in Griffel's article 'A Reappraisal of Schubert's Methods of Composition', where he quoted the theme incorrectly in a version which is two bars short, although he declares in the foreword to his dissertation, written before his article, that he had been the first person to make a careful study of the autograph.

Ex. 10

(bar 378)

Ex. 11

(bar 1046)

The only other work by Schubert in which the same progression is to be found is the Sonata Fantasia in G major op. 78, D 894, which he began in October 1826. It is interesting to observe that in the first movement, where the idiom seems to occur as though by chance, it is not employed by Schubert for the purpose of building a cadence (bars 155ff, and parallel passages: Ex. 12, p. 194). Clearly, only one note has been altered from the progression in Ex. 13, which was in common use long before the time of Schubert, and in which the outer parts move in contrary motion. Not until the last movement of the sonata is this progression used with cadential effect as in the symphony, although in a far more modest way (bars 203-6 and 301-4). Here too it rather playfully adds a sudden piquancy; instead of the expected minor $^{6}_{4}$ on C, Schubert presents us with a major $^{6}_{3}$ on E♭, and satisfies our disappointed expectations some four bars later by supplying the traditional resolution. In the symphony things are quite different: the new progression is introduced with

Ex. 12

Ex. 13

consummate craftsmanship, and makes it possible for him, as never before, to effect a return to the tonic from very remote harmonic territory. No earlier example of this progression has come to my notice.[11]

Whether the use of this chord in the G major Sonata D 894 should be regarded as anticipating the symphony or as following it is a question that cannot easily be answered. One feels inclined to interpret its rather playful treatment in the sonata as an indication that the latter preceded the symphony; yet such a view has no firm evidence to support it. It is of course astonishing that such a characteristic and significant turn of harmony should have made its first appearance in the symphony, without in any way making its influence felt in the other works composed in 1825, such as the three great piano sonatas D 840, 845 and 850. It is also strange that Schubert apparently was the first to discover this original progression and then forgot its existence for more than a year, only to take it up again at the end of 1826. It therefore appears worth mentioning that in the symphony it is used regularly only in the finale, so much so that it may be described as part of the movement's very structure. Before this it had appeared only twice, and precisely in those passages which, according to Robert Winter's examination of the paper (see pp. 260-1), were written on sheets that Schubert inserted later. From this one may put forward the following hypothesis: the first three movements could already have been in existence in 1825, whereas the appearance of this progression would seem to bring the finale's date of composition nearer to that of the G major Sonata of 1826.

The scherzo must originally have had another trio. This is evident from the fact that to make room for the newly added sheets a series of others have been removed. Schubert appears to have composed a new trio in a fresh burst of

11 After Schubert's death, this progression seems to have fallen into disuse; it was revived some decades later by Tchaikovsky, who employs it with great effect in the second movement of his Fifth Symphony at each of the two climaxes. Instead of the expected B minor $^6_4$ the second theme enters on a $^6_3$ in D major, preceded however by B minor $^6_4$ as an appoggiatura.

energy, as well as the most important part of the coda of the first movement. The introduction of the same turn of harmony found in the finale into each of the rewritten passages was perhaps intended to emphasize the work's stylistic unity. This revision might perhaps help to place the last phase of the composition somewhere between September–October 1826 at the earliest, and August 1827 (when the orchestral parts were copied) at the latest. Other stylistic peculiarities of these two passages point rather to the latter year.[12] The coda of the first movement on the inserted sheet shows another harmonic progression which likewise suggests a later date. This is a diminished triad or diminished seventh which resolves in an unusual way, one of the outer parts being sounded as a suspension before the succeeding perfect fifth and raised or lowered a semitone – Ex. 14. This progression appears in bars 614-18 of the first movement of the symphony – Ex. 15 – and a very similar example occurs later in the third of the Klavierstücke D 946 of 1828, bars 70-3 – Ex. 16. Comparable passages also occur in the Piano Fantasia in F minor for four hands D 940 (bars 64 and 90), in the scherzo of the B flat major Sonata D 960 (bars 67-8), and in other compositions. Since all these works are later than the symphony, the latter presumably contains the first use by Schubert of this progression.

Ex. 14 (a) (b)

Ex. 15

12 An examination of the paper of the inserted sheets in the first and third movements, which confirms that it was made in 1826 (see pp. 236-7), does not contradict this hypothesis outright. In 1827 Schubert could very well have used single sheets of paper bought but not used in 1826. There are several instances of Schubert's repeatedly drawing upon old stocks of paper. Brown has established that the F sharp minor Piano Sonata D 571/570 of 1817 was written on different types of paper, which include fragments of earlier works from 1815-16 (*Essays on Schubert*, pp. 206f). The autograph of the song 'Iphigenia' D 573, which dates from 1817, recently appeared at an auction. It consists of a four-sided sheet, on the first page of which a fugal study of 1813 is notated.

Ex. 16

Ex. 17 (a) Symphony in C major, trio of the scherzo

(b) Sonata in A major, trio of the scherzo

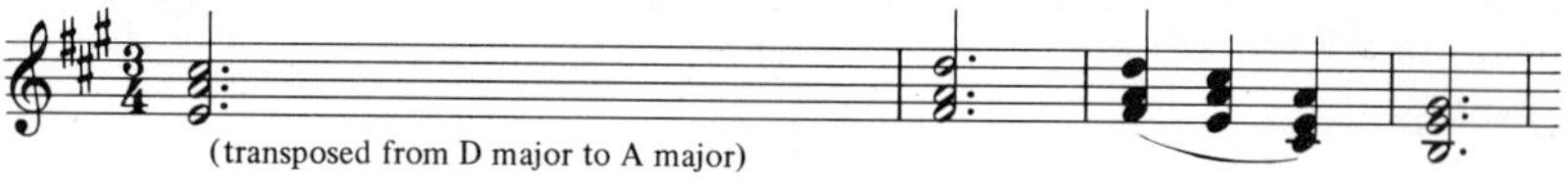

The elegiac quality of the newly composed trio too seems to tie in better with 1827. A certain melodic kinship with the trio of the scherzo from the A major Sonata D 959 is noticeable: Ex. 17. The poetic content of the symphony's trio, and its richness of harmony, have hardly any parallels in works written in 1825-6. The reader is here referred to the thoroughly reliable analysis of its harmony made by D. F. Tovey for the Schubert number of *Music and Letters* in 1928.[13]

Sometimes it is not only the later insertions but the bulk of the symphony which contains passages of stylistic interest that do not unequivocally point to the middle period of Schubert's creative activity. Thus in the late instrumental works suspensions occur with figuration at cadences, stemming from the church music tradition and thus readily available for Schubert to make use of in his early devotional compositions. He employed them also in secular works, thereby imbuing these too with a certain religious quality. Hans Gál underlines this in a striking way in his book on Schubert, when referring to Schumann's description of the Austrian landscape:

> There is no doubt that this is the style of church music; the suspended cadences are unmistakable . . . And likewise Schumann, that sensitive observer, immediately perceived and has described for us a distinctive feature of the Austrian scene – it is suffused with a gentle aroma of Catholic incense. Everywhere in Austria one finds holy places – crucifixes, wayside shrines, chapels

13 Reprinted in *Essays and Lectures on Music*, ed. H. Foss (London, 1949), pp. 134-59.

> by the roadside, . . . or in a woodland clearing he finds religious pictures hanging from the trees . . . Here, in the fresh Alpine air of this sonata movement [D 959], there must be such a 'Waldandacht' or woodland shrine, a manifestation of the unaffected and completely undemonstrative religious feeling which finds such beautiful and spontaneous expression in Schubert's masses.[14]

We find this devotional formula at many points in the A major Sonata D 959, e.g. first movement, bars 21 and 324 (Ex. 18); in the String Quintet D 956 it appears in the first movement, bars 76-7, 97-8, 125-6 and elsewhere, and also in the trio of the scherzo, bars 219-20. In the symphony it occurs in a related form several times during the first two movements – e.g. first movement bars 15-16 (Ex. 19).

Ex. 18 (a) (b)

Ex. 19

Another expressive melodic detail, which to my knowledge is otherwise only to be found in works written in 1828, might be described as a 'motif of ecstasy'. The E flat Mass D 950 has examples of this, as in bars 25 and 61 of the Benedictus. It also appears in the Rondo in A major for four hands D 951, bars 227-8 (Ex. 20), and at several points in the second movement of the C major Symphony, e.g. bar 275 (Ex. 21). If we did not know that this symphony was completed by the summer of 1827 at the latest, such coincidences could easily lead to false conclusions.

One of the boldest harmonic innovations of Schubert's last works is the juxtaposition of chords from widely distant keys, such as E♭ major with B

14 H. Gál, *Franz Schubert oder die Melodie* (Frankfurt am Main, 1970), pp. 139f.

Ex. 20

Ex. 21

minor, or C minor with E minor. One finds, intensified by chromaticisms, a leaning towards the key of the mediant which can hardly be explained in terms of functional harmony. For this very reason its psychological effect is extraordinarily powerful, and is perhaps to be labelled with such terms as 'lofty', 'exalted' or 'awe in the presence of the numinous'. This tendency towards the mediant, which was later taken up by Bruckner (as in the Credo of the F minor Mass at the words 'Sedet ad dexteram'), reveals itself in the first movement of the C major Symphony, bars 54-7, where the progression moves from D♭ minor to F minor – Ex. 22 – in the second movement of the A major Sonata D 959, bars 91-3, from D♭ minor to E minor, and in the Sanctus of the E flat major Mass, bars 1-7 (E♭ major - B minor - G minor, and thence to E♭ minor): Ex. 23. In this Sanctus Schubert has bridged the steps over a major third in the bass with a passing note, thus producing a whole-tone scale (E♭–D♭–C♭(B)–A–G–F–E♭), which has of course little in common with the later whole-tone scale of Impressionist harmony, as found in Debussy or the later works of Liszt. A similar whole-tone scale is to be found in the first movement of the symphony, bars 304-15, 328-39 (1st and 2nd violins): Ex. 24. Another example occurs in the second movement of the C minor Sonata D 958, bars 104-5. This could point to a close stylistic relationship between the symphony and the works composed in 1828, yet isolated ex-

Ex. 22

Ex. 23

Ex. 24 Symphony in C major, first movement, bars 328ff

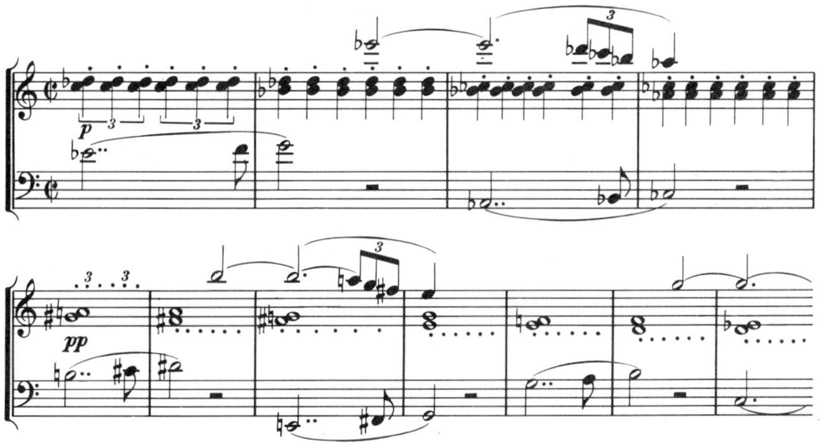

amples of the whole-tone scale are found even earlier: see bars 172-6 in the finale of the Octet D 803 and the first movement of the String Quartet in G major D 887, bars 374-8. In the finale of the String Quintet in C major, Schubert even presents us with a rising whole-tone scale:[15] Ex. 25.

Ex. 25

Ex. 26

Yet another characteristic trait, which makes an occasional appearance in Schubert's early works, occurs frequently during his last year and could almost be regarded as typical of his late compositions. This is the resolution of the dominant of the mediant chord on to the dominant seventh of the tonic, i.e. in the key of C from the chord of B major or minor to the dominant seventh on G. For this characteristically Schubertian progression see bars 27-8 of the first movement of the C major Symphony: Ex. 26. It recurs in bars 37-9, 155-8 and 185-8, and in similar passages in other works, e.g. in the opening chorus of 'Mirjam's Siegesgesang' of March 1828, bars 21, 26, 30, 69, 73, among others: Ex. 27. The progression in Ex. 28 is from the String Quintet D 956, where it is used repeatedly, e.g. first movement, bars 140 and 144, as also in bars 103-6 of the scherzo. Apart from the symphony I have found only one other instance of this harmony in works of 1825-6, namely in the unfinished last movement of the C major Sonata D 840, bars 86-7. It even appears in much earlier works, such as the last movement of the Sixth Symphony,

15 For directing my attention to these passages I am indebted to the late K. P. Bernet-Kempers (see *Mens en Melodie*, XVI (1961), pp. 179-81).

Ex. 27

Ex. 28

completed in 1818 (bars 469-70, 475-6, 521-2, and 527-8). A psychological change in the meaning of this progression is noteworthy: what in the earlier works is a last touch of spice added to the harmony in the building up of a final climax is in the later ones an unusual combination, but one now felt to be inadequate for any cumulative purpose. It is moreover remarkable that Schubert uses this almost exclusively in the key of C major, thus giving his use of this key a character which distinguishes it from all other tonalities.

Not only in melody and harmony but also in the instrumental layout, parallels can be drawn between the symphony and other works composed in 1828, which could lead to an incorrect dating on the basis of stylistic analogies. A technical detail often encountered in other late works is the preference given to cellos rather than to violas. With melodies in the tenor register, the fuller tone of the cellos is brought into play, by giving them the upper part and allotting the middle part to the violas, which mostly play a third below. An example of this romantic instrumentation occurs in the first movement of the symphony, bars 23-8 – Ex. 29 – and in various passages in the String Quintet D 956, such as bars 322-41 of the first movement[16] – Ex. 30. Similar melodic writing for the cellos had of course existed long before, as in Mozart's A major Rondo K 386 or in the 'Unfinished' Symphony (first movement, second subject). The novelty of this combination lies in the fact that the

16 Brahms, who was closely acquainted with Schubert's works, used the same refinement of orchestral technique in his Second Symphony (first movement, second subject).

Ex. 29

Ex. 30

viola does not keep to its usual role of playing the double-bass part an octave higher, but has a separate middle part.[17]

It is not only on the basis of many of the technical details already mentioned that one could accept the relationship of the symphony with other works known to belong to the last of Schubert's creative periods; the structure of the work as a whole reveals it to be a kind of opus ultimum. Yet this has even less claim than the other stylistic comments to be the foundation of a valid argument, or even a criterion in any objective estimate of its date. Most of Schubert's works from his last period are distinguished by an inward as

17 This individual trait is found occasionally in Schubert's early works, as when the strings have the lead in the second part of 'Gesang der Geister über den Wassern' D 714 (1821), which is accompanied only by the lower strings (two violas, two cellos and double-bass) and which therefore belongs to the realm of chamber music. This shows precisely that one must beware of arriving at a premature conclusion regarding dates of origin on the basis of isolated stylistic features. Only a number of these can enable us to ascribe a work to a particular period.

well as an outward abundance of creative power, which in earlier works can only be found exceptionally – as in the 'Wanderer' Fantasy. The clearest manifestation of this newly awakened energy during his last years seems to be Schubert's solution to the problem of composing finales which can be regarded as a match for or even a climax to the preceding movements. The C major Symphony in particular shows his success in constructing a last movement which, despite its great length of 1155 bars, seems to have been poured out in one flood of inspiration, thereby crowning the whole work with a conclusion well worthy of what has gone before. This sustaining of an unbroken line of tension is made possible by the invention and elaboration of themes of great amplitude, which are then propelled into the work as though from a great distance. At the very beginning of the finale the first subject with its vivid rhythm flashes like a rocket being launched into the vastness of space. The last movements of the well-known instrumental works of 1825 can hardly bear comparison with it. The charming rondo of the D major Sonata D 850 composed at Gastein is genial and episodic in character; the impression produced is that of a pleasantly aimless summertime ramble in the country. In the C major Sonata D 840 of spring 1825, the unfinished last movement cannot rise above a few short-winded and ineffectual flourishes, and was surely abandoned for this reason. The finale of the A minor Sonata op. 42, D 845, is best able to bear comparison with that of the symphony; yet it is scarcely half as long and its subject matter is far from displaying an equal intensity. Hence one feels inclined on stylistic grounds to settle, if not for 1827, at least for 1826 as the year of composition of the finale. The instrumental works of 1828, despite all other differences, have finales which exhibit the same sense of spaciousness and range as we find in the symphony. In the concentrated last movement of the String Quintet, it is the contrast between the defiant first subject and the mystical concluding theme that attracts our attention. Between them stands the earthiness and jollity of the second subject, which cannot however maintain its hold. The last word is contained in the tragic Neapolitan descent of a semitone from D♭ to C, a symbol of unbending defiance, which also plays an important part in the second movement of the quintet. We should also mention the monumental fugato in the Fantasia in F minor D 940 for four hands, and the lengthy concluding movements of the last three piano sonatas, of which the very last, with a serenity that has risen above the world, gives the impression of being a salute to Beethoven; to the latter's last composition – the final movement which was later added to the String Quartet op. 130 – this sonata finale in fact shows some astonishing parallels. All of these show Schubert at the very summit of his powers.

Another general characteristic of Schubert's last creative period lies in the universality of his musical subject-matter. The specific Viennese or Austrian elements in his style are pushed into the background by a more generally human content, which one might describe as European – as the musical substratum of an entire continent. In this respect it is interesting to compare the subordinate themes of the slow movements in both the D major Sonata D 850 of 1825 and the C major Symphony: Ex. 31. The burgeoning theme of the piano sonata is not without a certain local colour, which Alfred Brendel has aptly described as 'alpine'. It is just this folk element in the the rising sequence which has unfortunately been misunderstood by many fanatical lovers of 'pure music', who dismiss it as too 'crude' and too 'popular'; it is this that has contributed to a prolonged lack of the public recognition which Schubert deserves. On the contrary, the secondary theme in the C major Symphony's second movement is so sublimely and universally beautiful that it can only be compared to the greatest and most mature conceptions of Haydn, Mozart and Beethoven (whoever finds this theme unappealing would also repudiate those that Mozart introduces into his Clarinet Quintet). Its special kinship with the second theme of the 1828 Rondo in A major D 951 for four hands is unmistakable. Such connections between subjects in Schubert's late works are apparently not at all uncommon. The rhythmic flow of the introduction to the symphony is reproduced in the second subject of a short draft for a symphony in D major, doubtless written in 1828, and presumably just before Schubert's death; it displays throughout a joyous, festive character: Ex. 32. This passage for the horns belongs among those musical ideas which have a

Ex. 31 (a)

(b)

Ex. 32

classical stamp; it has far outgrown any merely 'alpine' quality, even though its 'Austrian' origins are perhaps still recognizable. Here too a superficial analysis could lead to false conclusions. Finally it is worthy of note that the radiantly optimistic mood of the tonality seems as appropriate to 1825 as to the year of Schubert's death, and should never be used as a basis for what can only be doubtful reasoning. It would be naive to expect a very close connection to exist between a composer's life and his work – that is, when things go well he expresses only happiness, and when they go badly, only tragedy. In 1825 Schubert composed the tragic A minor Sonata op. 42, D 845, and the 'weary unto death' second movement of the Sonata in C major D 840, the so-called 'Reliquie' Sonata; on the other hand in March 1828 he wrote 'Mirjam's Siegesgesang' – a radiantly joyful setting in C major, the style of which shows a number of parallels with that of the C major Symphony.

Even if, like Hilmar (see note 1 above), we take the last figure to be a '5' and consequently read 'March 1825' instead of 'March 1828', questions still remain unanswered, for the supposition that the work was begun in March 1825 is not borne out by the watermark. To solve this riddle two hypotheses offer themselves: either the watermark was in use earlier than Robert Winter concludes (see his essay in this volume, pp. 232, 266-7), or else Schubert made a slip of the pen, e.g. in erroneously putting 'March' instead of 'May' 1825. Another – hitherto unbroached – possibility is that Schubert wrote 'March 1826' on the autograph. I have been led to this suggestion by a careful study of holograph figures of the relevant years. The date on Schubert's autograph of the Allegretto in C minor D 915, '26. Aprill 1827', can be cited to show that the figure '6' in Schubert's handwriting sometimes resembles the figures '5' and '8'. Thus the trimmed first page of the symphony leaves open the possibility that the figure was originally '6'.

As stated above, we can see stages of development in the composition more clearly here than with other works, by examining the various colourings of the ink. (The variations in colour are explained by the fact that not until late in the nineteenth century did ink become an industrial product; it was mostly mixed as needed for domestic purposes.) On the autograph of the C major Symphony, the first entry in darker ink is only a full set of clefs and signatures indicating the instrumentation; this is followed by a correction to it, and some notes, in lighter ink; the reworking of the opening bars and later corrections are clearly written in ink of a darker colour. If the date on the first page were also written in darker ink than that of the rest, it would be recognizable as a later insertion, and could strengthen the theory that Schubert had handed over the symphony but left it undated, and did not supply a date until the supposed revision in 1828. This is unfortunately not the case; the ink and the style in which the date is written on the first page correspond exactly with those used for the signature directly underneath, as well as for the first notes, and therefore the notation of the most important parts (cf. Figure 1).

As the recent researches of Otto Biba have shown,[18] the last of Schubert's corrections to the final version must have been made at the latest by summer 1827, since the orchestral parts were fully copied out in their final form by August of that year. Although the first page of the score is comparatively somewhat faded (from which one may conclude that the manuscript was for years exposed to the sunlight in a showcase), corrections to the horn part were made in darker ink. An examination of the manuscript using normal graphological methods has so far yielded no satisfactory results.

The figures in Schubert's dates during 1825 also show an incredible variety of forms; while in many cases the '5' is clearly recognizable and could never be mistaken for '8', others are less clear on account of their flourishes. The date on the C major Sonata D 840 from the same year looks as though the '5' was written later, although we cannot give any reason for this. If Hilmar's analysis is correct, and the date on the autograph is to be read as 'March 1825', then Schubert began work on the symphony earlier than has hitherto been supposed. Since he composed the unfinished C major Piano Sonata D 840 in April 1825 and the A minor Sonata D 845 probably in May of the same year, this would mean that work on the symphony was soon interrupted – contrary to his usual practice – only to be taken up again during his stay at Gastein in the summer, and, as analysis of the paper tells us, yet once more at a later date – and not before 1826.

If we collate all the results of recent scientific investigation, the following picture emerges: a study of the documents and examination of the paper speak for 1825-6; this view is decisively supported by the fact that Schubert used five different kinds of paper dating from these years. An examination of the handwriting shows that several revisions were made, which must have been completed before August 1827. The set of parts copied in 1827 corresponds with the final version; no major alteration is visible in them. Many stylistic features however seem to point to a later date of composition, or at least of completion. If we accept that the 'Great' C major Symphony is identical with

18 'Concert Life in Beethoven's Vienna' in *Beethoven: Performers and Critics. The International Beethoven Congress Detroit 1977* (Detroit, 1980), pp. 77-93.

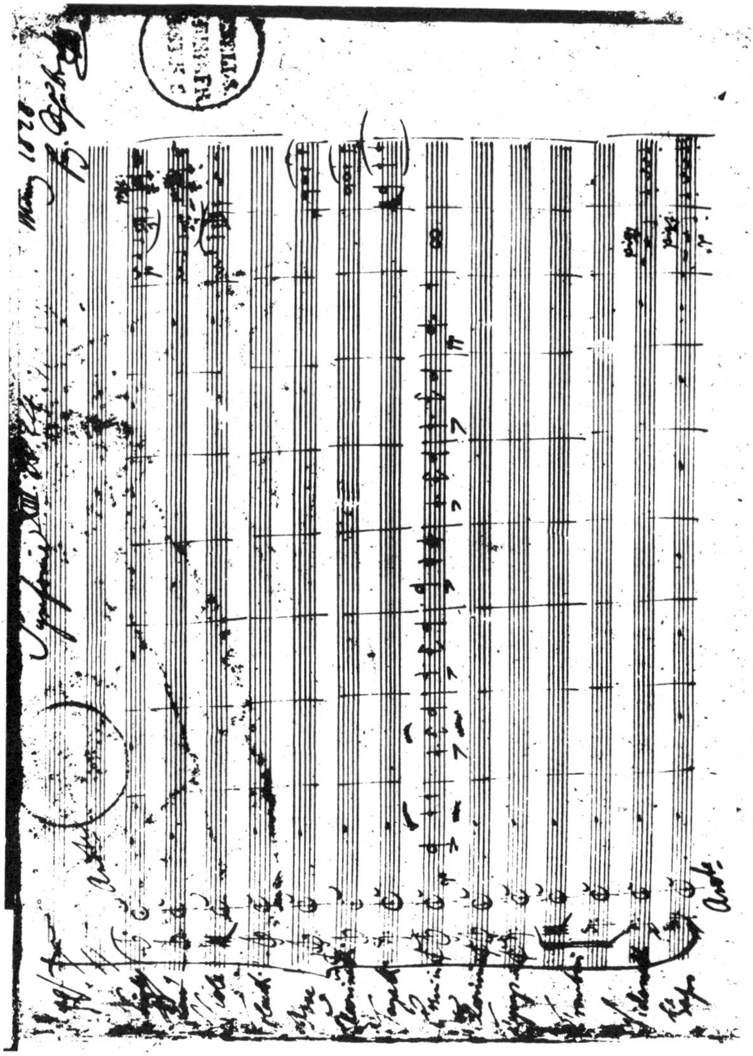

Figure 1. 'Great' C major Symphony, first page of the autograph (Vienna, Gesellschaft der Musikfreunde, MS A 245)

the 'Gastein Symphony', begun in 1825 and finished in 1826 (though he revised it later) – and there is sufficient documentary evidence for this – then we are dealing with one of Schubert's almost inexplicable intuitive feats, which again and again make the expert look upon him as one of the most mysterious and wonderful of all composers. The miracle becomes just a little easier to grasp if we accept that some at least of the corrections visible in the autograph are the result of several radical revisions, and perhaps a final perusal of the manuscript in the spring of 1827. In any event, the example of the 'Great' C major Symphony indicates with particular clarity the limits of the possibilities of establishing more exact chronological ordering of Schubert's works on the basis of stylistic criteria.

I am indebted to my wife, Eva Badura-Skoda, whose help in writing this article I gratefully acknowledge; and to Robert Winter, whose valuable advice was most welcome.

Paper studies and the future of Schubert research

ROBERT WINTER

The title of this essay might as readily have been 'Beethoven, Schubert, and the "Great" C major Symphony', though many readers would find it hard to believe that both that title and the one used can apply to the same essay. Yet the techniques for investigating paper that I propose to introduce are as fundamental to our overall understanding of Schubert's symphonies as is our understanding of his handling of the augmented-sixth chord, or of the re-transition, or of sonata form. And there is doubtless irony in the circumstance that Beethoven's relationship to Schubert proves to be far more intimate in the realm of paper than in any personal ties that may have existed between the two men. But even more important, it is only when the chronology (both external and internal, relative and absolute) of Schubert's works has been set on a firm foundation that we will be in a position to assess with confidence his stylistic development and artistic achievement. The welcome appearance in the sesquicentennial year of a revised German-language edition of Otto Erich Deutsch's monumental thematic catalogue[1] as well as Ernst Hilmar's ambitious survey of the extensive Schubert holdings in the Wiener Stadtbibliothek[2] have brought us closer than ever before to a reliable chronology. Yet in different ways each has also pointed up anew the pressing need for rigorous and imaginative application of paper studies to Schubert research.

My thesis is a simple one: the study of physical characteristics in music paper – until now largely ignored – proves to be not only a useful tool for approaching dating problems in Schubert, but in many cases the single most powerful technique available. Traditionally, studies in chronology have relied upon four criteria of widely varying authority:

(1) biographical data: correspondence to and from the composer, concert programmes, announcements in newspapers and periodicals, publications, etc.;

1 Otto Erich Deutsch, *Franz Schubert. Thematisches Verzeichnis seiner Werke in chronologischer Folge*, ed. by the Editorial Board of the *Neue Schubert-Ausgabe* and Werner Aderhold (Kassel, 1978): cited below as '*D2*'.

2 Ernst Hilmar, *Verzeichnis der Schubert-Handschriften in der Musiksammlung der Wiener Stadt- und Landesbibliothek*, Catalogus Musicus, VIII (Kassel, etc., 1978).

(2) analysis of musical style;
(3) handwriting characteristics, of both the composer and copyists;
(4) study of the physical aspects of autographs, contemporary sources, authorized copies: watermarks, staff ruling, gathering structure, datings supplied by the composer.

We are seldom granted the luxury of selecting the tool with which excavations will commence. The importance of each approach, in fact, varies widely from composer to composer, and from epoch to epoch. Although Josquin research stands to benefit substantially from comprehensive studies of contemporaneous sources and a deepening knowledge of the scantily documented events in the composer's life, until now the myriad of dating problems has been treated with liberal dosages of style analysis. The new chronology of J. S. Bach's vocal music included item 4, but was nourished largely by fresh study of the copyists charged with preparing parts for weekly performance. And even though Beethoven chronology is not the closed book many scholars assume, the combination of 1 and 4 proves sufficient to resolve all but the most Byzantine of riddles.

Schubert chronology contains its own problems, each of which demands equally individual strategies. Although we have the indefatigable Deutsch to thank for two invaluable biographical studies,[3] the ultimate utility of such contributions is restricted to those relatively few instances where specific works are tied to specific events and dates (hence we can date the 'Trout' Quintet provisionally even though the autograph is lost). When viewed against Beethoven's correspondence over thirty years with a large assortment of publishers, the eight such letters from Schubert's last months offer but a meagre showing. We have impressive contemporaneous collections of Lieder and part-songs – such as those commissioned by Josef Wilhelm Witteczek and Josef von Spaun – whose dates are frequently taken from autograph sources. With the help of Witteczek–Spaun, for example, more than forty works otherwise undatable can be placed with reasonable confidence. But even with the more than ninety *opera* of Schubert's music published in Vienna between 1821 and 1828, a level that placed him in the forefront of that city's musical life, the proportion of works (particularly orchestral works, whose performances the composer seems to have promoted only weakly) for which chronological documentation exists represents only a fraction of his output.[4] Only in such unsung circumstances could the genesis of a work like the 'Great' C major lie shrouded in mystery for a hundred and fifty years.

3 O. E. Deutsch, *Schubert. Die Dokumente seines Lebens* (Kassel, 1964), and *Schubert. A Documentary Biography* (cited below as '*Documents*'), transl. Eric Blom (London, 1946); Deutsch, *Schubert. Die Erinnerungen seiner Freunde* (Leipzig, 1957), and *Schubert. Memoirs by His Friends*, transl. Rosamond Ley and John Nowell (London, 1958).
4 For a fresh look at 'Schubert's Position in Viennese Musical Life', see Otto Biba in *19th Century Music,* III/2 (November 1979), pp. 106-13.

In this arid climate the temptation to slake one's thirst at the bubbling spring of style analysis is great. (Some of the potential applications are shown by Paul Badura-Skoda, pp. 187-208 above.) The incentives for restraint are perhaps equally great. While there is a sizeable and literate body of appreciative literature on Schubert's music today, we do not yet, in my judgement, possess the analytical sophistication required to discriminate among two-to-four-year segments (and nothing less than this degree of refinement will do for such a brief composing career). Recognizing the B flat Symphony D 125 as a youthful work and the B flat Piano Sonata as a mature work is one distinction. But surely it takes more than the ascending third cited by John Reed in both the song 'Die Allmacht' and the opening horn solo of the 'Great' C major to posit, much less confirm, any close chronological relationship between these two works.[5] Perhaps the shakiest assumption is that style moves like time or direct current – in one direction only. Aside from making no allowances for retrospective elements in an artist's palette, we run the extreme risk of focusing on just those quantifiable parameters – new resolutions to an augmented-sixth chord, or certain rhythmic configurations – which may be least intrinsic to the style. The lure of sleuthing after musical fingerprints must not blind us to the realization that they can lead into analytical abysses at once treacherous and absurd.

Style criticism nevertheless remains the most pressing challenge to, and responsibility of, the writer about music. The fascinating elixir of classical, post-classical and proto-Romantic ingredients in Schubert's music has yet to be explained in relation to Beethoven and subsequent generations, much less in terms of three-year periods in Schubert's life. I remain convinced that from a stylistic point of view the 'Great' C major Symphony could have been written any time after the 'Unfinished' Symphony. Once we know when it was in fact composed we are undeniably in a better position to understand Schubert's development. But this does not license us to reverse our stance and insist that, from a musical point of view, only this single moment of creation was possible.

With the exception of a few works (such as the first part of *Winterreise*, prepared for performance and/or publication in 1827), the issue of copyists in Schubert sources is restricted to largely straightforward collections like Witteczek–Spaun. Thus spared the nightmare of Beethoven's shifting clutch of scribes, we are left only with Schubert's enigmatic hand. There is no question that his musical orthography evolved considerably between 1812 and 1828. There is also no question that a decisive, if largely inexplicable, change in writing habits surfaces abruptly in 1820 (was it unconsciously related to the composer's first compositional confrontations with Beethoven around this time?), persisting until Schubert's death eight years later. A few other tendencies can be pointed to around 1813, 1815, 1817, 1823, and 1825.[6]

5 See John Reed, *Schubert. The Final Years* (London, 1972), pp. 95-7.

6 The most visible change, occurring around 1820, is the shift from the open

Occasionally terminology is an aid – Schubert writes 'Cembalo' before 1814, 'Fortepiano' into 1815, and 'Pianoforte' thereafter. But once these broad divisions are recognized – and none are so dramatic or unambiguous as those around 1820 – the next refinements are substantially more difficult. In his recent catalogue, Hilmar assigns scores of dates largely or entirely on the basis of handwriting, often down to the confines of a single month. Regrettably, he has not yet published any of the extensive network of evidence essential to support such sweeping claims. A full-scale investigation which draws upon the resources of the major Schubert collections, one which catalogues in detail common signs like clefs, accidentals, shapes of noteheads, stemming and beaming, and overall layout, would form a most welcome addition to efforts at building a reliable Schubert chronology. Alan Tyson's study of five Beethoven copyists supplies just the necessary standards for presentation and documentation.[7] Until such a study is forthcoming for Schubert we are bound to remain sceptical of every partial attempt.

What remains? It is that technique which in the Renaissance is generally useful for assigning provenance only, and which after 1835 shrinks drastically in value. But the leverage supplied by source studies in the Vienna of Mozart, Beethoven, and Schubert can hardly be overestimated.[8] It is ironic in another context that the relationships which prove so useful to us are ones of which the composers were almost certainly unaware. Not only are the primary criteria non-musical in nature, but they have little value when considered in isolation. To both Beethoven and Schubert the sole virtue of the music paper they purchased regularly must have been its ability to serve as a vehicle for their musical thoughts. If either found himself, in an idle moment, noting the variety of ways in which musical staves were drawn, or if one of them chanced to view a leaf while the strongest light source was behind it, he could scarcely have imagined the potential to us of systematized scrutiny of this kind.

Perhaps most surprising is that such scrutiny has not been in evidence long before now. The study of watermarks in handmade paper (so-called *Büttenpapier*) dates back to the dawning years of this century, and although the application to music papers has been slower to develop, we have examples like Joseph Schmidt-Görg's description of the Beethovenhaus holdings in the mid-1930s to remind us that such techniques were neither unknown nor un-

natural sign (♮) to the interlocked type (♮). Changes in the appearance of clefs (particularly the bass clef) and crotchet rests are useful during Schubert's teens, as are the positioning of stems in the early 1820s. Needless to say, the rate of change in the composer's musical hand diminished as he grew older.

7 Alan Tyson, 'Notes on Five of Beethoven's Copyists', *Journal of the American Musicological Society*, XXIII (1970), pp. 439-71.

8 See in particular the recent contributions by Alan Tyson to Mozart chronology: 'New Light on Mozart's "Prussian" Quartets', *Musical Times*, CXVI (1975), pp. 126-30; and '"La Clemenza di Tito" and Its Chronology', *Musical Times*, CXVI (1975), pp. 221-7.

appreciated.[9] However, the first thoroughgoing investigation of a large corpus of works was carried out by a small community of Bach scholars who arrived at conclusions about Bach's compositional activities – especially in the early Leipzig years – that seem no less remarkable today than twenty years ago.[10]

Alas, the nineteenth century has proved practically invulnerable to ventures of this kind, not least because it is still widely assumed in many quarters that they are unnecessary. The visionary and singular contributions of Douglas Johnson and Alan Tyson, for example, have yet to affect Schubert studies – even with the recent spate of catalogues – in any meaningful way.[11] But at a time when a new complete edition of the composer's works is cementing its still-fresh *Richtlinien*, it might be well to inquire into the conceptual bases which recommend paper studies to us. If I have singled out the 'Great' C major Symphony for special discussion, it is not because its general date is any longer disputed in informed circles. It is, rather, both because the discontinuous explanations offered by John Reed have received uncritical acceptance[12] and because this classic illustration of the application of paper studies to a seemingly insoluble problem has been accepted equally uncritically – for example in *D2* – without its ramifications being sufficiently understood.

Paper studies would seem to offer the advantage that they are completely objective. The letters 'GFA', for example, resist transformation into 'JAA' without wilful deceit. It is not a question of deceit but of veering toward self-deception when we judge on purely stylistic grounds a work of Schubert's to be 'before 1820' or 'after 1826'. But sceptics will quickly and rightly point out that the working conditions for source studies are often less than ideal,

9 Joseph Schmidt-Görg, *Katalog der Handschriften des Beethovenhauses und Beethoven-Archivs Bonn* (Bonn, 1935). To the sixty-three autograph items the compiler keyed a network of seventy-nine characteristics, corresponding in part to halves of the original sheet watermarks. The data itself remained undigested.

10 Alfred Dürr, 'Zur Chronologie der Leipziger Vokalwerke J. S. Bachs', *Bach-Jahrbuch 1957*, pp. 5-162; and Georg Dadelsen, *Beiträge zur Chronologie der Werke Johann Sebastian Bachs*, Tübinger Bach-Studien, ed. Walter Gerstenberg, Heft 4/5, Trossingen, 1958.

11 Douglas Johnson and Alan Tyson, 'Reconstructing Beethoven's Sketchbooks', *Journal of the American Musicological Society*, XXV (1972), pp. 137-56; Alan Tyson, 'A Reconstruction of the Pastoral Symphony Sketchbook' in *Beethoven Studies 1*, ed. Alan Tyson (New York, 1973), pp. 67-96; and Alan Tyson, 'The Problem of Beethoven's First *Leonore* Overture', *Journal of the American Musicological Society*, XXVIII (1975), pp. 292-334. In particular, readers are referred to the appendix of the last article, where Tyson's five 'ground rules' prove not only essential for understanding Viennese papers but adequate to even the most refined discussions. I wish to thank Dr Tyson for his instructive and patient counsel over the last nine years.

12 See Reed, *Schubert. The Final Years*, chapters III and VII; 'How the "Great" C Major Was Written', *Music and Letters*, LVI (1975), pp. 18-25. Reed first pondered the problem of a missing Schubert symphony in 'The "Gastein" Symphony Reconsidered', *Music and Letters*, XL (1959), pp. 341-9.

and just as prone to deception. In a poorly lit room, using a makeshift watermark lamp (the situation in all too many of our most important archives, a silent comment upon the esteem in which investigations like the present one are held), the viewer may indeed believe that the letters 'GFA' *are* 'JAA'. However, unlike refractory questions of style, virtually all problems of paper identification and organization in Beethoven's and Schubert's Vienna are soluble with moderate technical means. Once the initial sifting has been completed, a surprisingly limited number of paper types remains (the surfeit of illustrations in Hilmar obscures the fact that more than 90 per cent of Schubert's autographs were written on fewer than twenty main paper types); this very limitation turns out to be one of our strongest weapons.

Ultimately, the potential application of paper studies has little to do with us and everything to do with the composer. If he could afford the luxury of working in a haphazard manner, using one variety of paper today and another tomorrow, then all efforts at uncovering patterns will only end in frustration. If, on the other hand, detailed source studies suggest that his compositional habits were highly organized, then we are justified in proposing solutions to unresolved problems that conform to his observed habits. It is my contention that Franz Schubert, for all the persistent tales about his Bohemian life-style and madcap inspiration, was a creature of habit and order as much as, if not more than, the three other great representatives of the Viennese classical style.

To the composer we must add his environment. Even had he wished to, Schubert could not have stockpiled a thousand leaves – only a few years' supply – from retailers accustomed to dealing in *Lagen* (a pair of gathered bifolia). Perhaps even more than to Schubert we owe our thanks to the economic and technological system which nurtured and sustained him. Shortly after 1830, with the irreversible transformation of paper-making into a machine art, the usefulness of paper studies in music shrinks drastically. But the composers who lived and worked in Vienna between 1808 and 1830 helped underwrite a last great flowering of handmade paper manufacture around the periphery of Bohemia, one which was privileged to serve the two finest living representatives of European musical art, first Beethoven and then Franz Schubert.[13]

We do not yet know all of the details of this commerce, to which almost two hundred mills were party. We are ignorant, for example, of the reasons behind the meteoric rise of trade between the Kiesling firm and Vienna after 1809. (Convenience could not have played a great role, for the Kiesling mills lay in the extreme northeast corner of Bohemia. It may have been linked to the partnership from 1810 on of the brothers Anton-Ignaz, Gustav, and Wilhelm.) We are equally in the dark as to why for more than twenty years

13 The standard survey of this growth is Georg Eineder's *The Ancient Paper-Mills of the Former Austro-Hungarian Empire and Their Watermarks* (Hilversum, 1960).

only a single rival firm, the Welhartitz (also Welhartiez or Welhartiz) mills near the Bavarian border, was able to gain a secure foothold in the face of the *de facto* monopoly exercised by the Kieslings – and this only after 1815. What is certain is that for the almost two decades during which Beethoven and Schubert were both shopping for music paper they were restricted largely to a few brands.

This restriction means that instead of having to chart the sporadic growth of a large number of firms we need only plot the straight-line evolution of several interrelated chains of watermark families and paper types. (For the purposes of this discussion the term 'paper type' will be reserved for the watermark *plus* the staff ruling and any other unusual characteristics.) We should be able to assume, for example, that the disappearance of one watermark will be followed shortly by the emergence of another unique yet related strain.

It is just this plotting of watermark chains and paper types which has not been carried out in Schubert research. In his otherwise excellent introduction to the families of watermarks found in the manuscripts of Schubert songs, Walther Dürr does not even suggest that these and related properties of music paper can be a useful ally in solving questions either of chronology or compositional process.[14] Hilmar's catalogue provides no guidelines at all for the many watermark types – some grouped accurately, others less so – which are so liberally assigned dates.[15]

The manufacture of handmade paper is sufficiently well understood to require no elucidation here.[16] It must have been both the artistic impulse of the craftsman and the craftsmanship of the artisan that prompted most European makers not only to employ a practical second mould, but to create this twin in the mirror image of the original form. Hence a skilfully applied design could be associated with a specific form only if the 'mould side' (i.e. showing the watermark in tiny valleys) could be distinguished from the 'felt side' (where the watermark appears smooth). These manufacturers could scarcely have dreamt that their ingenuity would lead a century and a half later to the identification of missing leaves from Beethoven sketchbooks, or to the reconstruction of Schubert chronology.

14 See the *Kritischer Bericht* to *NGA*, Series IV (*Lieder*), Vol. 7, ed. Walther Dürr, especially pp. 8-16; and *Franz Schuberts Werke in Abschriften: Liederalben und Sammlungen*, *NGA*, Series VIII, Supplement 8, *Quellen* II, also ed. Walther Dürr; and the review of the latter by Tyson in *Fontes Artis Musicae*, XXIV (1977), pp. 53-4.

15 The 105 illustrations which make up more than 40 per cent of the catalogue are arranged – problems of accuracy aside – in clusters whose interrelationships are not chronological.

16 In addition to Eineder, see the accounts in Johnson and Tyson, 'Reconstructing Beethoven's Sketchbooks'; Tyson, 'The Problems of Beethoven's First *Leonore* Overture'; and also A.H. Stevenson's classic exposition, 'Watermarks are Twins', *Studies in Bibliography* (Charlottesville), IV (1951), pp. 57-91 and 235.

Each of these mould forms – like any manufactured product – had a certain life expectancy. From the moment they were pressed into service there commenced a process of inevitable disintegration. Yet with few exceptions the deterioration of moulds in this period is only an occasional (if no less valuable) aid in calculating life span. Rather, the Kiesling and Welhartitz firms seem to have used a particular pair of forms (or even a twin pair of forms) over a period of time with only minimal repairs, and then to have withdrawn them voluntarily. The reasons for this probably stemmed as much from pride in workmanship as from the facilitation of business records. At their extremes, the life spans of a pair of twin moulds used to make the paper delivered to Vienna in the second and third decades of the nineteenth century could range from a few months to almost three years. Yet the size of this spread proves enormously deceptive unless it is simultaneously stressed that the vast majority of watermarks enjoyed one *annus mirabilis* and then vanished, leaving only an occasional ghost – known bibliographically as a 'remnant' – behind. (Hilmar's assertion that 'die Fehlerquote in der Regel bei einem halben, höchstens aber bei einem dreiviertel Jahr liegt'[17] is simply in error.) This duration proves ideal. It is sufficiently brief to enable us to locate a work with reasonable specificity. It is sufficiently lengthy for even composers of Beethoven's sporadic productivity to be represented on the majority of papers.

The sheets destined to become music paper (measuring 40–50 x 60–70 cm.) probably arrived in Vienna unfolded, uncut, and unruled. Once there, they would have been parcelled out among a number of musical establishments (including, no doubt, those of Artaria, and Steiner/Haslinger) which then supplied the staves with their own hand-operated machines. Although these were constructed within conventional norms, each apparatus produced a slightly different group of staff-rulings whose distinguishing feature can be expressed most consistently by measuring the distance at each edge from the top line of the top staff to the bottom line of the bottom staff (identified as the *total span*).[18] Since the size of an individual paper shipment probably did not exceed several hundred leaves, it seems unlikely, for example, that the Kiesling firm would have maintained a number of different rastrals for ruling staves when only small quantities of paper were involved, especially since their product was also used for letters, album leaves, maps, and other applications. The theory that proposes that the ruling was done in Vienna also allows for the most efficient distribution: each individual retailer would be free to determine how much 8-, 10-, 12-, 14-, 16-stave or special-format paper he required.

17 *Verzeichnis*, p. vii. The actual time frame may vary anywhere from a few months to several years.

18 There will be slight variations in total span within a single type, but the range is rarely more than a millimetre for oblong papers, or 2 millimetres for larger upright-format leaves.

In the year 1824 Beethoven relied heavily upon paper with a watermark of an elaborate crown and the letters 'AK&S' (cf. Watermark II) for portions of the Ninth Symphony finale and for two copies of the same work, prepared shortly thereafter. This 16-stave paper displays a uniform total span of 195 to 196+ millimetres. At just this period Schubert was using paper that displayed the identical watermark and 16-stave layout for a group of works including the Introduction and Variations in E minor on 'Ihr Blümlein alle' for Flute and Piano, D 802 (January); the Wind Octet, D 803 (February); the songs 'Der Sieg' and 'Abendstern', D 805 and 806 (March); 'Gondelfahrer', D 808 (March); the first movement of the String Quartet in D minor, D 810 (March); the 'Salve Regina' in C, D 811 (April); and some of the incidental music to *Rosamunde*, D 797 (undated, but performed on 20 December 1823): this amounts to more than a hundred leaves. The arresting detail is that the total span on Schubert's 16-stave paper falls uniformly between 197+ and 198+ millimetres, or some 2 millimetres greater than that used by Beethoven. No other conclusion seems possible than that Beethoven and Schubert patronized different shops which employed similar but slightly different (or differently adjusted) rastrals. When we consider that a town without automobiles or public transport was supported quite literally by the walk-in trade, such a circumstance is probable; indeed, there is no evidence that the two composers ever made purchases of music paper from the same firm, Steiner's or elsewhere. Whatever the commerce between Beethoven and Schubert, it does not seem to have occurred while procuring compositional supplies.

Some day we may be in a position to describe more precisely the size and frequency of consignments of music paper between Bohemia and Vienna. At present we can infer only indirectly the scale and magnitude of these operations. (We know, for example, that the Kiesling firm maintained a warehouse in Vienna, but we lack information about the volume and type of trade.) But even exact data would not shed much light on the habits of Beethoven and Schubert; just as surely as they coveted paper so did the Carl Czernys and the Anton Halms of Vienna – and probably in greater quantities. The example of Schubert cited above suggests that individual purchases somewhat in excess of a hundred leaves were not unusual. When sketch leaves (including those discarded) are taken into account, the actual amount used during a given period may have been even larger. Pursuing the problem from this end, however, leads to the tail wagging the dog. The critical question is for how long a given paper type would have been available, for which I have already suggested a circumscribed time frame. It seems, in fact, that there were occasional paper shortages, or periods when there were no large runs of a uniform paper type available. We cannot, of course, rule out the possibility that at intervals Schubert simply ran short of funds, and the irregular nature of his income supports such a notion. Yet we uncover the same evidence of paper shortages among the autographs of Beethoven, who can scarcely be said to have been without money very often, whether his own or someone else's. This forced reliance upon low-grade papers and remnants until another major type reached the market supports my earlier hypothesis that papers bearing specific watermarks were introduced and withdrawn at regular intervals.

If we consider the entire network of dependencies that must have existed from manufacture to distribution, only a highly efficient operation could have yielded any profits. Even in large mills with a few dozen employees, the output still would have been too small to permit amassing any but modest reserves. (There was a regular network of post routes between Vienna and various parts of Bohemia, mostly by way of Prague. Twice- or thrice-weekly shipments required three to five days for delivery.) Hence most paper probably arrived in Vienna from the mills within a few months of its manufacture.

The same economic restrictions impinged upon the retailers of music paper as upon the manufacturers. What advantages could accrue from the hoarding of any particular consignment? The demand for music paper in this, the music capital of the world, must have been colossal, as both the expansion and proliferation of paper mills throughout the Austro-Hungarian empire at this time attest. Since there is evidence that sporadic shortages were a reality for the Viennese composer, there would have been even less reward for withholding supplies from musicians eager to commit pen to paper. And the simultaneous offering of two different paper types bearing the same watermark is inherently more believable as the common practice of retailers accustomed to issuing new papers shortly after receipt than as a simple coincidence.

Remnants, which surfaced in several varieties, performed a small but vital role in this scheme. It was natural that from time to time Schubert would seize an odd leaf from an earlier run on which to enter, perhaps, a single song (or even two strophic songs, one on the recto and one on the verso), or to fill in a small gap in a larger manuscript. Small quantities of unknown papers also occur, although their random appearance during major runs accounts for only about 2½ per cent of the leaves used by the composer after 1822. At other times, however, it appears that temporary scarcities forced him to rely on whatever papers he could round up, some of them of remarkably inferior quality. Two such periods assume pivotal importance in the heated controversy surrounding the 'Great' C major Symphony.

We can profile the kinds of leaves likely to be enlisted as remnants. In Vienna and elsewhere at the time, oblong was vastly preferred to upright format, and there is reason to believe that these preferred papers were the first to disappear from the shopkeepers' shelves – and hence from Beethoven's and Schubert's autographs. Less frequent upright-format gatherings, which proved ideal for vocal and instrumental parts, could surface several months after the main run of the paper had been exhausted. Finally, there were also periods – including, but not limited to, the summers of 1818, 1824, and 1825 – when Schubert relied (whether voluntarily or involuntarily) upon papers distributed chiefly outside of Vienna. We are aided in identification by their anomalous watermarks and generally blemished appearance.

What then of Schubert's own idiosyncratic habits of composition? Those few he developed and relied upon remain remarkably consistent throughout his eighteen-year career, from choirboy to economically independent composer. As Dürr has noted, Schubert preferred 16- or 12-stave paper for song composition, but the same also holds for the other genres he cultivated: orchestral, chamber, solo sonata, and dramatic music. From about 1820 on, however, Schubert showed a steadily increasing preference exclusively for 16-stave papers; these account for more than 80 per cent of the leaves used by the composer in the last eight years of his life.

Like his contemporaries, Schubert used upright format sparingly. It was (as today) obligatory for orchestral parts, numerous specimens of which exist in Schubert's hand. Otherwise only an occasional large work, such as the Fourth Symphony, utilizes upright format. It is important to remember that regardless of format the watermark with its twin forms was identical. If the sheet was ruled with the long side running horizontally, the result was oblong format; with the long side running vertically, the result was upright format. (There are in this period rare instances of oversize sheets in upright format, used almost exclusively for large orchestral works. Beethoven used such papers occasionally, as in the choral portions of the Ninth Symphony, but Schubert does not seem ever to have employed such varieties.) If nothing else, this survey should lay to rest once and for all the notion that Schubert 'employs whatever paper is available to him at the moment'.[19]

If Schubert's paper preferences manifest themselves clearly, so does his manner of organizing this material into functional bundles. Then, as even now in tradition-bound areas, paper was sold chiefly in units of gathered sheets (*zwei ineinanderliegende Bogen*). Such was Schubert's confidence in the trouble-free progress of a work that he routinely inserted one sheet inside another to produce a gathering of eight leaves. The 153-folio autograph of *Die Verschworenen*, D 787 (Add. MS 29802 in the British Library), for example, contains primarily double-sheet and even larger gatherings. Examples of this pattern could be multiplied many times over. The occasions on which these regular structures were disturbed during composition are isolated, though – as we shall see with the 'Great' C major – always of great interest. At the other extreme, Beethoven's inordinate caution is underscored by his almost habitual use of single bifolia, the smallest gathering unit available ready-made. The frequency with which even these entities were interrupted is an undeniable manifestation of compositional struggle. The autograph of the fourth-movement variations in the C sharp minor Quartet, op. 131, for

19 See Michael Griffel, 'A Reappraisal of Schubert's Methods of Composition', *Musical Quarterly*, LXIII (1977), p. 200.

example, contains seventeen single leaves along with six bifolia. Such overt signs of large-scale struggle are rare in Schubert.

It was Otto Erich Deutsch who first popularized a notion about the composer still widely held:

The present catalogue is the first list of all known and traceable works by Schubert in their chronological order. This order was comparatively easy to achieve because Schubert dated most of his manuscripts. In 1813 he sometimes dated a song at the beginning and at the end, and in 1814 even when he finished one on the same day. He dated each movement of a string quartet in 1814, and he dated as a rule each act of an opera. From 1815 onwards more and more manuscripts are dated with the month, and in rare cases with the year only.[20]

In practice neither Schubert's habits nor their ostensible motives seem to have been quite so quantifiable. If the underlying impulse was simply to provide a reliable guide to his own output, then it would have proved unnecessary to date works composed within a period of a few days (or even on the same day) at both the beginning and the end (D 52, 106, 114), or to provide each member in a group of songs on the same bifolium or gathered sheet with the identical date (D 160-162, 224-225, 286-287 and 289, 669-670). Along with the cataloguing function it must have served to reinforce the composer's perception of his own creative powers: each work begun and completed signified the solution of a particular set of compositional problems, regardless of how simple or complex. It is astonishing that this heightened awareness of productivity seems to have inhabited Schubert from the earliest juvenilia down to the works drafted during his final illness.

Even so, Schubert himself was not always sure of the date, as shown by the 'December' altered to 'November' 1814 in 'Schäfers Klagelied', D 121b; or the 'September' crossed out and then re-entered as 'September' 1816 on D 481, one of the 'Sehnsucht' settings. Nor can the date given, as we shall see, always refer to the manuscript on which it is found.

Because of the dearth of information in *D1*, it was impossible to determine just how many Schubert autographs were indeed 'Undated', though even a cursory survey suggested the number was far greater than the original thirty-four entries. In fact, of the almost eleven hundred surviving autograph sources, close to one-third carry no date in Schubert's hand. Even though many of these documents can be dated through association with other manuscripts, just as many defy easy placement. The problem is compounded in later years; in the last six years of the composer's life the proportion of undated autographs soars to almost half. For this large group *D1* provided unfailingly intelligent and informed surmises, though all too frequently relieved of any distinction between the compiler's and Schubert's contribution. Although both the new

20 Otto Erich Deutsch, *Schubert. Thematic Catalogue of All His Works in Chronological Order* (cited below as *D1*) (London, 1951), pp. xiv-xv.

German-language edition of Deutsch's catalogue (*D2*) and Hilmar's *Verzeichnis* set new standards of description, neither has enlisted the aid of paper studies as an equal partner in problems of chronology. If *D2* is still not sufficiently comprehensive, the catalogue of the Wiener Stadtbibliothek holdings too often resembles a confetti-like sea of raw data whose meaning is left for the user to puzzle out.

Any effort to improve upon past or present chronologies must be based upon a complete description of the autograph material, including the number of folios, the types of watermarks represented, the number of staves and the total span, and any remarks supplied by Schubert, particularly a dating. Otto Erich Deutsch worked in an era when simply confirming the whereabouts of autographs was a herculean undertaking, and when microfilm technology as we know it was still in its infancy. He would have welcomed the more intense focus on autograph materials, not least of all because he was acutely aware of the limitations inherent in the more traditional means of documentation (letters, contemporary performances, editions).

Although the following survey rests upon direct examination of more than five hundred Schubert autographs – half of those that survive – I have chosen to limit the discussion to some 120 manuscripts from Schubert's last six years. Aside from encompassing all known theories about the genesis of the 'Great' C major Symphony, there is scarcely a situation to be encountered before 1823 that does not find an echo in the last period. The strategy is simple: autographs displaying a uniform paper type are divided into dated and undated strains. The chronological spread of the dated works is then tested for its applicability to the undated group. In practice such a blueprint will carry authority only if papers were, on the whole, used successively. If we assume, as seems safe, that Schubert was almost continually involved in musical projects, then a pattern of smooth dovetailing between paper types ought to dominate the hundreds upon hundreds of sources which survive. The evidence of his last six years furnishes powerful testimony for just this conception.

Seven principal watermarks provide the framework against which the chronology of Schubert's compositional maturity may be viewed. Five of the seven know only a single staff-ruling, hence the watermark is equivalent to the paper type. The two exceptions prove nonetheless to be highly useful. Along with the title and signature of each autograph I have supplied three further items of information: any dates entered on the manuscript by the composer; the general physical structure; and any unusual features, including biographical knowledge relevant to the placement of undated works. Except for the C major Symphony – whose special problems demand more detail – the specific quadrants within the sheet watermark have been omitted; they are not central to most of the argument, and those who wish to pursue this dimension further will insist on first-hand examination anyway. The brief

Table 1. *Conspectus of paper types used by Schubert between 1823 and his death*

Type (watermark, staves, total span in mm)	*Number of MSS / number of leaves**	*Period of use*
Ia and Ib All 16-stave TS: 194– to 194.5	15/575	Jan.–Dec. 1823 (just under 12 months)
IIa and IIb All 16-stave TS: 197 to 198	11/165	*c.* Nov. 1823 – Sep. 1824 (11 months)
Remnants I 12; 16-stave	4/22	Nov. 1824 – April 1825 (6 months)
III All 16-stave TS: 195.5 to 196.5	6/125	May–Sep. 1825 (5 months)
Remants II 12-, 16-stave	2/6	*c.* Nov. 1825 – Jan. 1826 (2–3 months)
IV All 16-stave TS: 195.5 to 196.5	11/70	Jan.–Sep. 1826 (9 months)
Va and Vb 15 MSS are 16-stave TS: 205+ to 206.5 remainder have 12-, 14-stave rulings	23/155	Sep. 1826 – May 1827 (9 months)
VIa cut down from 16-stave upright format TS: 255 to 257	4/28 original-size leaves 26 used in pocket format	June–Aug.? 1827 (*c.* 3 months)
VIb 12-, 16-stave upright format	5/29	very likely Sep. 1827 in Graz
VIIa 16-stave TS: 193.5 to 194– (clear watermark)	7/60	June–Aug./Sep. 1827 (*c.* 3–4 months)
VIIb 12-stave TS: 185+ to 185.5 (less clear watermark)	13/165	Oct. 1827 – April 1828 (7 months)
VIIc 16-stave TS: 193.5 to 194– (unclear watermark)	12/100	*c.* March–June 1828 (3–4 months)
VIId 16-stave TS: 193.5 to 194– (barely visible watermark)	7/30	*c.* July–Oct. 1828 (*c.* 4 months)

Table 1 (contd)

Type (watermark, staves, total span in mm)	*Number of MSS / number of leaves**	*Period of use*
VIIIa and VIIIb 16-stave TS: 200.5 to 201–	5/70	Oct.–Nov. 1828 (*c.* 2 months)
Eight miscellaneous papers from 1823 to 1828: 8-, 9-, 10-, 12-, 16-stave leaves; 40 folios		

* Number of MSS includes only those in which the paper type is dominant or at least heavily represented; number of leaves over 50 rounded to nearest 5

description of the paper type(s) at the head of each section is supplemented by a schematic illustration of the watermark. In this era of beta radiography it is probably more useful to have an accurate description of a watermark – with measurements of critical dimensions – than a tracing which inevitably introduces distortions in the guise of absolute fidelity. The summary that concludes each classification also treats the usage of similar papers by Beethoven, with emphasis on their chronological implications. It goes without saying that an examination of the papers used by hordes of *Kleinmeister* during this period would doubtless prove very helpful; some tentative applications are suggested below with regard to the C major Symphony.[21]

A survey of these paper types is shown in Table 1. In the discussion that follows, paper types are designated by roman numerals, and the examples of each type are numbered consecutively; so a cross-reference in the form 'V/1' means the first numbered exemplar of paper type V.

Watermarks Ia and Ib

Although type Ia predominates, the papers bearing both of these watermarks were clearly manufactured and distributed together by the Welhartitz firm. The astonishing number of type I leaves filled by Schubert – almost six hundred – suggests that supplies were replenished periodically. All examples showing these related marks have 16 staves and a total span of 194– to 194.5 millimetres.

Dated Works on Types Ia and Ib

1. Twelve Ecossaises for Piano, D 781 Vienna GdM* A 261
January 1823. Two single leaves of type Ia from the same sheet.

21 A quick check of Viennese archives revealed dated autographs from the 1820s by Joseph Czerny, Peter Haensel, Friedrich Klemm, I. F. von Mosel, Alexander Pössinger, and Leopold Sonnleithner, as well as others of Schubert's contemporaries.

* Abbreviations are explained on p. 269.

2. Seventeen Deutsche, D 146, 779, 783 Vienna SB MH 163/c
February 1823. A sheet of type Ia.

3. Opera, *Die Verschworenen*, D 787 London BL Add. 29802
The manuscript, which does not include the overture, is dated April 1823 on fol. 153r, the last page. 147 of the leaves are type Ia; 6 are type Ib. Gathering sizes are generally double sheets and larger.

4. Song, 'Pilgerweise', D 789 Vienna SB MH 114/c
April 1823. The first two of the three leaves are type Ia. The third leaf is a remnant from the previous principal type, used for, among other works, the 'Unfinished' Symphony, the 'Wanderer' Fantasy, and the song 'Die Mutter Erde', D 788, also composed in April and part of the same remnant.

5. Twelve Ländler for Piano, D 790 Vienna GdM A 262
May 1823. A bifolium with a single leaf inserted, all of type Ia.

6. Sketches for an opera, *Rüdiger*, D 791 Vienna SB MH 11/c
May 1823. 32 leaves in five gatherings of type Ia.

7. Song, 'Vergissmeinnicht', D 792 New York PML Heineman
May 1823. Although now five single leaves, the original structure probably comprised a single leaf and two gathered bifolia from different sheets, all of type Ia. There is no hint as to who may have made the cuts in the bifolia.

8. Two songs, 'Das Geheimnis', D 793, and 'Der Pilgrim', D 794
Berlin SPK N.Mus.ms. 5
May 1823. Two single leaves followed by a bifolium, all of type Ia.

9. Opera, *Fierrabras*, D 796 Vienna SB MH 9
The autograph of the opera – minus its overture – is preserved in three volumes, one for each act. Fol. 1r of Act I bears the date 'den 25. May 1823'; however, 'den 25.' is clearly a later addition. The end of this act, on fol. 153r, is dated 'den 30. May 1823', and even taking into account Schubert's prodigious facility it is scarcely to be believed that these dates reflect accurately the period of composition; indeed, simply to have copied fifty pages a day for six days would have been a major feat.

The first 103 leaves contain a mixture of types Ia and Ib, with Ia predominant. The last 50 leaves of the first act and the first 24 leaves of the second act contain a mixture of four related Italian papers showing the letters 'VG' and various countermarks. Since the last 119 leaves of Act II and 97 of 98 leaves in Act III resume the mixture of types Ia and Ib, we can hypothesize either that Schubert temporarily exhausted his supplies, or that he undertook a wholesale revision of this portion of the opera. There are, to be sure, discrete changes in the musical orthography of these Italian leaves, although closer study of their period of availability would be needed to determine the significance of any such notational variations. No further examples after 1821 of the VG family are known in either Schubert or Beethoven autographs. At all events, the genesis of *Fierrabras* is doubtless more complex than that suggested by its author's datings. The 143-folio second act is dated 31 May 1823 and 5

June 1823 at its beginning and end, no more believable than the first act, while the shorter 98-folio third act required from 7 June 1823 to 26 September 1823, a snail's pace by comparison. The single inserted leaf, fol. 92, is identified wrongly by Hilmar; it is a type II leaf added to the finale no earlier than December. A thorough study of the internal chronology of *Fierrabras* – which without a doubt involves several compositional stages – would shed considerable light on Schubert as a man of the musical theatre.

10. Overture to *Alfonso und Estrella*, D 732 Berlin SPK N.Mus.ms. 49
The date of December 1823 is squeezed on to a title-page that was originally used for an interior portion of the overture. Considerably more puzzling, however, is the title: underneath the inscription *Alfonso* an earlier layer with *Rosamunde* can still be seen. There is no particular reason to doubt Schubert's dating of these 22 leaves of type Ia. But it is difficult to reconcile these facts: (1) the full autograph of *Alfonso* (Vienna GdM A 208) contains no overture; (2) a two-hand version of the Berlin manuscript, now in private possession, is purportedly dated 'November 1822' (see D 759A); (3) a four-hand version of same, D 773 (present whereabouts unknown), is dated 1823; (4) two days after the première of *Rosamunde* on 20 December 1823, Moritz von Schwind – who was there – wrote to his friend Franz Schober that 'Schubert has taken over the overture he wrote for "Estrella", as he thinks it too "homespun" for "Estrella", for which he wants to write a new one.'[22]

These items raise more questions than they answer. *D2* opines that with the commission for the *Rosamunde* music 'hat [Schubert] erst bei dieser Gelegenheit das Titelblatt der Ouvertüre geschrieben, sie als "Rosamunde" bezeichnet und mit Dezember 1823 datiert. Erst später wurde der Titel "Rosamunde" wieder in "Alfonso" geändert.'[23] But this scenario is impossible. The Berlin overture was – and only the paper can verify here – clearly written *after* the two-hand version of November 1822. So where is the original overture which presumably accompanied the autograph of *Alfonso*? If Schubert simply took over the opera overture for *Rosamunde*, why was it necessary for him to prepare another complete version (itself not entirely a *Reinschrift*, especially with the makeshift title-page) of a work that presumably had already existed for at least a year? How did Schwind know the overture to an opera that had not been performed? I am not so much proposing two separate overtures – although the possibility cannot be ruled out that Johann Nepomuk Fuchs, the editor of *Alfonso* in the old complete edition (*AGA*), was right in declaring this overture to have been first composed for *Rosamunde* – but simply pointing up contradictions in the historical record that require some explanation. Explanations there may be (Schubert could himself have con-

22 *Documents*, p. 309.
23 'Not until this occasion did [Schubert] write a title-page for the Overture, entitling it "Rosamunde" and dating it December 1823. Only later was the title "Rosamunde" changed back to "Alfonso".' See the *Anmerkung* to the entry for D 732 in *D2*.

fided in Schwind about the overture, for example), but they will have to take into account, as earlier attempts have not, the truths afforded by paper studies.

Undated Works on Types Ia and Ib

11. Nos. 8 and 13 from *Alfonso und Estrella*, with piano accompaniment, D 732 Berlin SPK Schubert aut. 13

D2 makes no attempt to date this arrangement, but it must have been made in 1823, possibly for a performance, though none has been documented. The manuscript is a gathered sheet of type Ia.

12. Sonata in E minor for Piano (Fragment), D 769A (*olim* 994) Vienna SB MH 173/c

This single leaf of type Ia has been placed correctly in *D2* in the year 1823. Hilmar's confining it to 'Frühjahr (März?)' is unjustified without supporting evidence.

13. Song, 'Greisengesang', D 778 Berlin SPK N.Mus.ms. 51

On the basis of Anton von Spaun's report of a performance in St Florian (*Documents*, p. 280), *D2* dates the song 'vor Juni 1823'. The paper used by Schubert permits us to narrow the range to January–May 1823. There are, however, two versions of the song. The Berlin manuscript shows the characteristics of an *erste Niederschrift*, while a version closely resembling a *Reinschrift* (Vienna SB, MH 1862/c; with D 649, 756) is dated 'Sommer (Juli?) 1822' by Hilmar. Aside from the complete improbability of such a chronological relationship, two further pieces of evidence – neither decisive by itself – conspire to suggest a more plausible date for the complex MH 1862/c. The watermark (cf. Hilmar, Illus. 99) is highly unusual; there is no traditional 'countermark', but instead a small cross clustered at the intersection of the horizontal and vertical folds. The imprint 'C Hennigsches Notenpapier N^O^ 2. Prag, bei Halla & Comp.' merely suggests a paper of Bohemian origin. Between the spring and autumn of 1826, Beethoven filled 45 leaves with score sketches for the quartets opp. 131, 135, and 130/6; the central piece in the watermark is the identical cross found in MH 1862/c (I have not been able to associate the letters 'GE' in quadrant 4 with any specific mill, although a Bohemian origin for these leaves seems equally assured). We know that figures for watermarks – often the very same ones – were sold to mills by travelling pedlars, hence the plethora of grinning half-moons, shields, coats of arms, fleurs-de-lis, etc. that populate these papers. Virtually all the important mills were within a hundred kilometres of Prague, but more than geographical proximity it is the rarity of this particular mark that suggests 1826 as an alternative to 1822. Here the matter might rest were it not for the coincidence of this new date with the announcements of editions by Cappi & Czerny and Sauer & Leidesdorf in June, September, and November of 1826. We do know that Schubert frequently prepared fair copies for submission to publishers, and even the slight discrepancies between MH 1862/c and the printed version of D 778 are not inconsistent with this hypothesis. (On at least two other occasions, Hilmar confuses papers from 1826-7 with 1822; see types IV/5 and V/16.)

14. Overture to *Die Verschworenen*, D 787 Vienna SB MH 11800/c
The initial gathering, which presumably contained the date, is missing; only the last 12 leaves remain. All are type Ia. Identical in paper to the rest of the autograph (see type I/3), the overture was probably removed later for a planned performance. Hilmar's date of 'Frühjahr (März?) 1823' is plausible, though February is no less so.

15. Sketches for the opera *Fierrabras*, D 796 Vienna SB MH 168/c
Of the 14 leaves, eight are type Ib; they include fragmentary drafts in score for nos. 6 and 20, and for a discarded trio. From the chain of dates in the autograph (see type I/9) all of the sketches in MH 168/c can probably be placed in the spring of 1823.

Beethoven and Type I

Beethoven did not himself use paper showing this watermark, largely because the homemade sketchbooks for the Ninth Symphony were made up from Kiesling papers early in the year, and these occupied him for the remainder of 1823. As a rule he used fewer Welhartitz types than did Schubert, further evidence that they patronized different establishments. But an interesting copy of the Kyrie and Gloria of the Missa Solemnis, op. 123 (Bonn Beethovenhaus), prepared by Tyson's Copyist E some time between 1822 (when the work was completed) and April 1825 (when the manuscript was dispatched to Ferdinand Ries), preserves just this mixture of types Ia and Ib. With assistance from Schubert autographs, then, the copy can be ascribed with some confidence to the year 1823. Finally, we can assert with equal confidence that not only did Schubert rely almost exclusively on watermark types Ia and Ib in 1823, but he relied upon them *only* in that year. Their life span was something less than twelve months, from January to the beginning of December.

Watermarks IIa and IIb

For most of 1824 Schubert was again supplied with paper bearing two contemporaneous watermarks – this time from the Kiesling firm. And, again like the Welhartitz varieties, the only known type contains 16 staves, but with a slightly larger total span of 197 to 198 millimetres.

Dated Works on Types IIa and IIb

1. Introduction and Variations in E minor on 'Ihr Blümlein alle' for Flute and Piano, D 802 Vienna SB MH 2035/c

January 1824. 11 leaves of type IIa with an irregular gathering structure.

2. Octet in F for String and Wind Instruments, D 803

Vienna SB MH 131/c

Dated February 1824 at the beginning and 1 March 1824 at the end. Fols. 1-42 and 57-60 are type IIa; beginning with the *Andante*, fols. 43-56 are type IIb. The gathering structure of single bifolia is found only rarely in Schubert, and suggests the composer was less assured in this medium. Hilmar's watermark description contains several inaccuracies.

3. Songs, 'Der Sieg', D 805, and 'Abendstern', D 806

Vienna GdM A 233

'Abendstern' is dated March 1824. The last ten bars of 'Der Sieg' with which this type IIa leaf commences were clearly joined originally to an earlier leaf (probably part of a bifolium) containing the remainder of the song.

4. Song, 'Gondelfahrer', D 808 Berlin DSB Schubert aut. 3

March 1824. A single leaf of type IIa.

5. String Quartet in D minor, 'Death and the Maiden', D 810

New York PML

March 1824 on the front title-page. All that survives from this autograph is the initial three-sheet gathering, with the 12 leaves divided between types IIa and IIb. The first movement occupies fols. 1v-9r; the first 142 bars of the second movement fill the rest of the manuscript. It contains no evidence of the kind of revisions cited by Deutsch (*Documents*, p. 506) as having been made during the second rehearsal on 30 January 1826.

6. 'Salve Regina' in C for Quartet (T.T.B.B.), D 811

Berlin SPK Schubert aut. 12

April 1824. A gathered sheet of type IIa.

7. Quartet, 'Gebet', D 815 Vienna SB MH 4078/c

September 1824. A double-sheet gathering (eight leaves) of type IIb.

Undated Works on Type IIa

8. Six Deutsche, D 146, 366, 783, 975 Vienna GdM A 266

The keyboard dances on this bifolium were all included in Schubert's op. 33, published on 8 January 1825. Neither *D1* nor *D2* dates the manuscript, which must have been set down between *c.* November 1823 and September 1824.

9. No. 1 from *Die Verschworenen*, D 787 Vienna SB MH 2034/c

This revised version of the duet 'Sie ist's' consists of two double-sheet gatherings (16 leaves). While neither *D1* nor *D2* dates the manuscript, Hilmar has recently assigned it, without supporting evidence, to 'Anfang April 1823'. The paper suggests a more probable time frame of *c.* November 1823 to September 1824. No external stimulus for this second version is known.

10. Nos. 1, 3a, and 5 from *Rosamunde*, D 797 Vienna NB S.m. 27.668

32 leaves in four irregular gatherings. These three entr'actes were part of the music premièred on 20 December 1823. Helmina von Chézy's play was not

known to Schubert until October at the earliest (*Documents*, p. 293); whether he began the composition of his incidental music then or – more probably – in November, *Rosamunde* almost certainly represents his earliest usage of type IIa.

11. Nos. 2 and 9 from *Rosamunde*, D 797 Vienna SB MH 10/c
18 leaves in four irregular gatherings. The comments on the preceding entry apply to these two ballet numbers as well.

Beethoven and Type II

Beethoven and his copyists consumed enormous quantities of paper showing these related watermarks at just the period when Schubert was using them. Beethoven brought 13 leaves of type IIa into the autograph of the Ninth Symphony finale (early 1824), and more than 200 of them were conscripted during the preparation of the *Stichvorlage* and of yet another copy of the symphony, both datable to the second half of 1824. Type IIb is found on 18 leaves of late sketches for the symphony (November–December 1823) and on a bifolium in the autograph of the finale. The copy of *Die Weihe des Hauses* in the Beethovenhaus (SBH 739), predominantly of type IIb, was also very likely prepared at the end of 1823. These powerful concordances with Schubert are not matched by an equal congruence in staff-ruling: the total span of Beethoven's 16-stave paper is consistently less than Schubert's, ranging from 195 to 196+ millimetres.

The period from June to October 1824, when Schubert was employed on the Esterházy estate in Zseliz (Hungary), produced nine known autographs (D 812-820, although D 819 may belong to the 1818 sojourn); of these, four are lost and only a single one – the quartet 'Gebet', D 815, probably Schubert's greatest part-song – survives in a major public collection. Its type IIb paper suggests that the composer carried with him supplies of Viennese paper while travelling to remote outposts; this consideration assumes special importance in the history of the 'Great' C major Symphony. At all events, nine datable autographs on type II papers distribute themselves smoothly over an eleven-month period. The slight overlap with type I is hardly surprising; Schubert would quite naturally have replenished his supplies before they were entirely exhausted.

Remnants I

Schubert's compositional activities following his return from Zseliz until at least April 1825 present a perplexing picture. The almost superhuman level of production of the previous two years slackens considerably. Although there are impressive achievements on a smaller scale, like the Arpeggione Sonata and the song 'Todtengräbers Heimwehe', the mood of these pieces is at once retrospective and anticipatory. Too few of the autographs between D 821 and D 848 survive (or can be ascribed convincingly to this period), but the four that do share a common feature: all are on anomalous paper types that suggest a composer either unable or unwilling to procure a run of a major variety. Included are papers with unusual staff rulings and damaged watermarks. Although it is tempting to postulate a connection between Schubert's compositional uncertainty in these months and the seeming scarcity of paper, my argument does not depend on any such connection.

1. Sonata for Piano and Arpeggione, D 821 Paris BN Ms 304
November 1824. The paper shows a watermark unique in Schubert autographs: quadrants 1-2 contain a large letter 'W', over which a forearm suited up for fencing raises a sword aloft; quadrants 3-4 contain only a single half-moon staring intently toward the vertical fold. All 12 leaves contain 12 staves with a total span of 185 millimetres. The gathering structure of the manuscript is regular: a double sheet followed by a single sheet. It is possible that Schubert purchased this paper in Zseliz.

2. Song, 'Des Sängers Habe', D 832 Paris BN Ms 303
February 1825. This bifolium is the first of three examples that clearly belong to the type II watermark family, but survive in such a state of disrepair (and frequently having undergone repair) that only the generic relationship – in this instance with type IIb – remains. The staff-ruling and total span are identical with those in the principal paper type of 1824.

3. Sonata in C for Piano, 'Reliquie', D 840 Vienna SB MH 4125/c
April 1825. Three leaves from the same sheet of a modified type IIa. There are 12 staves to the page with a total span of 187.5 to 188+ millimetres.

4. Songs, 'Der blinde Knabe', D 833, and 'Todtengräbers Heimwehe', D 842 Vienna SB MH 102/c
April 1825. A gathered sheet of the same paper type as the previous entry.

Watermark III

The quality of paper employed by both Beethoven and Schubert throughout their careers tended toward the medium grade. With the shift around 1808 from north Italian sources to Bohemian suppliers, a visible decline in the aesthetic appeal of Viennese papers takes place. Since virtually all paper manufactured before 1830 consisted of 100 percent rag content, there was no parallel decline in durability. Rather, most Viennese papers of the time display a brownish or greyish or greenish tinge, not easily confused with the alabaster complexion of earlier Italian types. The Bohemian papers also tended to be lumpier and less translucent than their Italian counterparts, though this doubtless caused less distress to composers than to present-day students of watermarks.

Hence the unexpected – and as yet unexplained – appearance of a high-quality series of paper types in the years 1825 and 1826 must have provided a source of special pleasure for Viennese composers. Although a species of class distinction between paper grades was observed all over Europe, the widespread distribution of watermark types III and IV among autographs of Viennese provenance and the scarcity of other paper types during this period offer persuasive evidence that the Kiesling firm had not undertaken to inaugurate an elite, low-volume line, but was for a period of almost eighteen months in the curious position of being able to sharply upgrade the quality of their standard music paper.

The month of May 1825 was full of happy anticipation for Schubert, for on the 20th he departed from Vienna in the company of his esteemed friend Johann Michael Vogl, the beginning of what was to prove the happiest and most productive summer of his short life. Bearing in mind that Schubert's pen was sustained by remnants through at least April, he probably laid in large supplies of music paper shortly before his departure, in the full knowledge that he would need all of it. As was his preference, all leaves had 16 staves; the total span varied from 197+ to 198 millimetres. What did the summer in Steyr and Linz and St Florian and Gmunden and Bad Gastein and Salzburg hold?

1. Song, 'Versunken', D 715 Vienna SB MH 2031/c

This Goethe text had already been set in February of 1821; the inscription 'transp. July 1825' on the present manuscript indicates the date of the transposition. It is not known for whom Schubert made this low-voice arrangement, which consists of a bifolium with a single leaf inserted.

2. Quartet (T.T.B.B.), 'Nachtmusik', D 848 Vienna NB Cod. 19.487

A front title-page with the inscription 'July 1825 / Gmunden' suggests the esteem in which Schubert held this charming work. It consists of a single bifolium. Schubert departed from Gmunden on 15 July.

3. Sonata for Piano in D major, D 850 Vienna NB Cod. 19.490

A full *Umschlag* title-page carries the inscription 'Sonate / für das Pianoforte', Another inscription on fol. 2r reads 'Gastein. Aug. 1825', where Schubert had arrived on the 15th. 18 folios are arranged into two uniform double-sheet gatherings around which the bifolium wrapper is placed. The particular spaciousness in the layout of this autograph indicates that the composer invested the sonata with special importance.

4. Song, 'Das Heimweh', D 851 Berlin DSB Schubert aut. 37

The manuscript carries the inscription 'Gastein. August 1825', where Schubert had arrived on the 15th. Its first layer consists of a sheet of type III. At some later point Schubert inserted a bifolium of low-grade greenish paper identical with secondary paper 3 in the 'Great' C major autograph, and containing an alternative ending of some 61 bars. The revision must have been carried out before May 1827, when an edition incorporating it was announced by Haslinger. A more likely date is September 1825 (see the discussion of the 'Great' C major autograph).

5. Songs, 'Fülle der Liebe', D 854, and 'Wiedersehn', D 855

Berlin DSB Schubert aut. 30

The first of these songs is inscribed 'August 1825', and the second 'Sept. 1825'. The manuscript consists of a single bifolium.

Type III and the 'Great' C major Symphony

While Beethoven might have been pleased with a summer's output of this magnitude, by Schubertian standards it was rather meagre, even if of unusually high quality. This picture is not modified significantly by the addition of a few masterpieces known to have been composed during the same period, for example the song 'Die Allmacht', D 852 (dated August 1825 by Witteczek–Spaun, and published together with D 851, whose autograph carries the inscription 'Gastein. August 1825'). It might well be argued that in the summer of 1825 Schubert was on holiday, and that a slackening in his level of production would have been a natural outcome to these leisurely months. The more than a dozen moves made between *c.* 19 May and 1 October, coupled with the near-constant companionship of the irrepressible Johann Michael Vogl, could hardly be thought to produce the ideal working conditions for a composer of even Schubert's easy-going disposition.

We know now, however, that Schubert had purchased almost a hundred additional leaves of type III paper before departing Vienna; there is a slim chance, of course, that he did so upon his return in October, but both his and Beethoven's patterns of usage throughout this period discourage such a hypothesis. What did he do with all of these remaining leaves? Regardless of when or in what surroundings he used them, the evidence is unequivocal: he composed most of the 'Great' C major Symphony. For the moment, the evidence of the papers will simply be entered on the record; only when the testimony from all 120 autographs has been presented can its ramifications be fully appreciated, and justice done to the biographical and style-critical aspects of the debate. To this it must be added that the apparent date 'März 1828' in the upper right-hand corner of fol. 1r of the C major autograph cannot be allowed to dominate the discussion; the primary importance of the inscription is obvious enough, but when unchecked it has led partisans as diverse in intent as Grove and Reed to untenable conclusions.

Two-thirds of the autograph consists of type III paper, with the remainder of the manuscript divided among no fewer than four different varieties. Three of these are represented almost nowhere else in Schubert, and will be viewed as secondary papers. The final species displays watermark type IV.

Symphony in C major, D 944 Vienna GdM A 245

folio	quadrant	paper	movement
1	4b	type III	I begins
2	3b		
3	2b		
4	1b		
5	4b		
6	3b		
7	2b		
8	1b		
9	4a		
10	3a		
11	4a		
12	3a		
13	2a		
14	1a		
15	2a		
16	1a		
17	2b		
18	1b		
19	4a		
20	3a		
21	2a		
22	1a		
23	4b		
24	3b		
25	3b		
26	4b		
27	3a		
28	4a		
29	1a		
30	2a		
31	1b		
32	2b		

folio	quadrant	paper	movement
33	4a		
34	3a		
35	2b		
36	1b		
37	2b	secondary 1	I, bar 591 in coda
38	3b		
39	4b		
40	3b	type III	I, bar 646, on fol. 40v
41	2a		
42	1a		I ends on fol. 42v
43	1a		II begins on fol. 43r
44	2a		
45	4b		
46	3b		
47	2b		
48	1b		
49	3a		
50	4a		
51	1a		
52	2a		
53	2b		
54	1b		
55	4b		
56	3b		
57	3a		
58	4a		
59	4a		
60	3a		
61	3a		
62	4a		
63	1a		II ends on fol. 63r
64	2a		III begins on fol. 63v
65	2a		
66	1a		

folio	quadrant	paper	movement
67	4b		
68	3b		
69	4a		
70	3a		
71	2a		
72	1a		scherzo proper ends on fol. 72v
73	4a		trio begins on fol. 73r
74	3a		
75	3b	secondary 1	trio, bar 43
76	4b		
77	1b		
78	2b		
79	2a	type III	trio, bar 122
80	1a		
81	2b		IV begins on fol. 81r
82	1b		
83	4a		
84	3a		
85	2a		
86	1a		
87	4b		
88	3b		
89	3b		
90	4b		
91	2b		
92	3b		
93	1b		
94	2b		
95	4b	secondary 2	IV, bar 326
96	3b		
97	2b		
98	1b		
99	4b		
100	3b		
101	2b		
102	1b		

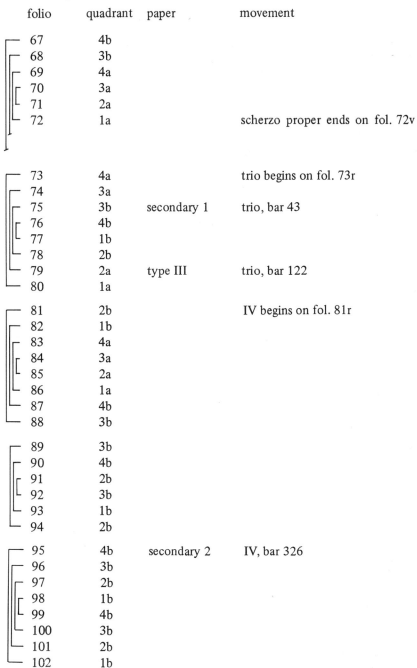

folio	quadrant	paper	movement
103	3a		
104	4a		
105	x	secondary 3	IV, bar 573
106	x		
107	x		
108	x		
109	1a	secondary 2	
110	2a		
111	x	secondary 3	
112	x		
113	x		
114	x		
115	x		
116	x		
117	x		
118	x		
119	x		
120	x		
121	x		
122	x		
123	x		
124	x		
125	3a	type IV	IV, bar 1025
126	4a		
127	4a		
128	1a		
129	1a		
130	2a		

Description of Secondary Papers in the 'Great' C major Autograph

(1) fols. 37-9, 75-8: 16 staves, total span of 197.5 millimetres (and drawn with a different rastral from type III). This three-quarter-sheet and gathered-sheet pair are the lone exceptions to the otherwise sequential use of paper types within the autograph, a circumstance that points to their service as vehicles for revision. The watermark, although found nowhere else among Schubert autographs, belongs to a Viennese paper employed by Beethoven in both the composing score and the fair copy of the new finale to the B flat major String Quartet, op. 130, a movement completed no later than the

beginning of November 1826; Beethoven's supply must have been purchased before he left Vienna for Gneixendorf at the end of September.

(2) fols. 95-104, 109-10: 16 staves, total span of 195– to 196– millimetres. It seems clear that Schubert consumed his remaining stores of type III while only partway through the finale. Under normal circumstances we would expect him to have procured a sizeable quantity of the next principal type available, and to have completed the autograph with only this single break in continuity (the most impressive such example from Schubert's last years is the E flat major Mass, D 950, begun in June 1828 on type VIIc and completed that autumn on types VIIIa and VIIIb). For whatever reasons, this was not possible in the symphony. The creamy smoothness of the preceding gatherings is abruptly replaced by a Kiesling variety of decidedly inferior cast. Although the general watermark family appears in scattered Viennese papers between 1818 and 1823 (cf. Hilmar, Illus. 66-71 passim), there are no specific concordances with any known Viennese types.

(3) fols. 105-8, 111-24: 16 staves, total span of 194 to 195 millimetres. Type 3, which was probably purchased and used simultaneously with type 2, is unquestionably the lowest grade of paper ever used by Schubert. The faint greenish tinge of the previous variety has deepened to a pea green. There is no decorative watermark at all. Those chain lines that can be at all discerned are bent, broken, and otherwise deformed. It is difficult to imagine even small quantities of such a low-grade paper having been available in Vienna.

Watermark IV

If the last paper found in the autograph of the 'Great' C major Symphony is represented there only sparsely, it completely dominates the first nine months of 1826. The outstanding quality of the previous year's offering from the Kiesling firm is mirrored right down to the similar watermark. All examples show 16 staves and a slightly smaller total span of 195.5 to 196.5 millimetres.

Dated Works on Type IV

1. Songs, 'Am Fenster', D 878, and 'Sehnsucht', D 879 — Washington LC
March 1826. A gathered sheet. Bars 1-71 only for D 879; see type IV/10 for continuation.

2. Song, 'Im Frühling', D 882 — Paris BN Ms 2194
March 1826. A bifolium now preserved as two single leaves.

3. String Quartet in G major, D 887 — Vienna NB S.m. 27.665
The date 20 June 1826 is found on fol. 1r, and the date 30 June 1826 on the last page, fol. 33v. The manuscript consists of 34 leaves in four largely regular gatherings.

4. Quartet, 'Grab und Mond', D 893 — Berlin SPK Schubert aut. 20
September 1826. A single leaf.

Undated Works on Type IV

5. Mass in A flat major, D 678 (Gloria sketches) Vienna SB MH 180/c
Quartet fragment, 'Nachklänge', D 873A
'Gesänge aus *Wilhelm Meister*', D 877 (sketches to nos. 1-3)
Hilmar's description of these six leaves (a bifolium followed by four single leaves) rests upon a fundamentally false assumption concerning the evolution of the A flat major Mass, one that has prevented us from recognizing the most extensive and longest-deferred compositional revision in Schubert's far-flung output. It is true that the Dresden fair copy of D 877 carries the date January 1826, and that the slightly earlier Vienna draft was probably set down in the same month. But how much sense does it make to then assign the fewer than a dozen bars related to the colossal fugue which concludes the Gloria of D 678 to the '1. Hälfte 1822', or the quartet fragment 'Nachklänge', D 873A, on another leaf in the same complex, to '1823'? Not only is there no evidence to support a chronology of such complexity; paper studies have now provided us with solid evidence that the fugue, which has hitherto been assigned to the year 1822 through guilt by association with brother Ferdinand's dating (apparently more compelling for Hilmar than the manuscript evidence), was recast not in that year but during the period from September 1826 to May 1827 (see type V/16). There is hence no evidence to challenge the premiss that all three works drafted on these leaves originated around January 1826 and thereby constitute the earliest datable use of type IV.

6. Melodrama, 'Abschied von der Erde', D 829 Vienna GdM A 213
A single leaf. This conclusion to the one-act play *Der Falke* had its première privately in Vienna on 17 February 1826.

7. Song, 'Todtengräber-Weise', D 869 Washington LC
Four separate leaves from at least three different sheets. The indexes to the Witteczek–Spaun collection date the song '1826', a frame that can now be narrowed to January–September.

8. Songs, 'Der Wanderer an den Mond', D 870, and 'Das Zügenglöcklein', D 871 Berlin SPK Schubert aut. 33
A gathered sheet. Both songs are dated '1826' in the indexes to the Witteczek–Spaun collection, a period that can now be limited to January–September. D 870 was one of five Lieder included in the programme of the all-Schubert concert on 26 March 1828.

9. Song, 'Nur wer die Sehnsucht kennt' (no. 4 from *Wilhelm Meister*), D 877
Vienna SB MH 2063/c
A single leaf. *D2* places the genesis of all four Mignon numbers from D 877 in January. Hilmar, 'aufgrund der Schriftzüge', assigns no. 4 to 'Frühjahr (April?) 1826', but fails to supply any supporting evidence. The only reliable frame is, once again, January–September.

10. Songs, 'Sehnsucht', D 879; 'Im Freien', D 880; and 'Fischerweise', D 881
Vienna SB MH 104/c

These two single leaves followed by a gathered sheet form the continuation of type IV/1, and may likewise be assigned to March 1826. Hilmar places D 881, without any supporting evidence, in April.

11. Fols. 125-30 of the Symphony in C major, D 944 Vienna GdM A 245
Like the other undated autographs on type IV, these six leaves were almost certainly not filled before January of 1826.

Having now accounted for every leaf which makes up the autograph of the 'Great' C major Symphony, we are at one level equipped with powerful new evidence concerning its compositional history. In fact, such data provides only the opening salvo in a longer campaign. The case history amassed thus far demands not just sifting and interpretation, but completion. What contemporaneous papers used by Schubert do *not* appear in the C major autograph? Most important, do the papers employed by the composer in the last two years of his life include varieties present in the autograph of the symphony? In the course of addressing these issues a number of other chronological questions can be raised and solutions proposed.

Remnants II

Although the evidence is less complete than for a year earlier, there is reason to suspect that a short period of paper scarcity greeted Schubert upon his return to Vienna in the early days of October 1825. The last dated example of type III occurs in September (D 893), while the earliest work on type IV cannot be confirmed before some time in January 1826 (D 877). Only two solitary remnants survive to fill this two-to-three-month gap:

1. Song, 'Um Mitternacht', D 862 Washington LC
December 1825. These two leaves display an unusual 12-stave ruling, with a total span of 186 to 186.5 millimetres. Traces of the letters 'EGA' in quadrant 1 and an eagle in quadrant 2 suggest affinities with papers used by both Beethoven and Schubert in 1812-2.

2. Quintet, 'Mondenschein', D 875 Berlin SPK Schubert aut. 21
January 1826. This gathered sheet shares all of the characteristics of secondary paper 3 in the 'Great' C major autograph (and in D 851; cf. type III/4): 16 staves, a total span of 194 to 195 millimetres, and a marked greenish tinge accompanied by an identical array of broken chain lines with no decorative watermark. Its possible origins are treated more thoroughly in the concluding discussion dealing with the chronology of the 'Great' C major Symphony (see below, pp. 257 and 260).

Watermarks Va and Vb

After almost eighteen months of offering Vienna's composers and music copyists a premium paper, the Kiesling firm returned in the autumn of 1826 to a medium-grade brand manufactured from a pair of twin moulds, a procedure already familiar from type II. On paper bearing this watermark Schubert was to draft more works, and in more diverse formats, than on any other variety from his last six years – no fewer than twenty-three separate autographs with three different staff rulings. The 16-stave variety appears throughout the run, but the two dated 12-stave examples are confined to January–February 1827, while the three dated 14-stave examples span February to May. There is nothing inherent in any of the works on either 12- or 14-stave paper that suggests such rulings represented pre-compositional choices on Schubert's part; hence the provisional placing of undated works within the time frame of their dated counterparts is unlikely to produce a significant amount of error, while measurably increasing the precision of our chronology.

Beginning with type V, Schubert no longer shared watermarks with Beethoven; the latter spent October and November at his brother's villa in Gneixendorf, and was bedridden upon his return to Vienna in December until his death the following March.

16-stave examples show a total span of 205.5 to 207 millimetres, the largest ever in an oblong paper used by Schubert. 14-stave examples are also ruled generously, ranging from 201- to 202.5 millimetres. Examples with 12 staves have a total span of 187 to 188.5 millimetres. More than two-thirds of the manuscripts on type V paper display 16 staves; unless otherwise noted, the following examples are of this variety.

Dated Works on Types Va and Vb

1. 'Nachthelle' for Tenor Solo, Male Chorus, and Piano Accompaniment, D 892
Vienna SB MH 31/c

Along with two leaves each of types Va and Vb, the autograph includes two leaves of type IV and a single leaf (16 staves, with a total span of 193.5 millimetres) which may well belong to the type VII family; regardless of its lineage, this inserted leaf represents a later compositional stage than the remainder of the autograph. The mixture of types IV and V is characteristic of the transition from one paper to another.

2. Sonata in G major (called 'Fantasia'), D 894 London BL Add. 36738

October 1826. 17 leaves of both types Va and Vb.

3. Rondo in B minor for Violin and Piano, D 895
New York PML Heineman

October 1826. Along with ten leaves of type V weighted in favour of the b variety, the autograph includes an internal sheet of type IV, again typical of the transition period.

4. Songs, 'Zur guten Nacht' (with T.T.B.B. chorus), D 903; 'Alinde', D 904; and 'An die Laute', D 905 Vienna SB MH 2014/c
January 1827. A sheet plus a bifolium of type Vb with 12 staves.
5. Song, 'Der Vater mit dem Kinde', D 906 Vienna GdM A 234
February 1827. A bifolium of type Va, also with 12 staves.
6. Variation on a Theme from Hérold's *Marie* for Piano, four hands, D 908 Berlin SPK Schubert aut. 24
February 1827. Three leaves of type Vb with 14 staves.
7. Song, 'Jägers Liebeslied', D 909 Dresden Sächsische Landesbibliothek
February 1827. Three leaves of type Va, also with 14 staves.
8. Song Cycle, *Winterreise*, D 911, Part 1 New York PML Cary
February 1827. 20 of the 21 leaves are type Vb. Fol. 15 is a leaf of type VIIa, and represents a major compositional revision to the song 'Rückblick', one that could not have been made before June of the same year. Revisions, in fact, rule the day in the autograph to Part 1, and account in large measure for its highly irregular gathering structure.
9. 'Schlachtlied', for Male Double Chorus, D 912 London Zweig Collection
28 February 1827. Five of the seven leaves are type V. A bifolium (fols. 3-4) of type VIIa has replaced two original folios; like the major revision in Part 1 of *Winterreise*, this could not have taken place before June of 1827.
10. Quartet, 'Frühlingslied', D 914 Vienna SB MH 60/c
April 1827. A gathered sheet of type Va.
11. Quartet, 'Das stille Lied', D 916 (sketch) Vienna SB MH 185/c
May 1827. A single leaf of type Vb.
12. Quartet, 'Das stille Lied', D 916 (complete score) Private owner
May 1827. 14-stave paper.

Undated Works on Types Va and Vb

13. Exercises, D 16; Quartet sketch, 'Ich hab' in mich gesogen', D 778B Vienna SB MH 191/c
A single leaf of type Va with 14 staves. *D2* offers the date '1823(?)'; Hilmar gives 'Herbst 1826' for the quartet and 'November 1828' for the counterpoint exercises. The paper type is found in dated examples between February and May 1827, and there is no reason for supposing either entry to have been composed outside of this frame. Hilmar's attempt to link the seven exercises in inversion to Schubert's last instruction with Simon Sechter remains unsubstantiated.
14. Trio, 'Die Advokaten', D 37 Stargardt, 1961 (bars 1-30)
Vienna SB MH 34/c (bars 31-174)
Cambridge Fitzwilliam Museum (bars 175-200)
Although the largest portion of this triply divided manuscript is undated, its initial segment carries in Schubert's hand the autograph inscription '1812', one whose literal meaning is not challenged by either *D1* or *D2*. There can be

little doubt that the entire autograph (six leaves of type Vb) was prepared as an engraver's copy shortly before the censor's approval of 12 May 1827, noted on the final leaf. Schubert's decision not to employ a copyist may have related to his commencing the 1812 version in F, moving up to G – the tonality throughout the later copy – only after the first section.

15. Song, 'Dem Unendlichen', D 291c Berlin DSB Schubert aut. 44
Unlike the two 1815 versions of this song, the present autograph – a bifolium plus a single leaf of type Vb, and largely a transposition from F into G – must date from September 1826 – May 1827, a circumstance not noted in either *D1* or *D2*.

16. Mass in A flat major, D 678
(a) Osanna, second version Vienna SB MH 24/c
A bifolium of type Va. *D2* allows 'bis September 1822' for the first completion of the mass, while Hilmar offers the vague dating 'nicht vor Sommer 1822' for this revised version of the Osanna. It must in fact date from September 1826–May 1827.

(b) Fols. 50-63 of the autograph score Vienna GdM A 204
The final witnesses to the later compositional stages in the A flat Mass are the 14 leaves of type Va in the autograph itself. It is now possible to affirm that the brilliant 'Cum Sancto Spiritu' fugue – one of Schubert's greatest achievements in the archaic sacred style – was recomposed not in 1822, as both Ferdinand Schubert and Deutsch (*D1* and *D2*) seem to imply, but some time between the autumn of 1826 and the spring of 1827 (cf. type IV/5). The nature of the restructuring of this fugue (it is not so much lengthened as filled out contrapuntally) is the subject of a separate study, but for now we can at least acknowledge its proper place at the head of an imposing list of contrapuntal *tours de force* from Schubert's last two years, a period that includes such Handelian homages as 'Mirjams Siegesgesang', the F minor Fantasy, and the E flat Mass.

17. Overture to *Fierrabras* for piano duet. D 798 Paris BN Ms 302
13 leaves of type Va. *D2*'s general reference of 'nach 2. Oktober 1823' (the date on the orchestral score from which the arrangement was made) can now be narrowed considerably to September 1826 – May 1827. No external stimulus for the keyboard version is known.

18. Quartet, 'Wein und Liebe', D 901 Berlin SPK Schubert aut. 19
A sheet of type Va with 14 staves. The autograph carries the date of the censor's permit, 2 June 1827, and was in all likelihood set down only shortly before (the earliest example of the 14-stave variety is in February).

19. Song for Male Voice, 'Il traditor deluso', D 902/2
Mass in E flat major, D 950 (Gloria sketches?) Vienna SB MH 107/c
A sheet of type Vb. The draft for the aria (on a Metastasian text) is complete only in the notes of the vocal part; text and accompaniment are incompletely represented. Because of the paper distribution in the autograph of D 902 (see

next entry), this first version of no. 2 was most likely conceived around May 1827. It is not at all clear that the brief twelve-bar entry (untexted and in G major) similar in outline to the 'Cum Sancto Spiritu' from the E flat Mass was already linked, at its writing down, to that work. At all events, there is no reason to suspect that the G major entry was penned outside of this time frame – for example, 'im Frühjahr 1828', as Hilmar has asserted without supporting evidence.

20. Three Songs for Male Voice, D 902/1-3
London BL Add. 41630, fols. 45-58

The co-existence of 12 leaves of type Va (score, 14 staves) with a bifolium of type VIIa (vocal parts) argues strongly for a compositional date of May–June 1827, a more precise one than the '1827(vor September)' offered by *D2* (based on the advertisement of 12 September 1827 for the first edition).

21. Cantata for Irene von Kiesewetter (for Quartet and Double Chorus with Piano Duet), D 936 Vienna SB MH 32/c

Three gathered bifolia from two sheets of type Vb. A chronology of this slight work provides a classic instance of the need to reconcile conflicting pieces of evidence: (*a*) fourfold reference to 'Irene' within the anonymous text virtually assures the connection with Irene von Kiesewetter (even so, Hilmar's attribution of the corner inscription 'Irene' on fol. 1r to Schubert is not shared by the editors of *D2*); (*b*) the date '1828' appears in red crayon in an unidentified hand on the same fol. 1r; (*c*) although the manuscript is otherwise undated, a copy in the Witteczek–Spaun collection (complete with parts) carries the date 26 December 1827; (*d*) a letter of 28 January 1828 from Johann Baptist Jenger to Frau Marie Pachler explains that Fräulein Kiesewetter 'kürzlich von einer bedeutenden Krankheit genesen [sei]';[24] (*e*) the paper used by Schubert suggests a time frame of September 1826 – May 1827. At this point speculation begins where the meagre facts leave off. Kreissle decided on the basis of considerations *a*, *c* and *d* that the cantata was written 'zur Feier der Wiedergenesung des Fräuleins [Irene Kiesewetter]'[25] – logic apparently sufficient for the editors of *D2*. As it is, no incontrovertible evidence exists linking these particular circumstances to the same narrative. Only the second of the four stanzas – 'Thy pains alone with cruel rigour / A jealous Fate would let us share' – could possibly be associated with an illness, and this is by no means unambiguously established. Likewise, Hilmar's date 'Jänner 1828' is simply beholden to *b* rather than *c*, relying otherwise on the same unestablished claim. Viewed against either approach, the evidence offered by paper studies must be taken seriously. For if Schubert did indeed hang on to three bifolia of type Vb for at least seven months after the main run was exhausted, using them only in December, then they are parties to a singular incident in the last

24 Cf. *Documents*, p. 726: 'recently recovered from a serious illness'.

25 'In celebration of the recovery of the young lady': see Heinrich Kreissle von Hellborn, *Franz Schubert* (Vienna, 1865), p. 408.

six years of the composer's life. Finally, if the claims of points *a-d* cannot at present be entirely reconciled with those of point *e*, their competing interests can now at least be placed on more equal footing.

22. Tenor Aria with Chorus, 'Intende voci', D 963

Berlin SPK Schubert aut. 14

Although the fair copy is dated October 1828 by Schubert, this early draft – eight leaves of type Va with 12 staves, and slightly less than half-complete – must date from the first months of 1827, a circumstance not noted by either *D1* or *D2*.

Watermark Types VIa and VIb

Although watermark types VIa and VIb and type VIIa were employed over a similar time span, their joint usage does not actually reflect a shift in Schubert's attitudes towards paper. The first instance signals a remarkable, though apparently temporary, modification in Schubert's compositional habits – one whose significance has gone entirely unremarked in the Schubert literature (including Hilmar's catalogue). Beethoven's penchant for tearing an upright-format bifolium in half so that it would fit into the ample coat pockets of the time has been well documented. These home-made booklets then served as the agents for sketching done with pencil while the composer was enjoying the out-of-doors. Although Beethoven maintained this practice from shortly after 1800 until the end of his life, the 52 pocket bifolia bequeathed by Schubert all date from the summer of 1827. We remain completely in the dark as to the motivating force behind this sudden preference and its equally sudden disappearance.

The watermarks of types VIa and VIb share an ornamental crown surrounding a fleur-de-lis in quadrants 1 and 2, and the letters 'AK&S' at the seam of quadrants 3 and 4. Type VIa displays the additional feature of the letter 'L' (doubtless representing 'Lauterwasser', the river on which the Kiesling mills were situated) in the lower left-hand corner of quadrant 1. The similarities with type Va are obvious enough, yet three small but crucial distinctions remain. First, the quality of these upright-format papers is consistently a notch below that of the preceding oblong-format varieties. Second, the watermarks themselves show small differences in layout. Third, the earlier folio sizes (width x height in oblong format) of 318-28 x 245-8 millimetres for untrimmed leaves are replaced by the smaller dimensions (height x width in upright format) of 304-9 x 242-8 millimetres. We can only conclude that the watermark selected by the Kiesling firm in the early summer of 1827 to replace type Va was in a sense cloned from its predecessor, skilfully enough to deceive Hilmar on two occasions (cf. his Illus. 36 and 37). This was the paper that awaited Franz Schubert when he sought out a variety – all in upright format with 16 staves and a total span of 255 to 257 millimetres – that could be easily converted into pocket format.

The relationship between types VIa and VIb turns out to be even more intimate, since b was very likely produced from the actual mould frames used for a; only a few repairs, such as the removal of a damaged 'L' in quadrant 1, and the alterations to '&' in both moulds, would have proved necessary. The sole dated example of this type is inscribed 'Grätz, Sept. 1827', and only one further example (D 872) can be verified. Given the circumstance that all the undisputed examples (with one easily explained exception) of type VIa are in pocket format, and that both clear-cut examples of type VIb are in standard upright format, I have assigned three further upright-format autographs to type VIb, without ruling out the possibility that their genesis may extend back to the early summer of 1827. At all events, Schubert's renewal in Graz of exhausted paper supplies provides a plausible scenario for type VIb.

Dated and Undated Works on Type VIa

1. Opera, *Der Graf von Gleichen*, D 918 (fragment) Vienna SB MH 169/c
The first of the oblong leaves (see type VIIa/3) in this two-format complex is dated 19 June 1827 by Schubert. Since these were filled concurrently with the 14 pocket bifolia and two standard leaves of type VIa that fill out the manuscript (the first use of a pocket leaf is for no. 5), the same general starting-point doubtless applies. But Hilmar's chronology of selected numbers – which he extends all the way into the late spring of 1828 – will continue to seem far-fetched until the grounds on which it is based are specified. There is at present no reason for proposing that work on D 918 extended beyond Schubert's summer months in Vienna.

2. Impromptu in C minor for Piano, D 899/1 Vienna SB MH 145/c
Four pocket bifolia in a single gathering. *D2* dates all four impromptus 'Sommer bis Herbst 1827(?)'; Hilmar dates the C minor draft 'Spätsommer oder Herbst 1827'. There is again no reason for pushing the composition beyond the summer months of 1827. The numbering 5–8 on the autograph of four further impromptus, D 935 – dated in December – does not inhibit the notion of a first draft of the C minor being complete by August.

3. Klavierstück in C major, D 916B Vienna SB MH 14276/c
Four pocket bifolia in a single gathering. Along with the following entry, this fragment was doubtless a candidate for inclusion in the group of four impromptus that now constitute D 899. The chronological considerations are identical with those for item 2.

4. Klavierstück in C minor, D 916C Vienna SB MH 14277/c
Four pocket bifolia in a single gathering. The same arguments apply as for items 2-3. Significantly, the drafts for both D 916B and 916C were found among the sketches for *Der Graf von Gleichen*. Otto Brusatti's published

solution for completing D 916C – with a literal repeat of its exposition, including the original modulation to the secondary key of the submediant! – cannot possibly reflect Schubert's intentions, as a cursory glance at the composer's late view of sonata style in D 935/1 (composed within several months of D 916C) or many other similar movements will show.

Dated and Undated Works on Type VIb

1. Songs, 'Heimliches Lieben', D 922, and 'Eine altschottische Ballade', D 923 New York PML

This gathered sheet in upright format (12 staves, total span 243 to 243.5 millimetres) is dated by Schubert 'Grätz, Sept. 1827'.

2. *Deutsche Messe*, D 872 Vienna SB MH 14/c

20 folios of upright-format paper in three gatherings with 16 staves and a total span of 255 to 257 millimetres. This fair copy includes a few leaves of a companion watermark used in parallel with type VIb (and not noted by Hilmar), but is otherwise identical to that of D 922 and 923. Schubert's letter of thanks to Johann Philipp Neumann on 16 October 1827 upon receiving his honorarium for this commissioned work offers additional support for a compositional frame of September 1827. At all events, no evidence can be cited to support Hilmar's date 'Anfang 1827'.

3. Song, 'Die Nebensonnen' (no. 23 from *Winterreise*, D 911) Vienna GdM A 235

Half of a single upright-format leaf (originally 16 staves with a total span of 255 to 257 millimetres). Positive identification of the watermark is impossible; the format suggests type VIb. A circumspect dating would place the draft between July and September 1827, with preference given to the later boundary.

4. Impromptu in F minor, D 935/1 Burlington, Vermont Wilhelm Raab
'Hymnus an den heiligen Geist', D 948

A single upright-format leaf with 16 staves. Although I have not seen the manuscript at first hand, the illustration given by M. J. E. Brown[26] appears to be of a type VI leaf. The 41 bars sketched for the Impromptu are followed abruptly by bars 60-108 of the hymn. Since the autograph of D 935 is dated December 1827, and that of D 948 May 1828, it is almost certain that Schubert reclaimed the leaf some eight to ten months after its initial usage to work out a problematic section in the hymn (he would scarcely have commenced the work in bar 60!). The sketch for the Impromptu falls into the same period as 'Die Nebensonnen' above.

5. Klavierstück in C major, D 946/3 Vienna SB MH 144/c

Three single leaves ruled like items 2 and 3. The watermark is too blurred to distinguish between types VIa and VIb, but the format again favours type VIb. In any event, the datings of May–June 1828 put forward by both Hilmar

26 Brown, *Essays on Schubert* (London, 1966), facing p. 20.

and *D2* cannot be reconciled easily with the evidence of the paper, which places the composition at least eight months earlier. Until concrete evidence is forthcoming that overrides the weight of arguments from paper, the latter will continue to take precedence. (The argument advanced in *D2* concerning 'die Ähnlichkeit . . . der musikalischen Faktur der drei Stücke' does not withstand scrutiny; the first two in the group share a common tonality, highly similar left-hand accompaniments in their A sections, and identical ABACA forms without coda. The third member of the set is not only in another key, but in Schubert's more favoured ABA ternary form with coda.)

Watermark Types VIIa, VIIb, VIIc and VIId

Sixteen of the last eighteen months of Schubert's life were dominated – in so far as paper was concerned – by a single watermark, one that marked the return of the Welhartitz firm, absent since the end of 1823. The most remarkable feature of this type is the gradual and irreversible fading of the watermark to near-illegibility, a phenomenon directly associated with wear due to extended life. It must be stressed that only the second of the four stages (type b, 12 staves with a total span of 185 to 185.5 millimetres, and dated examples from October 1827 to April 1828) is easily identified, thanks to its staff-ruling. The three remaining stages (all with 16 staves and a total span of 193.5 to 194– millimetres) represent points on a continuum, and although the progressive disappearance of the watermark is a very real phenomenon, the possibility of a one-stage error (either between a and c or between c and d) cannot be ruled out. In switching from 16- to 12- and finally back to 16-stave paper, Schubert presumably renewed his supplies at least three times during this period; there were no compositional prerequisites between October and April that would have prompted a change in staff-ruling. Indeed, it is almost certain that type VIIb – more than 150 leaves – was acquired in a single purchase upon Schubert's return to Vienna around the beginning of October. Within this context of periodic acquisitions, the distinctions among the 16-stave varieties assume considerable importance, and it is both possible and to be hoped that more refined techniques of comparative paper analysis in the future will facilitate improvements to the provisional chronology offered here.

Dated Works on Type VIIa (all with 16 staves)

1. Songs, 'Im Abendrot', D 799, and 'Der blinde Knabe', D 833

New York PML Cary

Although D 799 is clearly dated 'Febr. 1825', the two fair copies in this bifolium can have been prepared no earlier than June 1827, though probably no later than October of the same year (a circumstance not noted in either *D1* or *D2*). The composing score of D 833 is dated April 1825 by Schubert, so the date on the fair copy of D 799 doubtless refers to that of its composition (surely taken from an earlier autograph now lost).

2. Song, 'Das Lied im Grünen', D 917
Palo Alto, USA Stanford University Libraries
June 1827.

3. Opera, *Der Graf von Gleichen*, D 918 (fragment) Vienna SB MH 169/c
The first of the 34 oblong leaves (of which 22 are single bifolia) is dated 19 June 1827. Concerning their chronology, see type VIa/1.

4. 'Ständchen' for Contralto Solo and Chorus with Piano Accompaniment, D 920 Vienna SB MH 27/c
July 1827. A gathered sheet plus a single leaf.

Undated Works on Type VIIa

5. *Deutsche Messe*, D 872 Private owner
This first version, like the fair copy (see type VIb/2), lacks any title or date; the 'Schlussgesang' breaks off after eighteen bars. The draft was probably made shortly before Schubert's journey in September to Graz.

6. Song, 'Mut' (no. 22 from *Winterreise*, D 911) Vienna Hans Kann
A single leaf containing the first version of 'Mut', and datable to June–September 1827.

Dated Works on Type VIIb (all with 12 staves)

1. Song Cycle, *Winterreise*, D 911, Part II New York PML Cary
October 1827. This fair copy consists of 16 leaves in two double-sheet gatherings.

2. Piano Trio in E flat major, D 929
(a) Incomplete drafts for movements I–III Vienna GdM A 251
November 1827. These 11 leaves in score contain drafts for the first three movements (the longest is for the first movement, continued through the beginning of the development), and offer strong evidence that Schubert dated his manuscripts upon the commencement of composition.
(b) Fair copy Bottmingen bei Basel Frau Ria Wilhelm
November 1827. 38 leaves, of which the first 20 (for movements I–III) are in units of single bifolia, while those for the finale are in two larger groups.

3. Songs, 'Der Wallensteiner Lanzknecht beim Trunk', D 931; 'Der Kreuzzug', D 932; and 'Fischers Liebesglück', D 933 Vienna SB MH 1865/c
November 1827. A single leaf and a bifolium from the same sheet.

4. Fantasy in C major for Violin and Piano, D 934 Vienna SB MH 3977/c
December 1827. 13 leaves in four irregular gatherings.

5. Four Impromptus for Piano, D 935 New York PML Cary
December 1827. 16 of the 18 leaves are type VIIb, while pp. 13-16 are an inserted bifolium of type VIIc containing the second impromptu, and probably filled several months after the initial composition. Given the completely reg-

ular structure of four gathered sheets that results when the extraneous bifolium is omitted, the possibility that the group of four impromptus was originally a trio of pieces cannot be excluded.

6. Song, 'Der Winterabend', D 938 New York PML Heineman
January 1828. A gathered sheet.

7. Fantasy in F minor for Piano, four hands, D 940 Basel Floersheim
January 1828. Ten leaves containing an incomplete draft of more than 400 bars (Brown, *Essays*, p. 87, mentions two more leaves not cited in either *D1* or *D2*).

8. 'Mirjams Siegesgesang', D 942 London Zweig Collection
March 1828. 18 leaves made up from two double-sheet gatherings wrapped in a single bifolium.

9. Song for Voice, Horn, and Piano, 'Auf dem Strom', D 943
Cambridge USA Houghton Library, Harvard University
March 1828. A gathered sheet followed by a bifolium.

10. Fantasy in F minor for Piano, four hands, D 940
Vienna NB Cod. 19.491
April 1828. 23 leaves.

Undated Works on Type VIIb

11. Quartet, 'Der Tanz', D 826 Vienna SB MH 37/c
A bifolium. If the unattributed inscription '1828' in red crayon (cf. type V/21) at the head of fol. 1r issues from a contemporaneous witness, then this lightly satirical work must have been composed between January and April 1828. (There are no dated autographs from the month of February – see also below.) Like D 936, 'Der Tanz' was presumably a musical offering to Irene Kiesewetter.

12. Adagio in E flat Major for Piano Trio, D 897 Vienna NB S.m. 4.373
A gathered sheet plus a bifolium. The origins of this movement have long been surrounded by controversy, and can be considered only briefly here. The significance of the so-called 'Notturno' (as it was dubbed by Diabelli upon its first publication in 1846) extends beyond itself to a major chamber work of Schubert's maturity for which not a shred of autograph material remains: the B flat major Piano Trio. When all of the evidence is assembled – particularly that supplied by musical style working in concert with new physical data – Arnold Feil's 'Vermutung' in the *NGA* that the B flat Trio 'könnte . . . nach dem Es-dur-Trio entstanden sein' can be raised to a point of near certainty.[27]

The arguments identifying the 'Notturno' with a discarded slow movement to D 898 are several and strong. (1) Both the 'Notturno' and the present slow movement share not only a common key, but also a highly characteristic and

27 Feil, preface to *NGA*, Series VI, vol. 7, p. xi. For a different interpretation, see E. Badura-Skoda's essay in this volume, esp. pp. 291-4.

sensuous embroidering of the mediant degree in their opening periods. (2) The substitution of a movement in ternary form for one in a highly dramatic sonata style is wholly consistent with the musical developments in the last year of Schubert's life. Before D 898, the vast majority of slow movements make their peace with the claims of the sonata principle; beginning with the B flat Trio, six of the seven remaining such movements (including that in the symphony draft, D 936A) adopt the radically new formal aesthetic represented by ternary form, a central plank in the emerging Romantic platform. That the slow movement to the E flat Trio still retains sonata form is only one more argument for its earlier genesis (it is not even inconceivable that the lone exception, the C minor Piano Sonata, D 958, was sketched in the summer or early autumn of 1827). (3) An untitled instrumental movement of this scope must belong somewhere, and there is scarcely time for Schubert to have penned a third trio in this period.

Those who accept the common origin of the 'Notturno' and D 898 will not fail to notice that within the seven-month period of astonishing productivity – even for Schubert – mirrored in type VIIb, there is not a single work assigned to the month of February. In February, as we know from regular entries in Franz von Hartmann's diary, Schubert was well, if rather more withdrawn from the usual social addictions. February is also the month of renewed correspondence with the publishing firms of Probst and Schott, scarcely grounds for discouragement. Unless Schubert found himself inexplicably confounding the working habits of more than fifteen years' duration, he was commencing works in this month as well; however tentative, the provisional assignment of the B flat Trio to the gap that is February 1828 requires no further justification.[28]

Dated Works on Type VIIc

Comparison with the four dated members of this group facilitates identification of the eight undated ones. Nevertheless, the line between type VIIc and the two other 16-stave varieties is frequently difficult to establish. At the very least we can avoid the pitfall of placing 16-stave examples amongst a thicket of works displaying eleven consecutive dated autographs with 12 staves.

1. Klavierstücke in E flat major, D 946/1-2 Vienna SB MH 143/c
May 1828. A gathered sheet plus a bifolium.
2. 'Hymnus an den heiligen Geist', D 948 Berlin SPK Schubert aut. 17
May 1828. A gathered sheet containing the unaccompanied version.

28 That Schubert failed to mention a second piano trio in his letter of 21 February to Schott hardly condemns it to having been – as Reed would have it – 'finished and disposed of long before' (*Schubert. The Final Years*, p. 199). There would have been little point in offering a work begun very recently and still far from complete. It made excellent business sense, however, to dangle a piano duet, perhaps a publisher's most preferred medium; the F minor Fantasy had been more than three-quarters complete in January, and Schubert was doubtless confident he could deliver the remainder on short order.

3. Rondo in A major for Piano, four hands, D 951
Berlin DSB Schubert aut. 4 June 1828. Nine leaves in one double-sheet gathering with a single leaf inserted before p. 9.

4. Mass in E flat major, D 950, fols. 1-16 Berlin SPK Schubert aut. 5 June 1828. Only the Kyrie from this 80-leaf complete autograph is on type VIIc. With the Gloria and Credo on type VIId, and the Sanctus and Agnus Dei on type VIII, it now appears that the final stages in the composition of this masterpiece may have stretched out over almost five months.

Undated Works on Type VIIc

5. Quartet, 'Widerspruch', D 865 Vienna SB MH 4178/c
This bifolium has traditionally been dated earlier (both *D1* and *D2* give '1826(?)', and more recently Hilmar suggests 'Spätsommer 1827'). The watermark and staff ruling, however, point to the spring of 1828, a chronology more consistent with a first edition published three days after Schubert's death.

6. Vier Refrainlieder, D 866 Vienna Männergesang-Verein Ms. U
Piano Sonata in C minor, D 958 (16 bars for finale opening)
Two leaves. The dating 'Sommer 1828(?)' cautiously put forward in *D2* should probably be modified to late spring.

7. Songs, 'Fröhliches Scheiden', D 896 (fragment); 'Sie in jedem Liede', D 896A (fragment); and 'Wolke und Quelle', D 896B (fragment)
Vienna SB MH 182/c
Two gathered bifolia from different sheets. The dating 'zwischen Herbst 1827 und Anfang 1828' offered by *D2* is narrowed further by Hilmar to 'Anfang (Jänner?) 1828'. But unless 'Herbst' is limited to September, the odds are at least eleven to one against the verity of either conjecture. It was in September, at the home of Frau Marie Pachler in Graz, that Schubert became thoroughly acquainted with the poetry of Karl Gottfried von Leitner (of course the composer already knew the text to 'Drang in die Ferne', D 770). But in view of the eleven consecutive autographs on type VIIb, the possible periods of composition for the present trio of fragments are limited to either September (from which no dated examples on type VIIa survive) or – more likely – the early spring of 1828. Neither *D2* nor Hilmar offers reasons why Schubert could not have maintained his interest in setting Leitner beyond the very beginning of 1828.

8. 'Mirjams Siegesgesang', D 942 Vienna SB MH 198/c & MH 174/c
'Hymnus an den heiligen Geist', D 948
Mass in E flat major, D 950 (all movements but the Kyrie)
These five leaves (including two bifolia) of sketches, especially those for the mass, clearly belong to the same complex. The possibility that work on all three pieces commenced in the late summer of 1827 (even with *Der Graf von*

Gleichen, the month of August is not overburdened) cannot be entirely eliminated. With complete autographs begun in March, May, and June, however, more plausible choices are March 1828 for D 942 (particularly since the exclusively interior portions sketched in MH 198/c are best explained in conjunction with a complete version; cf. type VIIb/8); and shortly thereafter for the hymn and the mass. In this event, all five leaves might well be remnants of type VIIa.

9. Piano Sonata in C minor, D 958 Vienna SB MH 170/c

A single leaf and a bifolium from the same sheet, followed by a single leaf from another sheet. Each of the four leaves is devoted to a single movement; represented are the exposition to the first movement, slightly truncated versions of the second and third movements, and the exposition plus an extensive but discarded continuation for the finale. These drafts probably date from the spring of 1828.

10. Piano Sonata in A major, D 959 Vienna SB MH 171/c

Eight leaves, including a single leaf for a slightly abbreviated version of the *Andante*, and a gathered sheet containing a complete scherzo and more than 300 bars – most of them ultimately discarded – for the finale. Two further leaves, headed 'Sonata II', were filled somewhat later and begin what was probably intended to serve as the fair copy for the first movement; they break off at the recapitulation (there are a few coda sketches, and an intervening leaf with bars 66-128 has apparently been lost), and doubtless formed the basis of the final version. Without any supporting evidence, Hilmar's notion that the third and fourth movements were created before the first and second remains speculation. Until a much closer study of the sources for the late sonatas becomes available, the chronology of that last remarkable spring and summer will remain something of a puzzle. If they were indeed composed – as Schubert seems to indicate – in the order we know today, then the A major Sonata could well have been drafted in the late spring of 1828.

11. Piano Sonata in B flat major, D 960 Vienna SB MH 172/c + 171/c

The complex of sketches for the B flat Sonata is considerably more intricate than that for either of the preceding sonatas. Along with two leaves of type VIIc (containing portions of the first movement and a complete slow movement), there is also a leaf of type VIIb (for the scherzo) and two upright-format leaves (with more sketches for the first movement as well as interior portions of the finale) that can be identified with some certainty as type VI(?) with 16 staves (the type VII suggested by Hilmar is not possible). Finally, on four empty staves found on the verso of the earliest leaf of first-movement sketches for the A major Sonata, Schubert entered a draft for most of the recapitulation and the coda of the first movement of the B flat Sonata. Although this rich skein of interrelationships cannot be unravelled here, it is surely noteworthy that three of the six leaves on which these sketches are found enjoyed a principal period of use up to seven months earlier than the spring of 1828. The number of folios involved is too small for them to aspire beyond remnant status, but at the very least it now appears that the composition of the B flat Sonata may have stretched out over a time period considerably longer than hitherto suspected. Hilmar's assertion that the A major and B flat sonatas were 'Hand in Hand komponiert' over the same period from June to August remains unproved.

Dated Works on Type VIId (all with 16 staves)

1. Song, 'Glaube, Hoffnung, und Liebe', D 955 Vienna NB Cod. 19.487
August 1828. A bifolium.

2. Song Cycle, *Schwanengesang*, D 957 New York PML
August 1828. The first 19 leaves (of 21) are type VIId, which includes all fourteen songs except the ending of 'Die Taubenpost'. The assertion in *D2* that the autograph of this song is 'auf anderem Papier geschrieben' is incorrect. In fact, 'Die Taubenpost' begins with a bifolium of the same type VIId paper used for the first thirteen songs; the change in paper does not occur until the final bifolium of type VIIIa, which was probably inserted – if the shift in handwriting can be trusted – to replace an earlier ending (see also type VIII/3).

3. Sketches for a Symphony in D, D 936A Vienna SB MH 14275/c
Seven leaves, of which three are single leaves of type VIId. The discovery of extensive drafts for three symphonies worked on in succession within a complex long believed to include work on only one was made by Ernst Hilmar in 1978. The datings assigned to this third fragment in the group have lacked consistency in both argumentation and conclusions. *D2* assigns the work to 'Frühjahr – Sommer 1828(?)', citing – in addition to unspecified handwriting characteristics – thematic similarities with D 916B and 898; such foreground musical analogies are hardly reliable guides. Since Hilmar invokes virtually identical evidence in the 'Nachwort' to his facsimile edition of the symphony sketches, he is probably the source for most of the information in *D2* as well; however, the facsimile now slides the date forward to simply 'Sommer 1828'.[29] There can be no doubt that the D number assigned to the fragment in *D2* is incorrect, and should have been at least twenty entries later (for a combined dating of all seven leaves, see type VIII/4). Hilmar provides partial acknowledgement of this circumstance in his final dating, one that places all three movements '[nicht] vor Frühjahr 1828', with the first movement in 'Sommer 1828' and the slow movement 'im Herbst 1828'.[30]

Absent from these confusing deliberations are accurate evaluations of the two varieties of paper used by Schubert. The three loose leaves of type VIId include sketches for the scherzo and the slow movement; the almost total invisibility of their watermark links them to the latest examples of this sub-

29 Franz Schubert, *Drei Symphonie-Fragmente* (Kassel, 1978), 'Nachwort' by Ernst Hilmar, pp. [2-3].

30 Ernst Hilmar, 'Neue Funde, Daten und Dokumente zum symphonischen Werk Franz Schuberts', *Österreichische Musikzeitschrift*, XXXIII (1978), pp. 266-76, esp. p. 272.

species. When viewed together with the two bifolia of type VIIIb that fill out the manuscript, a chronology quite different from those hitherto put forward emerges.

4. Songs, 'Lebensmut', D 937; 'Liebesbotschaft', D 957/1 and 'Frühlingssehnsucht', D 957/3 Vienna GdM A 236

A bifolium, probably set down shortly before the commencement of work on the autograph of D 957 in August 1828.

5. Mass in E flat major, D 950, fols. 17-56 Berlin SPK Schubert aut. 5

These 40 folios for the Gloria and Credo inaugurate a marked change from the paper of the Kyrie: the texture is less transparent, partly as the result of a more greenish tint, and the watermark is extremely difficult to decipher beyond establishing the general type. A time frame of July–August 1828 seems most likely.

6. 'Tantum ergo' in E flat major, D 962 Vienna SB MH 178

A single leaf. Hilmar dates this complete draft to 'September (oder Anfang Oktober?)', a plausible time frame, although a genesis dating back to *c.* July cannot be ruled out.

7. 'Der Hirt auf dem Felsen' for Voice, Clarinet, and Piano, D 965 Vienna SB MH 197/c

A bifolium with bars 126-316, devoted largely to the vocal part (although untexted). Hilmar's dating 'Anfang Herbst 1828' is plausible, although a genesis dating back to *c.* July cannot be ruled out.

8. Song, 'Die Taubenpost', D 965A (formerly D 957/14) Vienna SB MH 4100/c

A single leaf. Hilmar gives no reasons for preferring 'August(?)' to a period closer to the 'October' found in the autograph of *Schwanengesang* (see type VIId/2), although a genesis dating back to *c.* July cannot be ruled out.

Watermark Types VIIIa and VIIIb

Schubert's 'swan song' to music paper included a pair of Kiesling watermarks (similar to types Va and Vb) dated only in the penultimate month of his life. All examples show 16 staves and a total span of 200.5 to 201 millimetres (about 5 millimetres less than the papers of type V).

Dated Works on Types VIIIa and VIIIb

1. 'Tantum ergo', D 962; Tenor Aria with Chorus, 'Intende voci', D 963; and 'Hymnus an den heiligen Geist', D 964 Vienna NB Cod. 19.488

The first two works in this unified 32-leaf complex are both dated October 1828. The 'Hymnus' carries the inscription 'May 1828 / Oct. instrumentirt', a clear reference to the unaccompanied autograph (cf. type VIIc/2). Both types VIIIa and VIIIb are represented.

2. 'Der Hirt auf dem Felsen' for Voice, Clarinet, and Piano, D 965 Vienna GdM A 237

October 1828. A gathered sheet plus a bifolium of type VIIIa. Cf. type VIId/7.

3. Song, 'Die Taubenpost', D 965A (formerly D 957/14) New York PML
The initial bifolium of type VIId, now attached to the end of the thirteen songs in D 957, is dated October 1828. The subsequent bifolium of type VIIIa – possibly a direct continuation but more likely a replacement for a discarded ending – cannot have been written earlier than October.

Undated Works on Types VIIIa and VIIIb

4. Sketches for a Symphony in D, D 936A Vienna SB MH 14275/c
Among the seven leaves in this complex are two bifolia of type VIIIb. The first is filled with two extensive and interrelated drafts for the first movement, while the second continues sketches for the scherzo and *Andante* begun on type VIId leaves. There is no reason at all to doubt that in the overall evolution of the symphony the first movement was conceived first; to commence work on a large-scale composition with its interior movements would have been as foreign to Schubert as to Beethoven. The paper of this bifolium is dated by Schubert no fewer than five times, and on each occasion dated October 1828. To be sure, the last dated example of type VIId in this study is in August (D 957); only an examination of the complete autographs for the three late piano sonatas (D 958-960) could tell us what paper(s) Schubert favoured with his muse in September. At all events, sketching on the symphony could scarcely have commenced before September 1828, and more likely in October. As the single incomplete work from this eventful autumn, there can be little doubt that Schubert carried these drafts with him to his deathbed; to single out only the slow movement, its Mahlerian sense of process supplies a transcendent musical epitaph to a career even richer in promise than we knew.

5. Mass in E flat major, D 950, fols. 113-60 Berlin SPK Schubert aut. 5
These final 24 leaves for the Sanctus and Agnus Dei are divided between both types VIIIa and VIIIb. It is unlikely that either movement was completed before September, or even more probably October.

Eight Miscellaneous Papers from 1823 to 1828

Of the almost 130 known autographs from Schubert's last six years, only eight are found on papers outside of the dozen main types and not falling into one of the two periods characterized by remnants.[31] None of the manuscripts contains as many as a dozen leaves, and five are on only one or two leaves. As

31 This figure does not include 60 leaves of closely related Italianate papers used successively by Schubert for the end of Act I and the beginning of Act II of *Fierrabras*. During the months of May and June 1823 Schubert was consuming paper so fast he may have been forced temporarily to procure supplies elsewhere.

a group they constitute less than 2½ per cent of the roughly 1,650 leaves that have survived from this period, a powerful testimonial to the reliability of paper distribution for determining Schubert chronology. The abbreviated descriptions in the following list are intended for identification purposes only.

1. Song, 'Viola', D 786 New York PML Lehman
March 1823. 11 leaves.

2. Song 'Die Mutter Erde', D 788 Vienna SB MH 101/c
April 1823. A single-leaf remnant of the main paper type preceding types Ia and Ib.

3. Songs, 'Trinklied', D 888; 'Ständchen', D 889; 'Hippolits Lied', D 890; and 'An Sylvia', D 891 Vienna SB MH 116/c
July 1826. Although the fact is not noted by Hilmar, these four songs are recorded on eight leaves of letter-paper.

4. Allegretto in C minor for Piano, D 900 Vienna SB MH 147/c
Undated. The handwriting on this bifolium suggests a genesis in the early 1820s, possibly as late as 1823; hence the work may or may not merit inclusion in the present group.

5. Song, 'Romanze des Richard Löwenherz', D 907 Vienna SB MH 103/c
Undated. Most of the six leaves are in a hand other than Schubert's, one possibly responsible for the procurement of the paper as well.

6. Song, 'Die Nebensonnen' from *Winterreise*, D 911/23
Vienna GdM A 253
Vienna, 12 October 1827. A bifolium of high-quality album paper.

7. Fugue in E minor for Organ or Piano, four hands, D 952
Paris BN Ms 305
Undated. The watermark on this bifolium is very similar to type Vb, but its 16-stave ruling shows a total span of only 196+ to 196.5 millimetres. If the story of the fugue's creation on 3 June 1828 is true (see *D2*, p. 611), then the paper supplied to Schubert may well have been purchased in Baden or provided by Franz Lachner himself.

8. Copy of Psalm VIII by Abbé Maximilian Stadler, *D2* Anh. II,4
New York PML Lehman
29 August 1823. The work was prepared by Schubert in Steyr, probably for performance by Johann Michael Vogl, and all eight leaves were very probably purchased there.

The watermark on two further leaves (Exercises in Thorough-Bass, *D2* Anh. I,32; Berlin SPK, Schubert aut. 22) is identical to that found in Beethoven manuscripts between the summers of 1825 and 1826; however, the exercises contained on them probably had nothing to do with Schubert. Finally, in only two of the instances enumerated above does a ready explanation for Schubert's use of marginal papers *not* suggest itself (nos. 1 and 4), and the second of these may not even belong to the group.

Two years and some seventy-five autographs ago we left the chronological fate of the 'Great' C major Symphony hanging in the balance, acting from the conviction that the evidence assembled after 1826 could prove just as essential to the unravelling of its origins as the data leading up to the summer in Gmunden and Gastein. Even so, there can be no illusion that the evidentiary web, particularly as it involves parallel testimony, has been spun in its entirety. Consider Beethoven's relationship to Remnants I and to watermark types III and IV. In the spring of 1825 he had just completed the first of the three quartets commissioned by Prince Nikolaus Galitzin, whereupon he commenced work almost immediately upon the A minor Quartet, op. 132. The first two movements were completed in Vienna before Beethoven was immobilized in mid-April by one of his chronic intestinal ailments. Removing himself to Baden on 7 May – as was his custom every spring – he drafted the celebrated 'Heiliger Dankgesang' and the finale. All of these sketches are found on one of four different leftover papers, the most prominent (20 of 29 leaves) and astonishing of which is that used for the choral portions of the Ninth Symphony, and containing no fewer than 23 staves![32] This oversize paper could not have been more ill suited to drafting a quartet, and only a general paper shortage would have left Beethoven with no other recourse. Can Schubert's use of remnants during the same spring be pure coincidence?

When it became time to organize the sketches into permanent form, Beethoven would have been required to return at least for the day to the city. Perhaps he purchased his type III paper with 12 staves and a total span of 187+ to 189+ millimetres on the same outing of 4 June that included an unannounced call on his physician, Dr Braunhofer, who was not at home. In any event, the parallel with Schubert's use of paper bearing the identical watermark is persuasive, extending even to the structure of the autographs themselves. Schubert's exhaustion of his type III supplies within the autograph of the 'Great' C major has already been noted; Beethoven, too, had to rely on a secondary paper for the final three bifolia and four other inserted leaves in the 72-leaf complex for op. 132 (Berlin SPK, Mendelssohn 11).

The year 1826 produced no less striking a parallel. The extensive sketches in score for the C sharp minor Quartet that dominated the first half of the year for Beethoven were begun in January–February on paper with watermark type IV, congruent once more with Schubert's own usage. These supporting examples, of course, are only the leading edge of a phalanx; there were hundreds of composers active in Vienna at the time, and an all-out assault on

32 In a letter to nephew Karl of 11 August, and at a time when Beethoven feared Karl Holz may have lost the autograph, the composer confided that 'the ideas for it are only jotted down on small scraps of paper, and I shall never be able to compose the whole quartet again in the same way' (*The Letters of Beethoven Chronologically Arranged*, transl. and ed. Emily Anderson (London, 1961), Letter 1410).

the archives of this musical capital and its surrounding principalities might well yield refinements to the usage patterns of Schubert and Beethoven. But when the evidence already assembled is viewed cumulatively, there seems little reason to doubt that its principal findings will receive only further confirmation.

All previous attempts to date the C major Symphony have proceeded without the slightest comfort from paper studies, beginning with the crusading Sir George Grove right up to the more recent – and somewhat more dispassionate – anti-crusade of John Reed. Reed was surely right to chastise Grove's barely concealed glee in seizing on the apparent date found in the upper-right-hand corner of fol. 1r for a wedge with which to promote the theory of a missing 'Gastein Symphony'. At the same time Reed himself refrained from admitting that the biographical legacy of Schubert's last symphony, whether drawn from Maurice J. E. Brown's ten documents or from more recent archival finds,[33] itself falls well short of 'proof beyond reasonable doubt'. The main protagonists in the drama are dead; moreover, the testimony they bequeathed is grounded in allusion and is often conflicting.

Leopold von Sonnleithner was a complex man whose ignorance of, or even complicity in, a lost Schubert symphony cannot be altogether ruled out. That Ferdinand Schubert might have been uninformed about the existence of another symphony from Schubert's last years should hardly surprise; he was not close to his brother's musical galaxy (his presence is not recorded at a single Schubertiad, for example), nor was the status of Schubert's instrumental works known at all well to even the friends of his innermost circle. In Schubert's last year and a half the single exception might have been Eduard von Bauernfeld, the librettist for *Der Graf von Gleichen* (begun in June 1827) and a close friend until Schubert's death. When Bauernfeld speaks, in the 'Nachtrag' to his 'biographische Notizen' of 1828 (*Documents*, pp. 893-5), of '1825 grosse Symphonie' and '1828 letzte Symphonie', he cannot simply be dismissed for introducing a confusion, nor can the sketches for a symphony made in the autumn of 1828 be added without explanation to a list of otherwise complete works.

Further, it is perfectly conceivable that Joseph von Spaun – one of Schubert's most trusted friends – would not have known of a work familiar to Bauernfeld, particularly since Spaun himself had gone on record praising Schubert's great genius as a song composer, while minimizing the importance of his instrumental works. It is Reed himself who characterizes the testimony of Ferdinand Schubert, Bauernfeld, and Spaun as 'mainly negative' in nature. His curious contention that 'for fifty years after the composer's death . . . it

33 Brown, *Schubert. A Critical Biography* (London, 1958), pp. 354-61; Biba, 'Franz Schubert und die Gesellschaft der Musikfreunde in Wien' in *Schubert-Kongress Wien 1978: Bericht*, ed. Otto Brusatti (Graz, 1979), pp. 23-36, and 'Schubert's Position in Viennese Musical Life' (cited in note 4 above).

was taken for granted that the Great C major was the only symphony of his mature years, and that it is the symphony begun in 1825 at Gmunden and Gastein and presented to the Philharmonic Society in 1826'[34] is simply unfounded. The fact is that Schubert's friends may or may not have assumed so, but their chain of murky recollections can lead only to a hung jury, no matter how brilliantly an advocate like Reed argues the case.

At a loss for more concrete evidence, some writers – including Reed – have reasoned that Schubert's prodigious output in the last nine months of his life excludes the possibility of another large instrumental work being squeezed into the same chronological space. But the addition or subtraction of a symphony is hardly decisive in a year that included more than twenty Lieder (among which are 'Auf dem Strom', *Schwanengesang*, and 'Der Hirt auf dem Felsen'), three sizeable four-hand compositions (the Fantasy, the Allegro in A minor, and the Rondo), a cantata, three piano sonatas, a mass, a string quintet, four large liturgical pieces, extensive sketches on yet another symphony, and very probably a second piano trio. Indeed, the inclusion of the 'Great' C major in this already crowded field swells the miracle of Schubert's last three hundred days by less than one-fifth; given the periods of equal or greater productivity that Schubert had already known (1815 and 1823, for example), we are scarcely in the position to deny the symphony a room in the inn.

The prognosis for a clear verdict by means of style analysis has been even bleaker. Reed's motto-hunting, which is happily not specified beyond the opening of the first movement, has little to do with significant stylistic parallels. Those 'four-times rhythmically repeated notes, the "run-up to the wicket" in triplet rhythm before a cadence back to the tonic, the ambiguous use of chromatically adjacent sevenths and sixths, these fingerprints of the years 1824 and 1825, and many others' leave for Reed 'no doubt where the internal evidence points on the question of the symphony's origins'.[35] But it is precisely these surface characteristics or 'fingerprints' that have almost nothing to do with the mysteries of composition or style. An equally strong defence, in fact, can be erected as easily on behalf of an 1828 genesis (see Paul Badura-Skoda, pp. 197-203 above) as one from three years earlier. Although we may some day acquire the wisdom necessary to make such refined distinctions, for now it would prove more prudent to admit that the Schubert of 1825 still shares too many musical traits with the Schubert of 1828.

There is nothing sacrosanct about paper studies. The circumstances that combine to grant these techniques nearly unrivalled jurisdiction in the Vienna of Mozart, Beethoven, and Schubert are accidents of history, not the result of mortal machinations. If the close scrutiny of music papers cannot provide answers to every outstanding question concerning the genesis of the 'Great'

34 Reed, *Schubert. The Final Years*, p. 73.

35 Ibid., p. 97.

C major Symphony, at the very least it can segregate the problems for which solutions are now available from those which remain elusive. It may be well to recall that the testimony handed down by the physical characteristics of Schubert's manuscripts derives its essential credibility from a quiet anonymity. There is no particular reason for believing that Schubert was conscious of the trail he was leaving behind. Year after year he transformed empty sheaves of paper into finished scores, and almost every one of them telegraphs – all considerations of musical style aside – something of its origins to us. Lest the composer's ignorance inspire misgivings, two observations are in order: any intuitions on Schubert's part about paper types would have exercised little if any effect on his own usage; and the court-ordered tap on a telephone is effective only if the suspect is not aware that it has been installed.

The considerations that exercise a direct influence on the chronological fate of the 'Great' C major Symphony are these:

(1) Throughout his life (and documented here for the last six years), it was Schubert's almost exclusive practice to consume music paper in large uniform runs, a circumstance altered, so the evidence suggests, only by infrequent paper shortages. Among the hundreds and hundreds of autographs examined, there is not a single example apart from the 'Great' C major Symphony that offers even a muted suggestion of hoarding on the composer's part.

(2) The type III paper used for the first two-thirds of the C major autograph survives in five additional dated manuscripts, all dated between July and September 1825. D 848 is dated 'July 1825 / Gmunden' on a full title-page. D 850 and 851 are each dated August, in Gastein. D 850 – the most ambitious of these summer offerings – includes a full wrap-around *Umschlag* with the inscription, 'Sonate / für das Pianoforte' on the front page; the location and date head fol. 2r. Although the earliest dated work on type III is in July, Schubert must have purchased his large supply before leaving Vienna around 19 May. (The probability of the composer's having procured another supply of type III upon his return to Vienna at the beginning of October is quite slim. Beethoven's last use of paper bearing this watermark is in late July, and a paper shortage seems to have greeted both of them in the autumn.)

(3) The 30 leaves (secondary papers 2 and 3) which succeed type III are among the lowest-quality papers ever included in a Schubert autograph. This circumstance suggests either that the composer was forced to replenish his stocks well outside the capital city, or that the paper shortage alluded to above left Viennese composers with no other recourse. Both of these conditions may, in fact, have prevailed. The concordance between secondary 3 and the autograph of D 875 (dated January 1826) links this development to the second half of 1825.

(4) The three bifolia of type IV with which the autograph concludes have their parallel in six manuscripts datable between January and September 1826. Six remnant leaves survive in the autographs of D 892 and 895, the

latest dated October 1826.

(5) The seven leaves of secondary paper 1 used to make large-scale revisions in the coda to the first movement and the trio of the scherzo show a watermark identical to that found in paper purchased by Beethoven in September 1826.

As the study of paper characteristics has achieved a limited recognition for its potential contributions to problems of chronology and compositional process, challenges to the validity of its findings have always centred on a single premiss: what would have prevented any composer – including Franz Schubert – from hoarding, even if just for once in his life, a large portion of a major paper run for use some three years later? To lend further support to this hypothesis the superior qualities of type III might be invoked: would these not have created sufficient inducement for caching a generous supply until the magical appearance of a worthy work like the 'Great' C major Symphony (recalling the vision at the end of *Die Walküre* of Siegfried as 'The Hero to Come')?

Leaving aside the great improbability of such behaviour, which scrutiny of several hundred Schubert autographs reaffirms, we can test this hypothesis by reconstructing the only possible scenario. It must reconcile the chronological demands of the paper with Schubert's presumed dating of March 1828. To begin with, during the summer of 1825 the composer would have set aside almost one hundred leaves of type III, designating them for later use. Some time between the late summer and early winter of 1825 he would have then laid in an additional store of 30 incongruously low-grade folios. During the first nine months of 1826 these would be further augmented by a gathered sheet and bifolium of type IV, another premium paper. Finally, in the early autumn of 1826 seven leaves bearing a watermark found only in contemporaneous Beethoven autographs would have been singled out as the last of the five paper types earmarked for the symphony. After collecting this heterogeneous ensemble over a continuous eighteen-month period, Schubert would then have waited almost another year and a half before using the whole lot at once (taking care, of course, to maintain their original chronology).

By the most generous stretch of the historical imagination, such a sequence of events is not even remotely possible. Had he taken the unprecedented step of reserving a large quantity of type III for use beginning in March 1828, he would surely have filled out the remainder of the manuscript with papers from that year. Any arguments from quality are quickly nullified by fols. 95-124. And even if we presume that it was Schubert's regular practice to set aside stores of paper in chronological sequence for later service, why are all five of them located in the continuous period between May 1825 and September–October 1826, and in a single work? Extrapolating from the composer's own working habits over almost two decades, the odds against his having composed the C major Symphony outside the general time frame established by the papers are many thousands to one. On at least this one occasion, then, we are compelled to acknowledge the priority of hidden evidence over what appears to be Schubert's own direct testimony.

We can now state with confidence that the 'Great' C major Symphony was begun shortly after Schubert's departure from Vienna around 19 May 1825. Since we possess no autographs dated before July, it makes good sense to suppose that Schubert was hard at work on the symphony in Gmunden, probably to the exclusion of any other works. Upon his arrival in Linz in mid-July, progress had apparently been sufficient for his friend Anton Ottenwalt to write enthusiastically to Joseph von Spaun that '[Schubert has] worked at a symphony at Gmunden, which is to be performed in Vienna this winter.'[36] (The epithet '"Gastein" Symphony' has always been inappropriate; not only were its initial stages carried out in Gmunden, but Schubert spent more than twice as much time there as in Bad Gastein.)

If Schubert had already drafted a good portion of his symphony by mid-July – and with two and a half months of the holiday still remaining – the likelihood of a finite paper supply exhausting itself is strong indeed. There has to be an explanation for the drastic plummet in quality between fols. 94 and 95, for even during a paper shortage Viennese standards remained above those set by secondary paper 3. The key is almost certainly the modest bifolium inserted into the song 'Das Heimweh', D 851 (a subject doubtless more on Schubert's mind than usual). It is unlikely that revisions of this kind would have been carried out more than a month or so after the original draft; 'Die Taubenpost', D 965A, is a case in point (see type VIII/3). The last dated example on type III is found in September, but in a bifolium whose first song is dated in August (see type III/5). Schubert's dating of 'Mondenschein', also on secondary type 3, in January 1826 is no proof of the paper's Viennese origin, for its appearance in D 851 is left unexplained. The burden of evidence points strongly to Schubert's purchase, probably between mid-August and mid-September in Bad Gastein or Gmunden, of a modest supply of paper intended to last until his homecoming. It may even have sustained him through the first weeks back in Vienna. At all events, the bifolia that conclude the finale could not have been added until after the new year.

The wealth of internal revisions within the autograph of the 'Great' C major Symphony has captured the attention of virtually all commentators. Yet only John Reed has noted the presence of two large-scale structural changes, though not fully appreciating their significance.[37] The perfect regularity of double-sheet gatherings is broken for the first time at fol. 36; hence it is not surprising to discover a change in paper type immediately thereafter. In this instance we can retrace Schubert's steps almost exactly. The composer first removed the original fol. 37 from the inner bifolium of the

36 *Documents*, p. 430.

37 Reed, 'How the "Great" C Major Was Written' (cited in note 12 above): see particularly p. 25, where neither the gathering structure nor the chronology of the inserted paper is taken into account.

gathering. He then added the three new leaves of secondary paper 1 (a bifolium followed by a single leaf), or the present fols. 37-9. Finally, he linked these to the second bar of fol. 40v, cancelling all of its recto. After the necessary additions and subtractions are made we discover that this first-movement coda had now grown by almost forty bars. Specifically, the bars added between bars 612 and 649 are both a repetition of the closing group that commences in bar 590 and a dramatic expansion of their original function. Without them both the affectionate embrace of Rossini at bar 650 and the electrifying transformation of the opening horn call at bar 662 are markedly weaker. Such revisions are the almost inevitable outcome of final reconsiderations just before a vine-ripened work is ready to be picked. The identity of the watermark in secondary 1 and that in papers used by Beethoven in the early autumn of 1826 constitutes strong evidence that this particular decision may have been made on the eve of Schubert's presentation of 'this, my symphony' to the Gesellschaft.

Yet another disturbance in the paper distribution points unmistakably to a revision of similar magnitude. The simple replacement of the inner sheet (fols. 75-8) containing the B section of the trio of the scherzo conceals the original layer entirely, but at least bars 295-360 were recomposed, and quite possibly portions of the A sections as well. As with the first-movement coda, these revisions to the trio could only have been entered after virtually all of the symphony was drafted. The two leaves lopped off after fol. 72 suggest that troubles with this quintessentially Viennese interlude may have begun considerably sooner, and that the trio caused Schubert a great deal more difficulty than we could have otherwise imagined.

The ambivalence that shines through the entries for D 849 ('Sinfonie') and 944 ('Sinfonie Nr. 8 in C') in *D2* is vastly preferable to the doctrinaire confessions of the original *D1*. Much of that ambivalence can now be tied up in bundles and put away. Certainly the general chronology established here for the 'Great' C major discourages the notion of yet another symphony having been either sketched or completed during that summer in Gmunden and Gastein. If Schubert proved unable to complete *one* symphony in that period, how much steeper the odds are against his having worked on two! ('Gastein' diehards, of course, will argue that the 'Great' C major remained unfinished in September because Schubert had first composed another symphony.) Yet one glaring, and scarcely hidden, contradiction remains: how can the immovable evidence of the paper be reconciled with Schubert's own celebrated inscription 'März 1828'? Attempts to untie this Gordian knot have proceeded along two divergent paths, neither of which owes anything to paper investigations.

In his 1972 study John Reed first put forward the attractive hypothesis that the date on the autograph represented that of its 'final recension', and that 'there was one symphony and one manuscript, written in 1826 [sic] and revised and dated in March 1828'.[38] Three years later Reed elaborated upon

38 Reed, *Schubert. The Final Years*, pp. 80, 194.

this notion in a preliminary study of 'How the "Great" C Major Was Written'.[39] He proposed that Schubert had put together an 'outline sketch' in Gmunden and Gastein, which was completed in all its details only in March of 1828.

The most serious problem with this idea is that it is almost certainly not true. We have already presented evidence that the two major structural revisions pointed to by Reed were carried out before Schubert offered a symphony to the Gesellschaft at the beginning of October 1826. In addition, a large number of the remaining revisions would have had to be completed before October if the symphony were to be turned over in anything like completed form. In his 1975 article – and doubtless now more aware of the inconsistency – Reed attempted to circumvent this issue by claiming that 'the probability is that the negotiations of October 1826 did not go beyond an exchange of compliments, and that the manuscript itself remained in Schubert's hands until March 1828'.[40] But Reed was apparently unaware of the *Sitzungsbericht* of the Gesellschaft for the year 1826, cited by C. F. Pohl, which includes the unambiguous statement: 'Schubert sandte gleichzeitig zwischen dem 9. und 12. Oktober seine Composition mit . . . Begleitschreiben ein'.[41] Although Pohl was thrust into the centre of controversy by Grove's theory, he would have had no incentive to forge or misquote such a document, for it was published a full decade before Grove's ideas took shape. If anything, Grove could have used the *Sitzungsbericht* as further evidence that the symphony presented in October 1826 was not the same one dated by Schubert in March 1828.

Even more devastating than either of these objections is a complete set of orchestral parts for the 'Great' C major preserved in the archives of the Gesellschaft. A full discussion of this fascinating complex must await another occasion, but it is already clear that a sizeable portion of the *Stimmen* prepared by the copyists Grams and Glöggl was completed *in the summer of 1827*. The archivist of the Gesellschaft, Dr Otto Biba, located not only these parts but also the receipts for their copying. Though only a 'Sinfonie von Franz Schubert' is specified, the inordinate size of the job – 301½ *Bogen* – can refer to only the 'Great' C major.[42] A preliminary check of these parts shows a complete correspondence with the version that we know.

39 See note 37 above, and especially p. 21 of Reed's article.

40 Reed, 'How the "Great" C Major Was Written', pp. 26-7.

41 'At the same time – between 9 and 12 October – Schubert sent in his composition with . . . accompanying letter': Carl Ferdinand Pohl, *Die Gesellschaft der Musikfreunde des Österreichischen Kaiserstaates und ihr Conservatorium, auf Grundlage der Gesellschafts-Acten bearbeitet* (Vienna, 1871), p. 16. It is not clear why Pohl introduces 12 October as the *terminus ante quem*. Otto Biba supplies additional details on the presentation and the honorarium in 'Franz Schubert und die Gesellschaft der Musikfreunde in Wien' (cited in note 33 above), pp. 27-8.

42 Biba has reported on some of these findings in 'Franz Schubert und die Ge-

Whether or not the symphony had taken up physical residence in the Gesellschaft then (and it seems very unlikely that the Society would have paid for the copying unless this were so), it was almost certainly complete in every detail when Schubert commended it to the directors of the Gesellschaft between 9 and 12 October 1826. This fits what we know of the composer's working procedures with other large works. I do not believe that Schubert stopped working on the symphony until he finished it. The initial completion was probably reached in the first several months of 1826. This was followed by the only other large-scale work before October, the G major String Quartet, D 887 (in the dominant key of the symphony, just like the Piano Sonata in G, D 894, composed immediately after the presentation to the Gesellschaft), for which Schubert wrote out a complete autograph in eleven days, but which he surely drafted beforehand. Until September there are only four sublime songs (D 888-891), the first two in the main key of the symphony and the last two in that of the slow movement (A minor) and the trio to the scherzo (A major). September is inhabited only by the exquisite quartet with tenor solo 'Nachthelle', D 892, and the tiny quartet 'Grab und Mond', D 893. If Schubert was creating at such a healthy pace during the last third of June, we can scarcely believe him to have produced less than 350 bars of vocal music as the entire output over the next three months. Not only do the extensive revisions and accompanimental fillings-in in the autograph of the 'Great' C major rush in impeccably to fill the breach, but they probably could not have been made at any other time.

The solution conceived most recently for the enigma of March 1828 forms a perfect epilogue to this inquiry, both for its ingenious simplicity and for its casual regard for the evidence of paper. In a sesquicentennial essay on Schubert's symphonic production, Ernst Hilmar offered a fresh assessment of the symphony's evolution.[43] Large portions of Hilmar's conclusions – for example, that the third and fourth movements were commenced only in 1826, or that the revisions were made in the autumn of 1827, and supplemented even later by further pencil corrections – are simply incorrect. But it is his novel interpretation of Schubert's enigmatic inscription that merits our attention. Starting from a comparison between the dates that head the 'Great' C major and the song 'Todtengräbers Heimwehe' (dated 'Aprill 1825' by Schubert), Hilmar writes: 'Stellt man nun die Schreibweise des Datums von D 944 jener von D 842 gegenüber, ist die erste Unterlänge der zweiten "8" fast deckungsgleich mit der Unterlänge der "5" von D 842. In beiden Fällen ist auch nach der Kreuzung der Linien eine kleine obere Schlinge zu sehen. Hat man sich dann aufgrund dieses Vergleichs und der oben genannten Beispiele

sellschaft der Musikfreunde', pp. 23-6. See also Biba's essay 'Schubert's Position in Viennese Musical Life' (cited in note 4 above).

43 'Neue Funde, Daten und Dokumente' (cited in note 30 above): on the C major Symphony see especially pp. 273-5.

mit Schuberts etwas ungewöhnlicher Schreibweise der "5" vertraut gemacht, kann man keinesfalls mehr mit Nachdruck behaupten, dass die Datierung 1828 lauten muss.'[44] From this stretch of inverse reasoning it is only a short step to the conclusion that 'das Jahr des Kompositionsbeginns der Symphonie D 944 nur 1825 – und zwar März des Jahres – lauten kann'.[45] While there are gross similarities between the final digits of each, the details that are not similar add up to much more. Judging from D 842, the sweeping horizontal flourish ought to be still visible below the trimmed edge of D 944. Further, unless the change was made after Schubert's death (and Hilmar does not speak at all to this crucial point), the half-loop which completes this beam would have necessitated a messy correction of a magnitude not found in hundreds of other dated Schubert autographs. Yet the slight correction invoked as a springboard in D 944 pales against that applied to a nevertheless clear '5' in D 845 (also dated 'Aprill 1825'), a contemporaneous autograph absent from Hilmar's deliberations. The size of the upper loop and the relative line thicknesses on each side (these are relative, not absolute, depending to some extent on the thickness of the quill immediately at hand) also prove incompatible when compared. There is, of course, everything to be said for pursuing such notions, as long as evidentiary standards are maintained and unproven hypotheses are not presented as facts. Sadly, however, the evidence in this particular realm is doomed to remain both partial and shadowy. For each correspondence a counter-example can as easily be found. Finally, we are left puzzling as to why Aloys Fuchs, the author of the title etiquette on the binding of the 'Great' C major Symphony and a collector as canny as his name, took no note of any irregularities in the date when he presumably had the manuscript bound in the 1840s. He was one of the last to see the full date before its decapitation, and for him it read clearly 'März 1828'.

In this context the evidence of paper takes on even greater importance. Few readers will have overlooked the circumstance that if the 'Great' C major was originally headed 1825, then the symphony must have been begun not only in that year, but in the month of March as well. I know of only a single example of Schubert's 'pre-dating' a work, and here reasons are not hard to find (see type VIIa/1). Moreover, the evidence so far available suggests that the type III paper with which the symphony opens was not on the market in March. Uses by neither Beethoven nor Schubert can be confirmed this early and – most telling – the two surviving autographs dated by Schubert between

44 'If one compares the writing of the date of D 944 with that of D 842, the first lower stroke of the second "8" is almost identical with the lower stroke of the "5" of D 842. In both cases a small upward flourish is visible after the crossing of the lines. Once one has become familiar, on the basis of this comparison and the above-mentioned examples, with Schubert's rather unusual way of writing the figure "5", it is no longer possible to maintain categorically that the date must read "1828"': 'Neue Funde', p. 274.

45 'The year of the beginning of composition of the Symphony D 944 can only be 1825 – and, to be more precise, March of that year': ibid., p. 274.

March and May (D 842 and 845) are both on the kind of remnant papers relied upon by the composer since the preceding November. We know of only a single instance (see miscellaneous paper 1) in his last six years where Schubert used more than eight leaves of an outside paper under apparently normal circumstances during a large run. The image of a half-year's paper shortage in which D 842 and 845 form an integral portion, however, cannot be easily dismissed. Once Schubert had acquired his type III supply we find him using it in the month of July for a simple transposition of the song 'Versunken', D 715; how much less likely, then, that he would choose a remnant paper for a piano sonata! The discovery of a type III example dated in March or even earlier by any of the innumerable Viennese composers could change all of this. Even so, my preliminary investigations have only further confirmed the patterns established by Beethoven and Schubert; here too a full report must await another occasion.

Alas, our present state of knowledge continues to taunt us with a contradiction. And yet however exasperating, this contradiction has been neutralized to a significant degree. Schubert's inscription – however it originally read – has been reduced to a problem in Schubert biography. We now possess a firm, broad outline of the symphony's genesis, one upon which long-overdue and detailed studies of the manuscript can build. (I strongly endorse John Reed's fervent call for a high-quality colour facsimile of this extraordinary art work; not only would such a publication facilitate study of the problems presented by the symphony, but it would spare an irreplaceable document any unnecessary handling.) At this juncture it is likely that only dramatic new evidence can solve the riddle of Schubert's dating to everyone's satisfaction.[46]

In concluding I should like to inject new life into a thesis put forward somewhat timidly by Reed in 1972. That writer concluded: 'an old symphony, and one in the possession of the Music Society, was obviously a less saleable property than a "new" one'.[47] Schubert's presentation of the symphony to the Gesellschaft was accompanied, as we know, by a heartfelt 'Begleitschreiben'. But the symphony must itself have been accompanied by an outer wrapper that included a title-page. (It is not inconceivable that the 'Begleitschreiben' was found on this wrapper.) Given the full title-pages for

46 Future studies of the manuscript will, it is hoped, argue from more sophisticated and established assumptions. Griffel, in the article cited in note 19 above, writes (p. 200): 'Brown ink shows the melody through the scherzo, the trio is all in black, black ink indicates the melody in the finale through measure 325, and brown ink is used for everything in the remainder of the finale.' But this simplification ignores the multitude of brown-ink entries in accompanimental voices, particularly the bass line. It also glosses over the complex interrelationship between the various shades of ink and the function of the filling-out or revision. Finally, it does not address itself seriously to questions of external or internal chronology. Until these basic procedural puzzles have been solved, all the imagination in the world will bring us no closer to the genesis of the symphony.

47 Reed, *Schubert. The Final Years*, p. 196.

the 'Unfinished' Symphony of less than three years earlier, or for the quartet 'Nachtmusik', D 848, from the summer in Gmunden; or given the full wrappers for the 'Wanderer' Fantasy, D 760, and the Piano Sonata in D, D 850 (also from the summer of 1825); or given that all four original works from the summer of 1825 are inscribed with their place of composition as well, it is simply inconceivable that a work of such colossal significance for Schubert would have been fitted out with the unassuming heading that we now know, and then committed with such pomp into the care of the Society.

Such a ceremonial bifolium could simply have been lost, though this seems unlikely. Much more likely is that Schubert removed it himself (possibly with the Society's permission and blessing). In the February correspondence with Schott Schubert does not exactly push the symphony, but in mentioning it at all he does place it in the public domain. Here the trail thins out, yet its continuation is obvious enough. Either in the hope of attracting interest, or in response to a lost expression of interest, Schubert supplied the symphony with a contemporaneous heading. I confess to a full awareness of all the questions which this proposed solution raises (why is the autograph today in the Gesellschaft? what about the expert testimony of graphologists that the heading was made simultaneously with the first compositional stages on fol. 2r?), and my present inability to answer very many of them. At the very least this line of reasoning proceeds without doing violence to central chapters in the symphony's history.

Such considerations remain, after all, secondary to the principal aim of this study. That has been to persuade the scholarly community, within which many Schubert-lovers can be counted, that the tools afforded by paper studies are not luxuries with which we can dabble at our convenience, but basic instruments in the formulation of any lasting chronology, whether relative or absolute. For so long as editors of *Gesamtausgaben* continue to pay awkward tribute to features like watermarks and paper types, we will continue to lull ourselves into thinking that the obligation has been met. The publishing of watermarks makes sense only if the context in which they originally appeared has been understood. The description of a gathering structure proves helpful only if the working habits of the composer have been established and their implications articulated. Finally, only when the student of compositional process comes to the realization that physical evidence forms the backbone of many of his investigations will he begin to see paper studies as an equal partner in the perennial quest for real knowledge and deepened understanding. These, after all, are the hallowed goals of humanistic inquiry.

The number of persons who have contributed materially to this study has grown steadily during its three-year gestation. Dr Eva Badura-Skoda both commissioned the piece and maintained a lively interest throughout; her encouragement was especially vital following the sudden loss of a thousand hours of research just as the project was nearing completion. She is also the source of information on autographs for D 912, 929, 942, and 943. Paul Badura-Skoda made time for several stimulating discussions, which benefited from both his encyclopedic knowledge of the Viennese classicists and a thoroughgoing study of problems surrounding the genesis of the 'Great' C major Symphony. Both Douglas Johnson and Alan Tyson read drafts of the manuscript and offered valuable suggestions, particularly concerning its organization; my debt to their seminal investigations of Beethoven sources will be obvious to all who know their work. Professor Joshua Rifkin not only double-checked many of the sources himself, but shared freely his findings growing out of a study of the primary materials for *Winterreise*, D 911; and it was he who provided the information on largely inaccessible autographs for D 866, 872, 909, 911/22, and 916. Walther Dürr and Arnold Feil of the *Neue Schubert-Ausgabe* responded generously to an earlier draft and shared a number of helpful insights; their *Hilfsbereitschaft* extended to providing me with a pre-publication copy of the revised Deutsch catalogue (*D2*). This study endeavours to reflect the spirit of friendly co-operation emanating from Tübingen.

Finally, I am deeply indebted to the many archives and institutions that have almost unfailingly supported this undertaking: the Deutsche Staatsbibliothek in Berlin DDR (abbreviated Berlin DSB), especially Frau Eveline Bartlitz; the Staatsbibliothek Preussischer Kulturbesitz (Musikabteilung) in Berlin BRD (abbreviated Berlin SPK); the British Library in London (abbreviated London BL); the Pierpont Morgan Library in New York (abbreviated New York PML), especially Mr J. Rigbie Turner; the Bibliothèque Nationale in Paris (abbreviated Paris BN); the Gesellschaft der Musikfreunde in Vienna (abbreviated Vienna GdM), especially its archivist, Dr Otto Biba, whose fresh researches into the holdings of that distinguished society have proved an invaluable stimulation and complement to the present study; and Dr Peter Riethus, also of the Gesellschaft, for sharing over the past eight years his extensive knowledge of Viennese music papers; the Österreichische Nationalbibliothek in Vienna (abbreviated Vienna NB); the Wiener Stadt- und Landesbibliothek (Musiksammlung) (abbreviated Vienna SB); the Music Division of the Library of Congress (abbreviated Washington LC); and the various private owners who have understood that scholarship can only enhance the value of their holdings.

A note on the watermark illustrations

The illustrations shown for the eight principal watermark families from Schubert's last six years are schematic, and not scale drawings intended for comparative use. Reproductions of tracings offer a dual disadvantage, both in perpetuating inaccuracies and in leaving the impression that the watermark shows up everywhere on the leaf with equal clarity (or, too often, lack of clarity). Only the comparatively recent application of beta-radiography to music papers has made it possible to carry out exacting comparisons thousands of miles apart. The potential gain from such investigations is enormous.

All drawings are presented according to the ground rules established by Alan Tyson (see note 11 above).

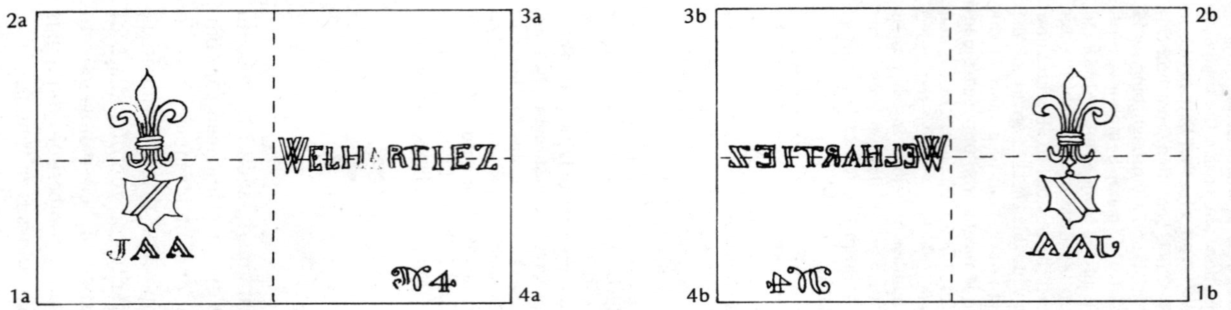

Figure 1. Type Ia (above) and Ib (below)

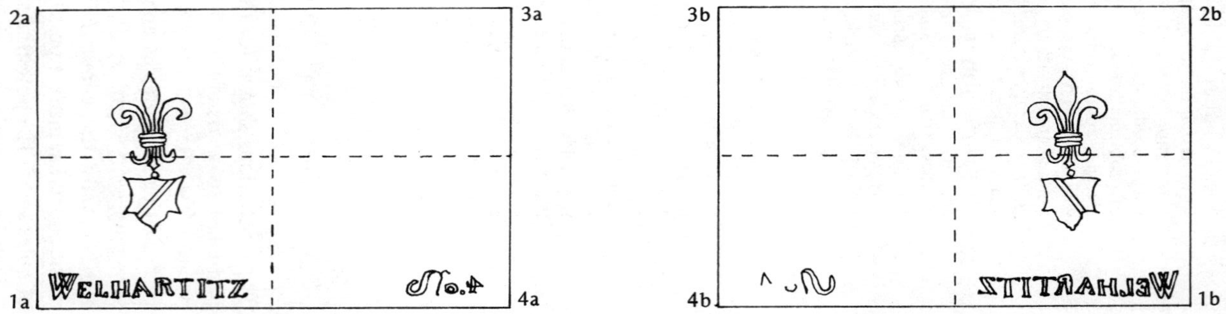

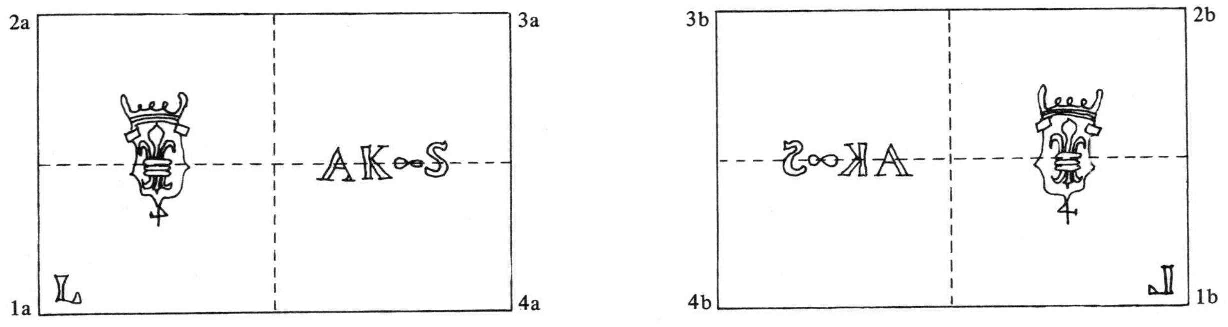

Figure 2. Type IIa (above) and IIb (below)

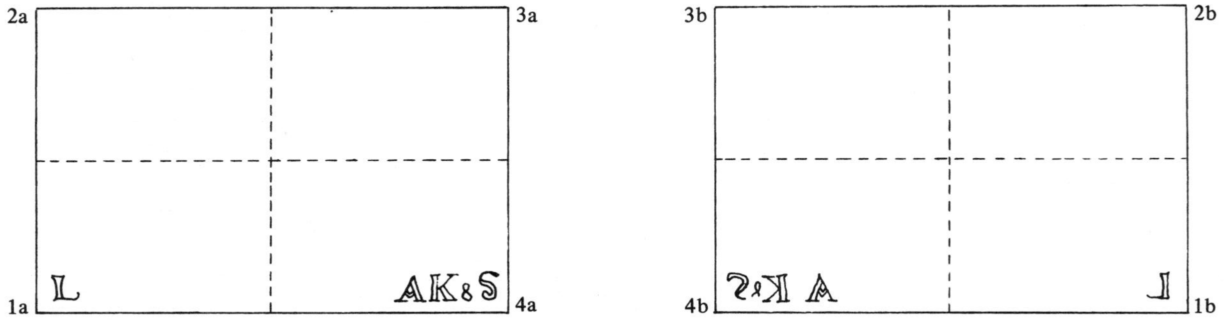

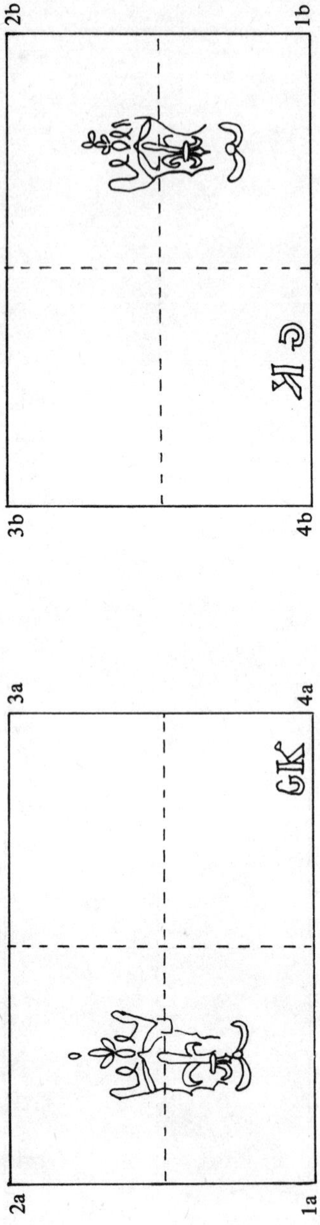

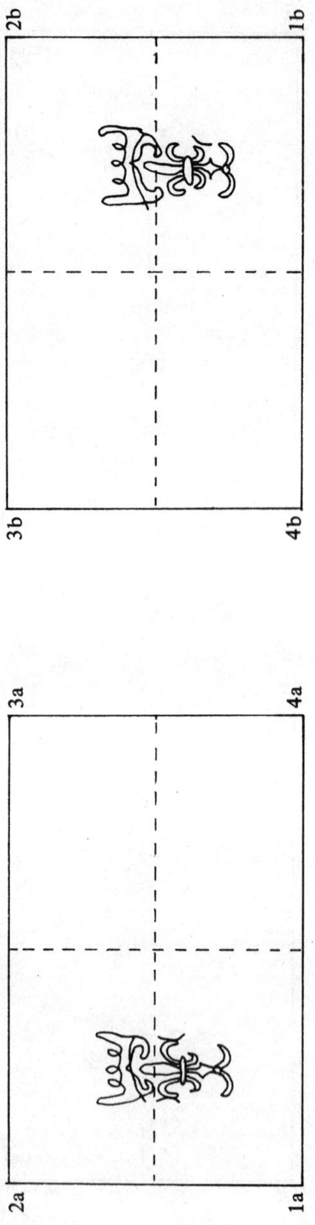

Figure 3. Type III (above), Type IV (below)

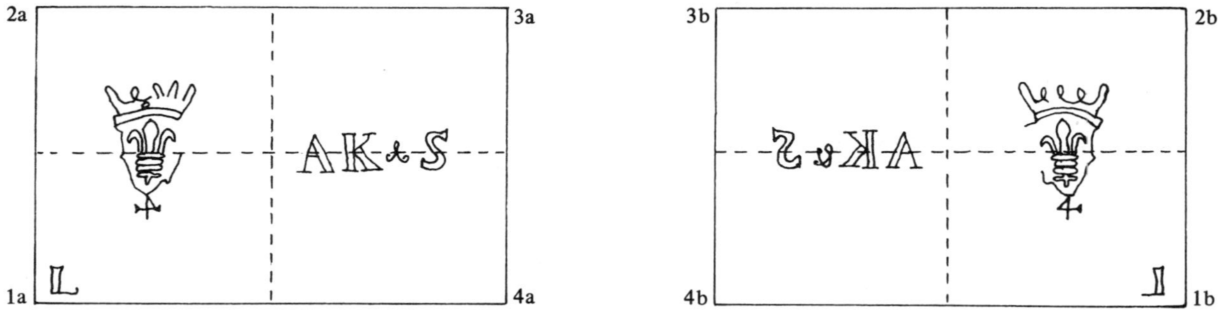

Figure 4. Type Va (above) and Vb (below)

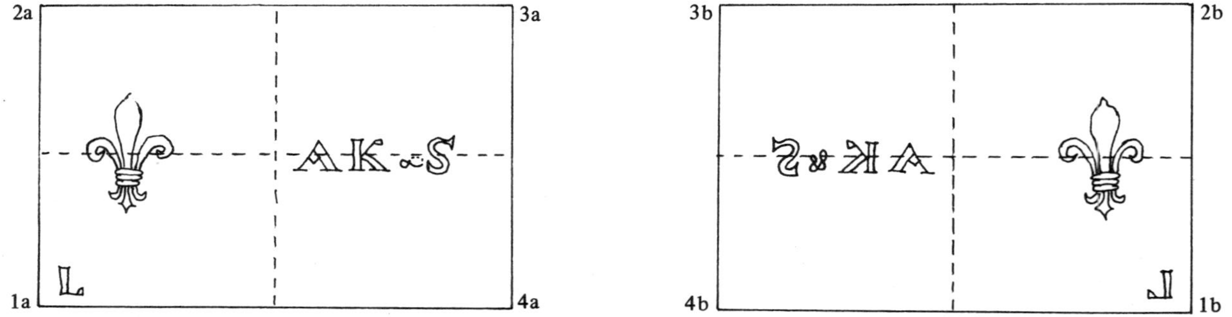

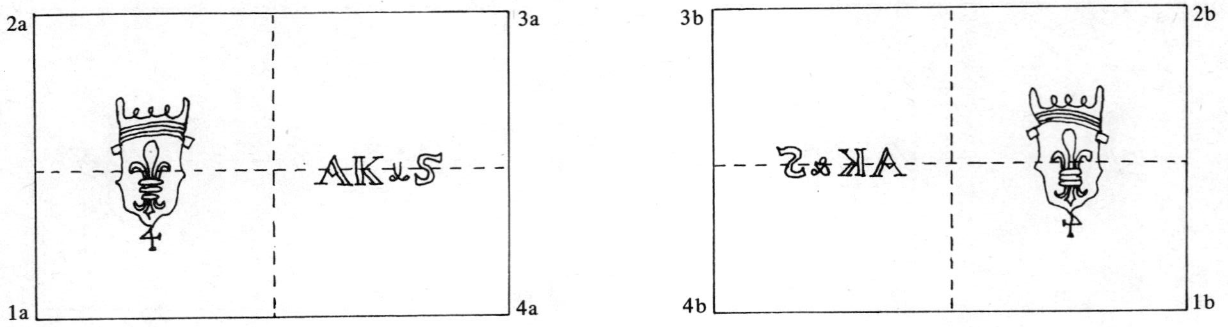

Figure 5. Type VIb (above), Type VIIa-d (below)

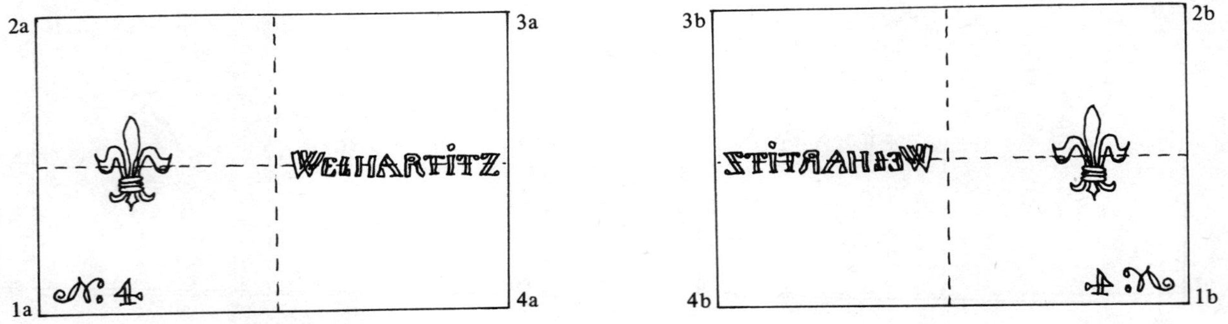

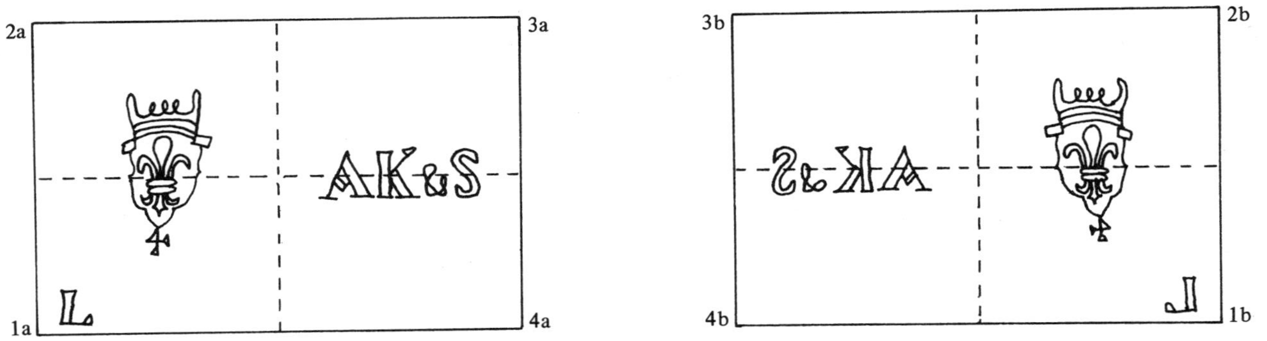

Figure 6. Type VIIIa (above) and VIIIb (below)

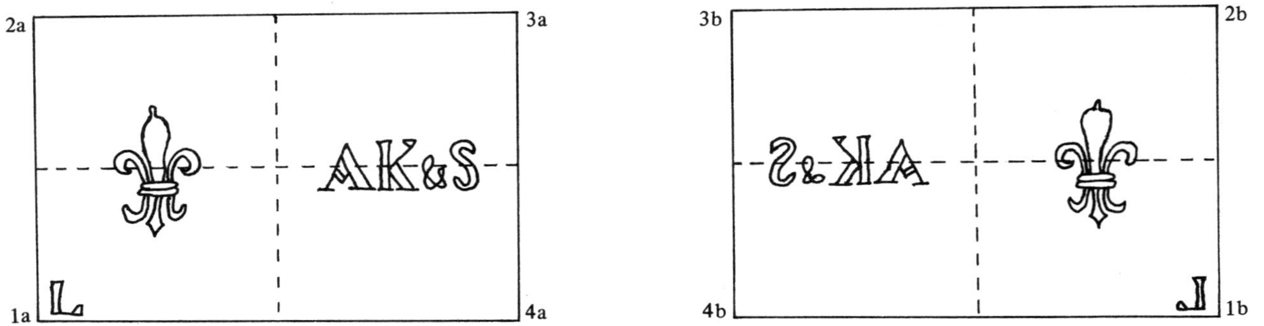

The chronology of Schubert's piano trios

EVA BADURA-SKODA

Schubert found his way to the piano trio late in his life. He probably knew the masterpieces in this genre by Haydn, Mozart and Beethoven. The last-named, more than anybody else, had perfected the art of composing for three equally important solo instruments.

For a long time Schubert apparently did not feel inclined to take advantage of the achievements of these masters. There exists an early composition for piano, violin and cello, a single movement in F major, dated July/August 1812 and entitled 'Sonata' (D 28). However, this piece can hardly be called a piano trio proper, not only because it remained a torso (Schubert abandoned it after completing the first movement, in sonata form – perhaps owing to the fact that during August 1812 his counterpoint lessons with Salieri started), but because it is indeed not much more than the pleasant but unimportant product of an early compositional exercise. Furthermore, the autograph of D 28 shows that Schubert originally planned to write a traditional church sonata: the violin part is headed 'Violino I^{mo}' and the piano part 'Cembalo'. However, Schubert's corrections on the first page indicate that he must have changed his mind soon after starting the composition: instead of a second violin part he decided to write a cello part. There are already some charming passages and even traits of genuine Schubert here and there in this movement; but altogether one can still feel Schubert's lack of experience. Probably on the advice of Brahms, D 28 was excluded from publication in the old complete edition of Schubert's works.

As will be shown in the discussion which follows, slightly more than fifteen years passed before Schubert became interested in the piano trio proper. I shall demonstrate that when he discovered for himself the special challenge and charm of this genre he immediately composed not just one but two great trios, the B flat major Trio op. 99 (D 898) and the E flat major Trio op. 100 (D 929), masterpieces which established his fame as an outstanding composer of chamber music earlier than did his string quartets or even the 'Trout' Quintet. Apart from these two well-known piano trios, there exists another single piano-trio movement in E♭ major (D 897), less familiar and less inspired but written with the same compositional skill as the two great trios. The first page of D 897 shows neither date nor signature, and no other title than 'Adagio' on the autograph. Schubert usually entitled in this way slow movements belonging to a sonata cycle. For this reason the piece has rightly been considered as a second movement for the B flat major Trio, later rejected and replaced by its *Andante un poco mosso* movement (also in E♭ major). The first edition of the rejected piece was brought out in 1845 by Diabelli as op. 148 under the title 'Nocturne' (which in later editions became 'Notturno'). Not only an external reason – namely that Schubert would have given the *Adagio* a proper title and would probably have written his signature and perhaps a date on the title-page if he had considered it a separate piece – speaks for the assumed connection with the B flat major Trio; internal reasons, too, make it probable that the *Adagio* movement D 897 was conceived at the same time as D 898. Consequently, O. E. Deutsch in his thematic catalogue of Schubert's works gave it the number just before that of the finished B flat Trio.

In spite of the mature style of the 'Notturno' and its apparent links with the inception of the B flat Trio, one can understand why Schubert replaced it: the new *Andante* movement, with its beautiful main melody introduced by the cello, certainly follows more fittingly the heart-warming and melodious first movement of the B flat Trio than does the *Adagio* movement D 897.

Today, the autograph of the *Adagio* movement D 897 is the property of the Österreichische Nationalbibliothek. The autograph of the B flat major Trio D 898, however, is missing. In its absence scholars began to find themselves – more than a hundred years after the composition of this trio – faced with a problem in dating the work. Its inception has been suggested for practically every year from 1825 to 1828. The riddle can be solved, however, as will be seen below. The autograph of the E flat major Trio D 929 fortunately survives and is presently in private possession in Switzerland. Moreover, an autograph draft of its first three movements also exists. It was once the property of Johannes Brahms and is now preserved in the archive of the Gesellschaft der Musikfreunde in Vienna. Both the draft of the three movements and the complete autograph were dated by Schubert 'November 1827'. On the title-page of the complete autograph Schubert wrote, in addition to date and signature, 'Opus 100' – an important fact, which shows inter alia that he was not as indifferent towards the question of numbering his works as has been claimed in the past.

Until the middle of the last century apparently nobody doubted that Schubert's B flat Trio was written just prior to that in E flat. This conviction may have been based only on the fact that Schubert gave the two trios successive opus numbers;[1] but it is possible that during the last century the compilers of worklists had other good reasons (unknown to us) for such dating.

1 Schubert took a lively interest in the numbering of his works; see (e.g.) his letters to Probst quoted below, or his letter to Schott of 2 October 1828.

Though the B flat Trio was published as late as 1836, nine years after the E flat Trio, it appeared with the title 'Premier Grand Trio op. 99'. This may well have been Schubert's own title on the lost autograph. The publisher of this first edition was Diabelli, who most probably had acquired the publication rights in a roundabout way. Prior to Diabelli, Leidesdorf and Weigl issued catalogues of Schubert's works in 1829 and 1830 respectively[2] in which they had already listed the B flat Trio under this title. It may well have been that Diabelli purchased manuscript and publication rights from Leidesdorf (see below).

Robert Schumann, Schubert's ardent admirer and herald in the musical world, welcomed in the *Neue Zeitschrift für Musik* the publication of the B flat major Trio with the following words:

A glance at Schubert's trio, and all miserable human commotion vanishes, and the world shines in new splendour. About ten years ago a Schubert trio in E flat went across ordinary musical life of the day like an angry thunderstorm. It was his hundredth opus. Shortly after, in November 1828, he died. This recently published trio seems to be an older work. To be sure, its style does not refer to any earlier period, and it may well have been written a short time before the famous one in E flat major. Intrinsically, however, they bear little resemblance to each other. The first movement, which in the other is inspired by deep indignation as well as boundless longing, is graceful and virginal in the one before us. The adagio, there a sigh tending to swell to anxiety, is here a happy dream, a rising and falling of genuine feeling. The scherzos somewhat resemble each other, but I give preference to that in the earlier published [second] trio. I cannot decide as to the last movements. In a word, the Trio in E flat major is more spirited, masculine, and dramatic; this one is more passive, lyric, and feminine. Let the work, which he bequeathed to us, be a precious legacy! Time, though producing much that is beautiful, will not soon produce another Schubert![3]

Schumann's opinion deserves careful consideration – he was an experienced reviewer of new music, and he was close to Schubert in terms of both time and natural sympathy. He probably could judge much better than any musician of our century whether or not the style of the B flat major Trio implies an earlier period than that of the Trio in E flat major, even if he did not have the (doubtful) advantage of historical distance.[4]

2 See notes 17 and 18 below.

3 Published in Heinrich Kreissle von Hellborn, *The Life of Franz Schubert*, transl. Arthur Duke Coleridge, 2 vols. (London, 1869), vol. 2, p. 233, and in a different translation in R. Schumann, *On Music and Musicians*, transl. Paul Rosenfeld and ed. Konrad Wolff (London, 1947), p. 121. (For the sake of accuracy, the present translation differs slightly from both versions.) On 26 August 1836 Schumann wrote in his diary (vol. V): 'The B flat Trio by Schubert. Prima vista. Extraordinary.'

4 John Reed, *Schubert. The Final Years* (London, 1972) is of a different opinion (p. 173) but fails to prove his point: 'But when Schumann goes on to suggest that in the style of opus 99 "there is absolutely no evidence of any earlier period" he is surely wide of the mark. It may have seemed so in the 1830s, but today the two works seem far apart in manner as well as matter.'

It could be that, regarding the question whether the two trios were composed in different years or at approximately the same time, doubts first arose through a simple misprint in Kreissle von Hellborn's biography of Schubert which appeared in 1865. In the German edition of Kreissle's biography one can read:

Das Es-Trio ist – sowie auch das etwas früher entstandene in B – eine der wenigen Instrumentalcompositionen Schubert's, die noch bei Lebzeiten des Meisters in Privatgesellschaften und auch in öffentlichen Concerten von ausgezeichneten, für den Componisten begeisterten Musikern vorgeführt und mit entschiedenem Beifall aufgenommen wurden.[5]

However, in Coleridge's English translation of Kreissle's biography, which appeared ten years later, the word 'etwas' before 'früher' is omitted. There the passage reads:

The Trio in E-flat, like that in B-flat, its earlier predecessor, is one of the few instrumental compositions by Schubert which, during the master's lifetime, was given with distinguished applause at private parties, and at public concerts also, by musicians who were enthusiastic worshippers of Schubert's genius.[6]

A more accurate translation would have inserted 'somewhat' before 'earlier predecessor' or would have used a less literal translation: 'The Trio in E flat – composed a little after that in B flat – . . .'

Coleridge's translation of the second relevant passage, in a later chapter of Kreissle's biography, is correct. This passage reads:

On the subject of Schubert's performance in chamber music, we should assign the foremost place to the two Trios (in B-flat and E-flat) . . . Both the trios, which were performed in private circles during the lifetime of the composer, are amongst Schubert's best-known works. They were written within a short time of each other, and belonging as they do to the last creative period of the composer,* are therefore conspicuous for all the peculiar graces and loveliness of Schubert's manner; both these works, indeed, bear on them the stamp of artistic ripeness and intense cultivation. Broader in conception, and more powerfully worked out in form and detail, is the E-flat Trio, when judged as an entire work – a work which the modest artist himself regarded with self-complacency.[7]

And in the footnote Kreissle added:

* The E-flat Trio, as we see from the original in the hands of the Countess Almasy, of Vienna, was written in November 1827, and engraved shortly afterwards at Leipsic. The B-flat Trio, although written before that in E-flat, was engraved at a later period.

For the appendix of his Schubert biography, Kreissle compiled a list of works. Here the B flat major Trio is listed on p. 613 as follows: 'Trio in B (1826), op. 99'. This '1826' in Kreissle's list could hardly be anything other

5 Heinrich Kreissle von Hellborn, *Franz Schubert* (Vienna, 1865), p. 408.
6 Op. cit. (see note 3), II, pp. 94f.
7 Ibid., II, pp. 232f.

than a printing error. If this suspicion is correct[8] then it was to prove a misprint with serious consequences, because – together with a misleading commentary in O. E. Deutsch's *Schubert. A Documentary Biography* – it gave rise to confusion over the composition date of op. 99. Since the 1940s there has been increasing uncertainty about the genesis of the B flat major Trio. In his Schubert thematic catalogue O. E. Deutsch dated the work '? 1827', which according to his preface means 'approximate year of composition is 1827'. This is correct, though Deutsch could have followed George Grove and could have dated op. 99 '?October 1827'; then the D numbers of the two trios would not have been separated by all the other numbers given to Schubert's works composed between January 1827 and October (November) 1827. But apparently in this case Deutsch did not trust Grove; his entry for the Trio D 898 in his thematic catalogue is followed by the note: 'There is no confirmation that this Trio was written in October 1827, shortly before 929, as stated in George Grove's Schubert article, in his Dictionary of Music and Musicians.'[9] Is there really no confirmation? The following pages seek to supply the answer to this question.

In 1952 the ethnomusicologist Karl Maria Klier[10] called attention to a folk-song from Upper Austria, a so-called 'Arbeitslied' (work-song) with such a regular musical rhythm that it was easy for a group of workmen to join in unison hammer blows on every second beat of a 3/4 metre. Klier pointed out that this song had a striking similarity to the melody of the Notturno D 897. He considered it possible that Schubert remembered this song from Upper Austria when composing the *Adagio* movement, because while in Gmunden in 1825 he is supposed to have watched piledrivers at work and to have listened to their singing. That led Maurice Brown to conclude that Schubert started to compose the Notturno in 1825:

> The 'Notturno' in E flat has always been considered a rejected movement from the B flat PF. Trio, and since Schubert is not likely to have delayed using the song he heard, it is possible that the PF. Trio was begun as early as 1825. There is no other means whatever of dating it: the manuscript is lost and there are no contemporary references to it: Two dates have been deduced for its composition, 1826 and 1827. The piledrivers' song and its tradition make the earlier one, 1826, more probable.[11]

8 The first victim of this possible printing error may well have been C. von Wurzbach, who around 1875 wrote an extensive article on Schubert in which he gives 1826 as the year of composition of op. 99 (see ***Biographisches Lexikon des Kaiserthums Oesterreich*** (Vienna, 1856-91), vol. 32, pp. 30-116). George Grove, however, who had personal contact in Vienna with relatives and publishers of Schubert (Schneider and Spina), reported in his ***Dictionary of Music and Musicians*** (London, 1884), 'October 1827' as the date of composition of op. 99 – correctly, as will be seen below.

9 Otto Erich Deutsch, ***Schubert. Thematic Catalogue of All His Works in Chronological Order*** (London, 1951), p. 435.

10 Karl Maria Klier, 'Österreichische Pilotenschlägerlieder', *Jahrbuch des Österreichischen Volksliedwerkes*, I (Vienna, 1952), p. 32.

11 Maurice J. E. Brown, *Schubert. A Critical Biography* (London, 1958), p. 168.

Therefore, according to Brown, we should assume that Schubert began to compose the trio in Gmunden in 1825, used the song he had heard there for the second movement, rejected it, abandoned the composition and (after a year?) finished the trio in 1826. Brown's uncertainty in this question can be seen from the fact that he first (p. 277) indirectly suggests May 1826 as the date of completion for the 'Premier Trio':

> If the story of the piledrivers' theme is sufficient grounds for giving the earlier Trio the date '1826', then something like eighteen months separated the two compositions; in Schubert's life that was a reasonably long period. The style of the first movement of the B flat Trio would confirm the date (although alone it would be insufficient evidence).

Later, however, in his list of Schubert's works in chronological order in the Appendix (p. 394), Brown dates the B flat major Trio 'end of 1826?', which would reduce the just-quoted eighteen months to twelve. Fortunately Brown admits his insecurity when referring to stylistic reasons in order to support his new dating of the trio.

Influenced by Brown, Harry Goldschmidt repeatedly expressed the opinion that biographical and stylistic reasons speak for a dating of the B flat Trio to 1825–6.[12] John Reed also took up the idea of an earlier composition date than 1827 for the B flat major Trio. In the preface (p. 13) of his book *Schubert. The Final Years*, he says that he has written

> a book which attempts, within a fairly strict chronological framework, to give a critical account of the composer's last years, on the assumption that the ['Great' C major] symphony (and, I would add, the B flat piano trio) are much earlier works than is commonly supposed.

When discussing the two piano trios, Reed also joined Brown and Goldschmidt in their opinion that the two great trios in B flat and E flat have so little in common with each other that in spite of the similarity of medium they do not appear to have been composed at the same time. This judgement is in flat contradiction to Schumann's opinion; and since it does not hold from a musical point of view, it may have caused Arnold Feil (the editor of the volume of the new complete edition in which the piano trios were published), to suggest yet another year for the composition of the B flat major Trio: according to Feil, the B flat Trio might have been composed *after* the E flat Trio during the late spring of 1828.[13] Apparently Feil, like Maurice Brown, thought the extant biographical data and documents to be insufficient for establishing the composition year of the B flat major Trio, an opinion which already in 1969, when preparing the Preface for my 'Urtext' edition of the Schubert trios,[14] I did not share. It seems that both scholars were misled by Deutsch's note on the programme for Schubert's concert on 26 December

12 See e.g. Harry Goldschmidt, *Um die Sache der Musik* (Leipzig, 1976), p. 105.

13 See *Franz Schubert. Neue Ausgabe sämtlicher Werke* (*NGA*), preface to Series VI, vol. 7 (Kassel, etc., 1975), p. XII.

14 Published as Urtext-Ausgabe by G. Henle Verlag (Munich, 1973). Originally,

1827; besides, some old catalogues were not considered carefully enough by these scholars. Apart from this, the most recent paper investigations supply us with important additional information, not available in previous years. Let us therefore once more examine all the extant documentary evidence concerning the two trios.

There is no reference to Schubert's pianoforte trios prior to autumn 1827. Dates which can be authenticated in connection with the trios are as follows:

(1) Schubert dated his autograph draft of the first three movements of the E flat major Trio 'November 1827'. Likewise the fair copy of these three movements is dated 'November 1827'.

There is no proof that the fourth movement of this trio was composed during this same month of November, since Schubert did not write a date at the end of the finale. No draft of this finale exists; perhaps there never was one. In Schubert's completed autograph the finale shows more corrections than do the other movements, some more far-reaching than usual: one whole page is pasted on top of another, and twice sections of some 50 bars occur in the autograph which Schubert later decided to cut – see below under (13).

(2) In addition to date and signature, Schubert wrote 'Opus 100' on the title-page of the completed E flat major Trio. Whether he supplied the trio with this opus number in November 1827 or at a later date we do not know.

It can be assumed that he decided to number his E flat major Trio 'Opus 100' at the time when he chose the opus number 99 for the B flat major Trio. That at this time of his life he took great care to number his works himself will be seen, inter alia, from the following correspondence excerpts.[15] It is more than probable that the lost autograph of the B flat major Trio showed Schubert's own indication 'Opus 99' on its title-page, since the catalogues of Schubert's works brought out by the publishers Leidesdorf,[16] Weigl[17] and Diabelli[18] between 1829 and 1831 already give this opus number for the

the reason for my dating of the B flat Trio had been explained in an extensive preface for this edition which, however, was drastically shortened owing to the late Dr Henle's firm conviction that musicians are not interested in historical questions and that prefaces to editions must therefore be very brief.

15 This also seems to be the only explanation for the fact that Schubert's Viennese publishers knew that they should not use the opus number 99 for another work by him.

16 *Franz Schubert's sämmtliche Werke, Wien bey M. J. Leidesdorf, Kärnthnerstrasse No. 941*. It contains a listing of *opera* 1-120 and was printed in 1829 (copy in the Archiv der Gesellschaft der Musikfreunde, Witteczek–Spaun collection, vol. 11 bound in with op. 119).

17 *Sämmtliche Werke von Franz Schubert, Wien in der Th. Weigl'schen Musikhandlung Graben No. 1144*, plate-number 2951 (July 1830). The list contains *opera* 1-128. Copy in the Gesellschaft der Musikfreunde, Witteczek–Spaun collection, vol. 12.

18 *Franz Schubert's sämtliche Werke, Wien, bey Ant. Diabelli und Comp. Graben No. 1133. Die Preise sind in Conventions Münze, der Gulden zu 3 Stück Zwanziger*, plate-number 2490 (1831). Diabelli was also the first to publish a thematic catalogue of Schubert's work (in 1851, plate-number 8932, copy in the possession of the author), thus preceding Nottebohm and Deutsch.

B flat major Trio in spite of the fact that the work was not published before 1836. Therefore at least one of them must have seen or heard of Schubert's indication.

(3) The first known performance of a piano trio by Schubert was a public performance in a subscription concert of the Schuppanzigh Quartet in the music room of the Gesellschaft der Musikfreunde on 26 December 1827. O. E. Deutsch lists this event in his *Documentary Biography*,[19] using as source the anonymous *Chronologisches Verzeichniss aller auf den fünf Theatern Wien's gegebenen Vorstellungen; vom ersten November 1827 bis letzten October 1828* . . . ('Chronological List of all Performances given in the five Theatres of Vienna from 1 November 1827 until the end of October 1828 . . .'), in a series which K. Voll brought out in the years 1826-9 (see Figure 1: the rarity of the relevant number of this publication justifies its facsimile reproduction here). The second number in the programme is listed as a 'New Trio': 'Neues Trio für Pfte., Violin und Violoncell, v[on] Schubert; die Principalstimme, vorg[etragen] v[on] Hrn. C. M. von Bocklet' (see Figure 2). No programme of this concert exists in the archive of the Gesellschaft der Musikfreunde or elsewhere, and no private report is known which tells us the key of the trio that was included in this programme (except for an unreliable one by Louis Schlösser, who recalled in his memoirs that Schubert played 'the first of his two piano trios'[20]).

In his commentary to this quotation from Voll's *Chronologisches Verzeichniss*, Deutsch (without justification) links it with a remark of Sonnleithner concerning the E flat major Trio and makes the following statements:

> This printed list, never before quoted from in these documents, contains several concerts known from other sources (cf. No. 1006). – Leopold von Sonnleithner told Kreissle that in the *andante* of this Trio (November 1827) Schubert had used one of the Swedish folksongs he had heard at the Fröhlich sisters' from the tenor Isaak Albert Berg . . . What is certain is that this theme has not so far been identified.

Sonnleithner does indeed relate the anecdote of Schubert's use of a Swedish folk song in the E flat Trio (the song in the meantime has been identified by Manfred Willfort[21]); but he does not say that the E flat major Trio was performed before March 1828. Deutsch's assumption that it was the E flat major Trio that was played in December 1827 is therefore erroneous.

(4) On 18 January 1828 Schubert wrote to Hüttenbrenner:

19 O. E. Deutsch, *Schubert. A Documentary Biography* (cited below as '*Documents*') (London, 1946), p. 698.

20 O. E. Deutsch, *Schubert. Memoirs by His Friends* (cited below as '*Memoirs*') (London, 1958), pp. 329 and 331-2.

21 See M. Willfort, 'Das Urbild des Andante aus Schuberts Klaviertrio Es-dur, D 929', *Österreichische Musikzeitschrift*, XXXIII (1978), 277-83.

Chronologisches Verzeichniß

aller

auf den fünf Theatern Wien's

gegebenen Vorstellungen;

vom

ersten November 1827 bis letzten October 1828.

Nebst Angabe aller

neuen Vorstellungen, Beneficien und Debüts

auf allen fünf Theatern.

Sammt einem Anhange,

enthaltend:

alle in diesem Zeitraume gegebenen

Akademien, Concerte und musikalischen

Unterhaltungen,

nebst vollständiger nahmentlicher Angabe aller dabey mitgewirkt habenden Individuen.

Vierter Jahrgang.

Wien, 1829.

Gedruckt bey J. P. Sollinger.

Figure 1. Voll's *Chronologisches Verzeichniss . . .* for 1827-8, title-page

Vienna, 18th January 1828.

My dear old Hüttenbrenner,

You must be surprised at my writing for once. I too. But if I do write, it is because I have a purpose. Listen, then: there is a drawing-master's post vacant at your Graz, and the competition for it is announced. My brother Carl, whom perhaps you know too, wishes to obtain this post . . . Recently a new Trio of mine for pianoforte, violin and violoncello was performed at Schuppanzigh's and pleased very much. It was admirably executed by Bocklet, Schuppanzigh and Linke. Have you done nothing new?[22]

(5) Next we know of a 'Schubertiad' which was held at Spaun's home on 28 January 1828. Spaun invited not only the usual group of friends but also, at Schubert's request, the performers Schuppanzigh, Bocklet and Linke. According to the description of this evening which Spaun wrote later, a piano trio was performed,[23] but unfortunately he did not say which one. It may

Im Saale des Mus. Ver. Quartetten des Hrn. Schup-anzigh. 1. Von Haydn, in Es. 2. Neues Trio für Pfte., Violin und Violoncell, v. Schubert; die Principalstimme, vorg. v. Hrn. C. M. von Bocklet. 3. Quator v. Beethoven, in moll, (Rasumoffsky).

Am 26. Im Vereins-Saale. Privat-Concert des Hrn. ranz Schubert, folgende eigene Compos., enthaltend. 1. Viol. uartett, vorg. v. d. Hrn. Böhm, Holz, Weiß und Linke. Vier Gesänge, mit Pfte. Begleit., ges. v. d. pens. k. k. Hofopern-zen, Hrn. Vogel. 3. Ständchen, vorg. v. Fräul. Jos. Fröh-ch und dem Frauen-Chor. 4. Neues Trio f. Pfte., Violin und ioloncell., ausgef. v. d. Hrn. von Bocklet, Böhm u. Linke. Auf dem Strome; Ges. mit Pfte. und Horn-Begl.; vorg. v. d. Hrn. Tietze und Lewy jun. 6. Die Allmacht; Ges. m. Pfte. Begl., ges von Hrn. Vogel. 7. Schlachtgesang, v. Klop-tock, Doppelchor für Männerstimmen.

Figure 2. Voll's *Chronologisches Verzeichniss* . . . for 1827-8, extracts showing the Schuppanzigh Quartet's concert on 26 December 1827 and Schubert's 'Privat-Concert' on 26 March 1828

22 *Documents*, pp. 713f.
23 *Documents*, pp. 724f, and *Memoirs*, p. 138.

well have been a first performance of the E flat major Trio, at this time still with the uncut finale which consisted then of more than 1000 bars if a (later deleted) repetition sign was also observed by the performers – certainly a unique length.

(6) 9 February 1828 is the date of two letters which were written to Schubert by the publishers Schott in Mainz and Probst in Leipzig inviting him to offer available compositions – a surprising coincidence. The letter of Probst remained unanswered until 10 April, since Schubert had had some unpleasant experiences with him. To Schott's letter Schubert replied on 21 February 1828:

Gentlemen,

I feel much honoured by your letter of 8th [*recte* 9th] February and enter with pleasure into closer relations with so reputable an art establishment, which is so fit to give my works greater currency abroad.

I have the following compositions in stock:

a) Trio for pianoforte, violin and violoncello, which has been produced here with much success.
b) Two string Quartets (G major and D minor).
c) Four Impromptus for pianoforte solo, which might be published separately or all four together.

Schubert then listed seven more works.[24]

It has always puzzled some scholars why Schubert in this letter to Schott offered only one piano trio and not two. The most plausible explanation is that Schubert had already sold one of the two trios to a Viennese publisher (probably in January 1828 after the successful public performance) hoping that he would bring it out quickly. Only Arnold Feil proposes another explanation, in his preface (p. XII) to the relevant volume of the *NGA*: he assumes that the B flat major Trio could not be listed because it had not yet been composed.

(7) Schott replied to Schubert's letter of 21 February on 29 February[25] and asked him to send a selection of eight of the ten available compositions. Among those selected was the 'Trio for pianoforte, violin and violoncello'.

(8) Schubert gave the first and only concert he arranged on 26 March 1828 in the music room of the Gesellschaft der Musikfreunde at 7 p.m., the programme consisting only of his own works (see facsimile reproduction of the programme in *Documents*, p. 755). In this concert he announced two instrumental compositions as being 'new': a movement of a string quartet (most probably the first movement of the last String Quartet in G, D 887) and a 'New Trio for pianoforte, violin and violoncello'. According to Viennese custom 'new' meant not only that it was not known through a printed edition

24 *Documents*, p. 739.
25 *Documents*, pp. 744f.

but that it was also unknown to the audience, not having previously been heard in a concert. And it would indeed have been unwise for Schubert to present a composition as 'new' which had already been performed publicly in December 1827.

Leopold von Sonnleithner reported about this concert:

> The result was a success in every way, and provided Schubert with a considerable sum of money. The criticisms are to be found in the papers of that time; I will only say that I cannot remember from which quartet it was that the first movement was played. The new *Trio* was the one in E flat major, Op. 100.[26]

(9) On 10 April Schubert wrote a letter to Schott:

> Vienna, 10th April 1828.
>
> Sirs,
>
> The arrangements for and performance of my concert, at which all the musical pieces were of my composition, have prevented me so long from replying to your letter. However, I have since had copies made of the desired Trio (which was received at my concert by a tightly packed audience with such extraordinary applause that I have been urged to repeat the concert), the Impromptus and the five-part male chorus, and if the said Trio is agreeable to you for 100 fl., A.C., and the other two works together for 60 fl. coinage, I can send them off at once. All I should request is publication as soon as possible.
>
> With all respect,
> Frz. Schubert.[27]

Schubert had apparently prepared copies for Schott of only three of the eight works requested, probably because he was most anxious to see these three works published first.

(10) The same day he also wrote to Probst, only now reacting to his letter of 9 February:

> Vienna, 10th April 1828.
>
> Sir,
>
> You have honoured me with a letter which, owing to the arrangements connected with my concert, has so far remained unanswered. It may perhaps not be without interest for you if I inform you that not only was the concert in question, at which all the pieces were of my composition, crammed full, but also that I received extraordinary approbation. A Trio for pianoforte, violin and violoncello in particular found general approval, so much so, indeed, that I have been invited to give a second concert (*quasi* as a repeat performance). For the rest, I can assign to you some works with pleasure, if you are inclined to agree to the reasonable fee of 60 florins, A.C., per sizable book. I need hardly assure you that I shall not send you anything which I do not regard as thoroughly successful, in so far as this is possible for an author and for some select circles [to judge], since, when all is said, it must be above all in my own interest to send good works abroad.
>
> With all respect,
> Your devoted
> Frz. Schubert.[28]

Schubert clearly did *not* offer Probst the Trio in E flat major for publication – he simply reported about the 'favourable reception' of the trio (for which he hoped to get 100 fl. from Schott); the success had filled him with justifiable pride. As can be seen from his letter to Probst, dated 10 May (see below under (13)), Schubert meant by a 'sizable book' a collection of songs or pianoforte pieces.[29]

(11) Probst – misunderstanding the offer – replied immediately (on 15 April) to Schubert's letter: 'I accept, upon your word, the Trio kindly offered me . . . please receive [the fee] enclosed . . .'[30] A letter from Leipzig took approximately a week to arrive, and therefore Schubert may have received it as well as the 60 fl. around 22 April. Understandably, he delayed his answer.

(12) Schott's reply was written on 28 April, and reads as follows:

Sir,

Your favour of 10th April acquaints us with the fee for your manuscripts. We note your wish to have these engraved very soon, in which case we would ask you for the moment only for the Impromptus and the five-part male chorus, the fee for which we shall settle with the amount of 60 fl., A.C.

The Trio is probably long, and as we have recently published several trios, and short of doing ourselves harm, we shall be obliged to defer that kind of composition until a little later, which might not after all be to your advantage.[31]

O. E. Deutsch commented on this letter that 'Schott fortunately did not ask for the pianoforte Trio, for which Probst had paid in the meantime'. However, as stated above, Schubert had not really offered the trio to Probst but had simply reported its successful performance. And he certainly was not happy about the idea of getting only 60 fl. for a trio for which he had asked 100 fl. from Schott.

(13) But he was probably in need of money. Therefore, after having received Schott's letter, Schubert answered Probst:

Vienna, 10th May 1828.

Sir,

Herewith I am sending you the desired Trio, although a song or pianoforte book was understood for the price of 60 fl., A.C., and not a trio, for which six times as much work is required. In order, however, to make a beginning at last, I would only ask for the speediest possible publication, and for the dispatch of 6 copies. The cuts indicated in the last movement are to be most scrupulously observed. Be sure to have it performed for the first time by capable people, and most particularly see to a continual uniformity of tempo at the changes of the time-signature in the last movement. The minuet at a moderate pace and *piano* throughout, the trio, on the other hand, vigorous

26 *Memoirs*, p. 115.
27 *Documents*, p. 764.
28 *Documents*, p. 765.
29 *Documents*, p. 765, Commentary.
30 *Documents*, p. 767.
31 *Documents*, p. 771.

except where *p* and *pp* are marked. In expectation of the earliest publication,

I remain,
respectfully,
your devoted
Frz. Schubert.[32]

(14) On 18 July Probst wrote to Schubert:

Not until to-day did I receive your favour of 10th May with the Trio, and you must therefore not be surprised, my valued friend, if this work is published somewhat later than perhaps you expected. However, work on it has started immediately, and it may be ready within about six weeks. In the meantime I would ask you further to let me know

1) the title as well as the dedication, if any,
2) the opus number,

as I should like to proceed as nearly as possible in accordance with your wishes in this respect.

All your further directions concerning this work shall be followed most faithfully.

As soon as it is ready, I shall send you the stipulated six copies as an enclosure.

My opinion of it I shall have the honour of communicating to you later, until which time I remain in

respectful devotion,
H. A. Probst.[33]

(15) This letter was answered by Schubert on 1 August:

Sir,

The opus number of the Trio is 100. I request that the edition should be faultless and look forward to it longingly. This work is to be dedicated to nobody, save those who find pleasure in it. That is the most profitable dedication.

With all respect,
Frz. Schubert.[34]

(16) Six weeks passed and Schubert did not hear from Probst. Therefore, he wrote to him on 2 October:

Sir,

I beg to inquire when the Trio is to appear at last. Can it be that you do not know the opus number yet? It is Op. 100. I await its appearance with longing . . .[35]

(17) To this letter Probst replied on 6 October:

In reply to your esteemed letters of August 1st and 2nd inst., I beg to apologize for the fact that your Trio, Op. 100, is not yet in your hands. My travels to France and Holland have doubtless had something to do with the delay, and moreover the work is somewhat bulky. However, its engraving is already

32 *Documents*, p. 774.
33 *Documents*, p. 793.
34 *Documents*, p. 796.
35 *Documents*, pp. 810f.

done, and also corrected as carefully as possible, and it will go to you, spick and span, with my next consignment to Diabelli & Co.[36]

Seven weeks later Schubert died, and it is unlikely that he lived to see a printed copy of the E flat major Trio, though it may have appeared in Leipzig during October or the first weeks of November. In Vienna the first copies were announced as being for sale on 11 December 1828.

(18) After Schubert's untimely death the family more or less agreed that Ferdinand Schubert should inherit the unpublished and as yet unsold compositions. Ferdinand eventually prepared a list of these compositions, in which neither of the trios is mentioned. Obviously this was due to the fact that the B flat major Trio had been sold previously by Schubert to a Viennese publisher and the E flat Trio had been sold to Probst.

We do not know which publisher it was who acquired the B flat major Trio. It could have been Pennauer,[37] but it is more likely that it was one of the three publishers who listed the B flat major Trio in their printed catalogues of Schubert's works: M. J. Leidesdorf, Thaddäus Weigl and Anton Diabelli. Most likely it was Leidesdorf, whose catalogue of 1829 lists op. 99 and op. 100 as follows:

Opus		Preis
99.	Premièr [sic] grand Trio p.1. Pianof., Violon et Violonc. in B	–
100.	Second grand Trio pour detto, in Es	4.30

Similarly, the catalogue of T. Weigl, printed in 1831, lists the two trios in this way. He may have simply copied the entry from Leidesdorf's catalogue (including the accent in 'Premier'). In 1835 Leidesdorf sold his small and not very successful publishing firm (including manuscripts and publication rights) to Diabelli.[38] One year later, in 1836, Diabelli brought out the first edition of the trio under the title 'Premier Grand Trio pour Piano-Forte, Violon et Violoncelle composè [sic] par François Schubert. Oeuvre 99', with the plate-

36 *Documents*, pp. 813f.

37 Pennauer (along with Leidesdorf and Weigl) later sold all his Schubert manuscripts to Diabelli. Regarding Pennauer see A. Weinmann, *Wiener Musikverleger und Musikalienhändler von Mozarts Zeit bis gegen 1860*, Österreichische Akademie der Wissenschaften, Sitzungsberichte, 230. Band, 4. Abhandlung (Vienna, 1956).

38 Kreissle, translated by Coleridge (see note 3), reports in a note (I, 269) that: 'In the contract, in which Leidesdorf surrendered to Diabelli the right of publishing compositions, mention is made of a trio by Lachner and Schubert.' However, so far as is known there never was a trio composed jointly by Schubert and Lachner. We do not know whether this mention of Lachner is anything more than a simple error on Kreissle's part. Joseph Czerny, who also later sold Schubert manuscripts to Diabelli, cannot have been in possession of the B flat major Trio because he made a catalogue of those compositions by Schubert which he owned, and op. 99 is not listed. For valuable help in connection with the catalogues I would like to thank most cordially my colleagues Peter Riethus and Alexander Weinmann.

number 5847. Diabelli had also managed to acquire Thaddäus Weigl's Schubert manuscripts; so Weigl may possibly have been the original owner of the B flat major Trio too. In Aloys Fuchs's catalogue of Schubert's works, compiled in collaboration with Ferdinand Schubert in or about 1830, the Trio op. 99 is also listed as 'Premier grand Trio'.

In Nottebohm's thematic catalogue of Schubert's published works – the most careful and elaborate catalogue to appear prior to O. E. Deutsch's – we find an interesting 'Note' in connection with the listing of the B flat major Trio. The text reads in German:

Anmerkung: Wahrscheinlich im Jahr 1827 und jedenfalls früher componirt als das Trio Op. 100. Oeffentlich gespielt zum ersten Mal um Neujahr 1828 von Bocklet, Schuppanzigh und Linke in einer Quartett-Unterhaltung Schuppanzigh's.[39]

(Afterwards Nottebohm's 'Note' gives precise details of the publication of the trio by Diabelli.) As well as asserting that the trio was 'composed probably in the year 1827 and in any case earlier than the Trio op. 100', Nottebohm leaves no doubt that he felt sure that it was this Trio op. 99 which was performed 'around New Year's Day 1828' by Bocklet, Schuppanzigh and Linke in one of Schuppanzigh's quartet concerts.[40]

My conviction in the past that the Trio in B flat major can be dated with certainty as having been composed before December 1827 and probably before late November 1827 was based on conclusions drawn from the cited documents, especially those under (3), (8), (15) and (18) above. Nottebohm has always enjoyed the reputation of having been a most reliable scholar. But even if one does not trust his confirmatory statement that the Trio op. 99 was performed at the end of the year 1827 (= 'around New Year 1828'), one should reach the same conclusion independently: it must have been the 'Premier Grand Trio' which was on the programme on 26 December because – quite simply – there is no other way to explain the programmes of the two public concerts, each announcing the performance of a 'new' trio. It is more than improbable that Schubert would have announced an important composition in this way in his first (and only) private concert, in March 1828, and then have played a trio which had already been performed publicly in Vienna a few months earlier. We know from the biographies of other musicians, especially Mozart and Beethoven, that in Vienna it was a matter of honour for a composer, if he arranged a concert himself, to present at least one or two compositions which had never previously been performed in public. Mozart wrote to his father on 3 March 1784 that he 'necessarily had to

39 Gustav Nottebohm, *Thematisches Verzeichniss der im Druck erschienenen Werke von Franz Schubert* (Vienna, 1874), pp. 116f.

40 Wurzbach (*Biographisches Lexikon*, vol. 32, p. 61) also commented in his list of Schubert's works that the B flat Trio was publicly performed at New Year 1828 in Schuppanzigh's 'Quartettunterhaltung'.

compose something new', since he wanted to give additional subscription concerts. Beethoven's own concerts, too, always included at least one new work which had not previously been heard publicly in Vienna. There is no known instance of one of these composers announcing as 'new' a work of his which had been played before in a public concert. Since in March 1828 it was without doubt the E flat major Trio which was performed, it must necessarily have been the B flat major Trio which was in the programme on 26 December 1827 in Schuppanzigh's concert.

We do not know the source of Nottebohm's information; however, though he may have had knowledge of a personal recollection or another document for his 'Note' which is unknown to us, it may be that he too came to his conclusion as the result of considering the fact that Schubert would never have announced the E flat major Trio as 'new' in the March programme if it had already been publicly performed.

Another important reason for accepting a composition date of approximately October/November 1827 for the B flat major Trio lies in the fact that Schubert assigned two successive opus numbers to the trios; and he not only gave the B flat Trio the earlier number but apparently himself entitled it 'Premier Grand Trio'. His Viennese publishers, who obviously never had doubts that it was composed earlier than the Trio in E flat, automatically then numbered the latter in their lists 'Second Grand Trio'.

(19) The most recent research now provides convincing support for the documentary evidence cited above. Robert Winter's paper investigations confirm the correctness of Grove's dating and Nottebohm's 'Note' and help us to narrow the period in which the Trio op. 99 must have been composed: the autograph of the *Adagio* movement D 897, the so-called 'Notturno', is written on paper which, it can now be stated, was not available before late summer or early autumn 1827 (see Winter, p. 247 above). The watermarks also make it clear that Schubert used the same Welhartitz paper as he used for the draft and the fair copy of the E flat major Trio D 929.[41]

When the late Maurice Brown, who assumed that the B flat major Trio was composed in connection with the *Adagio* movement D 897, redated the B flat major Trio, he could not know that the *Adagio* was written on paper which was not for sale in Vienna until September 1827. However, any scholar who nowadays believes, as Brown did, that this *Adagio* is a rejected slow movement for the B flat major Trio should note that this opinion rules out the possibility that the trio as a whole was composed before September 1827; and, unless he wants to assume that the first movement of the autograph of the B flat

41 I am very much indebted to Dr Günter Brosche of the Österreichische Nationalbibliothek, to Dr Otto Biba of the Gesellschaft der Musikfreunde, Vienna, and to Mrs Ria Wilhelm of Bottmingen near Basel, for permission to investigate the watermarks of the rather poor-quality paper on which the *Adagio* D 897 and the autographs (draft and fair copy) of the E flat major Trio are written, and to Prof. Robert Winter for helping to identify them. Regarding Winter's dating of the paper, see pp. 247-9 above.

Trio was written on different paper and thus theoretically could have been composed earlier, he will have to accept 'October 1827' as composition date for the other movements of the B flat major Trio as well as for the *Adagio* D 897 (in consideration of the fact that Schubert returned from Graz as late as 25 September).

As stated above, we do not know when the finale of the E flat major Trio was finished. We may assume that Schubert – when agreeing with Schuppanzigh (late October? November?) on the performance of a trio in Schuppanzigh's concert on 26 December – was perhaps not yet able to show both trios in their completed state to the performers Bocklet, Schuppanzigh and Linke. In this case it is most understandable that the musicians decided to perform first the B flat major Trio, which was probably already finished. Whether or not the Trio op. 100 was also finished (December? January?) and rehearsed, it seems that its long finale did not meet with the unreserved approval of the performers: it may well have been their wish to perform this piece privately to a circle of friends first and to have it judged by them, probably hoping thereby to persuade Schubert to shorten it. The fact is that Schubert did decide to make cuts in the finale, as can be seen from his letter to Probst, quoted above under (13), and from a comparison of the autograph with the first edition which contains the shortened version. Through these cuts, extraordinarily beautiful sections were omitted, inter alia a unique polyphonic combination of the cello theme from the slow movement with the *l'istesso tempo* subject of the finale. This cut in particular must indeed have been a hard decision for the composer. Most probably it was done after a performance which convinced Schubert of the undue length of the movement, and he then agreed to shorten it. Even with its shortened finale the trio is still one of the longest chamber-music pieces by any great composer. And though it is certainly to the advantage of the work that Schubert deleted the repeat sign, some lovers of his music certainly regret the other two cuts of approximately 50 bars each.[42]

As is borne out by other contributions to Schubert research, documentary evidence is always a more reliable guide to the chronological position of a work than are more or less vague impressions based on style. All the stylistic arguments regarding the date of inception of the B flat major Trio have centred, in the past, on the question whether the style of the trios allows a judgement as to which of the two masterworks shows a greater maturity and reflects a more refined compositional technique. Certainly Schumann's opinion that this is hard to say and that both works are equally admirable masterpieces

42 Even Schubert's shortened version apparently seemed too long to some listeners: Leopold von Sonnleithner wrote in 1857 that he considered the trio too long and was of the opinion that further cuts enhanced its effectiveness, cuts 'which have been tried out in recent times'. See *Memoirs*, p. 115.

is still valid today. Perhaps one should add that the two trios – in spite of their different character – form a 'unity' at least to the same extent as the last three great piano sonatas do: they differ from each other, but not more than for instance the highly dramatic C minor Piano Sonata D 958 differs from the great rhapsodic Sonata in A major D 959 and the last lyrical Piano Sonata in B flat major D 960. The apparent individuality of these masterworks as well as of the two trios is a sign of maturity and an essential part of their greatness.

The chronology of Schubert's fragments and sketches *

REINHARD VAN HOORICKX

It is obvious that not all the fragments and sketches for Schubert's works have the same value. His Symphony in B minor and the fragment of *Lazarus*, for instance, are among his greatest masterworks. Other fragments and sketches are small and may seem unimportant. Yet these too may be of considerable value, because at some periods Schubert re-used half-empty pages for new sketches, and so it has happened that parts of the same composition have been found on different manuscripts. This certainly contradicts the old legend that Schubert never made any sketches for his works and hardly made any corrections.

Although many of Schubert's manuscripts are dated, there are quite a number which are not. Yet in most cases it is possible to suggest an approximate date on the basis of external elements, such as the kind of paper and watermarks and, above all, the writing.

As far as the songs are concerned, it is known that Schubert often composed several songs to poems by the same poet in the same period; this may help where an exact date is missing. So, for instance, it is almost certain that all the Claudius settings except D 530-533 date from November 1816; not only those which are dated, that is to say 'Bei dem Grabe meines Vaters' (D 496), 'An die Nachtigall' (D 497), 'Wiegenlied' (D 498: author unknown, but wrongly attributed by the sources to Claudius), 'Abendlied' (D 499), 'Phidile' (D 500), 'Zufriedenheit' (D 501), and 'Am Grabe Anselmos' (D 504), but also the undated ones: 'Am ersten Maimorgen' (D 344), 'Zufriedenheit' (D 362) and 'Klage um Ali Bey' (D 496A, formerly D 140); in fact this last one is dated November 1816 in the copy in the Witteczek Collection.

This essay is by no means the answer to all Schubert problems in connec-

* The following abbreviations are used in this article:
AGA = *Franz Schuberts Werke. Kritisch durchgesehene Gesammtausgabe* (Leipzig, 1884-97)
NGA = *Franz Schubert. Neue Ausgabe sämtlicher Werke* (Kassel etc., 1964-)
D1 = *Schubert. Thematic Catalogue of All His Works in Chronological Order*, by Otto Erich Deutsch (London, 1951)
D2 = *Franz Schubert. Thematisches Verzeichnis seiner Werke in chronologischer Folge*, ed. by the Editorial Board of the Neue Schubert-Ausgabe and Werner Aderhold (Kassel etc., 1978)

tion with dates. Almost every year new documents are discovered to remind Schubert scholars that their work is never finished.

Earliest works: 1809-10

It is well known that Schubert's earliest work which is completely preserved is a long Fantasia for pianoforte duet (D 1), carefully dated 8 April – 1 May 1810.

At the end of 1968 and the beginning of 1969 Christa Landon discovered at the Vienna Männergesang-Verein a small pile of autographs and early copies; a large number of the copies had formerly been in the possession of Kreissle, Schubert's first biographer.[1] Among the autographs were some sketches for piano duet (or rather incomplete fragments) which are apparently connected with the Fantasia in G (D 1), and we can therefore presume that they were preparatory exercises or first drafts, made shortly before the Fantasia was written, i.e. probably in March and early April 1810. They are described in Christa Landon's article 'New Schubert Finds' (see note 1) and are listed as follows:

A. Fantasia (?) in G major for pianoforte duet (D 1B: MS C.2): *Adagio* (36 bars) and *Allegro* (148 bars); another version of bars 48-78 is in another manuscript (MS C.1).

B. Sonata (sic) in F major for pianoforte duet (D 1C: MS C.1) 32 bars only.

Another leaf (MS A.4), most probably written about the same time, is the last page (right hand) of a piano duet. Mrs Landon believed this to be the conclusion of a fast movement, possibly connected with the previous fragments. It was, however, identified recently as the ending of a piano arrangement of Gluck's overture to *Iphigénie en Aulide*. It is not clear whether this piece is simply a piano reduction or a kind of fantasia; this last possibility is suggested by some alterations in the music, which otherwise follows the original score quite closely.

Probably much older than these piano-duet fragments are two unfinished sketches of songs which were found at the same time.

The first one is a song fragment (D 1A), apparently a long ballad (fourteen printed pages) starting in C minor, without title or words. It is published in the *NGA*, Series IV, vol. 6, pp. 157-70. Bars 245-303 have a theme which also appears in the next item. Hence it is presumed that both sketches are of the same period.

The second one is part of an already known fragment which (in the manuscript) has only the first words of a song. Its title is 'Lebenstraum' (D 39); the poem is by Gabriele von Baumberg. Until recently, neither the author nor the

1 Hereafter these manuscripts are cited by letter (MS A, etc.) as in Christa Landon's article 'New Schubert Finds', *Music Review*, XXXI (1970), pp. 215-31.

title of the poem was known; hence the song was quoted with the first words as they appear on the manuscript, and it was dated by Deutsch *c.* 1813, following a pencil note on the manuscript, but it is apparently much older: on account of its style and 'imperfectness' it should rather be dated 1809 or even earlier. It illustrates the saying by Spaun that Schubert was always short of music paper and that he therefore tried to economize by writing very closely, as can be seen also in the first part of the Fantasia in G for pianoforte duet (D 1). This fragment consists of three loose leaves: the first one, already known to Deutsch, is in the Bibliothèque Nationale, Paris (MS 281), bars 1-140; the second leaf, in a private collection in the United States, was identified by Maurice J. E. Brown: it contains bars 141-231.[2] The third and probably final leaf was found among the manuscripts of the Vienna Männergesang-Verein (MS A.3). The first two leaves are printed in the *NGA*, Series IV, vol. 6, pp. 171-9, with the title as given in *D1*, i.e. 'Ich sass an einer Tempelhalle'. The last page is printed in the *Quellen und Lesarten* of vol. 6, Ex. 26 on p. 31.

When Schubert wrote his Fantasia in G major (D 1) he originally intended to end it with a fugue. Part of that original version still exists and is now in the Pierpont Morgan Library in New York (formerly owned by Dr Alwin Cranz of Vienna). The last (left-hand) page contains, besides 28 bars of the finale which are only slightly different from the final version, 65 bars of a fugue in C major. As the fragment breaks off at the end of the page, it is not certain whether or not Schubert completed this fugue; if he did, the remainder was probably destroyed after he had made the final version of his finale. This fugue in C major has now been published in a completion by the present writer in his article 'Counterpoint and Fugue in Schubert's Piano Music', *Piano Quarterly* (Wilmington, Vermont), XXVII (Spring 1979), pp. 48-9.

The fragment of a String Quartet in G major (D 2) is most probably not by Schubert but by Albert Stadler, his friend at the Vienna Stadtkonvikt.[3]

A Sonatina fragment (D Anh.I,11) is preserved at the Deutsche Staatsbibliothek (East Berlin) and is listed there as Mus. MS Autograph Fr. Schubert, Nr. 47. It is written in a childish hand and the writing (especially of the violin clef) does not resemble any of Schubert's later autographs. It is therefore doubtful whether it is an authentic Schubert autograph, but if it was written by the young Schubert, it must be one of his earliest compositions. In the catalogue of manuscripts in the Archiv für Photogramme musikalischer Meisterhandschriften, Widmung Anthony van Hoboken (Nationalbibliothek, Vienna), it is listed as 'Zwei Klavierstücke' among the doubtful works (PhA 1154, p. 405, no. 2506).

2 See M. J. E. Brown, 'Schubert: Discoveries of the Last Decade', *Musical Quarterly*, XLVII (1961), pp. 296-7.

3 See R. Van Hoorickx, 'Old and New Schubert Problems', *Music Review*, XXXV (1974), pp. 76-8.

1811

Several minuets were found among the autographs discovered at the Vienna Männergesang-Verein: three of them were written for wind instruments, and three others were only sketched in a piano score but most probably were intended to be arranged for wind instruments (MS D). The first two minuets were already known in a piano version (D 995). The last one in the set, in B♭, was left incomplete in the manuscript; fortunately, the same music appears in another manuscript (MS E) where the incomplete trio is written out, but with the title 'Menuet'. All these minuets were published in 1970 (the last three in an arrangement for wind instruments by Alexander Weinmann) by Bärenreiter, Kassel, nos. 19.109 and 19.110, with a foreword by Christa Landon. Some sketches for the Overture in C minor (D 8), which on the fair copy is dated 29 June 1811, indicate that they were written during the early summer of 1811.

Two unfinished sketches for the song 'Der Geistertanz' (D 15 and 15A) were probably made in 1811. Their experimental character even suggests that they might be older than Schubert's earliest preserved songs, 'Hagars Klage' (D 5) and 'Leichenfantasie' (D 7). The text must have appealed to the young Schubert, for he used it again in two more settings, one for a single voice (D 116) and one for male chorus (D 494).

Three unpublished fragments of instrumental compositions were acquired by Otto Taussig around 1950 (D 2A, 2B, and 2C: formerly D 996, 997, and 998). They were probably composed in the autumn of 1811. After composing some string quartets and smaller compositions for wind instruments during the summer, Schubert now tried his hand at larger compositions for full orchestra, probably at the time when he was occasionally directing the school orchestra: D 2A, 2B, 4, and 12. The first two remained fragments.

A. Ouvertura (sic) in D major (D 2A). A fragment of thirteen pages: *Adagio* (27 bars) and *Allegro* (35 bars) with many corrections; on p. 14 in the MS (a left-hand page) Schubert had already marked the instruments and written down the first note of each part. He then cancelled these notes and started to write the following fragment.

B. Sinfonie (sic) in D major (D 2B) for the same instruments, with only three trombones (the former item included two violas and four trombones!). Only five pages survive: an *Adagio* of 11 bars, and 19 bars of an *Allegro con moto*. At this point the score breaks off and it is most probable that at least part of the score was lost. As Maurice J. E. Brown puts it, 'The instrumentation is that of the beginner, being overladen and ornate, and the whole orchestra is kept going for long passages at full strength.'[4]

C. Fragment of a String Quartet in F major (?) (D 2C). Autumn 1811 (?).

4 Brown, 'Recent Schubert Discoveries', *Music and Letters*, XXXII (1951), p. 354.

This is a single leaf from which the beginning is missing; it is in 4/4 time with one flat: it could therefore be in either F major or D minor (most of it is in the minor). The first page contains 20 bars, the second page only 15 and remains unfinished. As the writing and the paper are the same as in former manuscripts, it is presumed that this fragment is of the same period.

1812

The fragment of an opera *Der Spiegelritter* (Kotzebue; D 11) may have been written in the spring of 1812; it is Schubert's earliest known work for the stage. It not only remained unfinished, but there are also certain parts missing.

A. The ensemble no. 2 is called unfinished in the printed score, but it seems to me more likely that part of it has been lost. In fact, the next item is also incomplete.

B. 'Arie des Königs' is the title of this unpublished fragment which comes in the score before no. 3. It was not printed with the rest because two leaves (four pages) are missing right in the middle of the aria.

The autograph, described in *D1* as 'Fragment of an orchestral score in D' (D 966), was sold in June 1972 and it could be identified as the last one of the missing leaves. Moreover, it is practically certain that the two 'Sketches of an opera' mentioned in *D1* in the note under D 982 are identical with the lost leaves from the 'Arie des Königs'.[5]

Three fragments, probably dating from the summer of 1812, were among the Männergesang-Verein manuscripts; they are:

A. Fugue in F major for two voices (MS G), only one page (D 24D).

B. The ending (eight bars) of a vocal trio in D major (without text).

C. Fragment of a Mass in F major (?), i.e. the ending of the Gloria and the beginning of the Credo, sixteen pages, probably from a complete Mass (D 24E: MS L). The fugue at the end of the Gloria is based on another fugue, discovered on the same occasion (D 24A: MS H).

It was already mentioned in a note in *D1* (p. 566) that 'recent identifications by Mr. Maurice J. E. Brown have made it necessary to add notes to nos. 3, 29 and 32, combining these numbers'. Maurice Brown had discovered that the fragments of D 3 belong to the String Quartet in C (D 32) and that they therefore date from the end of September or the beginning of October 1812. However, the first fragment, an *Andante* in C major, which at first sight seems to be a transcription of the Klavierstück in C (D 29) of 9 September, must be of an older date: according to Dr Walther Dürr, corrections in the MS and the type of composition clearly show that the piano piece was written after the string-quartet version, and not vice versa. That first fragment is incomplete,

5 Van Hoorickx, 'A Schubert Manuscript Identified', *Musical Times*, CXV (February 1974), p. 127.

but it is most probable that Schubert did finish it and that the second page of the manuscript was destroyed; this is suggested by the fact that this fragment too was crossed out by Schubert. The beginning is reminiscent of Mozart's overture to *Le nozze di Figaro*, and Schubert re-used it again (in F major) when he sketched a second movement for his String Quartet in B flat (D 36) in November 1812; no fewer than three different sketches were made before he composed the final slow movement to this quartet:

(*a*) *Adagio molto* in B♭, 4/4 time, 5 bars;
(*b*) *Adagio* in F, 2/4 time, 3 bars (the *Figaro* motive);
(*c*) *Adagio* in F, 3/4 time, 14 bars.

All these sketches were printed in the *Revisionsbericht* of the *AGA*, Series V, pp. 64-6, and are quite interesting.

In the manuscript which contains the fifth setting of the 'Aria di Abramo' (D 33) a short but complete melody without text and without accompaniment was written in pencil in the bass clef, apparently for a low voice, probably in October 1812. It is not mentioned in *D1* and was first published in A. Orel's book *Der junge Schubert*.[6]

The second version of the vocal quartet 'Te solo adoro' (D 34) is incomplete in the manuscript; it is quite different in detail from the first version, and it is most probable that it was continued on another leaf which is now lost. The first edition in Orel's book gives a combination of the second version with the ending of the first one, which was certainly faulty, as Schubert had made a mistake in putting the wrong accent on the last word, 'infini*ta*'. This could easily be corrected by changing the words from 'mente infinita' to 'fonte di verità' as in the second verse (this was probably done in the second version). The first version is dated 5 November 1812; the second version is not dated but was probably written shortly afterwards.

The manuscript containing a fragment of a pianoforte piece in C major, *Allegro moderato* (D 347) and three different sketches for a four-part fugue in B♭ major (D 37A, formerly D 967) may have been written at the end of 1812 or the beginning of 1813; this is suggested by the writing and the style of the fugues which are much more elaborate than the fugue-exercises of summer 1812. None of the three fugues is complete.

The autograph D 71C (formerly D 966A) contains a substantial fragment of an orchestral score, probably of an early Overture in D major. The manuscript is incomplete and consists in fact of two fragments:

(*a*) a single leaf (15 bars) which has been identified as an orchestral version of bars 209-23 from the first movement of the String Quartet in D major (D 74) dated August 1813;

(*b*) four bifolia and a single leaf, foliated 7-15 (151 bars). It is clear that both the beginning and the ending of this work are missing and that at least one leaf is lost in between (*a*) and (*b*) – if that is the right order. According to Dr

6 (Vienna, 1940), p. 8 of the musical supplement.

Walther Dürr, the corrections show that it was written after D 74, around the time when Schubert was writing his Symphony in D major (D 82).

The manuscript containing two different sketches for a concert aria 'Serbate, o dei custodi' (D 35) was destroyed during the war in 1945. It was dated 10 December 1812 (not, as in *D1*, 'October 1812'); both versions are described in Orel's book *Der junge Schubert*, which also contains his arrangement for voice and piano of the final version.

1813

According to his brother Ferdinand, Schubert in 1813 wrote a set of thirty Minuets for pianoforte (D 41) for his brother Ignaz. However, the extant manuscript at the Vienna Stadtbibliothek (MH 154), consisting of thirteen loose leaves, is incomplete and in my opinion is only a first draft; there are many corrections, and some half-empty pages were later used for sketches of other works: D 348, 349, 459A, and 516.

The ninth leaf contains the minuet no. 20 (this is no. 17 in *D1* and the *AGA*), and on the other side it has the sketch of a fugue in E minor: 14 bars, one in ink, the others in pencil. Ferdinand Schubert wrote on the same page (partly on top of the fugue) a piano arrangement of Schubert's 'Wiegenlied' (D 498).

The tenth leaf contains, besides the minuet no. 21 (no. 18 in *D1*), the ending of a piano piece in E major (eight bars, slightly different from the final version), i.e. the fifth of the Fünf Klavierstücke (D 459), as well as the beginning of the incomplete *Adagio* in C major (D 349) bars 1-31. In *D2* the first two movements of D 459 are called 'Sonata'; the other three movements are named 'Drei Klavierstücke' (D 459A). This suggests that the *Adagio* (D 349) was written shortly after the third of the Klavierstücke (D 459A), possibly in August 1816. It was continued on another leaf which was apparently added later and did not belong among the leaves with the set of minuets; this second leaf contains on the other side a first sketch of the song 'Sehnsucht' (D 516) which is also printed in the *Revisionsbericht* as well as in the *NGA*, Series IV, vol. 1, p. 290. A third leaf with the rest of the *Adagio* is probably lost.

The *Andantino* in C major (D 348), most probably written around the same time, i.e. August 1816, is partly written on the other side of the thirteenth leaf (bars 1-42) and partly on the twelfth leaf (bars 43-71). This piano piece, which is published as a fragment, is in my opinion not really unfinished. The last five bars are practically identical with the first five bars, and in Schubert's mind this probably meant a *da capo*. In this way, the piece can easily be played without any alteration, ending (after a *da capo*) with bar 29.

I have a feeling that this *Adagio* and *Andantino* were originally alternatives (or first drafts) for the slow movement of the Sonata in E major, generally known as Fünf Klavierstücke. In that sonata, the slow movement is in C major, typically Schubertian with its shift a major third below the tonic. When writing his fair copy, Schubert may have eliminated these first drafts, not being able to decide whether he would leave out the first or the second scherzo. Since the major part of the Fünf Klavierstücke does not exist (or is unknown) in manuscript, we cannot know whether Schubert intended to keep those five movements or whether this was the idea of the publisher (C. A. Klemm, Leipzig, October 1843).

An interesting fragment of a short cantata is the 'Dithyrambe' (Schiller) for solo – or soli? – and mixed chorus (D 47), which was left unfinished and is in part only sketched. Between the two extant fragments a certain part is missing, possibly only one leaf (the end of the first stanza). The fragment ends with a sketch of a mixed chorus on the last two lines of the second stanza. In the first part, the solo is marked 'Tenore' and the melody is written in the tenor clef; in the second part it is written in the bass clef without indication of the soloist. Both solo parts could be sung by a good baritone. It is a very lively piece, and the final chorus especially is very promising. It is dated 29 March 1813 at the beginning, and if Schubert had completed this work it would certainly have been one of his best vocal compositions of the period. There are 172 bars altogether, 88 in the first part and 84 in the second part.

The next work in the thematic catalogue is the Fantasia in C minor for pianoforte duet (D 48) of April 1813. In its first version it has also a couple of fragments and sketches which, so far, remain unpublished. There is no doubt that the Vienna manuscript is the first and only complete version of this work (MH 153).[7] On p. 4 some corrections were made on a separate piece of paper; this was not pasted on top of the page, as is often done in Schubert's manuscripts, but just inserted, so that one can see what is written on the other side. This shows a small fragment of an instrumental composition in Schubert's hand (but not necessarily his own composition!) probably for violin, viola and guitar. It has not been identified so far and it is reproduced in facsimile in my article (see note 7). On p. 15 and the following pages, there is a substantial fragment of a fugue in B♭ major (73 bars) which breaks off at the end of a page; this is still unpublished. Together with so many other exercises and attempts, it certainly shows that Schubert tried very seriously to master this form of composition and struggled with it – so to speak – throughout his career.[8] The fugue at the end of the fantasia, also in B♭, is based on the opening theme of the String Quartet in C (D 46), composed shortly before. The same theme had already appeared in another fragment of a fugue

7 See also my article 'Old and New Schubert Problems', pp. 77-80.

8 It would be interesting to make an extensive study of this subject. From his very first complete composition (D 1) up to his last ones, which were probably the fugal exercises for Simon Sechter (including the theme of D 952), he used this form many times in all kinds of compositions, vocal as well as instrumental.

(only 18 bars) which was, according to Dr Dürr, probably written in the summer of 1812 (D 24D). It is a C major *Maestoso* in 3/4 time, and it is written in a manuscript with the rough draft of 'Der Strom' (D 565) but is apparently much earlier.[9] This fragment was published in facsimile in the catalogue *Franz Schubert. Ausstellung der Wiener Stadt- und Landesbibliothek zum 150. Todestag des Komponisten* (Vienna, 1978), p. 25; and, with an additional three bars written by the present author, in *Piano Quarterly*, XXVII (Spring 1979), p. 52.

Among the many vocal works for three voices of this period we also find some fragments and sketches.

The trio 'Thronend auf erhabnem Sitz' (D 62), on a text by Schiller, was published only as a fragment in the *AGA*, and it was so described in *D1*. It is no longer a fragment: the second half was found by Fritz Racek in another manuscript and the whole composition[10] is now printed in the *NGA*, Series III, vol. 4, p. 22.

'Schmerz verzerret ihr Gesicht' (D 65) so far remains a fragment; this is certainly not a great loss, since we have Schubert's complete setting of the poem in his song 'Gruppe aus dem Tartarus' (D 583), which could hardly be surpassed. This first setting is only 19½ bars long, in a kind of fugal style.

Another poem by Schiller, 'Dreifach ist der Schritt der Zeit', was, as has recently become clear, set by Schubert three times on the same day! It seems that the fragment with a different title, 'Ewig still steht die Vergangenheit' (D 70), came first; this is in fact the ending (last 17 bars) of an 'Imitatio' or canon in the style of Haydn. Then comes D 69 and finally D 43 (the autograph is also dated 8 July 1813), which is quite elaborate and must be difficult to perform. The recently discovered opening of D 70 has already been listed in three sale catalogues, in New York, Marburg and Tutzing. The manuscript is now in a private collection in Vienna.

The empty space in the manuscript of the trio 'Die zwei Tugendwege' (D 71) was used by Schubert for some short sketches:

(1) Canon *a tre*: 'Alleluia' (D 71A), published in Racek's article (see note 9); this sketch is complete (six bars).

(2) Fugue in E minor (D 71B), a sketch of 12 bars. The same fugue, dated 'July 1813', was recently found in the manuscript which contains the autograph of 'Iphigenia' (D 573) where it has 20 bars, but both remained unfinished.

(3) Some pencil sketches are not very clear but might be for a minuet in C major and a trio. The trio is very reminiscent of a passage in Haydn's chorus 'Endless God' in *The Seasons*.

The next item in the catalogue is again a fragment, which however was

9 See Fritz Racek, 'Von den Schubert-Handschriften der Stadtbibliothek', *Wiener Schriften*, IV (1956), p. 107, where the incipit is given.

10 First published by Racek, article cited in note 9 above.

complete at one time. It is an octet (D 72) for wind instruments ('Harmonie-Oktett'), probably composed between 15 July and 18 August 1813. The beginning of the first movement as well as the whole of the second movement are missing. The second theme of the first movement already appeared in Schubert's Overture for orchestra in D major (D 26), written more than a year earlier.

In the autumn of 1812 Schubert had done several exercises on Italian texts by Metastasio, mainly for several voices (D 17, 33, 34, and 35). In September 1813 we again find some settings of Italian texts, this time as solo songs. Two of them are dated: 'Pensa, che questo istante' (D 76), 7 and 13 September 1813, and 'Son fra l'onde' (D 78), 18 September 1813. It is therefore probable that the settings of 'Misero pargoletto' (D 42) are also of the same period, possibly the beginning of September 1813. There are three different settings but only one is complete. According to Dr Dürr, there is no doubt that the unfinished settings were sketched first: the first setting has the complete melody (57 bars) but no accompaniment, whereas the second setting has the complete melody and some indications for the accompaniment (90 bars). Both are printed in the *NGA*, Series IV, vol. 6, pp. 180-3.

The fragment of an offertory 'Clamavi ad Te, Domine' (D 85) is not by Schubert. It is the beginning of a copy of an offertorium by Preindl, op. 16. This was discovered by Dr Karl Pfannhauser of Vienna.[11]

Among the manuscripts discovered at the Vienna Männergesang-Verein in 1968-9 are two fragments of compositions which had probably served in Schubert's family and were possibly made for name-days or birthdays in the family circle. One side of MS N seems to be part of a composition for voices and strings, of which only 32 bars of the second violin and cello parts are preserved, dated November 1813 (D 87A). The other side contains 30 bars of an accompaniment marked 'Allegretto' in A major, 6/8, of a similar work, presumably vocal solo with chorus (four-part canon), 'Drum Schwester und Brüder' (D Anh.I,25), dated October 1819, probably for his father's name-day (4 October).

NB: The String Quartet in B flat (D 68) of June and August 1813 has only two movements: the opening *Allegro* and the finale. Two other movements are most probably lost, but since the extant movements are complete the quartet is not counted as a fragment.

1814

The Guitar Quartet (D 96 = D Anh.II,2), an arrangement by Schubert of Wenzel Matiegka's Notturno op. 21 (originally for flute, viola and guitar),

11 See Pfannhauser, 'Kleine Köcheliana' in *Mitteilungen der Internationalen Stiftung Mozarteum*, XII (Salzburg, 1964), pp. 24-38, especially p. 35.

also remains a fragment: it breaks off in the middle of one of the variations. Schubert started to write it on 26 February 1814, probably for a special occasion. The comment in *D1* that Schubert (besides a second trio to the minuet) 'merely added a violoncello part' is not exact. Schubert rearranged the work and also added a new variation specially for the cello; he may have added other (new) variations, but if so these are lost.[12]

The String Quartet in C minor (D 103) was started on 23 April 1814. According to Alfred Orel, who arranged and completed the fragment for the first edition (Philharmonia, no. 350), this quartet may have been complete but is partly lost.

When writing his String Quartet in B flat (D 112) in September 1814, Schubert started to write a version for trio, which was abandoned after ten lines. This trio version, which seems to be quite different in detail, is lost (D 111A). The first 11 bars of it are reproduced in August Reissmann's book *Schubert. Sein Leben und seine Werke* (Berlin, 1873), pp. 67-8.

1815

According to *D1* and the *Revisionsbericht* of the *AGA*, the incomplete sonata movement in E major (D 154) dated 11 February 1815 is 'one of several sketches'. If this is correct, then the other sketches must be lost, for only this one is still extant.

The fragment 'Der Morgenstern' (D 172) is only one line (five bars) of the melody and the accompaniment of a song. It is dated 12 March 1815. Schubert cancelled this fragment and started to write the 'Trinklied vor der Schlacht' (D 169). If we compare this fragment with other sketches of Schubert's songs, it is obvious that this is the beginning of a fair copy, probably based on a sketch which is now lost. The right chronological order of the compositions D 168-172 is as follows:

'Begräbnislied' (D 168) 9 March 1815

'Osterlied' (D 168A) 9 March 1815 (The manuscript of this chorus, found only fairly recently in Scotland, shows the same date as D 168 with which it is apparently connected.)

'Der Morgenstern' (D 172) 12 March 1815 (Schubert probably first wrote a sketch of this song, which is now lost. Only the beginning of a fair copy, subsequently cancelled, is extant.)

'Trinklied vor der Schlacht' (D 169) 12 March 1815

'Schwertlied' (D 170) 12 March 1815

'Gebet während der Schlacht' (D 171) 12 March 1815 (The extant manuscript is slightly different from the printed version. It may be that Diabelli made

12 See my article 'Schubert's Guitar Quartet', *Revue Belge de Musicologie*, XXXI (1977), pp. 111-35.

some alterations, but it is also possible that another autograph was used for the first edition.)

'Liebesrausch' (D 164), the first setting of a song which Schubert composed again a few days later, is partly lost; only the last six bars are extant in the manuscript with the first setting of 'Das war ich' (D 174), which is dated 26 March; the fragment was therefore probably composed on the same day or shortly before.

The unfinished *Adagio* in G major for pianoforte (D 178b), which is written in the manuscript of another *Adagio* (D 178), may have been intended as a slow movement for a sonata. Although it is incomplete in the manuscript, it could easily be played without adding anything, simply by repeating the beginning (bars 3-24) at the end. It is clearly an alternative for or a second version of D 178 and was most probably composed right after it on 8 April 1815.

'Auf den Tod einer Nachtigall' (D 201) was also composed twice by Schubert. However, the first setting (25 May 1815) remained unfinished. The autograph seems to be lost, but a copy made by Ferdinand Schubert was found at the Gesellschaft der Musikfreunde in Vienna. It is in F♯ minor (not A major) and it was published in facsimile, together with a completion of the fragment by the present writer, in the *Revue Belge de Musicologie*, XXIV (1970), pp. 92-5. The melody is almost complete (only one bar short) and the accompaniment is not much shorter, so that it was quite easy to complete this attractive little song for practical use.

In the manuscript which contains the 'Jägerlied' (D 204), the lower half of a large oblong folio (26 May 1815), Schubert wrote the text of four stanzas from a poem by Hölty, 'Das Traumbild' (D 204A in *D2*). Although this could hardly be called a fragment, it seems likely that Schubert had set this poem – either as a duet or as a song – on the other half of the leaf, which is now lost, possibly also on 26 May 1815. It is called 'Lied' in *D2*.

The first setting of 'Die Nonne' (D 208), dated 29 May 1815, is partly unpublished. The greater part of this fragment is in the Vienna Stadtbibliothek and was published in the *Revisionsbericht* of the *AGA*. But the last leaf is in the Vienna Nationalbibliothek and was unknown to the *AGA* editors; it shows that Schubert did not finish this first setting. The empty space on the second page was later used for a first draft of the song 'Zum Punsche' (D 492). The unpublished fragment contains bars 112-58.

The first sketch for the setting of Schiller's poem 'Die Schlacht' is still unpublished (D 249); the manuscript is owned by Adolf Ibach, formerly of Vienna, now of Schwelm in Westphalia. A note under op. 27 no. 1 in Nottebohm's thematic catalogue[13] suggests that both settings used the first part of the *Marche héroique* as a piano introduction. According to Dr Dürr, this is

13 Gustav Nottebohm, *Thematisches Verzeichniss der im Druck erschienenen Werke von Franz Schubert* (Vienna, 1874).

correct. The second sketch is quite long (522 bars), and either the melody or indications for the accompaniment are written down for the entire work. It is dated March 1816 (D 387), and Schubert probably put it aside to compose other songs on texts by Schiller which were much more inspiring: 'Der Flüchtling' (D 402), 'Laura am Klavier' (D 388), a third setting of 'Des Mädchens Klage' (D 389), 'Die Entzückung an Laura' (D 390), 'Die vier Weltalter' (D 391), and 'Gruppe aus dem Tartarus' (D 396; see p. 310 below). The first setting of Schiller in March 1816 was probably 'Ritter Toggenburg' (D 397) which is precisely dated 13 March 1816.

The manuscript of the vocal trio 'Punschlied' (D 277) contains also a short sketch for quartet, published in the *Revue Belge de Musicologie*, XXX (1976), p. 151.

The unfinished *Allegretto* in C major (D 346) may well be the final movement of the Sonata in C major (D 279) of September 1815. Although there is no definite proof for it, Maurice J. E. Brown states: 'The paper on which this Allegretto is written is similar to that containing the Andante of the sonata [D 279] (same watermark, dimensions, etc.) and the handwriting of each suggests the same pen and ink.'[14] It seems that Schubert started to write another final movement, the Rondo in C major, dated 16 October 1815, which is mentioned in a note to D 310 in *D1*. However, the manuscript of this fragment is in private possession and its present whereabouts are unknown.

Although the sketch for a song 'An den Mond' (D 311) is not dated, it is almost certain that it was started on 19 October 1815, after Schubert had already written eight other songs that same day. The fragment, 12 bars of the melody, is on the other side of the last page of 'Luisens Antwort' (D 319) and normally it should therefore come after it, but Deutsch's way of citing works with uncertain date did not allow this. This song-fragment was published in facsimile and with a completion by the present author in Brussels in 1958.

The first setting of 'Lorma' (D 327) of November 1815 remains a fragment. The first part of it was privately published in a facsimile edition, but Maurice J. E. Brown discovered a further six bars of this song in a manuscript which contains part of the unfinished Sonata in F sharp minor (D 570/571).[15]

'Die drei Sänger' (D 329) of 23 December 1815 may have been a complete work, as is suggested in the *AGA*. The author of the poem was unknown until recently; Dietrich Berke of Kassel has identified him as Johann Friedrich Ludwig Bobrik, who was born in 1781 and died, almost 103 years old, in 1884.[16] The remaining fragment is 119 bars long; it is a quite pleasant song, though by no means to be compared to 'Der Erlkönig' (D 328), which was

14 Brown, 'Towards an Edition of the Pianoforte Sonatas' in *Essays on Schubert* (London, 1966), p. 201.
15 Brown, *Schubert. A Critical Biography* (London, 1958), p. 66.
16 The complete text is reproduced in Maximilian Schochow and Lilly Schochow, *Franz Schubert. Die Texte seiner einstimmig komponierten Lieder und ihre Dichter*, 2 vols. (Hildesheim and New York, 1974), vol. 1, pp. 43-4.

composed shortly before it.

The three settings of 'Das Grab' (D 330, 377 and 569) which were published in the *AGA* among the Lieder in Series XX (nos. 182, 186 and 323) are all indicated as 'Chorus' in the manuscripts or the early copies. *D1* states (under D 330) that 'the cancelled beginning of an earlier setting for mixed chorus' is written on the other side of the manuscript. (This second setting is numbered D 329A in *D2*.) However, from recent research it is clear that this cancelled fragment (13 bars) is not an earlier setting, but was most probably written right after the first setting: the same pen and ink were used. Schubert made another setting for mixed chorus (D 643A), which was discovered by Ignaz Weinmann and published by his brother Alexander Weinmann (L. Doblinger, VN 14229, Vienna, 1972).

1816

The Ländler D 354, 355 and 370 are in one manuscript of four pages (two loose leaves) in the Vienna Stadtbibliothek, MH.159, dated January 1816. The chronological order is:
(*a*) Nine Ländler in D major (D 370), treble part only. It is not clear whether they are first drafts for piano (one of them, the seventh, appears later in a version for piano as D 378/6), or were meant for violin solo; this last possibility is suggested by other Ländler which were written shortly afterwards, D 374. *D1* includes only eight Ländler under D 370, placing one (the seventh of the original nine) in the set D 378.
(*b*) Four 'Komische Ländler' (D 354) marked '1°' and '2°', meant for two violins. After these Ländler appears a sketch for an instrumental composition, but this is not in Schubert's own hand.
(*c*) Eight Ländler in F sharp minor (D 355), treble part only, with very beautiful melody, possibly for violin solo (?).

A Minuet in C major written (but left unfinished) on 22 February 1816 is not mentioned in *D1*; it is in the same manuscript with two Minuets D 380. It was first published in facsimile by F. Racek;[17] a version completed by the present writer appeared in the *Revue Belge de Musicologie*, xxv (1971), p. 79. Schubert wrote only the minuet and eight bars of a trio.

The first setting of 'Gruppe aus dem Tartarus' (D 396) may have been complete but the second leaf is missing. The extant fragment is on the other side of the Sonata for Violin and Piano (D 384), i.e. the last few bars of the final movement. It is printed in the *NGA*, Series IV, vol. 2, pp. 271-2.

The small fragment of the 'Romanze' (D 144), which is crossed out in the manuscript, is clearly dated April 1816 and is in the same autograph as 'Daphne am Bach' (D 411); they should therefore be adjacent in the thematic catalogue.

The incomplete song 'Lied in der Abwesenheit' (D 416) of April 1816 should probably come right after 'Stimme der Liebe' (D 412); this is suggested by the fact that both songs remained in the Schubert family until they were bought by Anton Dermota about twenty-five years ago.

From the printed version, it is not clear whether or not the opera fragment *Die Bürgschaft* (D 435) remained unfinished, but in the manuscript the last number (no. 16) is orchestrated only until bar 66; this shows that Schubert broke off the composition of this stage work, which contains many fine musical pages. It was started on 2 May 1816 and Schubert probably worked on it during the whole month; besides this substantial work, he wrote only some dances, the first version of his male-voice quartet 'Naturgenuss' (D 422) and a few short songs and trios.

According to a letter by Albert Stadler, Schubert wrote at the Konvikt 'a few little songs, canons, minuets and the like'.[18] In his memoirs, Stadler wrote that Schubert composed them while his friends were absent and he was waiting for them. He further writes: 'When we returned from church there was usually something finished and this he gladly let me have.'[19] He then cites some of these compositions: 'Widerschein' [*recte* 'Widerhall'] (D 428), 'Am Seegestad' (D 424) and 'Andenken' (D 423) of May 1816. Similar compositions of which only one part (either second tenor or bass) is preserved may well be of the same period:

(1) 'Sylphen' (Matthisson) D Anh.I,22 (formerly D 341)
(2) 'Lebenslied' (Matthisson) D Anh.I,23 (formerly D 425)
(3) 'Badelied' (Matthisson) D Anh.I,21 (formerly D 340)
(4) 'Amors Macht' (Matthisson) D Anh.I,20 (formerly D 339)
(5) 'Lied beim Rundetanz' (Salis) D Anh.I,18 (formerly D 132)
(6) 'Lied im Freien' (Salis) D Anh.I,19 (formerly D 133)

They appear in this order in the manuscript. They are all printed in the *NGA*, Series III, vol. 4, pp. 177-9, still numbered D 132 (number 5 above), 133 (6), 339 (4), 340 (3), 341 (1) and 425 (2) as in *D1*. In his foreword (p. xix), Dietrich Berke remarks that it is not certain whether these vocal pieces were composed by Schubert and it is equally uncertain whether they are vocal trios or quartets; they are therefore listed in the appendix (Anhang I) of *D2*.

'An Chloen' (D 363) is most probably of June 1816, as are all the other settings of poems by Peter Uz of which the date is known. According to Dietrich Fischer-Dieskau,[20] this is probably the best setting among the Uz poems. The beginning (first line) is missing in the manuscript, and attempts have been made to complete this fragment – by, among others, Kapellmeister Reinhold (1928) and the present writer (privately printed, 1972).[21]

17 'Von den Schubert-Handschriften der Stadtbibliothek', cited in note 9 above.

18 *Schubert. Memoirs by His Friends*, collected and ed. by Otto Erich Deutsch, transl. Rosamond Ley and John Nowell (London, 1958), p. 214.

19 Ibid., p. 147.

20 Fischer-Dieskau, *Schubert. A Biographical Study of His Songs* (London, 1971), p. 72.

The beginning of a second setting (only one line of the melody) of 'Das war ich' (D 174A) is apparently of June 1816. Schubert started to write it immediately after the 'Fragment aus dem Aeschylus' (D 450); he then probably realized that he had already set the poem during the previous year and cancelled the fragment.

The fragment of a Requiem in C minor (not, as in *D1*, in E♭ major) (D 453) was composed in July, probably right after the Mass in C major (D 452): the date is mentioned in Kreissle's list,[22] which means that the autograph was still complete in 1865. At that time it was in the possession of Johannes Brahms. The first leaf with the beginning has disappeared since, and it is strange that the first leaf of the Mass in C major also became separated from the rest of the manuscript and was lost for some time: the top of the page had been cut and the date looked like June 1810 (see *D1*, note on p. 203). This manuscript is now complete again and is, together with the other Wittgenstein family autographs, in the Library of Congress, Washington, D.C.

'Pflicht und Liebe' (D 467) is dated August 1816. As it is in the same manuscript as the first sketch of the song 'An die untergehende Sonne' (D 457), dated July 1816, we can presume that it was written at the beginning of the month.

The two fragments for pianoforte, an *Adagio* in C major (D 349) and an *Andantino* in C major (D 348), were most probably composed in August 1816. See under the set of Minuets (D 41) of 1813 (pp. 303-4 above).

Schubert composed a number of songs on poems by Goethe in September 1816. Some of these have been partly lost or were left unfinished by Schubert. The right chronological order is not certain but may be:

(*a*) 'Gesang der Geister über den Wassern' (D 484). Of this setting the beginning is missing (probably two pages), and it was left unfinished; it seems that it comes after 'Rückweg' (D 476).

(*b*) 'Mignon': 'So lasst mich scheinen' (D 469), probably composed after the second setting of 'Harfenspieler III' (D 478/2). There seem to be fragments of two different settings, the second of which may have been complete and is now partly lost. Both were printed in the *Revisionsbericht* of the *AGA*, respectively 7 and 11 bars (Series XX, pp. 86-7).

Maurice J. E. Brown discovered that the string-quartet fragment in B flat (D 601) is in fact part of a version for strings of the Overture in B flat (D 470) of September 1816, bars 87-118 of the *Allegro* movement. According to Dr Dürr, the writing and paper suggest that this version was written after the orchestral version, perhaps to be played in Schubert's family circle.

The String Trio in B flat (D 471) of September 1816 has an interesting second movement of 38½ bars, but it was left unfinished by Schubert. It is practically unknown, because it was printed only in the *Revisionsbericht* of

22 Heinrich Kreissle von Hellborn, *Franz Schubert* (Vienna, 1865), p. 618.

the *AGA*. The addition of two or three bars makes it possible to perform this attractive fragment. It was publicly performed for the first time (in a completion by the present writer) at the Palais Palffy in Vienna on 16 December 1966 by the Philharmonia Trio and has been played many times since.

The manuscript of 'Lebenslied' (D 508) of December 1816, which is preserved at the Gesellschaft der Musikfreunde in Vienna, contains the last six bars of a piano postlude in C major, probably the ending of a song which was written on a preceding leaf and has been lost.

The preliminary sketches for the aria 'Vedi, quanto t'adoro' (D 510) of December 1816 contain two different settings of this text. The first one was sketched twice before the final version which is printed in the *AGA*, Series XX, no. 573. The second sketch, only written out for melody and bass, is shorter but also more lyrical. It was published privately in a completion by the present writer in 1965.

The manuscript of the arietta 'La Pastorella' (D 528) of January 1817 contains the incipits of nine waltzes which were, according to Maurice J. E. Brown, probably composed shortly before the arietta, i.e. at the end of 1816 or at the beginning of 1817. Five of these waltzes could be identified and exist in another version in manuscripts or editions already known, but the remainder are otherwise unknown.[23]

1817

In January 1817 Schubert set a text by Zacharias Werner, 'Jagdlied' (D 521). Probably shortly afterwards he started to write another song, 'Nur wer die Liebe kennt' (D 513A in *D2*), on a text by Werner, which has no title in the autograph but is called 'Impromptu' in a printed edition of the poems. The melody is complete, but the accompaniment is written out only for the first 11 bars. It was published in a completion by the present writer in *The Music Review*, xxxv (1974), pp. 89-91.

The first setting of 'Mahomets Gesang' (D 549) on a text by Goethe, composed in March 1817, was probably completed. Unfortunately, only the first sheet (with 114 bars) is preserved.

The final version of the song 'An die untergehende Sonne' (D 457), which is dated May 1817, contains a song sketch without any words (D 555). When O. E. Deutsch published this sketch in 1934 in the magazine *Radio Wien* (x, no. 52, p. 13) he announced a competition to find a suitable text for the melody. The poems which Deutsch received were lost when he had to leave Vienna in 1938.

The magnificent song 'Gretchen' or 'Gretchens Bitte' (D 564) was most

23 Brown, 'Schubert: Discoveries' (cited note 2 above), p. 295.

probably complete at one time. The second leaf must have been lost quite early, since the song was published as a fragment as early as 1838, and the copy in the Witteczek Collection in the Gesellschaft der Musikfreunde (vol. 39, p. 30), made before that date, is also fragmentary. Among attempts to complete the song are those of N. C. Getty (1928), Benjamin Britten (1943), and the present writer (1976).

Maurice J. E. Brown wrote that 'The Goethe Haus [in Frankfurt] was destroyed during the Second World War and since then the manuscript of the song [D 564] has been lost; probably it was destroyed at the same time.'[24] Fortunately, that is not true. The manuscript was removed to a safe place during the war and has since been returned to the renovated Goethe Haus.

The unfinished Sonata in F sharp minor of July 1817 most probably consists of four movements, D 571, 604 and 570, of which only the slow movement and the scherzo are complete. It is one of the finest and most personal works of this period and it has been completed by several pianists, among them Walter Rehberg, Paul Badura-Skoda and Noel Lee.

'Die Entzückung an Laura' (D 577), dated August 1817, is one of those fragments which illustrate Brown's statement that 'Schubert evidently economised at that period [1816-17] by using up half-empty sheets of music paper from the previous years.'[25] For this particular song, Schubert used two (or more?) sheets with arrangements of duets by Johann Josef Fux. The title is 'Duetto. Fuga' although they are not really fugues, but just exercises in imitation. The fragment is incomplete (the second page is missing), and Schubert did not go on to complete the song.

'Lied eines Kindes' (D 596) of November 1817 is a fragment of which no autograph is known. It is probable that part of it has been lost.

1818

The Sonata in C major of April 1818 probably consisted of the three following movements:
(*a*) *Moderato* (the first part of D 613)
(*b*) *Adagio* in E major (D 612)
(*c*) a Rondo (presumably *Allegretto*, though without tempo indication: the second part of D 613).
In my opinion, it is not impossible that the Minuet in C sharp minor (D 600) and the Trio in E major (D 610) may also have been originally intended for this sonata: they would certainly fit in with the characteristic Schubertian key-scheme. This does not necessarily mean that he would have kept this scheme, if he had ever finished the sonata and made it ready for publication.

24 Ibid., p. 304.
25 Brown, *Schubert. A Critical Biography*, p. 66.

It is little known (because of its fragmentary condition), but truly fascinating and beautiful.

Even more fascinating are the sketches for a Symphony in D (D 615) which Schubert started to write in May 1818. They form a kind of sketchbook in which he may have written his ideas for a symphony whenever they came to his mind. It is very probable that his Symphony in E (D 729) originally consisted of similar sketches, and in fact the remaining sketches for the B minor Symphony (D 759) are written on similar paper. There is so much material on these pages that an extensive study (with music examples) would be needed to give a proper impression of them. An excellent article was devoted to them by Maurice J. E. Brown,[26] but much more could be written about them. Recent research by Ernst Hilmar, Director of the Music Department of the Vienna Stadtbibliothek,[27] has revealed that the sketches are of three different periods: 1818-20, 1821, and 1828. They have therefore three different numbers in *D2*: D 615 (the sketches of 1818-20), D 708A (those of 1821), and D 936A (those of 1828). One particular movement, an *Andante* in B minor (1828), is practically complete in sketched form. In the article referred to above, Brown said of it:

> This Andante is without doubt Schubert's first entry into that world of passionate and sustained lyricism that later produced the 'Quartettsatz', the first movement of the 'unfinished' Symphony and the slow movement of the string Quintet. It is, even in its first crude draft, incomparably more mature than any previous slow movement of his and than anything in the following sketched Symphony in E; and it cuts deeper, too.[28]

Brown transcribed it in piano score and gave an illustrated talk about it on the BBC's Third Programme. With a little imagination one could almost hear what a marvellous movement it would be when played by an orchestra.

Similar sketches for orchestral compositions were found among the manuscripts at the Männergesang-Verein (MS Q) and they could well be of the same period (D 966C). However, the paper is different and has only twelve staves, whereas the sketches of May 1818 have sixteen staves.

There are other sketches, apparently for some dances, which could be of the summer of 1818, judging from the writing and the manuscript paper. They are written with great haste and seem to be first drafts of an Ecossaise in G minor and two Ländler, respectively in F major and F minor (MS 0: D 980A).

26 Brown, 'Schubert's Unfinished Symphony in D', *Music and Letters*, XXXI (1950), pp. 101-9.

27 'Neue Funde, Daten und Dokumente zum symphonischen Werk Franz Schuberts', *Österreichische Musikzeitschrift*, XXXIII (June 1978), pp. 266-76; and *Franz Schubert. Drei Symphonie-Fragmente D 615 – D 708A – D 936A. Faksimile-Erstdruck der Originalhandschriften*, Documenta Musicologica, Zweite Reihe: Handschriften–Faksimiles, VI, ed. with afterword by Ernst Hilmar (Kassel, etc., 1978).

28 Brown, 'Schubert's Unfinished Symphony in D', p. 107.

Sketches for the Polonaises op. 75 (D 599) were written in July 1818, but one of the sketches (with the complete melody of the treble part) was not used in that set and was replaced by another polonaise (no. 2 in the set). The Polonaise in B flat (D 618A) was arranged for practical use by the present writer and was privately printed in Damascus in 1965; a corrected version was printed in Ghent in 1978.

The manuscript of the ballad 'Der Graf von Habsburg' (Schiller) is a rough draft on two staves (D 990). At first it was thought to be an early composition on account of the simplicity of both melody and accompaniment; but according to Dr Dürr the writing and paper point rather to 1818. Ignaz Weinmann discovered that the song was already printed in 1853 and had been published by Ferdinand Schubert (together with many other songs) as his own work! We can therefore presume that Schubert composed this song – and maybe others too – for his brother Ferdinand in order to help him in his position as a schoolteacher. The sketch on the other side of this song, described in *D1* as a pianoforte piece in B♭, was also found to be the first draft of a ballad on a text by Heinrich von Collin, 'Kaiser Maximilian auf der Martinswand' (D 990A). This had been published together with the previous song. Ferdinand's version, an arrangement for two voices and a bass line, is most probably based on a fair copy by Schubert which is now lost.

The unusual *Evangelium Johannis* (D 607), a setting from St John's Gospel, was composed in 1818. Although there is no indication on the manuscript which would suggest this date, according to Dr Dürr copies of it are dated. On the first staff of the autograph there is a short sketch for a vocal composition (eight bars only), possibly for four mixed voices, though only the two upper voices were written. Besides the facsimile in R. Heuberger's book *Franz Schubert*,[29] this small fragment was printed in the *Revue Belge de Musicologie*, XXVIII–XXX (1974-6), p. 162.

The Sonata in F minor (D 625), which is virtually complete, was written in September 1818. According to Maurice J. E. Brown, there is no doubt that the slow movement in D♭ major (D 505) really belongs to this sonata and was composed around the same time.[30]

1819

The sketch of a song 'Abend' (D 645) is in the manuscript of 'Die Gebüsche' (D 646) which is dated January 1819; the sketch is therefore probably of the same date. Schubert is not known to have set any other texts by the author of 'Abend', Ludwig Tieck. The manuscript was offered for sale by J. A.

29 Following p. 56 in the Berlin, 1902 edition; following p. 88 in the Berlin, 1920 edition.

30 See Brown, *Schubert. A Critical Biography*, p. 68.

Stargardt in April 1959. The fragment consists of five pages, with the melody and here and there an indication for the interludes (right hand only); the text is not written in beyond the first line, 'Wie ist es denn, dass'.[31]

The opera *Adrast* (D 137) was left unfinished by Schubert, and parts of it are still unpublished. Einstein dates it *c.* 1815, but Vetter and Brown give 1819 as a probable date; Brown suggests that Schubert started to write it immediately after he had finished *Die Zwillingsbrüder* (D 647). The sketches for *Adrast* are partly in the Vienna Stadtbibliothek and partly (unpublished) in the Nationalbibliothek. The more substantial part (152 pages) is in the Stadtbibliothek; but some pages are empty or remain unpublished (pp. 93-6 of the autograph). The Nationalbibliothek manuscript consists of two bundles each of 12 pages and a bifolium, marked pp. 21-68: pp. 55-66 are missing, as are also pp. 1-20. Einstein calls this opera fragment 'a noble experiment', and it is to be regretted that Schubert did not continue work on it.

Almost the same can be said of that other experiment, the sonata movement in C sharp minor (D 655) written in April 1819. It is incomplete and reaches only to the close of the exposition (73 bars), with a double-bar and repeat sign.

The beautiful Psalm XIII (D 663) of June 1819 was most probably finished, but the ending, which was apparently on another leaf, is missing. When O. E. Deutsch published it in facsimile in the *Festblätter für das 10. Deutsche Sängerbundesfest* (Vienna, 1928), together with a short article, he announced that it would be printed (completed by Eusebius Mandyczewski) in a further issue of the same magazine, but it did not come out. Schubert wrote 'XII. Psalm' which is an error, as it is numbered 'Der XIII. Psalm' in Moses Mendelssohn's translation; but the psalm is actually the twelfth in the Vulgate numbering. This work was published for the first time, completed by the present writer, in the article 'Schubert: Songs and Song Fragments' (cited in note 21 above), pp. 289-92.

1820

The autograph score of *Lazarus* (D 689) is – unfortunately – incomplete, and it is most probable that it was also left unfinished by Schubert. Yet, even in its actual state, it is to be counted among Schubert's greatest masterpieces. The fact that Acts I and II were performed in 1830 suggests that at least part of the score is lost, but also that Schubert never finished the third act. He started work on it in February 1820, and it probably kept him busy for the whole month since no other work is recorded for that period.

31 The complete poem is reproduced by Schochow and Schochow (see note 16 above), pp. 688-9.

The manuscripts with sketches for the dances D 980A and 980C (formerly D 640 and 680) are not dated. It is difficult to set a date for these sketches, but the paper seems to suggest that they were written after 1818, maybe in 1819 or 1820.

Die Zauberharfe (D 644) is generally believed to have been written in June and July 1820. It was the first opera to be published in the *NGA* (no. 5512, 1975), and the edition also contains, besides the main work, many fragments and sketches which hitherto had remained unpublished.

Schubert started to write the opera *Sakuntala* (D 701) in October 1820, and it is not clear for what reason he never tried to finish it. But, since he did not destroy the sketches and kept them quite carefully, it is not impossible that he intended to complete the opera at a later date. The fragment was arranged and completed for practical performance by Dr Fritz Racek and was given in concert form (with considerable success) at the Vienna Music Festival on 12 June 1971.

Another famous fragment of this year is the so-called 'Quartettsatz' in C minor (D 703) of December 1820. It is less well known that there is also a relatively important fragment of a second movement, *Andante* (40 bars), which, according to Vetter and Einstein, is among the most interesting of the fragments.[32] Einstein calls the *Andante* 'an indescribably rich and tragic movement', and he concludes that 'it is a major misfortune for our musical heritage that this movement at least was never finished'.[33]

Schubert had started a setting of Goethe's 'Gesang der Geister über den Wassern' (D 484) for a solo voice and piano in September 1816, but he never finished it. In March 1817 he wrote a setting (D 538) for four male voices without accompaniment. He was apparently not yet satisfied with it, for he started another setting for male chorus, this time with piano accompaniment (D 705), which was also left unfinished. Finally, he made a first draft of the setting for eight male voices and strings, probably immediately afterwards, and this was then completed (with minor alterations) in February 1821 with a view to Schubert's concert in the Kärntnertor-Theater on 7 March 1821 (D 714). It is without doubt one of Schubert's greatest vocal works, and if the first performance was a failure, it was certainly because the singers had underestimated its difficulty.

1821

The Fantasia in C major for Pianoforte (D 605) has no title in the manuscript; the title in the *AGA* is 'Pianofortestück' and the commentary in the *Revisionsbericht* (Series XXI, p. 3) is rather confusing: 'The appearance of the

32 See Walther Vetter, *Der Klassiker Schubert* (Leipzig, 1953), vol. I, pp. 159-61.
33 A. Einstein, *Schubert. A Musical Portrait* (London, 1951), p. 182.

autograph gives the impression that part of this composition is lost; yet it shows clearly that Schubert left this piece unfinished.'

On account of its experimental style, it was thought to be of 1818, maybe an alternative to the slow movement from the Sonata in C major of April 1818 (D 613 and 612: see above, p. 314); however, according to Dr Dürr the writing shows that this piece was written after 1820. It is a kind of set of variations on a theme, or rather on the notes which form the first chord (but without accidentals): G, B, C, E, in different tempos and keys. In his recording of this strange piece, the pianist Gilbert Schuchter plays it only up to the unfinished *Andantino*; Frederick Marvin adds at the end simply a full chord of F♯ major and, although the ending sounds a little abrupt and unexpected, one can at least hear the whole piece, which is certainly very interesting. There is no tempo indication at the beginning, but it is obviously a slow movement; it starts in C major and goes through different keys (51 bars). Then follows an *Allegro moderato* (bars 52-115) which also wanders through different keys and ends on the dominant of B (F♯). The last (incomplete) movement is in B (bars 116-47) and ends in F♯ major.

A second setting of Goethe's poem 'Mahomets Gesang' (D 721), for a powerful bass voice, dates from March 1821. The same impetuous rhythm as in the 'Gesang der Geister' depicts the mountain stream in the song's very promising opening. Unfortunately, after the first two stanzas (39 bars) Schubert stopped and cancelled the whole fragment. Schubert's alterations to the poem are quite interesting: at the end of each stanza he repeats the beginning, in the first stanza 'seht den Felsenquell!' and in the second one 'Jünglingfrisch'.

If Schubert had finished his ballad 'Johanna Sebus' (D 728), which he began in April 1821, it might well have been one of his very best vocal works for a solo voice. It has certain affinities with 'Der Erlkönig', and even in its unfinished condition (82 bars) it is quite impressive. It is the story of a young woman who, on the occasion of a terrible flood, helps to evacuate children and elderly people and is finally drowned herself. In the accompaniment one can hear the water rushing in the continuous semiquavers, and towards the end of the fragment there is a dramatic climax on the words 'sie sollen und müssen gerettet sein!' ('they shall and must be saved!').

A small and lyrical fragment is the duet 'Linde Lüfte wehen' (D 725) which Schubert started to write in the same month. Neither the title nor the author of the poem is known. It has the same sweet melancholy as the lovely song 'Die Mainacht' (D 194). As the first edition (in *Festschrift für Johannes Wolf* (Berlin, 1929), p. 36) is very rare, Maurice J. E. Brown reprinted this fragment (11 bars only) in his book *Schubert. A Critical Biography*, pp. 106-7.

The Symphony in E major (D 729) written in August 1821 is one of Schubert's most important fragments. It must have been virtually complete in Schubert's mind; it could well be that he put it aside when he left Vienna in September and started to write his opera *Alfonso und Estrella*, which kept him busy for the rest of the year. By the time he had finished his opera, he was occupied with the publication of his works (songs, dances for piano, and choruses). It is not a great loss that this symphony remained unfinished; yet most Schubertians all over the world would not want to be without it, and are grateful to Weingartner for having completed and published it for practical use. When it is well performed it certainly sounds very attractive, and it has a wealth of melody (although it can by no means be compared to the Symphony in B minor). This incomplete sketch has been realized by several composers in recent years: by Emile Amoudruz (Geneva 1950) after J. F. Barnett; and in new versions by Leonid Butir (Moscow 1969), Brian Newbould (Cheltenham 1978) and Boris Spassow (Sofia 1978).

1822

The quartet for male voices 'Der Wintertag' (D 984) is one of the most important works among the undated compositions. It was evidently written for some lady's birthday in winter-time, and the last stanza of the poem would suggest that it was composed for Schubert's stepmother:

Wir lieben dich so inniglich,
Und all die Deinen bitten dich,
Der Vater und die Kinder:
O liebe uns nicht minder!

However, Schubert's stepmother was born on 1 June 1783,[34] so it must have been written for another lady, probably a relative or a friend of the family. The four voice parts (copied separately) are complete, but Schubert's original piano accompaniment is lost. It is not included in the *AGA*, and besides the very rare first edition by Johann Herbeck (with a piano accompaniment by J. P. Gotthard: Spina, Vienna, *c.* 1865) there is only the more recent publication in the *Sämtliche Männerchöre* published in 1928 for the first centenary of Schubert's death, edited by Viktor Keldorfer (II, 156), who supplied a new piano accompaniment. Keldorfer indicates in a note that in his opinion the poem was probably written by Schubert himself. Maurice J. E. Brown dates the work 1822; it does indeed seem to be a mature piece.

In May 1822 Schubert started to write a *Missa* in A minor (D 755), according to the inscription on the autograph 'for his brother Ferdinand'. There are only four pages with the first Kyrie, a short interlude and the beginning of the Christe eleison. It is a very promising piece for mixed voices, soloists and strings, and it may be that Ferdinand had asked him to write this Mass for him, as he had previously (in 1818) the German Requiem (D 621). However, Schubert had not yet finished writing his *Missa solemnis* in A flat major

34 *Schubert. A Documentary Biography*, Otto Erich Deutsch, transl. Eric Blom (London, 1946), p. 30.

(D 678), and he probably interrupted this less important Mass in order to finish the great one first.

Sketches for the Symphony in B minor (D 759) are preserved: part of the first movement, the entire second movement, and most of the scherzo (inscribed simply *Allegro* in the autograph). It is a pity that the beginning of these sketches is missing, for it might have revealed the exact date when Schubert had started to write this most famous among his symphonies. The date on the score, 30 October 1822, is most probably the date when he started to write out the complete score. It is, however, very probable that he had already started to work on it after finishing his Mass in A flat in September 1822. Although it cannot be proved, in my opinion Schubert wrote sketches for all four movements. It is unthinkable that he could have had it in mind to compose a symphony in only three movements, and certainly not one in two movements since he already started to write out the scherzo, the sketches of which are virtually complete. There are no sketches extant for the finale, and this would not be so difficult to explain: he may have used them for the Entr'acte no. 1 in *Rosamunde*. The latter piece is not only in the same key and written for the same instruments as the 'Unfinished', but it is also much too long for its normal purpose as an entr'acte. I am, of course, not the first one to suggest that this entr'acte is in fact the finale which was originally planned for the B minor Symphony, but to me a strong point in favour of this theory is the fact that no sketches are left for the final movement, precisely because they were used for practical purposes. That he did not interrupt his work because of lack of inspiration (as is sometimes suggested) is sufficiently proved by the 'Wanderer' Fantasy which was written immediately afterwards. It still remains a mystery why he did not complete the symphony later.

1823

The small sonata fragment in E minor (D 769A, formerly D 994) was believed to be composed in June 1817. According to Dr Dürr, the writing and the paper suggest that it was written *c.* 1823 and certainly not before 1820.

A small fragment, the beginning of a chorus (or quartet?) for male voices, is included under D 16 in the thematic catalogue with the words 'Ich hab' in mich gesogen den Frühling treu und lieb' (D 778B). The words come from Rückert's poem 'Frühling' (which was set as a song by Schumann). The fragment is most probably from the beginning (February?) of 1823, like the other songs on poems by Rückert. (The date is suggested by Maurice J. E. Brown.)

Although the Singspiel *Die Verschworenen* or *Der häusliche Krieg* (D 787) is usually not counted among the fragments, it is in fact not complete. The overture was discovered among the so-called Krasser family relics (Krasser was related to Schubert's sister Theresa), but the beginning of it was missing. Dr

Fritz Racek was able to restore the overture, almost certainly as Schubert had written it, so that the loss of a few pages is not grave. The completed score was published in 1964 (Doblinger, Vienna, no. D.11.153), after it had been performed for the first time on 28 December 1963. It is the only overture by Schubert which is entirely based on themes from the stage work that follows. It was composed in March and April 1823.

Rüdiger (D 791) is the title of an opera which Schubert started to write in May 1823. The text is by Ignaz von Mosel ('Heroisches Operngedicht: *Rüdiger*') after Metastasio's *Ruggiero*, as was discovered by Theophil Antonicek.[35] It seems that only two numbers were sketched: an aria with chorus, and a duet. The first was published in an arrangement by Herbeck.

According to Maurice J. E. Brown, Schubert started to write another opera shortly after the former fragment; no title is known, but it may conveniently be referred to as *Sofie* (D 982) after the name of the principal character. The sketches are not much more extensive than those for *Rüdiger* (three numbers only) and this fragment too was abandoned before Schubert started to write his opera *Fierrabras* on 25 May 1823.

1825

One of Schubert's finest sonatas remained unfinished. It is the so-called 'Reliquie' Sonata in C major (D 840), written in April 1825. A strange reminiscence from an aria in *Die Zauberharfe* occurs in the second theme of the first movement.

1826

A substantial fragment of a chorus for mixed voices, 'Die Allmacht' (D 875A), was found in 1952. It was already mentioned by Kreissle among the unpublished works, but there it was erroneously called a quartet for male voices.[36] It is dated January 1826 and remained unfinished; there are seventeen pages, but on p. 5 the accompaniment is already interrupted, and on p. 14, after the exposition of a fugue, the text is also omitted.[37] This chorus was privately printed in Damascus (1965) and Beirut (1967), and it was performed for the first time at a concert in the East Berlin Opera House on 19 November 1978.

35 See his *Ignaz von Mosel (1772-1844). Biographie und Beziehungen zu den Zeitgenossen* (Vienna, 1962), pp. 133 and 661.

36 Kreissle, *Franz Schubert*, pp. 595-6.

37 The discovery was first published by Ladislav Mokry in the journal *Slovenskà Hudba*, April 1958; M. J. E. Brown mentions it in his article 'Schubert: Discoveries' (cited note 2 above), pp. 297-8.

A revised and corrected edition is being prepared by Breitkopf & Härtel, Leipzig.

Another (small) item which remained unpublished until recently is the 'Canon(e) a sei' (D 873), a canon for six voices without title or words. It was first privately printed, with the addition of the word 'Alleluia', in Beirut in 1967. It has now also appeared in the *NGA*, Series III, vol. 4, Appendix, pp. 181-7. In the manuscript it comes after the chorus 'Mondenschein' (D 875), and it should therefore appear after it in the thematic catalogue too. Schubert's original pianoforte accompaniment for 'Mondenschein' was lost for a long time. It was found again fairly recently in the archives of B. Schott's Söhne, Mainz.

A single staff of four bars with the title 'Nachklänge' (D 873A) was written by Schubert before he started to write the duet 'Nur wer die Sehnsucht kennt' in January 1826. It is the beginning of the first tenor part; it was published by Racek[38] before it was printed in the *NGA*, Series III, vol. 4, p. 187.

'Tiefes Leid' (D 876) is the title which was given – perhaps by Diabelli, who published it in 1838 – to Schubert's setting of this untitled poem, which can be attributed to Ernst Schulze. In the manuscript it is simply headed 'Im Jänner 1817', while Schulze's poem has 'Am 17ten Januar 1817'. It is known that Schubert set Schulze's poems in December 1825 and in 1826; hence the date 'January 1826' given for this song in *D1*. However, since the manuscript of 'Der liebliche Stern' (D 861) is of December 1825 (according to O. E. Deutsch), and is in the same manuscript with the rough sketch of 'Ueber Wildemann' (D 884) which is dated March 1826, this seems to suggest that Schubert interrupted his settings of Schulze's poems between December 1825 and March 1826. It is therefore more likely that Schubert composed 'Tiefes Leid', and the sketch which follows it in the manuscript, in March 1826. This song-sketch (D 874), again with no title, is apparently a dialogue between a flower and a spring; the first stanza starts with the flower saying 'O Quell, was strömst du rasch und wild' ('O spring, how fast and wildly you are running'), and in the second stanza the spring answers 'O Blume, kann ich ruhig sein?' ('O flower, can I be at peace?'), and this goes on for the remaining two stanzas which are again given to the flower and the spring. An appropriate title for this song would therefore be 'Die Blume und der Quell', and it was thus published by the present writer in a private edition (Ghent, 1968).

1827

The manuscript in the Vienna Stadtbibliothek which contains the sketch of a chorus for male voices 'Das stille Lied' (D 916) also contains a sketch of another composition, most probably a song with piano accompaniment

38 'Von den Schubert-Handschriften der Stadtbibliothek' (cited note 9 above).

(D 916A), which has no title or text; it was probably written in May 1827, i.e. immediately after 'Das stille Lied'. By a happy coincidence an unknown Schubert autograph came to light in the spring of 1977 and was sold at an auction in Paris. It contains the complete chorus 'Das stille Lied' for T.T.B.B. and is also dated May 1827. The melody is slightly changed and is somewhat longer than the original version (30 bars instead of 27). In the meantime, Fritz Racek had completed the sketch and published it in 1961 (Doblinger, Vienna, no. 10.312). The newly discovered complete version has now been published by Bärenreiter, edited by Walther Dürr (Kassel etc., 1978, no. VN 19317).

Although the libretto had been rejected by the censor, Schubert started to work at his last opera, *Der Graf von Gleichen* (D 918), on 19 June 1827. He worked on it at intervals until his death.

Together with the sketches for this opera, which are quite extensive, two sketches for piano pieces were discovered by Dr Ernst Hilmar in the Vienna Stadtbibliothek.

A. Klavierstück in C major (D 916B) written in pencil, 127 bars; a similar first sketch of the Impromptu op. 90 no. 1 (D 899/1) was published in an appendix to the Wiener Urtext Edition of the Impromptus and Moments Musicaux, edited by Paul Badura-Skoda (Vienna, UT 50001). It is possible that this and the following piece were first sketches for further impromptus and they were probably written down in the summer or autumn of 1827.

B. Klavierstück in C minor (D 916C), also written in pencil and unfinished; it breaks off after bar 182 at the beginning of the recapitulation.

Both pieces were published, D 916B as a fragment and D 916C in a completed form, by Otto Brusatti (Doblinger, Vienna, 1978, Diletto Musicale no. 804).

A similar composition is the *Allegretto* in C minor for pianoforte (D 900), which remained unfinished and is probably of the same period. According to Dr Hilmar, however, this piece was probably written in the autumn of 1823.

1828

The sketch of a song 'Fröhliches Scheiden' (D 896) on a text by Leitner may have been composed after the finished songs 'Winterabend' (D 938) and 'Die Sterne' (D 939) in January 1828. The sketch is written on the first leaf of a bifolium whose second leaf contains a sketch (without text) of another song, the beginning of which is missing; the melody is complete but the accompaniment is only indicated here and there. A second bifolium with the beginning of this song was recently found, and it also contains a sketch of yet another song, so that we now have two sketches of songs, without texts:

A. Sketch of a song in B♭ major (D 896A): the melodic line is complete but there are only occasional indications of the accompaniment (or interludes); there are 115 bars.

B. Sketch of a song in C major (D 896B): complete melodic line and indications for accompaniment; 96 bars.

There is no text in the manuscripts of these two songs; but the poems which Schubert intended to set (and which fit the music perfectly) were identified by the present writer in June 1978. In the 1825 Vienna edition of Leitner's *Gedichte*, 'Sie in jedem Liede' (D 896A) and 'Wolke und Quelle' (D 896B) appear only a few pages after the poem 'Fröhliches Scheiden' (D 896).[39]

The song 'Lebensmut' (D 937), to a text by Rellstab, was probably composed in April 1828, after 'Auf dem Strom' and 'Herbst'. It is not really a fragment (although Schubert did not write it out completely); the way it was printed in the Peters Edition (vol. 7, pp. 58-9) seems quite satisfactory, and that was most probably the way Schubert would have written it if he had made a fair copy. That it was finished in his mind is clear from the fact that he started another song on the next page, namely a first sketch of 'Liebesbotschaft' (D 957/1); this sketch occupies only two pages. The next page has a first sketch for 'Frühlingssehnsucht', but with a completely different melody from the one that was used in his final setting. It is printed in the *Revisionsbericht* of the *AGA*, Series XX, p. 115.

Finally, we have the fugal exercises (D 965B) which Schubert started to write (so it is believed) early in November 1828 when he was taking lessons with Sechter. Some of these sketches, or rather theme-expositions, are in the Landesbibliothek in Dresden, others in the Vienna Männergesang-Verein. Both manuscripts show the theme of the Fugue in E minor (D 952): in A minor in the Vienna manuscript, in E minor in the Dresden manuscript; both five bars: this (in my opinion) proves that the fugue (D 952) was in fact Schubert's last work and was not composed in Baden on 3 June 1828. That date was added in the manuscript by someone else.

The problem of attributing an approximate date to manuscripts which were not dated by Schubert himself is far from simple. Modern science and research have discovered new methods and additional devices to help establish approximate dates. For this reason, the new edition of O. E. Deutsch's thematic catalogue (*D2*), as well as Ernst Hilmar's catalogue of the Schubert manuscripts in the Vienna Stadtbibliothek,[40] will no doubt reveal a great number of surprises to all Schubert-lovers and scholars.*

39 See my article 'Further Schubert Discoveries', *Music Review*, XXXIX (1978), p. 99.

40 E. Hilmar, *Verzeichnis der Schubert-Handschriften in der Musiksammlung der Wiener Stadt- und Landesbibliothek*, Catalogus Musicus, VIII (Kassel, etc., 1978).

* I wish to express my heartfelt thanks to Dr Walther Dürr, the editor-in-chief of *NGA*, without whose help and advice this article could not have been written.

Rhythm in Schubert: some practical problems. Critical analysis, critical edition, critical performance*

ARNOLD FEIL

Concern for the reality of the work must prepare the ground, so that we may find art and the nature of art in the real work. Inquiry into the nature of art, and the path that leads to knowledge of it, must first be brought back to a firm basis.

Martin Heidegger, *Der Ursprung des Kunstwerkes*

Hypothesis: In the music of Franz Schubert, rhythm has its own special role – or, rather, it has a special function, unlike and more important than its function in the music of his contemporaries. If this hypothesis is valid, it is the task of the musical scholar as of the practical musician to see that this individual quality is given due acknowledgement.

In order to appreciate and understand Schubert's individual use of rhythm, it is necessary to have a clear idea of the rhythmic norm which prevailed during his lifetime, i.e. what the listener was able and indeed obliged to expect, and what the composer could count upon the listener's expecting and accepting. The works of art, as well as of theory, are there for consultation; but to render this norm perceptible, somewhat more information is required.

Between 1780 and 1830 not all treatises on musical theory and composition give equally reliable information on the subject of rhythm and the construction of musical periods. Heinrich Christoph Koch has been shown to surpass any other theorist of the time, since his pronouncements correspond, far more closely than most on the subject, to what we see in the works themselves (*Versuch einer Anleitung zur Composition*, Rudolstadt and Leipzig, 1782-93; *Musikalisches Lexikon*, Frankfurt am Main, 1802). Koch's understanding of the term 'rhythm' is very like our own; but for him rhythm is 'principally the relationship which the single melodic sections of subjects . . . bear to one another'. Accordingly we find under the headword 'rhythmopoeia': 'For the Greeks, rhythmopoeia was one of the most important aspects

* Revised version of a lecture given at the International Schubert Symposium 'Zur Aufführungspraxis der Werke Franz Schuberts', Vienna, 1974. The hypothesis has been put forward and demonstrated elsewhere with numerous examples, if in brief: see A. Feil, *Studien zu Schuberts Rhythmik* (Munich, 1966), and 'Zur Rhythmik Schuberts' in *Bericht über den internationalen musikwissenschaftlichen Kongress Kassel 1962* (Kassel, etc., 1962), pp. 198-200.

of music, namely the one which we today describe as the organization of bars, and which teaches the composer to bring into a proper relationship the tonal feet [i.e. the bars] and the melodic sections [i.e. the groups of bars] arising from their combination.' Also within the rhythmic sphere for Koch is something which for us it no longer includes, namely the organization of groups of bars and the weighing-up of their relative proportions. How should one build a four-bar phrase so that it produces a different effect? How does one build a five-bar phrase or a six-bar phrase? Answers to questions such as these are possible for Koch only according to the laws of musical rhythm. Similar questions are: How should one arrange groups of bars, i.e. sections of a composition, in such a way that the unity of the whole emerges from these groups of bars? How does one weigh up their proportions, how may they be combined or separated? Which parts fashioned in a particular way should go with which, and how should this be done to achieve this or that particular effect? The construction of the parts, and their combination into a whole, are likewise for Koch questions of musical rhythm. It is not surprising that the structures which we call four-bar phrases, eight-bar periods, and the like were described by Koch and his contemporaries as 'a rhythm of four bars', 'a rhythm of eight bars', etc. This mode of expression is as unfamiliar to us as it was common to his contemporaries. If we take these terms seriously, and regard them as having significance, then we must treat the problem of the organization of a composition as one of rhythm. We shall talk not of four- and five-bar phrases, nor of periodic and aperiodic sections, but of the possibilities and problems which arise when parts of a composition or groups of bars are regarded as rhythms, and also of the manner of (indeed, the very fact of) Schubert's use of such possibilities in his own musical art.

Koch's phrase 'a rhythm of four bars' and the theory of phrase-construction which follows from it were intended in the first place only to assert that a work is made up of many sections; the smaller form the larger ones, and these in turn the yet larger sections out of which the whole is constituted. All such sections are interrelated, and the nature of the relationship is rhythmic, for the musical work takes place in time, musical time must be organized, and the organization must be perceptible as music, able to be grasped musically.

The relationship of bars or sections in combination must therefore not be now the same and now different, or be almost chaotic, for as soon as the number of combined tonal feet [i.e. bars] becomes too irregular with respect to their proportions, the period [i.e. a longer section, such as a sonata exposition] which is built from them is not comprehensible enough; the relating of part to part demands too much of the listener.

This means that when listening to a piece of music we unconsciously relate its sections to each other and estimate them rhythmically, as it were. That this problem preoccupied both the musician and his audience, how it did so, and how seriously it was taken may be seen from the extent to which the publisher

Hummel tampered with the works of Haydn, as Georg Feder has pointed out.[1] Hummel was so disturbed by irregularities in periodic structure, particularly in Haydn's early works, that he frequently inserted or removed bars for his own editions, thereby interfering with the musical substance – and in many editions these alterations have persisted even to the present day, since so well-informed a man as Carl Ferdinand Pohl could show more faith in Hummel's regular bar-group structures than in Haydn's irregular ones.

'If . . . groups of bars are regarded as rhythms', general rhythmic principles must govern them: if not in the strict sense of the word, then in the broader sense. According to Hugo Riemann, they were applicable in the strict sense. Riemann's *System der musikalischen Rhythmik und Metrik* (Leipzig, 1903) is here neither criticized nor discussed, but it should be mentioned that while there is no general consensus that his system is entirely sound, there is none that it is entirely false either. We know today that in the music of Viennese classical composers – and Riemann takes his examples from Haydn, Mozart and Beethoven – metric laws prevailed, and that these were often obligatory when bars were to be combined into sections – often, but not always. Moreover, we know that Haydn, Mozart and Beethoven worked with the possibilities thus made available. A simple but impressive example may be found in Beethoven's Piano Sonata op. 7. The first movement is based upon a two-bar section, in which the second bar is metrically subordinate to the first. Within the bars, each of which follows a stressed/unstressed (or heavy/light) metrical pattern, Beethoven places the motif of the first movement – chords falling by thirds – on a downbeat at the beginning, on an upbeat at the end: Ex. 1.

Ex. 1 (a)

(b)

1 *Musicae Scientiae Collectanea. Festschrift Karl Gustav Fellerer zum 70. Geburtstage* (Cologne, 1972), pp. 88-101.

The classical composers worked with such possibilities. Yet not every two-bar section is so constructed that one bar is subordinate or superior to the other; any more than one finds metrical organization in every four-bar phrase or period. Rather, there are groups of bars that give no hint of such construction, and others that are metrically linked together. In opposition to Riemann and all his disciples in the field of rhythmic research, and despite all systematic theory, the point must be maintained: Riemann described as universally valid what is merely one possibility in the Viennese classical style.[2]

All therefore depends upon the compositional possibility of subjecting the 'rhythms of bars' to the general laws of metre and rhythm. Schubert of course saw the possibility, and used it, but differently from Haydn, Mozart and Beethoven, pushing forward beyond them into the uncharted land of rhythm and metre, and thereby into new fields of music; but before we can discuss this we need to know, at least in brief, what these general laws are which might be used for the organization of bars or rhythms of bars. The first of them, in force at the time of the Viennese classicists and Schubert, and fundamentally sacrosanct, states: Elements of the same rhythmic weight should invariably preserve the same distances when they recur; or, in the original terminology, the long (modern usage prefers to say 'strong' or 'heavy') internal time-units of a rhythmic organization should recur at the same intervals of time. The second law states: Between two long internal time-units at least one shorter (in modern parlance 'lighter') time-unit must be inserted; which means that an odd bar of only one period is excluded, as are two long internal time-units in succession followed by short ones in the same bar. Contemporary theory describes it in these words:[3]

If one tries to pronounce at regular intervals a series of long monosyllabic words – the only kind which might illustrate the necessity for such barring, as for example 'Kraft, Macht, Ruhm, Lob, Ehr, Preis' [strength, might, fame, praise, rank, prize] – a tiny rest or pause will be noticed after each word, which takes up the second half of the interval from one word to the next, as:

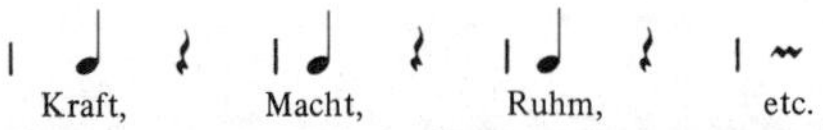
Kraft,
Macht,
Ruhm,
etc.

This becomes clearer if the short conjunction 'and' is placed between two of the words: the preceding word with its conjunction then takes up as much time as every other word alone, as:

Kraft,
Macht,
· · · Ehr
und
Preis.

2 See A. Feil, 'Mozarts Duett "Bei Männern welche Liebe fühlen". Periodisch-metrische Fragen' in *Festschrift Walter Gerstenberg* (Wolfenbüttel and Zurich, 1964), pp. 45-54.

3 Johann Abraham Peter Schulz, article 'Tact' in J. G. Sulzer, *Allgemeine Theorie der schönen Künste*, 1771-4.

Only to a limited extent does the same apply to the higher law of rhythm, i.e. when bars are grouped together to form rhythms of bars. Now, Kirnberger describes it in the following words:

When the nature of a melody is such that only one unit of time is felt throughout the bar, two bars must of necessity be taken together to make up the one, of which the first part is long, the second short. If this were not the case, the inevitable weight of the downbeat would cause the ear to hear a melody made up only of heavy beats, which would be as unpleasant as it is to hear a spoken passage made up only of monosyllabic words, all of which are accentuated.[4]

But this rule does not hold good at all times or in all places, as the works themselves prove; here theory deceives. Where whole bars make up the time-units, it is not at all correct to say that two must always constitute one, to satisfy the demands of a higher law of rhythm. Rather does one find, in the interrelationship of whole bars, that formal points of view have to be taken into account, as well as the principle of bar groupings on a higher plane; and finally it is possible to construct a movement according to neither rhythmic principles nor any other structural classification, simply by joining bars or bar-groups within the unit of the whole. If groups of bars are subject to rhythmic law, then presumably they must obey the rhythmic law within the bar – repetition of the same elements must be at the same intervals of time, in which between each two internally long bars a shorter one must be inserted. But this assumption is incorrect. The law which insists that a movement must be constructed from bar-group structures is only something analogous to the bar, not of the same kind; the concepts to be used in referring to the bar or the motif should not therefore immediately be applied to these analogous structures.[5] How these last words apply to Schubert I shall show by reference to the scherzo (*Allegro vivace*) of the great Octet in F major (D 803, op.posth. 166, 1824).[6]

In scherzo movements the listener naturally expects a symmetrical layout, and feels it to be irregular if this is broken; he is as it were surprised that the smallest time-units only are subordinate to the bar, not the bars themselves to some higher principle, be it one like the bar or one which is symmetrical and formal. If symmetrically constructed sections alternate with unsymmetrical, as in Ex. 2 (finale, *Allegro molto*, from Mozart's String Quartet in C major, K 465), the listener accepts this as offending against a supposedly binding law of rhythm, even if he notices the latter only at the very moment in which it ceases to be obvious.

With the bar-group which starts at bars 17ff the symmetrical arrangement is broken; the make-up of the four-bar structure, out of one isolated bar and three others sharply contrasted yet closely related, destroys at a blow the

4 *Die Kunst des reinen Satzes in der Musik*, II/1 (1776), 131.

5 Ewald Jammers, 'Takt und Motiv. Zur neuzeitlichen musikalischen Rhythmik', *Archiv für Musikwissenschaft*, XIX–XX (1962/3), pp. 194-207.

6 *Franz Schubert. Neue Ausgabe sämtlicher Werke* (cited below as '*NGA*'), Series VI, vol. 1, ed. A. Feil (Kassel etc., 1969).

Ex. 2 (a)

(b)

illusion of continuous and perceptibly symmetrical arrangement. It is precisely because no other arrangement but the one given claims the attention – because the motifs and sections derive their significance from their own character and from their place and function in the movement, i.e. in the whole – that this music is so bold in its effect, calling forth that indescribable impression of freedom.

In the scherzo of D 803, Schubert presents us with something similar, but not the same, for he has a different effect in mind; his musical concepts are characteristically different from Mozart's, and accordingly he employs a different technique, or, more accurately, he modifies the technical means of the classical composers for his own purposes.

The motion of Schubert's scherzo is carried along in whole bars. These are, at least in the first part, always grouped into four-bar structures, and – especially with the repeats – they are so striking that some design may be supposed to exist behind them. Because the grouping is so unequivocally in 'four-bar rhythms' and remains thus, in any case to begin with, the attention of the listener can be directed to other things. Using the simplest melodic and harmonic means, Schubert directs the attention towards the rhythm – not the rhythmic interplay of the bar-groups, but the inner rhythmic structure of each individual four-bar structure. This rhythm is moreover one which contradicts the general law of rhythm:

Such a rhythm, which corresponds basically to no accepted musical rhythm, cannot be indicated by musical notation alone; supplementary signs are needed in addition to the written notes, i.e. signs which can be added to them to make their rhythm recognizable. Schubert uses the accent for this purpose, and from bar 17 onwards the *fz* sign, and also the two together. Elementary four-bar structuring and a few additional accents would naturally not have sufficed to achieve the effect that Schubert desires and succeeds in realizing; the whole movement must be constructed and carried out in accordance with this principle. Schubert works at it through the motifs – or, rather, through the rhythmic motifs, to put it more aptly. With a few characteristic exceptions, only bars in the rhythm ♩. ♪ ♩ are provided with accent signs and thereby with a special emphasis; and all bars in that rhythm are provided with accents (again with a few characteristic exceptions). The dotted rhythm is mostly repeated, either once or several times; almost everywhere it begins the bar-group, and it is always in contrast with those bars which have no dotted-crotchet movement. From all this the bars with dotted rhythm are given such emphasis that their effect is that of a special impetus, followed by movement in a definite direction. With the repetition of the dotted rhythm and therefore of the impetus, this motion seems to have been set going twice in one direction. If within one and the same bar-group there then follow bars with crotchet movement which have no special impetus, the whole bar-group gives the impression of having a compound movement, thrusting forward and swinging out. A corresponding bar-group introduces the counter-movement, and with the literal repetition of both bar-groups the image of movement is mirrored symmetrically, as in the first two four-bar pairs of our movement (bars 1-16).

In the ensuing phrases (bars 17ff) we find the succession of accents altered (as well as the indication of accents – sforzatos are added to the accents, reinforcing them):

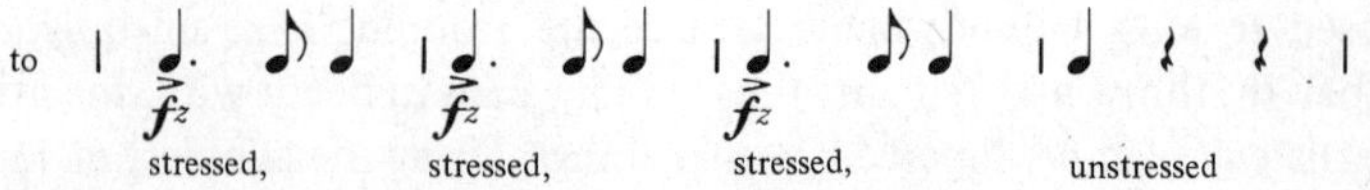

With this alteration the periodicity of the stress, the repetition of the similar material at the same intervals of time, and with it the impression of a rhythmic repeat, are all removed. Evidently it is not so much a particular rhythm as a particular presentation of movement by musical means which is being put into effect. This leads however to a free and independent rhythmic movement.

Such rhythmic freedom in music is possible only in a strict rhythmic context: i.e., the realization of rhythmically free movement in music presupposes a strict basic structure. This is provided by the movement of the measure, the as it were inaudible beat of the 3/4, and the regular articulation of uninterrupted movement through the bar-groups. On to the latter Schubert weaves that individual freedom of movement which the accentual signs indicate. Different strata of movement therefore lie one upon another in the rhythmic texture, bound together by the impetus of the whole, in which one sense of movement predominates.

The rhythmic freedom and its context appear most vividly when the movement of one of the rhythmic layers breaks into or forces its way up into one of the others. This happens at the decisive points of the composition, as here in the final group of phrases: in order to arrest the movement, and to prevent the ever-renewed impulses of the accented bars of each group from imparting their driving momentum, Schubert turns the movement around, almost forces the inversion of the rhythmic phrasing and with it the displacement of the accent (bars 118ff):

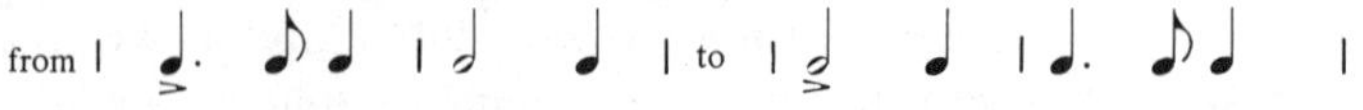

In order to achieve this, he breaks in upon the regular and symmetrical bar-groups with freely placed accents (bars 115ff).

What critical analysis has demonstrated, a critical performance – i.e. one given by thoughtful and careful musicians – must realize in sound. Yet the practical musician cannot analyse every work as the musicologist can (or should be able to). The performer must therefore expect more from the music in front of him – is entitled to expect more from the published scores of modern critical editions – than the bare notes themselves can provide; in a word, he must acquaint himself with an edited text based upon original sources and a critical analysis of the work. This text must reflect the original critically, as it were, and provide the incentive and the stimulus for a conscious, critical performance, which it alone makes possible. A modern edition therefore not only must offer a readily legible score, but must at the same time and with consistency make clear the structure of the work as a whole. It will of course be objected, 'As far as this is possible!' Even the critical edition

Ex. 3

cannot help being bound by its sources, and for the music of earlier periods these do not as a rule permit the combination in one single text of original source material and performing edition. For editions of music since Beethoven, however, much more is possible than is commonly accepted, admitted and offered. In our case, for example, some confusion has been caused both visually and audibly by the difference, in the old complete edition, between short accent marks and the long decrescendo signs in the second part of the scherzo (bars 43ff): Ex. 3. Apparently the editor felt compelled to have Schubert's relatively long accent marks engraved as decrescendo signs; he did not realize that these signs have rhythmic significance, that they are intended here not to be read as merely dynamic, but to indicate something that can be shown in no other way. They are a guide to performance; yet they are to be regarded as referring not to the dynamic but rather to the rhythmic parameter. Accordingly, in the new complete edition we have decided to use the accent signs and the corresponding *fz* and *fp* in such a way that they virtually provide the accentuation as well as the rhythm. This is also the reason for reprinting signs used by Schubert which, because they are unfamiliar, may not at first glance seem very sensible to the musician, but which nevertheless have a great deal of sense in them. In bar 95 the *f* in the violoncello and double-bass is necessary, sensible and correct, despite the presence of *fz* in all the parts, and the converse is also true, for the one is a dynamic sign, the other a rhythmic sign: Ex. 4.

To mention a final example: frequently it is only the perception of a movement's structure arrived at by analysis that makes possible the correct interpretation of Schubert's often hurried script, or guards against misunderstanding. The slur in bars 119 and 127 covers the whole bar (unlike the partial slurs in bars 114 and 122, which only appear to be the same): Ex. 5. Bar 119 is, as it were, the pivot or cardinal point of the underlying structure; it cannot be split up into the final note of the phrase and an upbeat; in performance one must not so divide it, or let the listener feel that it is capable of being so divided – for this reason the printed text must be unambiguous: Ex. 6.

To return to rhythmic considerations: in this example from the Octet, Schubert has employed the element of rhythm on not one but two planes of composition in shaping the musical development – that of the bar and that of groups of bars. He uses the opportunity provided by the whole-bar movement in the *Allegro vivace*, and similarly introduces a rhythmic law for the groups of bars. At the same time he makes use of another possibility. Since the arrangement of the groups of bars dictated by the law of rhythm is not the same as but only analogous to that of the bar (see above, p. 331), rhythmic figures are possible on the plane of groups of bars which are excluded from that of the bar. A rhythmic series such as stressed/stressed/unstressed/unstressed is not possible for the bar but is perfectly possible as a rhythm of groups of bars.

Ex. 4

Nevertheless, in arriving at this unusual rhythm Schubert has combined both planes, by making evident on the level of the bar, through the use of rhythmic motifs, what was destined to become operative on the level of groups of bars. If they are so combined, as here, if they derive mutual support and completeness from their inherent qualities, and therefore work together in the shaping of time as music, being bound together in the structure of the composition, why should they not, shall we say, influence each other? To take the strict law of rhythm from the plane of the bar to that of groups of bars, where it can have no validity, would be a foolish limitation of means. The opposite process – exploiting within the bar the possibilities of rhythmic structuring of groups of bars – this, on the other hand, opens up new horizons. Schubert saw this and utilized it.

In this respect we shall study the last movement (*Allegro vivace*) of the Piano Trio in B flat major (D 898, op. 99, 1828(?)).[7] This movement also

7 *NGA*, Series VI, vol. 7, ed. A. Feil (Kassel etc., 1975).

Ex. 5

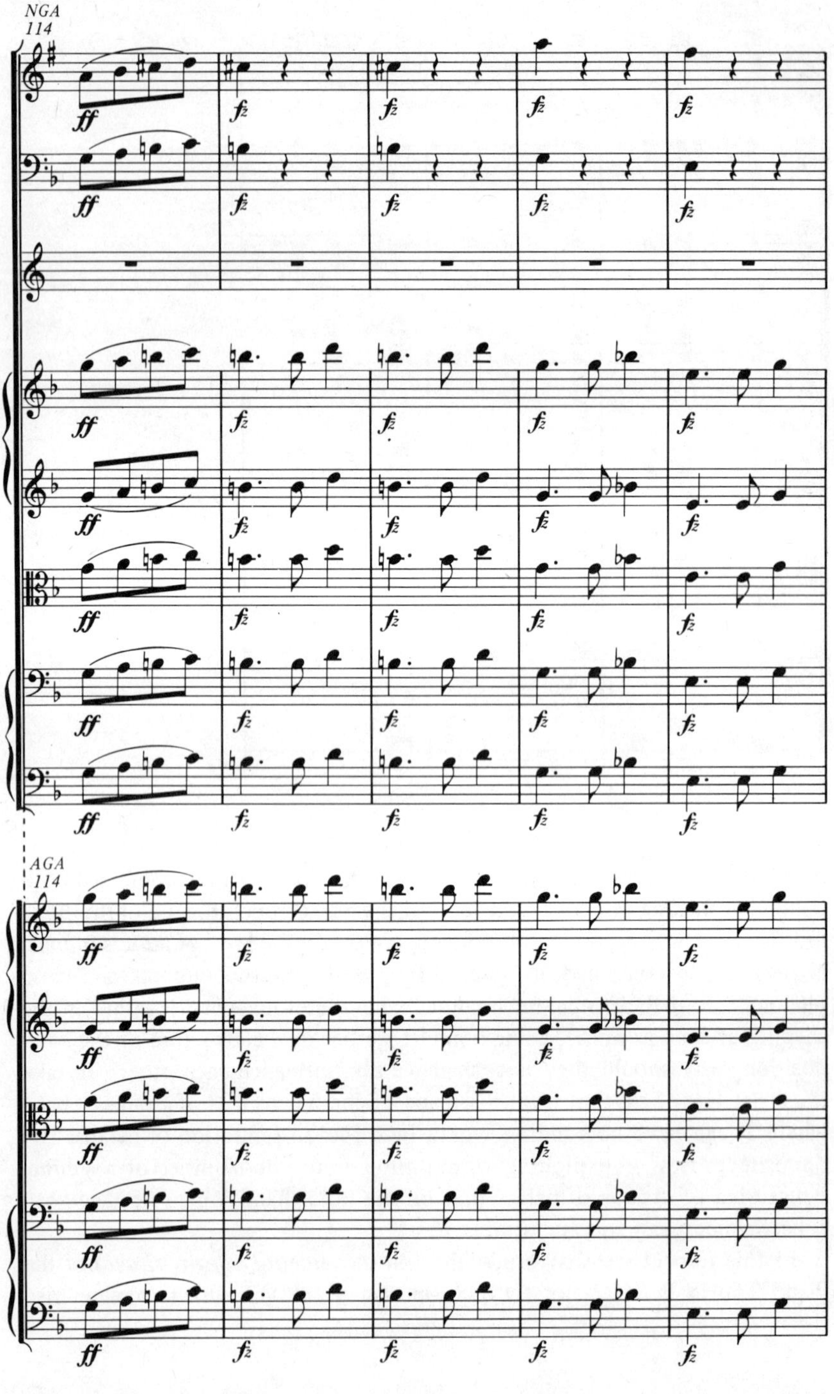

119
fz
fz
fz
fz
fz
fz
fz
fz
fz
fz
fz
fz
fz

Ex. 6

128
fz
ffz

runs in whole bars, yet not as plainly as the Octet movement just discussed; the groups of bars are not symmetrically built up in the same way. As an archetypal rondo, this movement has a 'real' theme, sharply delineated, 26 bars long. The first eight bars, in two groups of four, make up the principal part of what, since Hugo Riemann, has been called a 'period'; the second part begins in the same way, but is considerably enlarged despite its unchanged material. The two parts are made up of four-bar and two-bar groups; Schubert has carefully indicated their rhythm by accents. But the phrase 'their rhythm' is misleading: unlike the rhythm in the scherzo of the Octet (which follows the well-defined traditional scherzo type) there is here not one single rhythm, subject to variation; rather, Schubert has placed the accents much more freely, if not absolutely freely. He handles the element of rhythm in such a way that one is tempted to look upon it as his true thematic concern, his musical subject-matter, which must be worked at and developed.

This is not the place to describe and interpret the structure and layout of the movement as a whole. Yet in this context certain things should be pointed out. The first four bars announce the rhythm which is to acquire special significance in the course of the movement: Ex. 7. The continuation (bars 5-8)

Ex. 7

does not repeat this rhythm, and in the further course of the movement other bar-groups, of which the listener becomes conscious, are differently accentuated (7-8 unstressed/unstressed; 19-20 unstressed/stressed; 23-6 four-bar group with the accent on the third bar; 49-51 shortened group obtained by 'smothering' a bar, with crescendo to the first bar of the following group). For these reasons the rhythm of groups of bars fails to crystallize, as it were; the effect is that of a variously accented, free rhythmic movement, in which the 2/4 time pulsates in a lively manner, and which therefore does not unambiguously move in whole-bar phrase-groups. At bars 52-5 Schubert introduces a phrase, as though to say briefly and to the point, 'This is our rhythm, and thus it remains! Or, rather, it doesn't, for now the working-out is just beginning!' We know where the working-out was to lead him; let us recall two of the variants. Schubert plays the rhythm so to speak against itself, by making the four-bar group in violin and cello enter at an interval of only two bars (for the first time at bars 76ff): Ex. 8(a). He welds the four-bar group which is fundamental to the rhythm into a five-bar group (in its final form bars 234ff): Ex. 8(b). He shortens it into a three-bar group (bars 250ff). But if it becomes a three-bar group, he must shorten or alter the four-bar

Ex. 8 (a)

(b)

group stressed/stressed/unstressed/stressed, and we are left with stressed/stressed/unstressed. In fact Schubert no longer treats this rhythm as a bar-group rhythm at all, but as a 3/2 bar (bars 250ff): Ex. 9.

By so doing Schubert has overstepped that boundary of the general laws of rhythm which the composer of his time felt obliged to observe (see above, p. 330): 'Elements of the same weight should preserve the same distances.' Here they fall at varying distances, on the first beat and immediately on the second, but then not again until the first beat of the next bar. 'Between two long internal time-units at least one shorter time-unit must be inserted.' Here two long periods stand together without a short time-unit between them. In brief, we are concerned here not with a genuine three-beat bar, in which two short time-units would have to be subordinated to one longer one, but with a bar made up of three time-units, with two equally heavy centres of gravity

Ex. 9

at the beginning. Such a three-beat bar originates not from musical rhythm in the narrow sense, but rather from the rhythm of movement. In contrast to musical rhythm, rhythm of movement permits varying distances between the constituent centres of gravity;[8] and in the rhythm of movement one can also have a series of centres of gravity with no unstressed time-units between them.

If this is the case, then in addition to the bar-line a special sign will be needed for the transcribing of the rhythm, since musical notation provides signs only for musical conditions, or musical rhythms. The extra sign used here is Schubert's accent; but we also know that this sign has no dynamic significance, and is used to point the rhythm alone. In editing this *Allegro vivace* for the *NGA* we have therefore placed the accents not over the note-heads, as modern notational practice requires, but on an imaginary line below the violin and cello staves, and – wherever possible – between the treble and bass staves of the piano (as in Ex. 9). For the accent is a direction to the performer, so that a special aspect of the composition, namely its individual rhythm, can come into being as a musical reality; the accent is as much a direction to the player as is the bar-line.

If all this is correct, then the performance of such music calls for special attention, because something must be brought into effect that was new in Schubert's time, that lay outside the traditional domain of art music, beyond the accepted norm. This 'beyond' was by no means unfamiliar to the good musician, nor is it today; whenever he plays music for dancing, he is aware of it; but here the player must apply his knowledge consciously, and in the field of art music, where normally he does not apply it, or does so only exceptionally. If we turn our attention to dances in varying rhythms (for example

8 This can only be hinted at here, not enlarged upon. See Feil, *Studien zu Schuberts Rhythmik*, pp. 110ff.

the Bavarian *Zwiefache*, which alternate between common and compound time), and play these rhythms so that they can be danced to, we have a valuable model for performing Schubert too. Of course, neither the scherzo of the Octet nor the last movement of the B flat Piano Trio is dance music. Nevertheless in both one feels that Schubert has realized a sense of bodily movement through his special kind of rhythm, and has notated it by the use of a special sign. Both the individual rhythm and the bodily movement it is intended to suggest as a basic mental image (no more and no less) must still be 'turned into music' by the musician. The critical edition must serve to make this evident, and thereby enable him to bring the music to life.

Colour drawing of Schubert, by Moritz von Schwind, undated (collection of Wilhelm Kempff)

Schwind made several drawings of Schubert, but this sketch seems to be the only one which shows Schubert's hands.

'Father Leopold Puschl of Seitenstetten' and 'Schubert's sojourn at Zseliz': the late Ignaz Weinmann's last contributions to Schubert research

ALEXANDER WEINMANN

There is never an end to research; it continues to be alive and actual. The human mind is always restlessly active, not only thinking of the future, as with inventions and discoveries, but also – in historical research – peering into the past, rummaging through archives and unearthing all kinds of information. For the specialist, both kinds of investigation are attractive and even fascinating; but they also appeal to the educated layman, and often indeed to the man in the street. Every science has its well-known and not-so-well-known representatives in the academic field, but inventors and discoverers are not invariably recruited from among the circles of specialists – they are often non-professionals, dilettantes, who from time to time bring a breath of fresh air into research; and this is true also of historical studies.

There is of course a serious difficulty here: the more profound and the more 'scientific' a contribution is, the less likely it will be to have general appeal. Fortunately there are writers who know how to present the history of an invention, a discovery or a piece of research in a popular manner; they interpret scientific knowledge to the general public. To underrate such activity would be a great mistake; on the contrary, acting as intermediaries between the experts and the incomparably more numerous lay public – and in most fields we are all laymen – such writers fulfil a very important function. Today especially, at this time of reorientation and radical upheaval in physics, chemistry, medicine and biology, as in all the arts, there is a danger that the vast majority of people are made to feel insecure by a handful of specialists who are shaking daily life to its foundations; the latter perhaps do not realize the significance of their discoveries, and so will go merrily on, until the whole edifice of our traditional culture collapses.

These thoughts, as they pertain to the field of historical research, are retrospective. There is of course no immediate danger of a negative influence on the future, yet there is a danger of falsification, of lack of objectivity, which is no less serious. Artists, composers, writers, philosophers and scholars are simply forgotten, or are seen in the wrong light, according to the attitude of their commentators or biographers, who all too often cobble together their judgement according to the prevailing fashion or the taste of the time.

This article discusses two contributions made to Schubert studies, the completion of which coincided by chance with the Schubert anniversary year of 1978. My brother Ignaz Weinmann, who died on 16 October 1976, had for many years patiently worked towards their completion; at the time of his death they existed as manuscripts in a few photocopies; sadly, he was not destined to see their publication in book form. One of them has since appeared.[1] The other work has not yet found a publisher. As his brother I feel that it is my duty to see to its publication, and to give scholars advance notice of its existence.

A brief sketch of how the first study, entitled 'Die Schubertsammlung im Musikarchiv der Benediktinerabtei Seitenstetten', came to be written may be of interest. I work for the Austrian section of the International Inventory of Musical Sources (RISM) and am presently occupied with a survey of musical material in the archives of monasteries and private collections. In 1971 my work led me somewhat off the beaten track to the Abbey of Seitenstetten;[2] its archives are uncommonly rich in musical material, which attests to a strong musical tradition ranging from medieval to modern times. On my very first visit we discovered a box which was found to contain a complete collection of works by Schubert, with numerous first editions and early editions, manuscripts and records, as well as relevant literature. I immediately informed my brother, who had a great deal of experience in the field of Schubert studies, and thus began a series of weekly visits together to the abbey, which extended over a period of more than two and a half years; my brother studied the Schubert material while I was occupied with the affairs of RISM.

It soon became apparent that the Schubert collection had been established through the efforts of Father Leopold Puschl (1802-74); he was a fervent admirer of Schubert, and from 1825 till the year of his death he amassed all the Schubert editions he could get hold of, together with numerous manuscript copies. Taken as a whole, the study that Ignaz Weinmann completed just before his death gives a description of the collection itself and how it attained its present form, under the following chapter headings:

1. Introduction.
2. The Schubert collection: printed scores, first and early editions; collected editions; copies (in particular of the most important works); books and other writings; pictures.
3. Father Leopold Puschl, O.S.B.
4. Supplement and Index.

1 Ignaz Weinmann, 'Die Schubert-Sammlung im Musikarchiv der Benediktinerabtei Seitenstetten' in ***Schubert-Studien***, ed. F. Grasberger and O. Wessely (Vienna, 1978), pp. 167-298.

2 I would like once again to express my thanks to the keeper of the archives, Father Benedikt Wagner, O.S.B., for his invaluable help in placing at our disposal the relevant documents from both the music archive and the abbey's general archives.

In the dating of Schubert's works, Ignaz Weinmann's study has new information to offer to present-day scholars. Especially worthy of mention is the discovery of a hitherto unknown work by Schubert in one of Puschl's own copies – the fifth version of a setting of the poem 'Das Grab' by Baron J. G. von Salis-Seewis (1762-1834), which is listed in the new edition of O. E. Deutsch's catalogue as D 643A.[3]

A problem of particular importance today, a burning question in Schubert studies – namely, how many symphonies Schubert wrote – is affected by the discovery of the Seitenstetten collection. During the investigation an apparently insignificant scrap of paper came to light, with a note in Puschl's unmistakable handwriting; this clearly stems from Puschl's attempts to make a survey of Schubert's entire output. On one side the following groups of works are mentioned:

1. Franz Schubert's extant string quartets in manuscript
2. Two string trios
3. Piano sonatas

On the other side the symphonies are arranged in the following order:

1813	1st Symphony in D
1815	2nd and 3rd Symphonies in D and B flat
1816	4th Symphony in B flat
	5th Tragic Symphony in C minor
1817	6th Symphony in C
1825	7th Symphony in C minor, composed at Gastein

This is the first mention of the key of C minor for the symphony written at Gastein – a somewhat disturbing piece of information which understandably gave rise to a vigorous search through the Seitenstetten archives, including the library, since Puschl's exemplary precision raises him above all suspicion of having invented such a precise indication of the key. There must certainly have been a source for his information. Unfortunately he omitted to give it in this case, as in many others.

This circumstance gave rise, as may well be imagined, to a plethora of speculation and further research. In the first place we have to bear in mind that if Puschl had seen an autograph or a copy of the symphony, he would certainly have made a copy for himself; but none such is to be found in this collection. There could be more than one explanation for this: for example, Puschl certainly must have possessed the first editions of *Winterreise* and *Schwanengesang*, since his name appears in the lists of subscribers. Neither of these sizeable editions is represented in the collection, which leads us to

3 *Franz Schubert. Thematisches Verzeichnis seiner Werke in chronologischer Folge*, edited by the Editorial Board of the Neue Schubert-Ausgabe and Werner Aderhold (Kassel, etc., 1978).

This mature version for unaccompanied mixed choir was first performed in a choral concert given on Austrian Radio on 1 April 1972; it was published shortly before that date by Ludwig Doblinger, Vienna.

conclude that Puschl regarded them as particularly worthy of preservation – that is, he kept them somewhere especially safe. The score of the symphony may have been treated with equal care. Had he kept his special treasures in his office when he later became the headmaster of the Gymnasium, then in 1939, when the monastery was dissolved and the school moved to Waidhofen an der Ybbs, they would have been taken there and then perished, along with all the other archive material which was deposited there at that time. It would be possible to follow up this line of inquiry, although there is little hope of success. Further clues led to the vicinity of Seitenstetten, for example to the church of St Peter in der Au; but here again our efforts yielded no result. Another possible explanation for Puschl's note is that he got the information from a colleague in one of the numerous monasteries which he kept in touch with throughout his life and with which (as can be demonstrated) he frequently exchanged material. Of these the most important were the foundations at Lambach, Göttweig, St Florian, Melk, and Salzburg, along with several others; Steyr should be mentioned too, where Sylvester Paumgartner was active, at whose house Schubert had been a guest. It was Paumgartner to whom the 'Trout' Quintet was dedicated, the autograph of which must also be written off as lost. A relative of Paumgartner, with the same name, was magistrate (*Marktrichter*) at Seitenstetten and a cabinet-maker by profession; he made many splendid cupboards, tables and other pieces of furniture for the monastery. Puschl himself copied out two letters to Sylvester Paumgartner (the second was from Mozart's widow), which shows how much importance he attached to them, and also how wide were his interests and connections *in causis musicis*.

For the present, all attempts to follow up Puschl's clues relating to Schubert's symphony written at Gastein have proved fruitless, both positively and negatively. The point at issue is not only the whereabouts of such a symphony but even its existence, and this has already occupied many Schubert specialists and amateurs. There is an impressive number of printed articles on the subject, and although it has been proven recently that the autograph of the 'Great' C major Symphony was written on paper from the years 1825-6, and was probably finished and copied before August 1827, no final answer seems as yet to have been reached with regard to whether this symphony is indeed identical with the 'Gastein Symphony'. It is another matter that Schubert's date on the manuscript of the C major Symphony ('März 1828') has still not been satisfactorily explained; the possibility that at Gastein Schubert began a symphony in C minor cannot be ruled out completely. This makes the present discovery even more interesting and gives the problem a new lease of life.

It remains to be said that Puschl's note with the interesting statement concerning the key of a symphony 'composed at Gastein' was found tucked into a copy of volume x/1 of the *Neue Zeitschrift für Musik* (Leipzig, 1839). It was with the issue of 23 April 1839 that there began a series of articles entitled 'From the Life of Franz Schubert', and in the penultimate one (pp. 138-40) the author – Ferdinand Schubert – gives a list of his brother's unpublished works. We also know that four years before, on 3 April 1835, in the same periodical, he had called attention to seven symphonies by his brother and offered them for performance:

Concerning the larger posthumous works of Franz Schubert

We hasten to bring the following information to the notice of our readers and earnestly beg them both to let others know and to take advantage of it themselves.

Franz Schubert, the musician of genius who died all too young, and the composer of affecting songs, has left many works which are in his brother's keeping. The latter, partly because he does not wish to withhold them from the public, and partly in order to use his brother's spiritual heritage to his own best advantage and according to the wishes of the deceased, is willing to allow theatre managers and musicians the use of these scores on payment of a small fee. The works are:

I. Operas: *Des Teufels Lustschloss* in two acts (finished in 1814); *Fernando* in one act (1815); *Die Freunde von Salamanca* in two acts by Mayrhofer (1815); *Der vierjährige Posten* in one act (1815); *Die Bürgschaft* in three acts (1816); *Die Zwillingsbrüder* in one act; *Die Zauberharfe*, melodrama in three acts (1820); [*Der*] *häuslich*[*e*] *Krieg* in one act by Castelli (1823); *Fierrabras* in three acts by Schober [*recte* Kupelwieser] (1823).

II. Symphonies: in D (1813), in D (1815), in B flat (1815), in C minor (1816), in B flat (1816), in C major (1818), in C minor (his last).

III. Masses: in F for four vocal parts and large orchestra (1814); in G for four vocal parts and small orchestra (1815); in B flat for four vocal parts and medium-sized orchestra; in A flat and in E flat, both for four vocal parts and large orchestra (1822 and 1828).

Anyone wishing to receive one of these works should kindly make application in writing to Herr Ferdinand Schubert, teacher at the K. K. Normal-Hauptschule in Vienna.

In the list of symphonies given here, the 'Tragic' in C minor stands in fourth place, the B flat Symphony in fifth, while with Puschl the order is reversed. A symphony in C minor is given as his seventh (and last); no mention is made of Gastein, and the date of composition is not given as it is with the others. In volume X of the *Neue Zeitschrift für Musik*, in which the first of Ferdinand's series of articles appears with the catalogue of his brother's works, nothing is said of a symphony written in 1825, and thus there is naturally no mention of the key of C minor.

The objection that Puschl's notes may simply be a careful presentation of Ferdinand Schubert's list of the works may seem to have much to commend it. A closer look reveals Puschl's tendency to classification, here shown in his use of Ferdinand's list for the purpose of making a personal inventory, a kind of stock-taking. He writes of the quartets, for example: 'in all fourteen string quartets'; or of the piano sonatas: 'we may expect a further eleven (thirteen) sonatas'. Under 'the symphonies of Schubert', however, there are discrepancies. Ferdinand's catalogue of works is laid out chronologically, and Puschl seems to take this system over for each group of compositions; yet Ferdinand records for 1825 only one piano sonata in C (in the possession of Diabelli), but not the (last) symphony in C minor, which he had mentioned in 1835, whereas Puschl includes 'im J[ahre] 1825 7te Symph: in C-moll in Gastein componiert' (in the year 1825, Seventh Symphony in C minor, composed at Gastein). Although it cannot be definitely concluded that Puschl's information points in a specific direction concerning the 'Gastein Symphony', it does seem that such testimony as Puschl's should be taken notice of, even though its date is so long after the event and although the 'Gastein' riddle seems recently to have been solved. Puschl's note for 1825 does allow the possibility that he had sources of information now lost to us; one indication of such sources is found in his note 'Im Jahr 1811 also in seinem 14ten Jahre komponierte er sein 1tes Quartett' (in the year 1811, i.e. in his fourteenth year, he composed his first quartet). No quartet of such an early date was known until 1968, when Christa Landon found new Schubert manuscripts in the archive of the Vienna Männergesang-Verein, among them a page of the third movement of the 'Unfinished' Symphony and this early quartet of 1811.[4]

To be sure, Puschl's document – or Ferdinand Schubert's – might simply embody a reasonable human error. Yet a simple mistake on Puschl's part seems to me the least likely possibility. As one acquainted with the Schubert collection and with the writings of Father Puschl I know him to have been an extremely careful, almost pedantically exact man; there is no other evidence of his having made mistakes – on the contrary, he recorded many dates from Schubert's career that had hitherto been unknown. In the light of this, we regarded such an explanation as too simple and too convenient.

My brother Ignaz Weinmann, an authority on nineteenth-century Schubert literature – especially first editions – characterized the hitherto unregarded Benedictine father as a man of decisive importance in the realm of Schubert scholarship and remarked in the following words on the way in which Puschl handled the material to which he devoted himself as a pioneer from the 1830s to the 1850s: 'He deserves to be ranked as the first among Schubert bibliographers.'

Ignaz Weinmann characterized his study *Franz Schuberts Beziehungen zu Zseliz*, which still awaits publication, as a summary of the relevant literature and of the results of the most recent research. Schubert's two visits to the castle of Count Esterházy as music teacher to his two daughters is certainly recorded in letters and various documents, and has even been regarded as a

4 Christa Landon, 'Neue Schubert-Funde', *Österreichische Musikzeitschrift*, XXIV (1969), pp. 299-323 (transl. in *Music Review*, XXXI (1970), pp. 215-31).

good subject for fiction. Ignaz Weinmann's book gives a comprehensive account of all dates, events and persons connected with Schubert's time in Zseliz.

Part One concerns the families of Schubert, Count Johann Karl Esterházy von Galántha and Count August Ferdinand von Breunner-Enkevoerth, together with the estate of Zseliz and properties appertaining to it. Part Two deals with Schubert's early years and his two visits to Zseliz (in 1818 and 1824). Part Three, entitled 'Parerga Esterházyana', gives details of the music owned by Countesses Caroline and Marie Esterházy, and also discusses two of Schubert's successors in Zseliz.

The first of these is Leopold Eustach Czapek, who was born on 15 November 1792 at Krumau (Český Krumlov) in Bohemia; music historians have completely forgotten him, and he is not even mentioned in the two volumes of the fairly recent Czech encyclopaedia of music,[5] although forty-five published works by Czapek have been traced. We are indebted to the Czech writer on music Marie Tarantová (born in 1894) for an account of Czapek's life which has furnished us with some important information. He went to Vienna in about 1818, worked for a time in Warsaw, and proved himself a good friend to Chopin; he helped the latter with his travel arrangements and offered to advance him a loan for his journey to Paris. In 1819 Czapek took the post of music teacher at Zseliz in place of Schubert. All this seems reason enough for taking a deeper interest in this minor composer.

Schubert's second successor at Zseliz was Joseph Edmund Petzina. The discovery of his name was again a result of my brother's collaboration with me. My survey of the music archives of the Augustinian foundation at Herzogenburg brought to light a considerable number of sacred works by Petzina, who proved to have been the private tutor of Count August Breunner at the castle of Grafenegg near Krems. In the parish of Haitzendorf, in which the castle is situated, numerous other works by Petzina were found. In the cemetery by the church at Haitzendorf his grave may be seen near the tomb of the Breunners. Petzina's employment in 1838 as tutor to the Countess Caroline Esterházy in Zseliz is attested by a manuscript volume of music from the archives of the foundation at Herzogenburg, which bears an amusing title-page:

FOR THE FORTEPIANO

TO THE HIGH-BORN COUNTESS CAROLINE
ESTERHÁZY DE GALÁNTHA
THIS BOOK IS DEDICATED
WITH GREATEST RESPECT

Here you will find things
Unwanted by any;
Too trivial are they

5 *Česko Slovenský Hudební Slovník* (Prague, 1963-5).

They're meant to while the time away
When *Caroline* sits down to play.

May she a little kindness show
Else the composer's shame must grow.
And who is he that thus fears shame?
Joseph Petzina is his name.

1st Volume
Zelez in Hungary 10 October 1838

This rather naive title-page presents an enchanting picture of former times with a clarity scarcely to be surpassed. A remarkable coincidence in the world of research was to complete this picture. My colleague Dr Otto Biba kindly informed me of a sequel to the above manuscript, a 'Book Two', which Petzina likewise introduced with a few lines of verse; it is dated 'Presburg [Bratislava] 30 December 1838', and I was able to include it in the manuscript of my brother's book. The table of contents in Book Two refers to a third volume, which begins on page 182 and contains sections XII–XVI. It would be nice if this third book too could be located, and if its owner, or anyone who knows its whereabouts, could fill out the picture by providing this information.

The last chapter describes Zseliz in 1972. The castle was still inhabited during the Second World War by the descendants of Count Esterházy. After 1945 the area north of the Danube and Gran (Esztergom) was ceded to Czechoslovakia and Zseliz was renamed Želiezovce. Today part of the castle has been renovated as a museum dedicated to the memory of Schubert.

Ignaz Weinmann's book, which is richly furnished with illustrations, brings together all documentary references to Zseliz and will assuredly help us to form a clear picture of Schubert's life and work in these idyllic surroundings during the period of his sojourns there.

As the brother of Ignaz Weinmann, whose modesty inclined him to avoid the limelight, I consider it my duty to do after his death and in brief what he himself forbore to do. As the two studies described in the present article indicate, he saw it as his task to devote every spare minute of his life to the cause of Schubert scholarship. Close ties bound him to O. E. Deutsch until the latter's death. And it was to Ignaz Weinmann, appropriately, that Maurice Brown dedicated his *Essays on Schubert*.

A project close to his heart was a complete catalogue of all printed editions of Schubert's works; this volume, with the present writer as collaborator, is planned as the final volume of the new complete edition. The material for this 'new Nottebohm' (the passage of more than a century since Gustav Nottebohm's original *Thematisches Verzeichniss der im Druck erschienenen Werke von Franz Schubert* was published in Vienna in 1874 has brought abundant new material for inclusion) is assembled in its entirety and requires only to be prepared for the printer; when published it will make an essential and long-overdue contribution to Schubert bibliography.

Ignaz Weinmann's Schubert research also took him to the workshop of Anton Diabelli, Schubert's principal publisher. My own still incomplete series of publishers' lists of Viennese music firms from the first excluded the house of Peter Cappi/Cappi & Diabelli/Diabelli & Co./C. A. Spina, which in scope far exceeded all the other music publishing houses. My brother had planned to assemble a complete catalogue of this firm's publications, and indeed he worked at the project for many years. The vast quantity of music brought out by the firm in its various manifestations accounts for the time this work took; it is sad that Ignaz Weinmann did not live to see its completion. It is to be hoped that a suitably equipped successor will eventually be able to bring this huge task to a successful conclusion.

Index

by FREDERICK SMYTH

Bold figures indicate the more important references; *italic* figures denote illustrations or their captions. 'q.' stands for 'quoted'; '*passim*' conveys that references to the subject are scattered throughout the group of pages; 'n' ('nn') means 'footnote(s)' and 'Ex.' ('Exx.') 'music example(s)', which are serially numbered within each essay.

Librettists and dramatists are, where necessary, identified as such. It can otherwise be generally taken that the stage works listed appear under the names of their composers.

Aderhold, Werner, 61n, 139n, 143n, 209n, 297n, 349n
Allgemeine Musikalische Zeitung (1805), 140
American Musicological Society, 25n
Amoudruz, Emile, 320
Antonicek, Theophil, 322
'Arbeitslied' (Austrian folk-song), 281
Aristophanes: *Lysistrata*, 87
Arnstein, Fanny von, 50n
Artaria (publishers), 216
Aspelmayr, Franz: *Pygmalion*, 106
Assmayr, Ignaz, 4n

Bach, Johann Sebastian, 210, 213
Badura-Skoda, Eva, xiii, 178n, 208n, 249n, 269n
Badura-Skoda, Paul, xiii, 178n, 211, 259, 269n, 314
Baer, Abraham, 55
Bärenreiter (publisher), 324
Barnett, J. F., 320
Bäuerle, Adolf (dramatist)
  Aline (Müller), 113
  Verwunschene Prinz, Der (Müller), 114 and n
Bauernfeld, Eduard von (poet), q.**10**, 10n, 11, 258
  as librettist, *Der Graf von Gleichen* (Schubert), 104, 258
Baumberg, Gabriele von, 298
Baumgarten, Gotthilf von, 107
Beethoven, Ludwig van, 173-4, 204, 232, 240, 293, 329
  chronology, 210
  commissions refused, 52, 60, 140
  his copyists, 211-12, 229
  his MS paper, 217-19, 224, **226-7**, **229**, 230-44 *passim*, 257-66 *passim*
  his publishers, 210
  and Schubert, 9n, **39-45**, 81, 87, 209, 211-12, 217
  his sketchbooks, 215
  chamber music
    piano trios, 277
    quintets and sextets, 184
    string quartets, 177, 184, 257;
      op. 59/2 in E minor, 177 and n; op. 127 in E flat, 169n; op. 130 in B flat, 203, 236; op. 131 in C sharp minor, 219-20; op. 132 in A minor, 257
  Missa Solemnis, 227
  overture, *Die Weihe des Hauses*, 229
  Piano Sonata op. 7 in E flat, **329** (Ex. 1)
  songs, 3
    'Adelaïde' (Matthisson), 82
    An die ferne Geliebte (Jeitteles), **39-40**, 50n
  stage works
    Egmont, 108
    Fidelio, 66 and n, 87, 108, 110, 129, 141
    König Stephan, 108
    Leonore Prohaska, 108
    Ruinen von Athen, Die, 108
  symphonies
    no. 3, op. 55 in E flat ('Eroica'), 40-1 (Ex. 5(a))
    no. 6, op. 68 in F ('Pastoral'), 169 and n
    no. 7, op. 82 in A, 81

Beethoven: symphonies (contd)
no. 9, op. 125 in D minor ('Choral'), 60, 217, 219, 227, 229, 257
Benda, Georg, 106-9
Ariadne auf Naxos, 106-7
Medea, 105-7
Pygmalion 106-7
Theone (*Almansor und Nadine*), 106
Berg, Isaak Albert, 284
Berke, Dietrich, 309, 311
Berlioz, Hector, 51n
Biba, Otto, 187 and n, 206, 210n, 258n, 264 and nn, 269n, 354
Biedermann, Lazar, 49, 50 and n, 51
Binz, J. G. (publisher), 107n
Bloch, Ernst: *Sacred Service*, 47-8n
Blom, Eric, 1n, 38n, 53n, 210n
Blume, Friedrich, 62n, 79n, 80
Bobrik, Johann Friedrich Ludwig, 309
Bocklet, Carl Maria von, 284, 286, 292, 294
Boieldieu, François Adrien, 88
Jean de Paris, 109-10
Brahms, Johannes 184, 201n, 277-8
Branscombe, Peter, xiii, 114n
Breitkopf and Härtel (publishers), 323
Brendel, Alfred, 62n, 204
Breunner-Enkevoerth, Count August von, 353
Breuning, Gerhard von, 61
Britten, Benjamin, 314
Brody, Elaine, xiii
Brown, Maurice J. E., 70, 293, 301, 312, 317, 320-2
articles, 38, 299, q.300, 313, q.315, 322n
Essays on Schubert, 83 and n, 119 and n, 188n, 191-2 and nn, 195n, 246, 249, 309, 354
Schubert. A Critical Biography, 164, 173, 185, 258, q.**281-2**, 309, 314, 316, 319
Bruchmann, Franz von, 7n, q.8, 10
Brusatti, Otto, 144n, 187n, 245-6, 324
Bruckner, Anton, 198
Burney, Charles, 52n
Butir, Leonid, 320

Caigniez, Louis-Charles, 112
Capell, Richard, 25 and n, 78 and n
Cappi, Peter (publisher), 355
Cappi and Czerny (publishers), 226, 355
Cappi and Diabelli (publishers), 144n
Castelli, Ignaz Franz (dramatist/librettist), q.87, 113
Die Schweizerfamilie (Weigl), 87-8
Die Verschworenen (*Der häusliche Krieg*) (Schubert), 87-90, 351
Catel, Charles-Simon: *Sémiramis*, 115
Cherubini, Luigi, 88
Deux journées, Les, 109
Faniska, 109
Lodoiska, 109
Médée, 109-10
Chézy, Helmina von (dramatist): *Rosamunde* (Schubert), 228-9
Chopin, Frédéric, 353
Chusid, Martin, 164n
Claudius, Matthias (poet), 5, 143
collected works, *Asmus omnia sua*, 143-7, *146*
Schubert settings, 5, **143-59**, 297; 'Der Tod und das Mädchen', **144-59**
Coignet, Horace: *Pygmalion*, 105-6
Coleridge, Arthur Duke, 44n, 279n, q.**280**, 291n
collections
Cary, New York, 30n
Weinmann (Ignaz), 116n
Witteczek-Spaun, Vienna, 19n, 59, 139n, 210-11, 297
Zweig, London, 241, 249
Collin, Heinrich von, 316
Cone, Edward, q.44, 45n
Cranz, Alwin, 299
Czapek, Leopold Eustach, **353**
Czerny, Joseph, 223n, 291n

Dahlhaus, Carl, 162n, 169n
Dahms, Walter, 62n
Dalmonte, Rossana, 119n, 129
Debussy, Claude, 198
Dermota, Anton, 311
Deutsch, Otto Erich, xii, 8n, 210, 282-3, 289, 299, 313, 323, 354
Schubert. A Documentary Biography, 38, 44, 110-11, 115, 140-1, 210, 281, 284; and nn to 8, 53, 95, 144, 158-9, 171, 188, 288, 289
Schubert. Die Dokumente seines Lebens, 8n, 38 and nn, 44 and n, 119n, 210
Schubert. Die Erinnerungen seiner Freunde, 210
Schubert. Memoirs by His Friends, q.41, q.61, 110-11, 115, 210; and nn to 77, 108, 188, 284, 288, 311
Franz Schubert. Sein Leben in Bildern, 51n
Schubert. Thematic Catalogue, 30n, 47n, 62, 139, q.**220**, 242, 278, 281, 297n; and elsewhere, cited as '*D1*'
Franz Schubert. Thematisches Verzeichnis, 62, 64, 139, 143n, 209, 221, 242, 297n, 325, 349; and elsewhere, cited as '*D2*'

Diabelli, Anton (publisher), 38 and n, 278-9, 283 and n, 291 and nn, 292, 352, 355; *see also* Cappi and Diabelli
Dietrich, Anton, xiv, *186*
Doblinger, Ludwig (publisher), 349n
Drechsler, Joseph, 50, 52-3
Duncker, Friedrich (dramatist): *Leonore Prohaska* (1815), 108
Dürr, Walther, xiii, 5nn, 9n, 15n, 63 and n, 215, 219, 269n, 294n, 301-24 *passim*, 325n

Eberl, Anton, 108
Pyramus und Thisbe, 105
Einstein, Alfred, 11n, 39, 47-8n, 78-9nn, q.164 and n, 173, 317-18
Ense, Varnhagen von, 42
Eszterházy von Galántha, Count Johann Karl, 352-4
Eszterházy von Galántha, Countess Caroline, 353-4
Eszterházy von Galántha, Countess Marie, 353

Feder, Georg, 329
Feigl, Rudolf, 188 and n
Feil, Arnold, xiii, 2n, 249, 269n, 282, 287, 327n, 330-1nn, 337n, 344n
Fischer-Dieskau, Dietrich, 311
Förster, Friedrich, q.**70-1**
Francis I, Emperor of Austria, 49-51, 59 and n
Friedländer, Max, 38n, 144n
Fröhlich, Anna, 94n, 47, **61**, 62, 284
Fröhlich, Josephine ('Pepi'), 61, *142*, 284
Fuchs, Aloys, 266, 292
Fuss, Johann: *Judith*, 112
Fux, Johann Josef, 314

Gál, H., 180n, q.**196-7**
Galitzin, Prince Nikolaus, 257
Gelber, N. B., q.59n
Getty, N. C., 315
Gleich, Joseph Alois (librettist)
Herr Josef und Frau Baberl (Müller), 111, 113
Moses in Egypten (Tuczek), 112
Gleim, Johann Wilhelm Ludwig, 81
Glöggl (copyist), 264
Gluck, Christoph Willibald, 88
Alceste, 106, 115, **156-8** (Ex.7)
Iphigénie en Aulide, 298
Iphigénie en Tauride, 110, 115
Orfeo, 115
Goethe, Johann Wolfgang von, 3, 5, 10, 81, 83-4
and Schiller, 62n
and Schubert, **5-6**
Schubert settings, 6, 15, **64-70**, **75-82**, 143, 312-13, 318-19
Egmont, 108
Gedichte, 16n, 17n, 19-20
Werther, 145n
West-Östlicher Divan, 80
Wilhelm Meister, 17 and n, 66
Goldschmidt, Harry, 282
Gosmar, Louise, 61
Gotthard, J. P., 60, 320
Grams (copyist), 264
Grétry, André Ernest Modeste
Richard Coeur-de-Lion, 109
Zémire et Azor, 114, 128n
Griffel, L. Michael, 188n, 191-2nn, 219n, 267n
Grillparzer, Franz, 9n, 61, 105
Grimm, Baron Melchior von, 106
Grob, Therese, 81
Grove, Sir George, 47n, 232, 258, 264, 281, 293
Gülke, Peter, xiii, 173-4nn, 176n, 184n
Gyrowetz, Adalbert, 85, **86**, 92
Agnes Sorel, 86
Augenarzt, Der, 86

Haensel, Peter, 223n
Hallmark, Rufus, xiii
Hammerstein, Reinhold, 145n
Handel, George Frideric, 115
Hanslick, Eduard, q.89
Harmonicon (London, 1825), q.86
Harrán, Don, 60n
Hartmann, Franz von, 7, 250
Haslinger, Tobias (publisher), 20n, 140, 216, 232
Haydn, (Franz) Josef, 3, 105, 169n, 204, 329
on quintet writing, q.**177n**
oratorio *The Seasons*, 305
piano trios, 277
Heidegger, Martin, q.327
Heine, Heinrich, 5, 9, 10
Schubert settings, 21-3, 174
Heimkehr, Die (*Buch der Lieder*), 21n
Reisebilder, 7
Henle, G. (publisher), 282-3n
Herbeck, Johann, 89, 320-1
Herder, Johann Gottfried von, 145 and n
Hérold, Louis-Joseph-Ferdinand, 88
Heuberger, R., 316
Hiller, Johann Adam, 107
Hilmar, Ernst, 144n, 187n, 205-6, 209-16 *passim*, 221, 225-7, 237-46 *passim*, 251-4, 265-6, 315 and n, 324-5

Hoffmann, Ernst Theodor Amadeus, q.3
Hofmann, Georg von (librettist), 87
  Zauberharfe, Die (Schubert), 119
  Zwillingsbrüder, Die (Schubert), 87
Hofmann, Isaac Loew (Edler von Hofmannsthal), 49, 50 and n
Hofmannsthal, Hugo von, 50
Hölderlin, Friedrich, 182
Holländer, Hans, 66, 164n
Holly, Andreas Franz, 107
Holmes, Edward, 51n, q.88
Holschneider, Andreas, 83 and n
Hölty, Ludwig Heinrich Christoph, 5-6, 81, 143, 308
Holz, Karl, 257n
Hoorickx, Reinhard van, xiii, 5n
Höslinger, Clemens, 139, 139-40n, 158n
Humboldt, Alexander and Wilhelm von, 50n
Hummel, J.J. (publisher), 328-9
Hüttenbrenner, Anselm, 4 and n, 81, q.114, 284

Ibach, Adolf, 308
Isouard, Nicolò, 89
  Cendrillon, 109-10

Jeitteles, Alois (poet), 50n
  An die ferne Geliebte (Beethoven), 39 and n, 45n
Jeitteles, Barouch, 50n
Jenger, Johann Baptist, 243
Johnson, Douglas, 213, 215n, 269n
Joseph II, Emperor of Austria, 49n
Josquin Desprez, 210

Kalb, Charlotte von, 70
Keldorfer, Viktor, 320
Kerman, Joseph, 45n
Kiesewetter, Irene von, 243, 249
Kiesling, Anton-Ignaz, Gustav and Wilhelm (paper-makers), 214-17, 227, 231, 237, 240, 244
Kind, Friedrich (librettist): *Der Freischütz* (Weber), 90
King, A. Hyatt, 116n
Kirnberger, Johann Philipp, 176, q.331
Kleist, Heinrich von, 7 and n
Klemm, C. A. (publisher), 304
Klemm, Friedrich, 223n
Klier, Karl Maria, 281
Klingemann, Ernst August, 112
Klopstock, Friedrich Gottlieb, 5-6
Koch, Heinrich Christoph, **327-8**
Kollmann, Augustus F. C., 169n
Körner, Christian Gottfried, 169n
Körner, Minna, 70-1
Körner, Theodor (librettist): *Der vierjährige Posten* (Schubert), 118
Kornhäusel, Joseph, 51
Kosegarten, Ludwig, 5, 7, 143
Kotzebue, August von (dramatist)
  Adelheit von Italien (Seyfried), 113
  Ariadne auf Naxos, 107
  Kluge Frau im Walde, Die (Seyfried), 113
  König Stephan (Beethoven), 108
  Ruinen von Athen, Die (Beethoven), 108
  Spanier in Peru, Die, 86n
  Spiegelritter, Der (Schubert), 301
  Sultan Wampun, 114
  Teufels Lustschloss, Des (Schubert), 116-17
Krasser family, 321
Kreissle von Hellborn, Heinrich, 43, 44n, 139 and n, 243 and n, 279n, q.**280**, 284, 291n, 312, 322
Kreutzer, Rodolphe: *Libussa*, 111
Kringsteiner, J. F. (dramatist): *Johann Faust* (Volkert), 113n
Kupelwieser, Josef (librettist): *Fierrabras* (Schubert), 94, 98, **116n**, 131n, 351
Kupelwieser, Leopold, 94, 171

Lachner, Franz, 256, 291n
Landon, Christa, xiii, 59n, 60n, 298 and n, 300, 352
Lannoy, Eduard Freiherr von: *Ein Uhr*, 113
Lee, Noel, 314
Leidesdorf, M. J. (publisher), 38 and n, 279, 283 and n, 291 and nn; *see also* Sauer and Leidesdorf
Leitner, Karl Gottfried von, 8, 10, q.10-11n, 251, 325
Lessing, Gotthold Ephraim, 145 and nn
Lewis, M. G., 113
Lewy, Josef Rudolf, 44
Ley, Rosamund, 1n, 53n, 210n, 311n
Lindgren, Lowell, 37n
Linke, Josef, 38n, 286, 292, 294
Liszt, Franz, 49n, 91 and n, 198
Litterick, Louise, 37n
Luib, Ferdinand, 4

McKay, Elizabeth Norman, xiii, 114 and n
Macpherson, James ('Ossian'), 5
Mainzer, Joseph, 51n
Mandyczewski, Eusebius, 25n, 38 and n, 45n, 70, 317
Mannheimer, Isaak Noah, 51-2
Maria Theresa, Empress of Austria, 49-50nn
Marvin, Frederick, 319
Matiegka, Wenzel, 306
Matthisson, Friedrich, 5 and n, 6-7, 143, 311

Mayrhofer, Johann (poet and librettist), 5, q. 9, 10, 143
Die Freunde von Salamanca (Schubert), 351
Mederitsch-Gallus, Johann, 105
Méhul, Etienne Nicholas Henri, 89
Joseph, 112
Uthal, 109
Mendelssohn, Moses, 47 and nn, 317
Mendelssohn-Bartholdy, Felix, 84, 174
Metastasio, Pietro, 306, 322
Metternich, Prince Clemens, 89
Meyerbeer, Giacomo: *Il crociato in Egitto*, 111
Milder(-Hauptmann), Anna, q.8, 93, 158n
Mohn, Ludwig, 7n
Mokry, Ladislav, 322n
Moscheles, Ignaz, 50
Mosel, Ignaz Franz von (librettist): *Rüdiger* (Schubert), 223n, 322
Mozart, Constanze, 350
Mozart, Leopold, 292
Mozart, Wolfgang Amadeus, 3, 86, 204, 212n, 292-3, 329, 332
influence on Schubert, 87, **183-4**
Clarinet Quintet (K 581), 204
piano concertos, **178-9n**
Piano Sonata in D, four hands (K 381), 178n
piano trios, 277
Rondo for piano and orchestra (K 386), 201
stage works, 86, 88, 108
Don Giovanni, 115, **158-9** (Ex. 8)
Così fan tutte (*Die Zauberprobe*), 115
Entführung aus dem Serail, Die, 115
Idomeneo, 115, 158n
Nozze di Figaro, Le, 115, 302
Schauspieldirektor, Der, 115
Semiramis, 108
Thamos, König in Ägypten, 108
Zaide, 108
Zauberflöte, Die, 110
Mozatti,__, 4n
Müller, Wenzel
Aline, 111, 113-14
Herr Josef und Frau Baberl, 111, 113
Verwunschene Prinz, Der, 114
Müller, Wilhelm, 9, 10 and n

Neefe, Christian Gottlob, 107
Nettl, Paul, 52n
Neue Freie Presse, Die, q.89
Neue Zeitschrift für Musik, Die, q.**279**, 350, q.**351**
Neumann, Johann Philipp, 246
Newbold, Brian, 320
Nottebohm, Gustav, 59-60, 292-3, 308, 354
Novalis (Friedrich Leopold von Hardenberg), 7
Nowell, John, 1n, 53n, 210n, 311n

Orel, Alfred, 302-3, 307
'Ossian' (James Macpherson), 5-6
Ottenwalt, Anton, 262

Pachler, Karl, 10-11n
Pachler, Marie, 10-11n, 243, 251
Paer, Ferdinando, 89
Agnese, 112
Maître de chapelle, Le, 109
Paganini, Niccolò, 89n
Paradies, Maria Theresia von, 108
Paumgartner, Sylvester, 350
Pennauer (publisher), 291 and n
Perinet, Joachim: *Ariadne auf Naxos travestirt*, 107
Peters (publishers), 38n
Petrarch (Francesco Petrarca), 70
Petzina, Joseph Edmund, **353-4**
Pfannhauser, Karl, 306
Pfitzner, Hans, 78
Philharmonia Trio, 313
Piccinni, Nicola, **88**
Pixérécourt, Guilbert de, 113
Platen, Karl August, Count von, 7-8
Pleyel, Ignaz Joseph, 177
Pohl, Carl Ferdinand, 264 and n, 329
Pössinger, Alexander, 223n
Pratobevera, Adolf von (poet and dramatist): *Der Falke*, 139-40 and n
Pratobevera, Franziska von, 140n
Pratobevera, Karl Josef von, 139
Preindl, Josef, 306
Presse, Die (Vienna), 10n
Probst, H. A. (publisher), 250, 278n
correspondence with Schubert, 287, **288-91**, 294
Puschl, Father Leopold, **348-52**
Puttlingen, Vesque von, 40-1n

Racek, Fritz, 305 and nn, 310, 318, 324
Raimund, Ferdinand, 113
Rameau, Jean-Philippe, 156
Reed, John, 43n, **188** and n, 189-91, 211, 213 and n, 232, 258-64 and nn *passim*, 267, 279n, 282
Rehberg, Walter, 314
Reichardt, Johann Friedrich, 3, 51n, 77-8, 107
Reinhold, Kapellmeister, 311
Reissmann, August, 307

Rellstab, Ludwig (poet), 9, q.9n, q.**42-3** and n, q.**43-4**
Schubert settings, 9n, 21, 27n, 42, 42-3nn; 'Auf dem Strom' **25-46**
rhythm in Schubert's time, **327-31**
rhythmopoeia, 327-8
Riem, W. F., 3n
Riemann, Hugo, 329-30, 342
Ries, Ferdinand, 177n, 227
Riethus, Peter, 269n, 291n
Rifkin, Joshua, 30n, 37n, 269n
Ringer, A. L., 49n, 51n, 55
Rochlitz, Friedrich, **140-1**
Rosen, Charles, 45n
Rossini, Gioacchino, 87, **88**
Barbiere di Siviglia, Il, 115
Elisabetta, regina d'Inghilterra, 115
Inganno felice, L', 88
Mosè, 112
Otello, 111
Tancredi, 111-12
Zelmira, 115
Rousseau, Jean-Jacques: as composer, 85, 105-6; as dramatist, *Pygmalion* (Aspelmayr, Benda, Coignet, Schweitzer), **105-6**
Rückert, Friedrich, 7, 321

Sachs, Curt, 56n
Salieri, Antonio, 277
Axur, rè d'Ormus, 115
Danaïdes, Les, 115
Salis-Seewis, Baron Johann Georg von (poet), 5, 7
Schubert settings, 5-6, 143, 311, 349
Satzenhofen, Friedrich: *Ariadne auf Naxos*, 107
Sauer and Leidesdorf (publishers), 226
Schauffler, R. H., xiv
Schiller, Johann Christoph Friedrich von, 3, 175
correspondence with Goethe, 62n
Schubert settings, 5-6, 10, **70-4**, 81-2, 143, 305, 308
Schindler, Anton, 9n, q.**41-2**, 43 and n, 44, 45n, q.108
Schlegel, August Wilhelm, q.1, 2, 5, 7, 50n
Schlegel, Friedrich, q.2, q.3, 5, 7, 50n
Schlösser, Louis, 284
Schmidt-Görg, Joseph, 212, 213n
Schneider (publisher), 281n
Schober, Franz von, 7 and n, 10, 95, 225
as librettist: *Alfonso und Estrella* (Schubert), **90-4**
Schochow, Maximilian and Lilly, 5n, 27n, 309n, 317n
Schönkopf, Käthchen, 81

Schott (publishers), 60 and n, 250 and n, 268, 278n, 323
correspondence with Schubert, q.**278-9**
Schubert, Andreas, 144n
Schubert, Carl, 286
Schubert, Ferdinand, 38, 238, 242, 258, 291-2, 303, 308, 316, 320
and Franz Schubert's unpublished works, **351-2**
Schubert, Franz Peter
and Beethoven, **39-45**, 209, 212, 217
and Goethe, **5-6**
and Salieri, 277
Beethoven and Schubert's songs, q.41, 42
compared with others: Beethoven, **39-40**; Mozart, 332; Schumann, 18-19, 37n; Wolf, 18-19
his death-mask, *frontispiece*, xi, xiii-iv
his diary, q.6
doubtful and erroneous attributions, 299, 306
fragmentary and sketched compositions, xiii, **297-325**
influenced by: Beethoven, 39-40, 87; Gyrowetz, 85-6; Mozart, 87, **183-4**; Rossini, 87; Weigl, 85-7, 108-9
his letters, q.7 and n, q.141, q.**284-90**, 294
his MS paper, xiii, **209-75**
portraits of, *142*, *186*, *346*
as reviser of his own works, **61-84**
and rhythm, xiii, **327-45**
as a teacher, 352-3

chamber music
Adagio ('Notturno') in E flat for piano trio (D 897), 249-50, 277-8, 281, 293 and n, 294
Fantasia in C for violin and piano (D 934), 189 (Ex. 3), 248
Guitar Quartet (D 96), 306
Introduction and Variations in E minor for flute and piano (D 802), 159n, 217, 227-8
Minuets for wind instruments (arr. Weinmann), 300
Octet in F (D 803), 159n, 170, 171, 200, 217, 228, **331-41** (Exx. 3-6)
Piano Quintet in A ('Trout', D 667), xii, 188, 210, 277, 350
piano trios, **277-95**; in B flat (D 898), **179n**, 191n, 249-50, 253, 277-95 *passim*, 337, **342-4** (Exx. 7-9); in E flat (D 929), 63n, 248, 250, 277-95 *passim*
Quartettsatz in C minor (D 703), 100, 188, **318**

Schubert: chamber music (contd)
Rondo in B minor for violin and piano (D 895), 240
'Sonata' in F major for piano trio (D 28), 277
Sonata in A minor for arpeggione and piano (D 821), 229-30
string quartets, 352; in G major (D 2, probably by Stadler), 299; in C (D 32), 301; in B flat (D 36), 302; in C (D 46), 304; in B flat (D 68), 306; in D (D 74), 302; in C minor (D 103), 307; in B flat (D 112), 307; in A minor (D 804), 171 and n, 176; in D minor ('Death and the Maiden', D 810), xii, **159-71** (Exx. 9-17), 176, 188, 191, 217, 228, 287; in G (D 887), 162n, 173-4, 176, 181, 183, 188, 200, 237, 265, 287
String Quintet in C (D 956), xiii, 47, 60, **173-85** (Ex. 1), 189, 191n, 197, 200-3 (Exx. 25, 28, 30)
String Trio in B flat (D 471, unfin.), 312-15
Violin Sonata (D 384), 310
fragments, **300-1**, 306, 312-13
choral works, part-songs, etc.
'Advokaten, Die', trio (Engelhart, D 37), 241-2
'Amors Macht', trio or quartet (Matthisson, D Anh.I,20, formerly 339), 311
'Am Sëegestad' ('Erinnerungen'), trio (Matthisson, D 424), 311
'Andenken', trio (Matthisson, D 423), 311
'Badelied', trio or quartet (Matthisson, D Anh.I,21, formerly 340), 311
'Begräbnislied', chorus (Klopstock, D 168), 307
'Canone a sei' (textless, D 873), 323
Cantata for Irene Kiesewetter (anon., D 936), 243
'Dreifach ist der Schritt der Zeit' (Schiller, D 43, 69, 70), 305
'Frühlingslied', quartet (Pollak, D 914), 241
'Gebet', quartet (Fouqué, D 815), 228-9
'Geistertanz, Der', male chorus (Matthisson, D 494), 300
'Gesang der Geister über den Wassern' (Goethe, D 538, 714), 202n, 318
'Grab, Das', quartet (Salis-Seewis, D 643A), 349 and n
'Grab und Mond', quartet (Seidl, D 893), 237, 265
'Ich hab' in mich gesogen', quartet sketch (Rückert, D 778B), 241
'Intende voci', tenor aria with chorus (D 963), 244, 254
'Jägerlied' (Körner, D 204), 308
'Klage um Ali Bey', trio (Claudius, D 140), 143n, 297
Lazarus, religious drama (Niemeyer, D 689), 119 and n, 297, 317
'Lebenslied', trio or quartet (Matthisson, D Anh.I,23, formerly 425), 311
'Lied beim Rundetanz', trio or quartet (Salis-Seewis, D Anh.I,18, formerly 132), 311
'Lied im Freien', trio or quartet (Salis-Seewis, D Anh.I,19, formerly 133), 311
'Mirjam's Siegesgesang', soprano and mixed chorus (Grillparzer, D 942), 190, 200-1 (Ex. 27), 205, 242, 249, 251-2
'Mondenschein', quintet (Schober, D 875), 239, 262, 323
'Nachklänge', quartet sketch (textless, D 873A), 238
'Nachthelle', tenor solo with chorus (Seidl, D 892), 240, 265
'Nachtmusik', quartet (Seckendorf, D 848), 231, 268
'Naturgenuss', quartet (Matthisson, D 422), 311
'Osterlied', chorus (Klopstock, D 168A), 307
'Punschlied', trio (Schiller, D 277), 309
'Schlachtlied', male double chorus (Klopstock, D 912), 241
'Ständchen', contralto solo and chorus (Grillparzer, D 920), 248
'Stille Lied, Das', quartet (Seegemund, D 916), 241, **323-4**
'Sylphen', trio or quartet (Matthisson, D Anh.I,22, formerly 341), 311
'Tanz, Der', quartet (Meerau?, D 826), 249
'Te solo adoro', quartet (Metastasio, D 34), 302
'Thronend auf erhabnem Sitz', trio (Schiller, D 62), 305
'Wein und Liebe', quartet (Haug, D 901), 242
'Widerhall', trio (Matthisson, D 428), 311
'Widerspruch', quartet (Seidl, D 865), 251

Schubert: choral works, part-songs, etc. (contd)
'Wintertag, Der', quartet (anon., D 984), 320
'Zur guten Nacht', solo baritone and male chorus (Rochlitz, D 903), 241
'Zwei Tugendwege, Die', trio (Schiller, D 71), 305
fragments, 304-5, 309, 322-3
church music, xi, xiii
'Benedictus' (D 961) 189
Deutsche Messe in F (Neumann, D 872), 246, 248
Evangelium Johannis (D 607), 316
German Requiem (Schmidt, D 621), 320
'Hymnus an den heiligen Geist' (Schmidt, D 948), 246, 250-2, 254
masses, 197, 301; in F (D 105), 81, 351; in G (D 167), 351; in B flat (D 324), 351; in C (D 452), 312; in A flat (D 678), xi, 164, 238, 242, 320-1, 351; in E flat (D 950), xi, 47, 58, 60, 189-90 (Ex. 6), 197-9 (Ex. 23), 237, 242-3, 251-5 *passim*, 351
Psalm XII (XIII) (D 663), 47, 317
Psalm XXIII (D 706), 47
Psalm XCII (Hebrew setting, D 953), xiii, **47-60** (Exx. 1-2)
'Salve Regina' in A (D 676), xi
'Salve Regina' in C (D 811), 217
'Tantum ergo' in E flat (D 962), 254
fragments, 312, 320
melodrama, 'Abschied von der Erde' (Pratobevera, D 829), 116 and n, **139-40**, 238
miscellaneous works
Andante in B minor (of 1828), 315
'Aria di Abramo' (Metastasio, D 33), 302
Ländler (D 354, 355, 370), 310
Minuets (D 380), 310
'Serbate, o dei custodi', aria sketches (Metastasio, D 35), 303
'Vedi, quanto t'adoro', aria (Metastasio, D 510), 313
operas and other stage works, xi, 85-104
Adrast (unfin., Mayrhofer, D 137), 116n, 317
Alfonso und Estrella (Schober, D 732), 8, 86, **90-4**, 97, 99-100, 103, 129, 225-6, 319-20
Bürgschaft, Die (unfin., anon., D 435), 86, 119, 311, 351
Fernando (Stadler, D 220), 86 and n, 92, 351
Fierrabras (Kupelwieser, D 796), **94-103** (Exx. 1, 2(a), 3(a)), 104, 116, **116n**, **129-39** (Ex. 4), 224-7, 255n, 322, 351
Freunde von Salamanka, Die (Mayrhofer, D 326), 85, 103, 351
Graf von Gleichen, Der (sketches, Bauernfeld, D 918), 104, 245, 248, 251, 324
Rosamunde (Chézy, D 797), xii, 95, 111, 120, 217, 225 and n, 228-9, 321
Rüdiger (sketches, Mosel (?), D 791), 100, 224, 322
Sakuntala (sketches, Neumann, D 701), 100, 129, 318
[*Sofie*] (sketches, D 982), 322
Spiegelritter, Der (fragment, Kotzebue, D 11), 301
Teufels Lustschloss, Des (Kotzebue, D 84), **116-18** (Ex. 1), 129, 351
Verschworenen, Die (*Der häusliche Krieg*, Castelli D 787), **87-90**, 100, 219, 224, 227-8, 321-2, 351
Vierjährige Posten, Der (Körner, D 190), 116 and n, **118-19**, 129-30, 351
Zauberharfe, Die (Hofmann, D 644), 94, 100-1, 106, 108, 114, 116 and n, **119-29** (Exx. 2-3), 318, 322, 351
Zwillingsbrüder, Die (Hofmann, D 647), 87, 90, 93, 111, 317, 351
overtures
in C minor (D 8), 300
in D (D 26), 306
in D (fragment, D 71C, formerly 966A), 302
in B flat (D 470), 312
piano works, solo
Adagio in C (D 349), 303-4, 312
Allegretto in C minor (D 900), 256, 324
Allegretto in C minor (D 915), 205
Andantino in C (D 348), 303-4, 312
Deutsche (D 146, 366, 779, 783, 975), 224, 228
Ecossaises (D 781), 223
Fantasia in C (D 605), 318-19
Fantasia in C ('Wanderer', D 760), xii, 191n, 203, 224, 268, 321
Impromptu in C minor (D 899/1), 245
Impromptus (D 935), xii, 246, 248-9
Klavierstück in C (D 29), 301
Klavierstücke (D 459A), 303-4
Klavierstücke (D 916B, 916C), 245-6, 253

Schubert: piano works, solo (contd)
Klavierstücke (D 945), 350
Klavierstücke (D 946), 190-1 (Ex. 7), 195-6 (Ex. 16), 246-7
Ländler (D 790), 224
Minuets (D 41), 303, 312
Minuets (D 995), 300
sonatas, 47, 203, 352; in E (D 157), 188; in C (D 279), 309; in A minor (D 537), 188; in F sharp minor (D 570/571), 195n, 309, 314; in F minor (D 625), 316; in E minor, fragment, (D 769A), 226; in A minor (D 784), xii; in C ('Reliquie', D 840), 194, 200, 203, 205, 206, 230, 322; in A minor (D 845), 190 (Ex. 4), 194, 203, 205, 206, 266-7; in D (D 850), 188, 194, 203-4 (Ex. 31(a)), 231, 260, 268; in G (Fantasia, D 894), 193-4 (Exx. 12-13), 240, 265; in C minor (D 958), 188, 198, 250-2, 255, 295; in A (D 959), 188, 196 (Ex. 17(b)), 197 (Ex. 18), 198, 252-3, 255, 295; in B flat (D 960), 188-9, 195, 211, 252-3, 255, 295
fragments, 299, 302-5, 307-9, 314-15, 317-19, 321, 324-5
piano works, four hands
Allegro in A minor (D 947), 259
Fantasia in G (D 1), 298-9
Fantasia in C minor (D 48), 304
Fantasia in F minor (D 940), xiii, 47, 195, 203, 242, 249, 250n, 259
Fugue in C major (incomplete), 299
Fugue in E minor (also for organ, D 952), 256, 325
Overture to *Fierrabras* (D 798), 242
Polonaises (D 599, 618A), 316
Rondo in A (D 951), 197-8 (Ex. 20), 204, 250-1, 259
Sonata (Grand Duo) in C (D 812), 188, 191n
Variations in A flat (D 813), 159n
Variations on a Theme from Hérold's *Marie* (D 908), 241
fragments, 298-9
songs
'Abendlied' (Claudius, D 499), 144n, 297
'Abendstern' (Mayrhofer, D 806), 217, 228
'Abgeblühte Linde, Die' (Széchényi, D 514), 144n
'Abschied' (Rellstab, D 957/7), 81
'Abschied von der Erde', melodrama (Pratobevera D 829), 116 and n, **139-40**, 238
'Ach um deine feuchten Schwingen' ('Suleika II') (Goethe, D 717), 8, 158n
'Alinde' (Rochlitz, D 904), 140, 241
'Allmacht, Die' (Pyrker, D 852), 189 (Ex. 2), 211, 232
'Altschottische Ballade, Eine' (Edward/Herder, D 923), 246
'Am ersten Maimorgen' (Claudius, D 344), 297
'Am Fenster' (Seidl, D 878), 237
'Am Flusse' (Goethe, D 160, 766), **80-1**, 83
'Am Grabe Anselmos' (Claudius, D 504), 144n, 297
'Am Meer' (Heine, D 957/12), 189
'Amalia' (Schiller, D 195), 6
'An Chloen' (Uz, D 363), 311
'An den Mond' (Goethe, D 259, 296), 62n, **78-80**
'An die Laute' (Rochlitz, D 905), 140, 241
'An die Nachtigall' (Claudius, D 497), 144n, 297
'An die untergehende Sonne' (Kosegarten, D 457), 312-13
'An eine Quelle' (Claudius, D 530), 144n
'An Sylvia' (Shakespeare, D 891), 256
'Auf dem See' (Goethe, D 543), 67, **75-7** (Exx. 5-6), 83
'Auf dem Strom' (Rellstab, D 943), xiii, **25-45** (Exx. 1-4, 5(b)), 249, 259, 325
'Auf den Tod einer Nachtigall' (Hölty, D 201), 308
'Aufenthalt' (Rellstab, D 957/5), 42
'Baches Wiegenlied, Des' (Müller, D 795/20), 102-3 (Ex. 3(b)), 182
'Bei dem Grabe meines Vaters' (Claudius, D 496), 144n, 297
'Blinde Knabe, Der' (Cibber/Craigher, D 833), 230, 247-8
['Blume und der Quell, Die'] (Schulze, D 874), 323
'Daphne am Bach' (Stolberg, D 411), 310
'Das war ich' (Körner, D 174), 308, 312
'Drang in die Ferne' (Leitner, D 770), 251
'Drei Sänger, Die' (Bobrik, D 329), 309-10
'Du liebst mich nicht' (Platen, D 756), 8

Schubert: songs (contd)
'Entzückung an Laura, Die' (Schiller, D 390, 577), 70, 309, 314
'Erlkönig, Der' (Goethe, D 328), **9**, 79n, 169n, 309-10, 319
'Fischers Liebesglück, Des' (Leitner, D 933), 248
'Fischerweise' (Schlechta, D 881), 238-9
'Flüchtling, Der' (Schiller, D 402), 309
'Flug der Zeit, Der' (Széchényi, D 515), 144n
'Forelle, Die' (Schubart, D 550), xii
'Fragment aus dem Aeschylus' (Mayrhofer, D 450), 312
'Fröhliches Scheiden', fragment (Leitner, D 896), 251, 324-5
'Frühlingsglaube' (Uhland, D 686), 83
'Frühlingssehnsucht' (Rellstab, D 957/3), 254, 325
'Fülle der Liebe' (Schlegel, D 854), 232
'Gebet während der Schlacht' (Körner, D 171), 307-8
'Gebüsche, Die' (Schlegel, D 646), 316
'Geheimnis, Das' (Schiller, D 793), 224
'Geistertanz, Der' (Matthisson, D 116), 300
'Gesänge aus *Wilhelm Meister*' (Goethe, D 877), 238
'Gesänge des Harfners aus *Wilhelm Meister*' ('Harfenspieler I–III') (Goethe, D 478-480), 15, 17n, 62, 312
'Glaube, Hoffnung und Liebe' (Kuffner, D 955), 253
'Gondelfahrer' (Mayrhofer, D 808), 217, 228
'Grab, Das' (Salis, D 330, 377, 569), 310
'Greisengesang' (Rückert, D 778), 226-7
'Gretchen am Spinnrade' (Goethe, D 118), 64
'Gretchens Bitte' (Goethe, D 564), 313-14
'Gruppe aus dem Tartarus' (Schiller, D 396, 583), 305, 309-10
'Hagars Klage' (Schücking, D 5), 300
'Harfenspieler I–III' (Goethe, D 478-480), 15, 17n, 62, 312
'Heimliches Lieben' (Klenke, D 922), 246
'Heimweh, Das' (Pyrker, D 851), 231-2, 262
'Herbst' (Rellstab, D 945), 42n, 325
'Hippolits Lied' (Johanna Schopenhauer, D 890), 256
'Hirt auf dem Felsen, Der' (Müller and Chézy, D 965), 254-5, 259
'Im Abendrot' (Lappe, D 799), 247-8
'Im Freien' (Seidl, D 880), 238-9
'Im Frühling' (Schulze, D 882), 237
'Iphigenia' (Mayrhofer, D 573), 195n
'Jagdlied' (Werner, D 521), 313
'Jäger, Der' (Müller, D 795/14), 101-2 (Ex. 2(b))
'Jägers Abendlied' (Goethe, D 215, 368), **77-8**
'Jägers Liebeslied' (Schober, D 909), 241
'Joanna Sebus' (Goethe, D 728), 319
'Jüngling und der Tod, Der' (Spaun, D 545), **153-6** (Ex. 6), 165n
'Klage um Ali Bey' (Claudius, D 496A, formerly 140), 144n, 297
'Kreuzzug, Der' (Leitner, D 932), 248
'Kriegers Ahnung' (Rellstab, D 957/2), 42
'Laura am Klavier' (Schiller, D 388), 68, **70-4** (Exx. 3-4), 309
'Lebenslied' (Matthisson, D 508), 313
'Lebensmut' (Rellstab, D 937), 42n, 43n, 254, 325
'Lebenstraum' (Baumberg, D 39), 298-9
'Leichenfantasie, Eine' (Schiller, D 7), 300
'Leiermann, Der' (Müller, D 911/24), 168 (Ex. 18)
'Liebe hat gelogen, Die' (Platen, D 751), 8
'Liebesbotschaft' (Rellstab, D 957/1), 42, 254, 325
'Liebesrausch', fragment (Körner, D 164), 308
'Liebliche Stern, Der' (Schulze, D 861), 323
'Lied des Orpheus, als er in die Hölle ging' ('Orpheus') (Jacobi, D 474), **74-5**, 83
'Lied im Grünen, Das' (Reil, D 917), 248
'Lied in der Abwesenheit' (Stolberg, D 416), 311
'Lied vom Reifen, Das' (Claudius, D 532), 144 and n
'Lindenbaum, Der' (Müller, D 911/5), 181
'Lorma' (Ossian, D 327), 309
'Luisens Antwort' (Kosegarten, D 319), 309

Schubert: songs (contd)
'Mädchens Klage, Des' (Schiller, D 389), 309
'Mahomets Gesang' (Goethe, D 549, 721), 313, 319
'Mainacht, Die' (Hölty, D 194), 319
'Misero pargoletto' (Metastasio, D 42), 306
'Mondlied' (Goethe, D 259, 296), 62n, **78-80**
'Mut' (Müller, D 911/22), 248
'Mutter Erde, Die' (Stolberg, D 788), 224, 256
'Nähe des Geliebten' (Goethe, D 162), **68-70**, 83
'Nebensonnen, Die' (Müller, D 911/23), 191, 246, 256
'Nonne, Die' (Hölty, D 208), 308
'Nur wer die Liebe kennt' (Werner, D 513A), 313
'Nur wer die Sehnsucht kennt' (Goethe, D 877), 238, 323
'Orpheus' (Jacobi, D 474), **74-5**, 83
'Pastorella, La', arietta (Goldoni, D 528), 313
'Pensa, che questo istante' (Metastasio, D 76), 306
'Pflicht und Liebe' (Gotter, D 467), 312
'Phidile' (Claudius, D 500), 144n, 297
'Pilgerweise' (Schober, D 789), 224
'Pilgrim, Der' (Schiller, D 794), 224
'Prometheus' (Goethe, D 674), 66
'Rastlose Liebe' (Goethe, D 138), 6, 15
'Ritter Toggenburg' (Schiller, D 397), 309
'Romanze des Richard Löwenherz' (Scott, D 907), 256
'Rückblick' (Müller, D 911/8), 241
'Rückweg' (Mayrhofer, D 476), 312
'Sänger, Der' (Goethe, D 149), **66-9** (Ex. 2), 83
'Sängers Habe, Des' (Schlechta, D 832), 230
'Schäfers Klagelied' (Goethe, D 121b), 220
'Schlacht, Die' (Schiller, D 249), 308
Schöne Müllerin, Die (Müller, D 795), 101-3, 181
Schwanengesang (D 957), 10, 20n, 21, 25, 27n, 42-4, 253-5, 259, 349
'Schwertlied' (Körner, D 170), 307
'Sehnsucht' (Goethe, D 481), 220
'Sehnsucht' (Mayrhofer, D 516), 303
'Sehnsucht' (Schiller, D 52, 636), **81-2**
'Sehnsucht' (Seidl, D 879), 237-8
'Sie in jedem Liede', fragment (Leitner, D 896A), 251, 325
'Sieg, Der' (Mayrhofer, D 805), 217, 228
'Son fra l'onde' (Metastasio, D 78), 306
'Stadt, Die' (Heine, D 957/11), 20-3 (Exx. 9-11), 23-4
'Ständchen' (Grillparzer, D 920, 921), **61-2**, 83
'Ständchen' ('Horch, horch! die Lerch') (Shakespeare, D 889), 256
'Sterne, Die' (Leitner, D 939), 324
'Stimme der Liebe' (Stolberg, D 412), 311
'Strom Der' (Stadler, D 565), 305
'Suleika I' ('Was bedeutet die Bewegung') (Goethe, D 720), 188
'Suleika II' ('Ach um deine feuchten Schwingen') (Goethe, D 717), 8, 158n
'Szene aus *Faust*' (Goethe, D 126), **64-6** (Ex. 1), 83
'Täglich zu singen' (Claudius, D 533), 144 and n
'Taubenpost, Die' (Seidl, D 965A, formerly 957/14), 253-5, 262
'Taucher, Der' (Schiller, D 77), **11-15** (Exx. 1-4), 23
'Täuschung' (Müller, D 911/19), 92
'Tiefes Leid' (Schulze, D 876), 323
'Tod und das Mädchen, Der' (Claudius, D 531), xii, xiii, **144-59** (Exx. 1-5)
'Todtengräber-Weise' (Schlechta, D 869), 238
'Todtengräbers Heimwehe' (Craigher, D 842), 229-30, 265-7
'Traditor deluso, Il' (Metastasio, D 902/2), 242, 243
'Traumbild, Das' (Hölty, D 204A), 308
'Trinklied' (Shakespeare, D 888), 256
'Trinklied vor der Schlacht' (Körner, D 169), 307
'Trockne Blumen' (Müller, D 795/18), 181
'Ueber Wildemann' (Schulze, D 884), 323
'Um Mitternacht' (Schulze, D 862), 239
'Unendlichen, Dem' (Klopstock, D 291c), 242
'Vater mit dem Kind, Der' (Bauernfeld, D 906), 241
'Vergissmeinnicht' (Schober, D 792), 224
'Versunken' (Goethe, D 715), 231, 267
'Vier Refrainlieder (Seidl, D 866), 251

Schubert: songs (contd)
'Vier Weltalter, Die' (Schiller, D 391), 309
'Viola' (Schober, D 786), 256
'Wallensteiner Lanzknecht beim Trunk, Der' (Leitner, D 931), 248
'Wanderer, Der' (Schmidt, D 489), xii
'Wanderer an den Mond, Der' (Seidl, D 870), 238
'Was bedeutet die Bewegung' ('Suleika I') (Goethe, D 720), 188
'Wegweiser, Der' (Müller, D 911/20), 191
'Wer sich der Einsamkeit ergibt' ('Harfenspieler I') (Goethe, D 478), **15-20** (Exx. 5-8), 23-4
'Wiedersehn' (Schlegel, D 855), 232
'Wiegenlied' (? Claudius, D 498), 144n, 297, 303
'Winterabend, Der' (Leitner, D 938), 249, 324
Winterreise (Müller, D 911), 9, 10 and n, 168, 174, 191, 211, 241, 248, 349
'Wolke und Quelle', fragment (Leitner, D 896B), 251, 325
'Zogernd leise' ('Ständchen') (Grillparzer, D 920), 9n
'Zufriedenheit' (Claudius, D 362), 297
'Zufriedenheit' (Claudius, D 501), 144n, 297
'Zügenglöcklein, Das' (Seidl, D 871), 238
'Zum Punsche' (Mayrhofer, D 492), 308
'Zwerg, Der' (Collin, D 771), xii
'Goethe Songs', 8
Three Songs for male voice (Metastasio, D 902), 243
fragments, 298, 305-25 *passim*
symphonies
no. 1 in D (D 82), 303, 349, 351
no. 2 in B flat (D 125), 349, 351
no. 3 in D (D 200), 349, 351
no. 4 in C minor (D 417), 219, 349, 351
no. 5 in B flat (D 485), 211, 349, 351
no. 6 in C (D 589), 200-1, 349, 351
no. 8 in B minor ('Unfinished', D 759), 100, 119n, 181, 184, 188, 201, **321**; its MS, 224, 268, 315, 352
no. 9 in C (D 944) 184, 210-11, 221; its date, xiii, 171n, **187-208** (Exx. 1-31(b) *passim*), 213; its MS, 218-19, 229, **232-7**, 239, **257-68**, 350
in D (sketches, D 615), 315
in E minor (sketches, D 729), 100, 315, 319-20
in D (draft, D 936A), 204-5 (Ex. 32), 250, 253-5
in B minor (? fragment), 297
in C minor (? 'Gastein), 349-52
the 'Gastein' symphony, 188, 207-8, 262-3, 349-52
Schubert, Heinrich, 10-11n
Schubert, Ignaz, 303
Schubert, Theresa, 321
Schuchter, Gilbert, 319
Schuh, Willi, 78 and n
Schulz, Johann Abraham Peter, 6n, 330n
Schulze, Ernst, 7, 323
Schumann, Robert, 18-19, 37n, 40-1n, 321; on Schubert's B flat Trio, q.**279** and nn, 282, 295
Schuppanzigh, Ignaz, 286, 292-4
Schuppanzigh Quartet, 284, 292 and n
Schuster, J. A. (dramatist): *Samson, Richter in Israel* (Tuczek), 112-13
Schwarmath, Erdmute, 153n, 164-5n
Schweitzer, Anton: *Pygmalion*, 106
Schwind, Moritz von, xiv, 10, 169 and n, *170*, 225-6, *346*
Scott, Sir Walter, 10, 95
Sechter, Simon, 241, 304n, 325
Seidl, Johann Gabriel, 10, 21
Senn, Johann, 10
Seyfried, Ignaz, Ritter von, 52, 53 and n, 114 and n
Abraham, 112
Adelheit von Italien, 113
Faust, 112
Hund des Aubri de Mont Didier, Der, 113
Kluge Frau im Walde, Die, 113
Moses, 112
Noah, 112
Saul, König von Israel, 112
Timur, der Tarter-Chan, 113
Seyfried, Joseph, Ritter von, 112-13
Shakespeare, William, 90
Sheridan, Richard Brinsley, 86n
Smetana, Bedřich: *The Two Widows*, 129
Solomon, Maynard, 45n
Sonnleithner, Joseph (librettist), 112
Agnes Sorel (Gyrowetz), 86
Fidelio (Beethoven), 86
Sonnleithner, Leopold von, 223n, 258, 284, q.288, 294
Souchay, Marc André, 84
Spassow, Boris, 320
Spaun, Anton von, 226
Spaun, Josef von, 210, 258, 262, 286
and Goethe, q.**6**, 79-80
as a poet, 10, 153, 156

Spaun, Josef von (contd)
on Schubert, 5n, q.7, q.9, q.42 and n
Spina, C. A. (publisher), 281n, 355
Spohr, Louis, 114 and n, 174
Faust, 112-13
Spontini, Gasparo Luigi Pacifico, 89
La Vestale, 110
Stadler, Albert, q.4, 70, 299, 311
as librettist, *Fernando* (Schubert), 86n
Stadler, Abbé Maximilian, 256
Staël, Madame (Anne Louise, Baroness de), 50n
Stargardt, J. A., 316-17
Steiner (publisher), 216-17
Stockhammer, Count Franz von, 105
Sulzer, Salomon, 47-60 *passim*
Süssmayr, Franz Xaver, 112

Tarantová, Marie, 353
Taussig, Otto, 300
Tchaikovsky, Pyotr Ilyich, 194n
Thayer, Alexander W., 43, 44 and n
Tieck, Johann Ludwig, 7 and n, 316
Tietze, Ludwig, 44
Tomášek, Václav Jan, 78
Tovey, Sir Donald, 196
Treitschke, Friedrich (librettist), 109
Fidelio (Beethoven), 87
Trollope, Frances, 49n, 51n
Tuczek, Vinzenz
Moses in Egypten, 112
Samson, Richter in Israel, 112-13
Tyson, Alan, 45n, 212-13 and nn, 215nn, 269 and n

Uhlig, Ludwig, 145n
Umlauf, Michael, 52-3
Uz, Johann Peter, 81, 311

Verdi, Giuseppe: *La traviata*, 129
Vetter, Walther, 317-18
Vogel, P. W., 113
Vogl, Henriette, 4n
Vogl, Johann Michael, q.4, 19n, 91, 93, 95, *142*, 144n, 231-2, 256
Vogl, Kunigunde, 4n, 70n
Volkert, F.: *Johann Faust*, 113n
Voll, K., 284, *285-6*

Wagner, Richard, 100
Der fliegende Holländer, 99
Waldmüller, Ferdinand Georg, xiv, *142*
Wandsbecker Bothe, Der (newspaper), 143
watermarks, 209-69 *passim*, *270-5*
Weber, Carl Maria von, q.86, 88, 93-4, 99
choral work *Der erste Ton*, 140
operas
Euryanthe, 94-6, 111
Freischütz, Der, 90, 94, 100, 108, 111, 129, 141
Preciosa, 141
Weigl, Joseph, **85-6**
operas, 88-9, 92, 108, 141
Adrian von Ostade, 108
Baals Sturz, 112
Bergsturz, Der, 108
Schweizerfamilie, Die, 85, 87-88, 108, 110
Waisenhaus, Das, 85, 88, 110
Weigl, Thaddäus (publisher), 279, 283 and n, 291 and n, 292
Weingartner, Felix, 320
Weinmann, Alexander, xiii, 291nn, 300, 310
Weinmann, Ignaz, xiii, 310, 316, **347-55**
Weisgras, Nitza, 60n
Welhartitz (paper-makers), 30n, 215-16, 227, 247, 293
Werner, Zacharias, 313
Weston, George B., 30n
Wiener Allgemeine Theaterzeitung, q.**10n**
Wiener Zeitung, 140
Willemer, Marianne von, 80
Willfort, Manfred, 284
Winter, Peter von, 108
Winter, Robert, xii, xiii, 30n, 171n, 187, 194, 205, 208n, 293 and n
Witteczek, Josef Wilhelm, 70, 210
Wolf, Hugo, 18-19, 40-1n
Wolff, Christoph, xiii
Wranitzky, Paul, 107
Wurzbach, C. von, 281n, 292n

Zelter, Carl Friedrich, 3, 77-8
Zumsteeg, Johann, 107
Zwiefache (Bavarian dance), 345